INTRODUCTION TO THE STUDY OF LAW
Cases and Materials

THIRD EDITION

LEXISNEXIS LAW SCHOOL ADVISORY BOARD

INTRODUCTION TO THE STUDY OF LAW

Cases and Materials

THIRD EDITION

Michael Makdisi
Juris Doctor
Florida State University School of Law

John Makdisi
Professor of Law
St. Thomas University School of Law

978-1-4224-2873-3

Library of Congress Cataloging-in-Publication Data

Makdisi, John.
Introduction to the study of law : cases and materials / by John Makdisi, Michael Makdisi. -- 3rd ed.
p. cm.
Includes bibliographical references
ISBN 978-1-4224-2873-3 (perfect bound : alk. paper) 1. Law--United States--Cases. 2. Law--Study and teaching--United States.
I. Makdisi, Michael. II. Title.
KF385.A4M35 2008
349.73071'1--dc22
2008049558

This publication is designed to provide accurate and authoritative information in regard to the subject matter covered. It is sold with the understanding that the publisher is not engaged in rendering legal, accounting, or other professional services. If legal advice or other expert assistance is required, the services of a competent professional should be sought.

LexisNexis, the knowledge burst logo, and Michie are trademarks of Reed Elsevier Properties Inc, used under license. Matthew Bender is a registered trademark of Matthew Bender Properties Inc.

NOTE TO USERS
To ensure that you are using the latest materials available in this area, please be sure to periodically check the LexisNexis Law School web site for downloadable updates and supplements at www.lexisnexis.com/lawschool.

Editorial Offices
744 Broad Street, Newark, NJ 07102 (973) 820-2000
201 Mission St., San Francisco, CA 94105-1831 (415) 908-3200
www.lexisnexis.com

MATTHEW◆BENDER

2009-Pub. 3552

DEDICATION

For June Mary Zekan Makdisi whose love as a Wife and Mother has embraced, supported, and encouraged us.

PREFACE

This coursebook is designed for use by beginning law students. The first three chapters provide background reading for the summer months preceding law school. The four topics following these chapters provide several assignments for teaching an orientation course. Since different law schools offer orientation courses of varying length, these assignments have been arranged so that a course may be planned to run anywhere from one to six days. Each assignment has been limited to roughly twenty pages to provide sufficient reading material for one class. The assignments focus on the techniques of the case method of study in the areas of Contracts, Property, Torts and Criminal Law. The purpose of the orientation course is not to teach substantive law but to initiate the student into the methods of legal reasoning that are the basic tools of every lawyer.

The first of the three introductory chapters begins with an introduction to the basic law school curriculum and the goals of a legal education. This is fairly light reading to integrate the particular goals an individual student may have within a more holistic framework. Law students, especially during the first year, will read many judicial case opinions. To help place those cases within the context of the judicial system, the remainder of the first chapter will provide a bird's-eye view of the structure of the court system in the United States and will introduce the appellate process.

Chapter 2 is a longer chapter, intended to introduce the basic concepts of legal reasoning, legal logic and legal decision-making in a concrete fashion, and to explore the more abstract theories on the nature of law and their impact on judicial decision making. The first section of the third chapter focuses on the mechanics of legal reasoning and logic, which law students and practitioners use on a daily basis. The second section extends the discussion of legal reasoning into the thought process behind judicial decisions and takes a look at how the common law changes. The final, and third section examines major theories on the nature of law, and builds upon the concepts in sections one and two by illustrating how the various theories on the nature of law impact judicial decisions.

Chapter 3, the final introductory chapter, is a practical and mental guide for approaching and dealing with the cases that will be the focus of much of the reading during the first year of law school. The first section of this chapter details the case method of study and explains the value of such a study within the context of a common law system such as in the United States. The remaining sections aim to make the first year learning curve less steep by explaining the basic study techniques of reading, annotating, highlighting and briefing cases.

It is important for the student to realize that these materials are designed only to introduce various aspects of the law and the legal system. Some materials are fairly easy reading while others are quite difficult to comprehend in full at this initial stage. A deeper understanding will come with time. For purposes of the orientation course, the student should work to assimilate what he or she can. The orientation is not meant to teach all that law school has to offer. It is designed to provide a foundation on which to begin building an intellectual framework for the study of law.

This third edition adds a number of new readings while at the same time streamlining the existing readings to provide a greater focus on what a student needs to prepare for the unique method of study found in law school. The previous edition split the nature of law and legal reasoning into separate chapters; this edition combines them in order to show their integrated nature. The final chapter continues to introduce the student to the unique case method of study with a selection from the classic *Bramble Bush*, but this edition has added material to provide further guidance on the mechanics of reading, annotating, and briefing cases.

PREFACE

The Topics at the end of the book have remained mostly the same with a few exceptions. The discussion in the first assignment of Topic 1 has been revised. Topic 3 has been replaced with a new topic in the area of criminal law, which provides practice comparing statutes from different jurisdictions. Also, the second assignment of Topic 4 has been removed because it requires more time and effort to digest than is warranted by an introductory course.

We would like to thank the faculty who used the second edition and provided valuable feedback. Their suggestions, especially on Topic 1, have helped us create a more accurate and useful third edition. Overall, this edition has reduced the length of the book to make it more manageable for summer reading. It has changed headings, reworked some of the existing material in order to make it an easier read, and updated and replaced a number of older articles with more modern material.

It should be noted that section identifiers, such as "A," "1," or "i" have been removed from headings within the quoted articles to avoid confusion. Footnotes, with some exceptions, have been omitted from the cases and materials without indication by ellipsis. All footnotes are the editor's unless indicated otherwise. Case citations, as well as the words "[citations omitted]," within cases are generally omitted without indication by ellipsis, unless the case cite is important for understanding. When a case citation within a case is included, the information following the case name is sometimes omitted. Finally, an ellipsis is used to show the omission of text in a paragraph. If the text that is omitted starts within, or at the end of, a paragraph and extends to include another paragraph or paragraphs, the ellipsis appears only in, or at the end of, the paragraph where the omission begins. If the text that is omitted starts at the beginning of a paragraph and extends to include part of another paragraph, the ellipsis appears only in the paragraph where the omission ends.

The credit for the changes that have been incorporated into this new edition belongs to Michael Makdisi, who has joined John Makdisi as a new author and editor for the book. Michael recently graduated from law school and is a licensed attorney in the state of California. His experience as an honors student at Florida State University, where he was a member of Moot Court and editor-in-chief of the *Journal of Land Use and Environmental Law*, has provided this book with the unique insights of a recent student fresh from the three years into which the reader of this book is about to enter. Michael spent several months revising the book for the third edition, at the end of which time he was joined by John to do the final edits and a review of the entire book before submission to the publisher. Both authors are pleased to be working together not only as colleagues but also as father and son.

TABLE OF CONTENTS

Chapter 1	**LAW SCHOOL BASICS**	**1**

A.   THE BASIC CURRICULUM AND SETTING YOUR EDUCATIONAL
GOALS 1
ROY STUCKEY & OTHERS, BEST PRACTICES FOR LEGAL EDUCATION 2
Eric A. DeGroff & Kathleen A. McKee, *Learning Like Lawyers: Addressing the
Differences in Law Student Learning Styles* 5
B.   STRUCTURE OF THE AMERICAN LEGAL SYSTEM 6
Timothy Dixon, *Structure and Process in* THE JUDICIAL BRANCH OF FEDERAL
GOVERNMENT: PEOPLE, PROCESS, AND POLITICS 6
a.   The Federal System 8
b.   The State Court Systems 9
C.   APPELLATE REVIEW 10
DELMAR KARLEN, THE CITIZEN IN COURT 10

Chapter 2	**LEGAL REASONING AND THE NATURE OF LAW**	**17**

A.   LEGAL REASONING AND LOGIC: THE BASICS 17
a.   The Process of Legal Reasoning 17
KENNETH J. VANDEVELDE, THINKING LIKE A LAWYER: AN INTRODUCTION TO
LEGAL REASONING 18
b.   Legal Logic: Analogy, Deduction and Induction 26
EDWARD H. LEVI, AN INTRODUCTION TO LEGAL REASONING 26
Ruggero J. Aldisert, Stephen Clowney & Jeremy D. Peterson, *Logic For Law
Students: How to Think Like a Lawyer* 30
B.   LEGAL REASONING IN THE COURTS 41
BENJAMIN N. CARDOZO, THE NATURE OF THE JUDICIAL PROCESS 42
NEIL MACCORMICK, LEGAL REASONING AND LEGAL THEORY 45
KENNETH J. VANDEVELDE, THINKING LIKE A LAWYER: AN INTRODUCTION TO
LEGAL REASONING 49
C.   THE NATURE OF LAW AND JUDICIAL DECISIONMAKING 53
HAROLD J. BERMAN, WILLIAM R. GREINER, SAMIR N. SALIBA, THE NATURE AND
FUNCTIONS OF LAW 55
R. RANDALL KELSO & CHARLES D. KELSO, STUDYING LAW:
AN INTRODUCTION 60
Marin Roger Scordato, *Post-Realist Blues: Formalism, Instrumentalism, and the
Hybrid Nature of Common Law Jurisprudence* 66
Stephanos Bibas, *Originalism and Formalism in Criminal Procedure: The
Triumph of Justice Scalia, the Unlikely Friend of Criminal Defendants?* 69
Jeff Bleich, Anne Voigts & Michelle Friedland, *A Practical Era: The Beginning
(or the End) of Pragmatism* 73

TABLE OF CONTENTS

Chapter 3   **THE CASE METHOD OF STUDY** **79**

A.   CASES, PRECEDENT, AND THE COMMON LAW SYSTEM 79

     KARL N. LLEWELLYN, THE BRAMBLE BUSH: ON OUR LAW AND ITS STUDY . 79

B.   HOW TO READ A CASE 95

     KENNETH J. VANDEVELDE, THINKING LIKE A LAWYER: AN INTRODUCTION TO

     LEGAL REASONING 96

C.   HOW TO BRIEF 99

D.   EXTRACTING THE RELEVANT INFORMATION: ANNOTATING AND

     HIGHLIGHTING 101

Topic I: **LANDLORD'S DUTY TO PROTECT A TENANT** **105**

     W. KEETON, D. DOBBS, R. KEETON & D. OWEN, PROSSER AND KEETON ON THE

     LAW OF TORTS 105

     Corpus Juris Secundum *Care Required and Liability for Injuries to Licensees* . 109

     Assignment 1 Briefing: Examples in Tort Law 111

        LEVINE v. KATZ 111

        KENDALL v. GORE PROPERTIES, INC. 114

        GOLDBERG v. HOUSING AUTHORITY OF THE CITY OF NEWARK 121

     Assignment 2 Answering Questions: Examples in Contract Law 128

        PINES v. PERSSION 128

        QUESTIONS 130

        SAUNDERS v. FIRST NATIONAL REALTY CORPORATION 135

        QUESTIONS 136

        LEMLE v. BREEDEN 137

        QUESTIONS 141

     Assignment 3 A Synthesis in Property Law 145

        JAVINS v. FIRST NATIONAL REALTY CORPORATION 145

        QUESTIONS 151

        KLINE v. 1500 MASSACHUSETTS AVENUE APARTMENT CORP. 153

        QUESTIONS 159

Topic II: **MITIGATION OF DAMAGES** **163**

     Assignment 1 Briefing: Examples in Contract, Tort, and Property Law 163

        ROCKINGHAM COUNTY v. LUTEN BRIDGE CO. 163

        ROY v. ROBIN 167

        WRIGHT v. BAUMANN 170

        LEFRAK v. LAMBERT 174

Topic III: **ATTEMPT** **179**

     Assignment 1 Briefing & Statutory Interpretation: Examples in

     Criminal Law 179

TABLE OF CONTENTS

COMMONWEALTH v. PRATHER 179

PEOPLE v. HIRNIAK 183

STATE v. CLARK 187

STATE v. STEWART 190

Topic IV: **UNCERTAINTY** **195**

Assignment 1 Briefing & Statutory Interpretation: Examples in
Criminal Law 195

COOPER v. SISTERS OF CHARITY OF CINCINNATI, INC. 195

MANGE v. UNICORN PRESS, INC. 201

LOCKE v. UNITED STATES 203

RIDEAUX v. LYKES BROS. STEAMSHIP CO., INC. 207

Appendix A   **How to Read a Case Citation** **211**

Appendix B   **Additional Reading** **213**

Appendix C   **On the Lighter Side** **219**

Chapter 1
LAW SCHOOL BASICS

By now everyone has probably heard the expression, "You get what you give"; this is true of the law school experience. While the expression is simple, the application is not. In order to focus your time and energy effectively, it will help you to know a little about what the next three years will look like. Part A of this chapter will introduce you to the basic law school curriculum and skills that you can expect to develop. It should help you to prepare mentally for what is to come, to set your goals, and to make better decisions about what activities are most valuable.

Parts B and C of this chapter will begin to establish your bearings. Before proceeding with a discussion of law, legal reasoning, and the mechanics of studying the law, it will be helpful to understand the framework in which the law operates. If you are not already familiar with the structure of the American legal system and the process of appellate review, these sections will orient you to both.

A. THE BASIC CURRICULUM AND SETTING YOUR EDUCATIONAL GOALS

During the next three years, you can expect a very challenging curriculum. The expectation of success is not unrealistic but you will need to devote a serious effort to achieve that success. Remember that you get what you give; while a little effort might get you a degree, a little effort will not make you a good lawyer. Take advantage of the many opportunities that law school provides to hone the skills that will comprise the tools of your trade. A constant effort to hone these skills and not merely to pass your classes is one of the most important things you can do to enhance the value of your education.

As your studies progress, keep in mind that many students will get caught up in competition with each other, but grades are not everything! Grades do not necessarily determine how good a lawyer you will become. Your ability to learn, use, and master the skills of a lawyer, on the other hand, will make you a strong attorney. Expect training in the essential tools of a lawyer such as legal writing. Also expect training in the core legal subjects such as property, torts and criminal law. Law school is a three-year opportunity to learn your craft; take advantage of it, regardless of whether you soar with ease to the top of your class or find yourself somewhere in the middle. In the end, the substantive and practical knowledge that you absorb in law school will serve you better than any grade you are given.

The first article below was published by the Clinical Legal Education Association in order to aid law schools in developing better legal programs. The selection discusses an ideal curriculum for your first, second and third years. While it was intended for use by legal educators and administrators in order to make their programs better, it nonetheless will give you a good idea of the kinds of courses and activities you are likely to encounter in your experience. In laying out the curriculum, the selection identifies some of the skills that the curriculum is intended to impart. Even though different professors will attempt to impart the wisdom of a subject to you in different ways, if you understand the ultimate purpose of a course, or a course of study, the purpose behind the professors' questions or teaching methods (no matter how odd or frustrating) will allow you to take what you need from the class in order to do well both on the test and as a professional.

While the first article might describe the ideal law school curriculum, ideality is usually not reality. One critique of modern legal education is that law school is not sufficient to prepare the student for the profession. The MacCrate Report, a well-known publication put out by the American Bar Association, stated "that the task of educating students to assume the full responsibilities of a lawyer is a continuing process that neither begins nor ends with three years of law school study . . . ."[1] Although law school may not provide you with the kind of real-world experience that employers might desire, it will provide you with most of the essentials. The second article, "Learning Like Lawyers," will introduce you to the essential skills needed as a lawyer and will therefore help you set realistic goals by providing knowledge about what you can expect to gain from your legal education. If, during the course of your studies, you find that your required curriculum does not provide all the skills listed, you may want to consider enhancing your education with extra-curricular activities such as moot court, mock trial, a summer clerkship, or a semester externship. Remember that you get what you give; be sure to give of your time to the activities that will best enhance your ability to practice the law.

ROY STUCKEY & OTHERS
BEST PRACTICES FOR LEGAL EDUCATION
275–80 (2007)[2]

Components of a "Model" Best Practices Curriculum

This chapter describes one vision of a curriculum that seeks to implement best practices for legal education. The purpose of including it is simply to present ideas for consideration, discussion, and debate. We do not intend to suggest that this is the only way to design an effective program of instruction.

. . . .

The vision of legal education described in this chapter is consistent with that of the authors of the Carnegie Foundation's report on legal education. We envision a curriculum with three parts that interact with and influence each other.

> Those elements are first, the teaching of legal doctrine and analysis, which provides the basis for professional growth; second, introduction to the several facets of practice included under the rubric of lawyering, leading to acting with responsibility for clients; and third, a theoretical and practical emphasis upon inculcation of the identity, values, and dispositions consonant with the fundamental purposes of the legal profession.

We particularly like the description of best practices for developing students' professional identity and values contained in the Carnegie Foundation's report.

> [I]t is possible to imagine a continuum of teaching and learning experiences concerned with the apprenticeship of professional identity. At one end of the continuum would be courses in legal ethics, in particular those directly oriented to the "law of lawyering" that students must master in order to pass the bar examination. A bit further along would fall other academic courses, including those of the first year, into which issues concerning the substantive ends of law, the identity and role of lawyers, and questions of equity and purpose are combined with the more formal, technical issues of legal reasoning. Approaches of this sort are often called the "pervasive method" of teaching ethics. Further along the continuum we encounter courses that directly explore the identity and roles of lawyers, the difficulties of adhering to larger purposes amid the press of practice, and the way professional ideals become manifest in legal careers. Further still fall lawyering courses that bring questions of both competence and responsibility to clients and to the legal system into play. Finally, at the continuum's other end, we find externships and clinical courses in which direct experience of practice with clients becomes the focus.

---

[1] American Bar Association, Section of Legal Education and Admissions to the Bar, Legal Education and Professional Development – An Educational Continuum 8 (July 1992).

[2] Reprinted by permission of Roy Stuckey. All rights reserved.

. . . .

The First Year Program of Instruction.

The first year should provide the building blocks for the progressive acquisition of knowledge, skills, and values in the upper class curriculum and in law practice. The program of instruction should continue the current practice of emphasizing the development of analytical skills (how to think like a lawyer), research and writing skills, and basic legal knowledge. The goals of the first year should also include beginning the process of helping students develop their legal problem-solving expertise, self efficacy, and self-reflection and lifelong learning skills. First year students should be introduced to jurisprudence, the history and values of the legal profession and professions in general, notable figures in the law, the roles of lawyers, the ways in which legal problems arise and are resolved in our society and other societies, and challenges facing the legal profession such as commercialization, accountability, and access to justice. This instruction should occur in the classrooms and co-curricular programs.

. . . .

Simulations should be incorporated into every course to strengthen students' understanding of legal concepts and to give them opportunities to assume professional roles. Some simulations can be conducted during class time, while others may be conducted outside of class. . . .

Participation in study groups should be required or strongly suggested, and students should be assigned group projects, some to take place during class meetings and others outside of class. Students should be trained how to work in collaborative groups and be closely supervised to ensure these experiences reflect aspects of law practice collaboration and build their collaborative skills.

Students should also receive instruction in how to be expert self-regulated learners so they develop the skills of controlling their learning process; managing their workload, time, and stress; self-monitoring their learning process while it is in progress; and reflecting on their learning afterward, thereby continuously improving themselves as learners. Students should be required to maintain reflective journals in at least one course.

Academic responsibility should be taken seriously by everyone at the school, and students should be expected to conduct themselves as professionals from the moment they enter law school guided by a student code of professionalism. . . .

Students should have contact with practicing lawyers and judges from orientation throughout their first year in law school. This can occur through a variety of methods, including preceptorships or other forms of mentoring arrangements, inviting practitioners to be guest speakers in classes or at events open to all students, and requiring students to participate in "field trips" which at a minimum should include observations of actual appellate court arguments. . . .

A law school should not allow a student to stay enrolled beyond the first semester unless the student demonstrates the intellectual skills expected of a first semester student or the school has reason to believe that, with academic support, the student will achieve an acceptable level of proficiency by the end of the second semester.

The intellectual skills to be demonstrated are those that constitute the ability to "think like a lawyer." This includes the ability to understand the holdings of appellate cases, to distinguish among appellate cases, and to apply legal doctrine to a set of facts and predict what a court would decide. More generally, "thinking like a lawyer" involves broader problem-solving skills, including the grounding of analysis in facts, the comprehensive spotting of relevant issues and concerns, the search for governing rules, principles, or standards by which to make decisions, the weighing of competing policy considerations in light of their consequences, the value placed on consistency and deference to past decisions, the utility of reasoning by analogy, the importance of reasoned justification, and the need to reach a conclusion and make a decision even if not perfect.

These are core abilities that are essential to continued learning in law school and the practice of law. If a student cannot demonstrate these abilities by the end of the first semester, it would likely be a waste of the student's time and money to continue in law school.

The Second Year Program of Instruction.

The second year should continue helping students develop legal problem-solving expertise, self efficacy, and self-reflection and lifelong learning skills. Whereas the first year focuses on legal analysis, the second should focus on fact analysis. The school should continue providing instruction about core legal knowledge, including knowledge that is essential to all lawyers and foundational information that students will need to pursue specialized interests or tracks in the third year. Schools should consider developing courses that provide an overview of various related subject areas that give students an acquaintance with multiple subjects rather than a more in depth understanding of one subject. This will enable students to acquire a general understanding of a wider range of subjects, any of which they could learn in more depth if needed in practice.

Emphasis in the second year should be placed on helping students develop their knowledge and understanding about professional skills and values, including sensitivity to client-centered practice. Basic introductory courses in professional skills, especially transactional and pretrial skills, should be offered to all students during both semesters. Instruction in legal writing, drafting, and research should continue. Pre- or co-requisite courses might include professional responsibility, evidence, remedies, and civil procedure.

. . . . Co-curricular and extra-curricular programs, including competitions and the pro bono program, should be coordinated with curricular offerings.

Externship courses or required observation programs should be organized to give students opportunities to observe and reflect on law practice. The primary educational goal of such experiences should be to develop students' understanding of professional values and commitment to those values, including seeking justice, fostering respect for the rule of law, and dealing sensitively and effectively with diverse clients and colleagues. In furtherance of these objectives, a school might select externships with public interest lawyers and lawyers who handle pro bono cases to give students role models of lawyers who take seriously the profession's obligation to provide access to justice. Another option is to place students at agencies that provide services to under-represented segments of society or perhaps in disciplinary counsels' offices. Schools with sufficient resources should offer students opportunities to enroll in in-house clinics that provide legal services to under-represented members of our society, either as second chairs to third year students or as lead counsel on cases they are qualified to handle.

Students should be required to write reflective journals or papers in all experiential education courses. Assessment practices should continue as in the first year.

The Third Year Program of Instruction.

The emphasis in the third year should be to continue helping students develop their problem-solving expertise and cultivate "practical wisdom." The school should give special attention to helping students refine their self-reflection and lifelong learning skills. Rather than having discrete subject specific courses, multiple subjects should be taught in integrated contexts. Most courses could be organized as simulated law firms in which students work individually and in groups to resolve legal problems. For example, one course might be organized as a general practice firm, while others might be organized, for example as a corporate firm, a family law firm, a criminal defense firm, or prosecutor's office. The specific subjects should reflect the most probable settings in which the school's students are likely to enter practice. Practicing or retired lawyers should be recruited to assist in these courses.

Students should be required to participate in externship courses or in-house clinics in which students represent clients or participate in the work of lawyers and judges, not just observe it. Care should be taken to ensure that the externships and in-house clinics have clear, achievable educational objectives that cannot be adequately replicated in the simulated law firm courses or other courses. One option is to continue giving students opportunities to participate in the public interest practice settings such as those described in the second year curriculum. Another option would be to give students opportunities to work in the types of legal settings in which they are most likely to find themselves in their first years of practice.

Students should be required to write reflective journals or papers in all experiential education courses.

Eric A. DeGroff & Kathleen A. McKee
Learning Like Lawyers: Addressing the Differences in Law Student Learning Styles
2006 BYU Educ. & L.J. 499, 507–08 (2006)[3]

The Goal of Legal Education

There is considerable overlap among authors regarding what skills need to be developed in law school to prepare students for the challenge of legal practice. The Task Force Report of the American Bar Association (ABA) Section on Legal Education and Admissions to the Bar, issued in 1992, delineated what it deemed to be basic lawyering skills and professional values that students should have developed by the time they are ready to represent their first clients professionally. These fundamental skills and values include: (1) problem solving; (2) legal analysis and reasoning; (3) legal research; (4) factual investigation; (5) communication; (6) counseling; (7) negotiation; (8) litigation and alternative dispute resolution procedures; (9) organization and management of legal work; and (10) recognizing and resolving ethical dilemmas.

In practical terms, students who have acquired these skills and professional values in the course of their legal education should have mastered the controlling principles of individual areas of substantive law. They should also have a basic understanding of how the different areas of substantive law relate to each other and impact each other within the seamless web of law as a whole. The ultimate goal is students' mastery of a fully integrated body of skills and knowledge that support effective legal analysis, problem solving, and advocacy on behalf of clients in real-world situations.

In sum, legal education requires the integration of substantive law, practical lawyering skills and diverse learning strategies. Ideally, the end product is a student who is proficient in carrying out the mental processes of decoding, cataloging, retrieving, and encoding relevant legal concepts and related factual information.

B. STRUCTURE OF THE AMERICAN LEGAL SYSTEM

Timothy Dixon
Structure and Process in
The Judicial Branch of Federal Government: People, Process, and Politics
53–55 (Charles L. Zelden ed., 2007)[4]

Structure and Process

A court is an entity created by the government and given the authority to resolve disputes through the application of the laws and rules of a society. Courts are reactive institutions. They do not decide what issues or controversies upon which they will rule. They only act when someone files a suit requesting their help. When they do take a case, the objective is to provide litigants (both private and public) a level playing field in which to work out the disputes, problems, and crises of everyday life. In doing this, courts serve to preserve order and provide predictability in society, to provide for the general welfare, and to protect individuals and property.

Overview of the American Legal System

In the American judicial system, broadly speaking, two types of cases are heard: criminal and civil. Criminal law governs individual conduct with a set of rules enforced by government. The primary objective is the maintenance of social order. Criminal law does this job by punishing what society perceives as deviant behavior and, in so doing, sets standards of proper behavior by which it can define and discourage antisocial behavior. There are different levels of severity in criminal offenses — infractions, misdemeanors, and felonies — dealt with by progressively more severe punishments. Criminal law makes the government a party to the action as the representative of the entire society. Most criminal law actions take place in state courts, but the federal criminal caseload has grown with the increase in federal criminal laws.

Civil cases are those that relate to the conduct of and relationship between individuals or business enterprises. People who think that they have suffered a loss at the hands of a business or another individual represent themselves in the action. Litigants in civil cases usually seek compensation for a loss or the return of something valuable that was taken from someone. The government does not act as a representative of the society for the loss suffered by an individual. Rather, the courts serve as impartial forums for private dispute resolution. Civil law judges serve a similar role to that of umpires or referees in sports. While they have no personal interest in the outcome, it is their job to see that the process goes smoothly and that the interests of the wider audience (in the case of the law, the people) are protected.

Most cases in the American judicial system never get to trial. Trials are expensive, time-consuming, and unpredictable. Most civil cases are accordingly settled by the agreement of the parties themselves outside a courtroom on the basis of their lawyers' expectations as to the likely outcome should the case go to trial. In criminal actions, pleas, plea bargains, and diversion programs account for the failure to go to trial.

The judicial system in the United States consists of both a federal court system, established under the U.S. Constitution, and the judicial systems of each of the fifty states. Civil and criminal cases are heard in both of these systems, and both are basically systems with three levels or tiers. For both systems, the bottom level consists of trial courts, where actions are first filed and litigated. One step up from that, in the middle tier, are the intermediate appellate courts of the states and the courts of appeals

---

[4] Reprinted by permission of ABC-CLIO ©2007. All rights reserved.

in the federal court system. On top sits the highest court of the respective systems, most often named by states as the supreme court (though some states use other names), while in the federal system it is called the United States Supreme Court.

It is not a misnomer to talk about fifty-one American court systems as opposed to simply *the* American court system. While there are many similarities between the various state and federal courts, their rules — both substantive and procedural — vary widely. The differences tend to be greatest at the level of content (rules). The structures by which these courts are organized, in terms of both procedures and organization, are much more similar than they are different.

In order to hear and decide a case, for instance, the court (state or federal) must have jurisdiction to do so. This means the legal authority to hear and grant relief in particular cases. This authority is usually conferred by the statutes or constitution that apply to each court system, or both. In the federal system jurisdiction is governed by federal law and the U.S. Constitution. There are two basic types of jurisdiction, original and appellate.

Original jurisdiction refers to the ability of a court to hear a case as a trial court. This usually refers to the court that hears the case first in the judicial system. Under original jurisdiction a court will hear and determine the facts of a case in addition to applying the law to the facts of the case. Trials can take two forms: trial by jury or a trial by a judge. In a trial by a judge (called a "bench trial") the judge has control of all aspects of the trial: he determines the facts of the case and then applies the law to those findings. In a jury trial, there is a division of tasks between the judge and the jury. They judge will rule on issues of law (admissibility of evidence, for example) and provide the jury with instructions on the law that it is to apply. The jury hears the witnesses and evaluates the evidence to determine what facts have been successfully proven. The jury resolves conflicts in the testimony of witnesses and determines who is to be believed. It assigns weight to different items of evidence and testimony, then applies the law given in the judge's instructions to the facts it finds. The jury reaches a verdict favoring one side or the other in the case.

After a trial, an unsatisfied party may request a review of the finding of the trial court by appealing the trial court decision. Appellate jurisdiction is a court's ability to review and alter the decision of a trial court. Usually the appellate court will limit its review to the application of the law in the trial court and not conduct a review of the record of facts found in the lower court. The appellate court decides whether the trial court properly applied the correct law in the case or whether an error was committed. There is no jury in the appellate court, and no witnesses are heard. The court's review is limited to the facts and legal theories developed in the trial court by the parties to the case. No new arguments or proof is allowed at the appellate level; the court relies on the record of proceedings sent to it by the trial court and the briefs of legal arguments submitted by the parties. (The record of proceedings is a complete file containing all of the pleadings and documents filed in the case as well as a transcript of the trial itself.) If, after an appeal is heard an decided, a party is still unsatisfied with the decision on the appeal, he may have the right to take a further appeal to the highest appellate court in the state or federal system.

Generally, in both state and federal systems, litigants are guaranteed only a single appeal on the merits of their case. This guaranteed appeal is usually provided by the intermediate courts of appeals such as the federal circuit courts of appeals. Appeals beyond this level — in the federal system, to the U.S. Supreme Court — are at the discretion of the court. Only those cases deemed most important get a second hearing by an appellate tribunal. . . .

DISCUSSION

Names of the courts. On the federal level, the trial courts are the district courts, the intermediate courts are the circuit courts, and the high court is the Supreme Court. While these names are straightforward, the names on the state level may cause confusion. For example, in Florida, the trial courts are called the circuit courts, while the intermediate courts are called the district courts; this nomenclature is exactly opposite that of the federal system. Another example of name variation, which you are likely to encounter in your studies, occurs in New York. New York trial courts are called supreme courts, the intermediate courts are called the appellate divisions, and the high court is named the court of appeals.

Do not try to memorize all these distinctions. Just keep in mind that differences do exist, and if you ever need to look it up, the following website provides easy reference to all the state courts and their names:

http://wlwatch.westlaw.com/aca/west/statecrtorg.htm

a. The Federal System

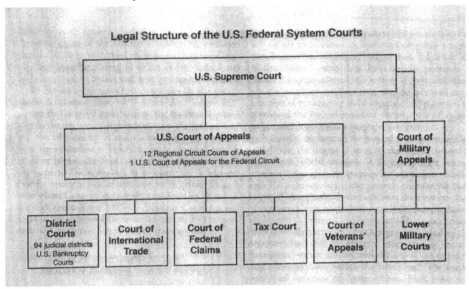

HERBERT M. KRITZER, ED., LEGAL SYSTEMS OF THE WORLD: A POLITICAL, SOCIAL, AND CULTURAL ENCYCLOPEDIA, Vol. IV (S-Z) 1703 (ABC-CLIO, Inc. 2002). Reprinted by permission of ABC-CLIO. All rights reserved.

United States Supreme Court[5]

The United States Supreme Court consists of the Chief Justice of the United States and eight associate justices. At its discretion, and within certain guidelines established by Congress, the Supreme Court each year hears a limited number of the cases it is asked to decide. Those cases may begin in the federal or state courts, and they usually involve important questions about the Constitution or federal law.

United States Courts of Appeals[6]

---

[5] United State Supreme Court, http://www.uscourts.gov/supremecourt.html (last visited June 11, 2008). The Official Website for the Supreme Court is http://www.supremecourtus.gov.

[6] The Federal Judiciary — United States Courts of Appeals, http://www.uscourts.gov/courtsofappeals.html (last visited June 11, 2008).

The 94 U.S. judicial districts are organized into 12 regional circuits, each of which has a United States court of appeals. A court of appeals hears appeals from the district courts located within its circuit, as well as appeals from decisions of federal administrative agencies.

In addition, the Court of Appeals for the Federal Circuit has nationwide jurisdiction to hear appeals in specialized cases, such as those involving patent laws and cases decided by the Court of International Trade and the Court of Federal Claims.

United States District Courts[7]

The United States district courts are the trial courts of the federal court system. Within limits set by Congress and the Constitution, the district courts have jurisdiction to hear nearly all categories of federal cases, including both civil and criminal matters. Every day hundreds of people across the nation are selected for jury duty and help decide some of these cases.

There are 94 federal judicial districts, including at least one district in each state, the District of Columbia and Puerto Rico. Three territories of the United States -- the Virgin Islands, Guam, and the Northern Mariana Islands -- have district courts that hear federal cases, including bankruptcy cases. . . .

Bankruptcy courts are separate units of the district courts. Federal courts have exclusive jurisdiction over bankruptcy cases. This means that a bankruptcy case cannot be filed in a state court.

There are two special trial courts that have nationwide jurisdiction over certain types of cases.

1. The Court of International Trade addresses cases involving international trade and customs issues.

2. The United States Court of Federal Claims has jurisdiction over most claims for money damages against the United States, disputes over federal contracts, unlawful "takings" of private property by the federal government, and a variety of other claims against the United States.

Discussion

You probably noticed that the federal system includes more than just the district, circuit and Supreme courts (such as the bankruptcy courts). Article III, Section 1, of the U.S. Constitution originally gave the Supreme Court all the power of the judiciary, but provided Congress with the ability to establish lower inferior courts. Just as Congress established the circuit and district courts, they also established other courts, such as the Bankruptcy court, as shown in the diagram above.

b.   The State Court Systems

For each of the fifty states, there exists a separate judicial system. The structure of each may vary slightly; however, the similarities outweigh the differences. Similar to the federal courts, most state courts have a three-tiered structure, with a tier of trial courts, and two tiers of appellate courts. Like the federal system, most states have only one high court, with the exception of Oklahoma and Texas (each of which have a separate high court for criminal appeals). While most state courts have a middle tier of intermediate courts, a few do not, including Delaware, Maine, Montana, Nevada, New Hampshire, North Dakota, Rhode Island, South Dakota, Vermont, West Virginia, and Wyoming. All states, without exception, have trial courts. Trial courts can be of general, limited, or special jurisdiction. In some states, a single trial court may hear a variety of different cases, regardless of the subject matter. In other states, different trial courts may each be designated to hear a specific type of case. Whether a state has one trial

---

[7] United States District Courts, http://www.uscourts.gov/districtcourts.html (last visited June 11, 2008).

court, or many, each state has its own nomenclature. Some examples of the various trial court names include: Superior Courts, District Courts, Circuit Courts, Courts of Common Pleas, Municipal Courts, Juvenile Courts, Probate Courts, Environmental Courts, and Small Claims Courts. The important thing to keep in mind is that all these courts, whatever their name, are trial courts whose function is to find and establish the facts and make an initial ruling.

If you would like more information on a specific state, the following website for the National Center for State Courts contains a comprehensive list of links for all 50 states:

> http://www.ncsconline.org/d_kis/ info_court_web_sites.html.

C. APPELLATE REVIEW

As a first year law student, a large portion of the assigned material will be either appellate court decisions or material that discusses those decisions. As described above, appellate courts are very different from trial courts. While trial courts focus on finding the facts and coming to a resolution of the dispute, appellate courts focus on issues of law and whether a trial court's process of reaching its decision was proper and justified. The next article will introduce you to the appellate process. Although it dates back over forty years, Delmar Karlen's description of the appellate process remains relevant today and provides some valuable insight into the decisions which will comprise a large amount of your first year materials.

DELMAR KARLEN
THE CITIZEN IN COURT
87–98 (1964)[8]

Appellate Review

. . . [N]ot many cases are actually contested. Most criminal prosecutions result in pleas of guilty and most civil actions are settled or defaulted. The relatively few contested cases are likely to be fought vigorously and to result in judgments that leave one side or the other unhappy. When this happens the aggrieved party may want to appeal to a higher court.

No automatic review is provided; it must be sought and initiated by one of the litigants. Appellate courts, like trial courts, are not self-starting mechanisms. The right of appeal, although not constitutionally guaranteed, is provided by legislation for virtually every type of case, large or small, civil or criminal. There is one very important qualification, however: In most states, in a criminal case the government may not appeal. If the defendant has been acquitted that is the end of the matter. Only where there has been a conviction may an appeal be taken and then only by the defendant. In Connecticut and Wisconsin a variation from this theme exists: The government may appeal on a question of law, such as a judge's erroneous instruction, although as in other states, it may not appeal on the basic factual issue of guilt or innocence.

The fact that a litigant may have a right to appeal does not mean that he will take advantage of it. Very few appeals are taken — less than 10 percent on the average — compared to the number of cases tried. Unless there is some reasonable likelihood that the judgment will be reversed, unless, in other words, it is demonstrable that the trial court reached a wrong result on the law or the facts, there is no point in spending further time and money on the litigation. Appeals are expensive as well as time consuming.

---

[8] Reprinted by permission of Delmar Karlen, Jr., Executor of the Estate of Delmar Karlen. All rights reserved.

Minor Case Appeals

Before considering the ordinary type of appeal we should first look briefly at a special type provided for those minor cases which are tried in justice of the peace courts and similar inferior tribunals. In such cases the aggrieved party — meaning the convicted defendant in a criminal case or either party who has lost in a civil case — is entitled to a retrial in a higher tribunal, one where the judges enjoy greater prestige and where there is more time for deliberation. The retrial takes place in a trial court of superior jurisdiction and follows the same pattern as the trial of a more serious case that is brought there originally. Witnesses are heard in the usual fashion and a jury may even be empaneled. Little or no attention is paid to what transpired at the first trial, for the whole job is done anew as if the first trial had never taken place. This type of proceeding, which is called by lawyers a trial *de novo*, is vastly different, as we shall see, from the ordinary appeal about to be discussed.

Ordinary Appeals

For the more serious civil and criminal cases tried originally in courts of superior jurisdiction, a retrial upon demand of the loser would make little sense. Where would it take place? If the judge who presided agreed that error had been committed he could grant a new trial and conduct it in such a way as to avoid the mistake the second time through. But if he considered the first trial properly conducted in every respect and the result right, what would be the point in going through the same performance again before him or one of his peers?

Because no satisfactory answer can be given to such questions, a different type of review is provided. It consists of the scrutiny of the record of the original trial by a group of judges bent on discovering whether any error was committed that would vitiate the result. If such an error is found the judgment must be upset. If not, it stands. Not all errors are subject to successful challenge on appeal. Those committed by the jury (if there was one) are constitutionally insulated against review except insofar as they may have been caused or permitted by erroneous rulings of the judge, for instance, if he failed to direct a verdict in a crystal-clear case. Ordinarily only the errors of the judge are open to appellate scrutiny, and furthermore, before the appellate court can order a reversal it must be satisfied that whatever error is found was prejudicial, thus affecting the final judgment. This means that if the judge made an erroneous ruling in excluding a piece of evidence but then in effect canceled it by a subsequent ruling admitting the same evidence when offered later the error would be considered harmless and disregarded. Finally, an appellate court will not interfere in areas of acknowledged trial court discretion, like sentencing in criminal cases. If a sentence is illegal it will be set right, but if it is merely excessive, though within legal limits, it will in most states not warrant appellate court interference.

An appellate court is vastly different from a trial court. Instead of a single judge there are several — at least three, sometimes five or seven or nine. There is no jury. No witnesses are heard or evidence taken. Even the parties themselves are rarely present, for this is a proceeding that the lawyers and judges can perfectly well manage alone.

Beyond the value of saving time and concentrating attention upon the critically important steps of the trial where mistakes are claimed to have been made, there is another value in this type of review, not present in trial *de novo*. This is uniformity in the interpretation of the law. With one central appellate court a statute or rule can have only one meaning in all the trial courts. Uniformity is accomplished in part by direct action upon the judgments of the various trial courts throughout the state; in part, it is accomplished by opinions handed down by the appellate court in the course of reaching its decisions. Decisions . . . become guide lines for the future, binding all lower courts that are confronted by substantially similar cases.

The Record on Appeal

Since the object of an appeal is to discover and appraise errors that may have been committed in the trial court, the record of proceedings there becomes a matter of prime importance. The record consists of a stenographic transcript of the testimony taken in the court below, the formal papers used there (pleadings, and so forth), and the verdict and judgment. These papers, or relevant excerpts from them — depending upon the questions to be argued on the appeal — are printed or otherwise duplicated to allow one copy for each of the judges in the appellate court. The job of preparing the papers and submitting them to the clerk of the appellate court for distribution to the judges normally falls on the *appellant*, the party who, having lost below, is taking the appeal.

The legal fees involved in taking an appeal and the mechanical costs of preparing the necessary papers pose a serious problem for the indigent litigant. It is partially solved, however, by a combination of devices designed to put him, as nearly as possible, on a par with a man of means. One is that permission is given him to appeal *in forma pauperis*, meaning, as a practical matter, that he is allowed to dispense with the printing of the appeal papers. Another, applicable only in criminal cases however, is furnishing him with a free copy of the stenographic transcript of his trial. Finally and most important, the indigent defendant in a serious criminal case is required to be provided with counsel free of charge for the taking of his appeal. This requirement is the result of a 1963 decision of the Supreme Court of the United States.

Use of Briefs

Along with the record, each judge receives *briefs*, or written arguments, from both sides. The one submitted on behalf of the appellant points out the errors claimed to exist and argues that they are of such a nature as to require reversal of the judgment. The brief of the *appellee*, or *respondent*, the winner below, who is trying to save the judgment, is defensive, arguing that the rulings objected to by the other side are not errors, or, if they are, that they are not sufficiently serious to warrant upsetting the judgment. Both sides cite authorities in the form of statutes and previous cases thought to justify their positions. Though arbitrary limitations on length are imposed by some courts, each brief is likely to run to fifty, sixty, or more printed pages, with the consequence that substantial printing or duplicating expenses may be involved. Sometimes the appellant files a reply brief in rebuttal of the respondent's argument. The briefs are exchanged between the lawyers (the appellant's is due first, then the appellee's, then the reply brief, if any) and filed in court in advance of the time for oral argument. The process ordinarily requires several months after the judgment in the court below.

Oral Argument

With written arguments available for study by the judges, one may wonder why there is need for oral argument as well. One or the other would seem to be enough. Such is the philosophy in England where there are no written briefs and where oral arguments are of unlimited duration, often lasting several days, sometimes even weeks.

In the United States the judges want both types of argument, although most of them tend to rely more on the briefs and to limit oral argument. In the Supreme Court each side ordinarily is allowed one hour; in many other courts considerably less time is allowed — sometimes no more than fifteen or thirty minutes for each side. Part of the time may be consumed by questioning from the judges, but this practice depends upon the mental habits and personalities of the judges and upon whether they make it a practice to study the briefs in advance. Rarely is any time spent reading to the court from the record, the briefs, or the legal authorities relied upon. Most judges object to counsel reading anything aloud, preferring to read for themselves at their own pace and in the privacy of their chambers. What they chiefly want from oral argument is a quick understanding of the case presented to them for decision, with a clear delineation of the issues and the principal lines of reasoning relied on by both sides.

The judges do not attempt to reach a conclusion immediately upon the close of argument. Almost invariably, they reserve judgment until they have had time to study the papers and to carefully formulate a decision. Arguments are heard in groups, several cases being scheduled each day over a period of a week or two. Then the judges adjourn for two or three weeks for the preparation of opinions. Several weeks or months may elapse between oral argument and decision in a given case. In this respect again, American practice differs sharply from English. There, the judges hear one case at a time and customarily deliver their opinions orally and extemporaneously immediately upon completion of oral argument.

Appellate Opinions

Reaching a correct decision is not considered the full discharge of an American appellate court's responsibility. The court is also expected to explain its reasons in writing. Partly this is to satisfy the disappointed litigants that their contentions have been carefully considered. Partly it is to improve the decisional process itself by forcing the judges into the discipline of written explanations and away from snap judgments. Partly it is to clarify and mold the law, for each decision becomes a precedent, governing like cases that may arise in the future.

After a group of cases has been argued, the judges customarily hold a private conference to reach tentative agreement as to decisions to be rendered. Views expressed and votes cast at this time are understood to be subject to later revision. Then, for each case, one of the judges assumes the responsibility of drafting an opinion for court. His selection may be pursuant to a prearranged system of rotating cases between the judges in numerical sequence or by special assignment of the presiding judge, depending upon the custom of the particular court. It is not the custom for each judge to prepare his own opinion. Rather, the ideal is a single opinion representing the view of the entire court, or, failing that, one which represents the view of a majority of the judges, possibly accompanied by a dissenting or concurring opinion for the judges in the minority. Occasionally there is an even greater fragmentation of viewpoints necessitating several dissenting and concurring opinions, but this is rare.

The judge to whom an opinion is assigned first studies the record and the briefs, sometimes supplementing such study by independent research into the law, and then drafts an opinion that he hopes will meet the approval of his colleagues. He circulates his opinion among them for criticisms and suggestions. Further conferences and interchanges of memoranda may ensue, formal or informal, until all of the judges who have to be satisfied (the whole court, the majority, or the minority) are content. The final language of the opinion may be the result of many compromises and not correspond to that which would have been used by any one of the judges writing independently. Furthermore, sometimes what started out to be a minority viewpoint may come to represent the view of the majority or even the entire court. The judges feel free to change their minds at any time until their decision is publicly announced. While each has the responsibility of drafting opinions in the cases assigned to him, he also has the responsibility of studying the cases assigned to his colleagues and the opinions drafted by them. The decision in every case is intended to be the composite result of the deliberations of all the judges.

Publication of Opinions

If appellate opinions are to serve their intended purpose as precedents, they must be available to the bench and bar for guidance. The simple solution is to publish them. This is done on a massive scale in the United States, where hundreds of volumes of opinions are printed each year, some officially, some privately. In general, no attempt is made to separate wheat from chaff, and all opinions of all appellate courts are published without discrimination. Here again is a sharp contrast with the practice in England, where only selected opinions — those which enunciate new principles of law — are published. In the United States, important opinions enunciating new legal principles tend to become buried among the hundreds that do nothing more than apply well-settled ones to particular fact patterns.

There are advantages as well as disadvantages in the American approach. On the positive side is the fact that the vast accumulation of judicial rulings upon concrete situations makes the law highly specific and limits the discretion that judges would otherwise exercise if they were guided by nothing but a set of broad, general principles. On the negative side is the complexity of the law resulting from treating as precedents a wilderness of single instances. Citations in briefs are multiplied to an unreasonable extent until one can scarcely see the forest for the trees. The work of judges and lawyers is increased and so is the expense to clients. . . .

Further Review

The procedure described above applies not only to state supreme courts, but also to intermediate appellate courts where those bodies exist. In some states, therefore, double appellate review becomes possible, and indeed necessary to resolve differences of opinion that inevitably arise between the intermediate courts. Some cases may be allowed to go up as a matter of right (such as those involving an interpretation of the state constitution), but most cases are allowed further review only in the discretion of the state supreme court, which chooses between those offered upon the basis of their importance.

Within the federal judicial system are found intermediate appellate courts also. These are the eleven[9] United States courts of appeals to which the judgments of the ninety-one[10] federal district courts can be appealed as a matter of right.

Unique Position of the Supreme Court

At the summit of appellate tribunals is the Supreme Court of the United States. It has power to review not only decisions of the lower federal courts but also decisions of the highest courts of the various states. While it decides only about 125[11] appeals a year, the cases are likely to be of great significance.

Almost all cases that reach the Court have already been through at least one stage of appellate review, either in one of the fifty state supreme courts or one of the eleven[12] federal courts of appeals. A few, however, come directly from trial courts. In some special situations (for example, where an act of Congress has been held unconstitutional), a direct appeal may be taken from a United States district court. Similarly, direct review of the decision of a lower state court is possible in exceptional circumstances. In 1960 a case of this kind arose. A man was convicted of loitering and disorderly conduct in a police court of Louisville, Kentucky, and fined $10. He claimed that the proceedings violated the due process clause of the Fourteenth Amendment, but under the statutes there was no higher state court to which he could appeal in so seemingly trivial a case. In these circumstances the Supreme Court of the United States granted review of the case and reversed the conviction. Such situations are exceedingly rare.

---

[9] The federal courts now have 12 regional circuit courts, and one court of appeals for the Federal Circuit.

[10] The federal courts now have 94 district courts.

[11] Today, the Supreme Court listens to approximately 100 cases a term, out of a total docket of more than 10,000. *See* THE SUPREME COURT OF THE UNITED STATES, THE JUSTICE'S CASELOAD, http://www.supremecourtus.gov/about/justicecaseload.pdf.

[12] The federal courts now have 12 regional circuit courts, and one court of appeals for the Federal Circuit.

A state case can reach the Court only if it involves a question of federal law of controlling importance. State courts are required to apply federal law wherever it is applicable, but since the scope of such law is limited relatively few of their cases are affected by it. Most state cases involve torts, contracts, real property, and other areas of private law where there is no federal legislation and where, moreover, no federal constitutional question is raised. With such cases the Supreme Court has no concern, for it acknowledges that state courts have the final word on questions of state law.

In a relatively small proportion of state cases, federal questions are present, which may or may not be controlling. Thus a litigant might challenge a state statute as being in conflict with both the state constitution and the federal Constitution. If the highest court of the state invalidated the statute on the ground that it violated the state constitution or on the ground that it violated both constitutions the Supreme Court of the United States would have no interest in the case. The state ground of decision would be adequate to support it, and the federal question would have become moot. If, on the other hand, the state court upheld the statute under the state constitution but invalidated it under the federal Constitution the case would be appropriate for review in the Supreme Court. The federal ground of decision, in other words, would be controlling. Similarly if a claim predicated upon a federal statute (like the Federal Employers' Liability Act) were brought in a state court and if the highest state appellate court interpreted the statute in such a way as to bar the claim, and if that were the sole basis for its decision, the case would present an appropriate question for review in the Supreme Court of the United States.

Insofar as its cases come from the lower federal courts, the Supreme Court again is a specialized tribunal, concentrating on the same kinds of questions. Potentially all cases in federal courts are eligible for ultimate review in the Supreme Court, regardless of the questions litigated. Nevertheless, the jurisdiction of these courts is such as to ensure that the only questions they yield for review are federal questions. The only criminal cases they handle are those involving violations of the federal criminal statutes; and about half of their civil cases arise under the Constitution, laws or treaties of the United States. It is only in the remaining half of the civil cases — those based solely upon diversity of citizenship — that nonfederal questions might be expected to develop. Insofar as such cases involve incidentally questions of federal law (the constitutional right to trial by jury, for example), they are on a par with the cases already discussed. Insofar as they involve questions of state law, such questions are important to decision in the lower federal courts, but they are of little concern to the Supreme Court. There is no dispute as to the general proposition that on such questions state decisions and state statutes are controlling, so that the only problem for the Supreme Court is to see that the lower federal courts respect state sources of decision.

Today relatively few cases reach the Supreme Court as a matter of right. At one time many did, but the press of business was such that Congress gave the Court a very large measure of control over its own docket. The objective was to allow it to concentrate its energies on crucial questions of nationwide concern. Today, as a consequence, most cases reach the Court only by its permission. A litigant seeking review serves on the other parties and files with the court a *petition for certiorari*, in which he seeks not so much to show that an error was committed below as to demonstrate that the question presented is one of general interest, deserving consideration by the highest tribunal of the land. The Court grants or denies review on the basis of its estimate of the importance of the case, measured not in terms of money or penalties but in terms of national significance. Less than 10 percent of the cases that seek review are accepted by the Court.[13]

The few cases that do reach the Court as a matter of right are called *appeals*, and they lie in the following circumstances:

---

[13] The percentage is even lower today.

From a United States court of appeals if a party is relying on a state statute held to be invalid "as repugnant to the Constitution, treaties or laws of the United States."

From a state court if its decision is against the validity of a treaty or statute of the United States; or if it upholds a state statute against the contention that it is "repugnant to the Constitution, treaties or laws of the United States."

The difficulties of arriving at decision are great in the Supreme Court because of the large number of judges whose views must be consulted (nine judges as against five or seven in most appellate courts) and because of the nature of the questions presented, involving, as they do, profound questions of national policy. In the Supreme Court, the lawgiving function of appellate review assumes greater importance than the function of ensuring correct decisions in individual cases. Its emphasis is exactly the reverse of that found in trial *de novo* where reaching the correct result is all that counts. The two types of review are at opposite poles, though both are important and both serve useful purposes.

Chapter 2

LEGAL REASONING AND THE NATURE OF LAW

What is legal reasoning? What is law? What is the Nature of Law? How do courts come to decisions based on the law? What do we get from studying the law? What does all of this matter to you, a student of the law? The answers to these questions should matter to you because they will help you to understand what you are about to learn, why the professors teach in the manner that they teach, and what role you will eventually play as a legal practitioner. This chapter will help you understand legal reasoning and logic and how to use them, will illustrate how the different theories on the nature of law can have a dramatic impact on legal decisionmaking, and will provide insight into the profession in order to help you more effectively learn, understand, and practice the law.

Upon entering law school, many students might anticipate an education filled with concrete rules and instruction on how to apply those rules to the facts of a case; this is only partly correct. During your studies, you will more than likely have a professor who likes to "hide the ball" or asks questions that may seem irrelevant to you. You may feel that this method of teaching is a waste of time since it provides neither a rule nor a solution to the immediate problem. Keep in mind, however, that law school is not merely about learning rules (whether from common law or enacted law), it is also about learning a new way of thinking (a legal way of thinking). Whether or not a question that a professor proposes will ultimately be relevant in a real case is irrelevant to the value that you will gain from the process of answering the question. Learning to answer questions, no matter how irrelevant they may seem at the time, will help you develop the thought process that is vital to finding and addressing relevant issues, and dismissing the irrelevant ones. The process of thinking like a lawyer is as valuable to learn (if not more so) as the law itself.

The first section of this chapter will introduce you to legal reasoning, and will detail the mechanics of logic in the legal reasoning process, including the methods of deduction, induction, and analogy. The second section will focus on the legal reasoning and logic that guides judicial decisions and will describe the different ways that our common law changes. Finally, the third section will discuss various theories on the nature of law that attempt to answer the question "what is law" and will illustrate through examples the impact that these various theories have on legal reasoning and judicial decisionmaking.

A. LEGAL REASONING AND LOGIC: THE BASICS

Legal reasoning is hard to define because it applies in such a wide variety of ways. Start by thinking of legal reasoning as the process that legal professionals use in order to analyze, synthesize, and apply the law. This includes everything from gathering and understanding the facts, to forming arguments, and to ultimately making decisions.

a. The Process of Legal Reasoning

As you will soon find out, if you have not already, lawyers think in terms of rights and duties. If someone has a duty to another, that other has a corresponding right, and a legal consequence may result if the duty is not satisfied. Therefore, when analyzing a conflict, a lawyer will determine the rights and duties of the people involved before deciding how to proceed with the case.

The first article by Kenneth J. Vandevelde will introduce you to the process of legal reasoning by providing and elaborating on five steps that lawyers use to identify a person's rights and duties. The only step in the process that law school does not emphasize is the fourth — researching the applicable facts. Of the five steps listed, law school emphasizes the last step the most — the application of rules to facts. The professors will want you to demonstrate repeatedly that you understand how to apply the law to a given set of facts and reach a conclusion.

KENNETH J. VANDEVELDE
THINKING LIKE A LAWYER: AN INTRODUCTION TO LEGAL REASONING
1–3, 7–8, 11–13, 16, 19–22, 25, 35–40, 57, 65 (1996)[1]

HOW LAWYERS THINK

The phrase "to think like a lawyer" encapsulates a way of thinking that is characterized by both the goal pursued and the method used. The method will be discussed momentarily. The goal of legal thought, which is addressed first, is generally to identify the rights and duties that exist between particular individuals or entities under a given set of circumstances.

As an illustration of the difference between lay thought and legal thought, imagine that two friends — a lawyer and a nonlawyer — are discussing a newspaper reporter who promised an informant anonymity and then published the informant's name. The nonlawyer, astonished by the reporter's conduct, may say to the lawyer, "He can't do that, can he?" The nonlawyer's conception is that the law tells you what you "can" or "cannot" do.

Lawyers rarely think that way, although they may occasionally speak in those terms as a kind of shorthand for a more elaborate thought process. A lawyer would ask instead, "Has the reporter breached any legal duties to the informant, and if so, what rights to relief from the reporter does the informant have?" That is, a lawyer's goal is to identify the rights and duties that exist between the reporter and the informant in the situation described.

As the illustration suggests, thinking like a lawyer essentially requires beginning with a factual situation and, through some process, arriving at a conclusion about the rights and duties of the persons or entities involved in the situation. Let us turn now to the method used by lawyers — a method known as legal reasoning.

Identifying a specific person's rights and duties requires a process of legal reasoning that includes five separate steps. They can be summarized briefly as follows: The lawyer must

1. identify the applicable sources of law, usually statutes and judicial decisions;

2. analyze these sources of law to determine the applicable rules of law and the policies underlying those rules;

3. synthesize the applicable rules of law into a coherent structure in which the more specific rules are grouped under the more general ones;

4. research the available facts; and

5. apply the structure of rules to the facts to ascertain the rights or duties created by the facts, using the policies underlying the rules to resolve difficult cases.

A lawyer may perform these steps in any of several different settings. A litigator may gather facts concerning events that have already occurred to determine whether the client has certain rights or duties with respect to the client's adversary. A business lawyer may be shown a contract and asked for advice concerning the rights and duties that the contract creates. In these two examples, the facts are fixed, and the lawyer's task is to identify the legal consequences of those facts.

In other cases, the process is reversed: The desired legal consequence is already known, and the lawyer's task is to identify the facts that would result in the desired

---

[1] From Thinking Like a Lawyer by Kenneth Vandevelde ©1996. Reprinted by permission of Westview Press, a member of Perseus Books Group.

consequence. A businessman may tell his lawyer, for example, that he wishes to obtain the right to purchase a thousand widgets for $1 each. The lawyer's task now is to create a set of events, such as the negotiation of a contract, that will give rise to a purchase right.

The rights and duties that lawyers identify through the legal reasoning process are those they believe would be enforced by a court of law. Regardless of how convinced a lawyer may be that a particular right or duty *should* exist, if a court would not enforce the right or duty, then it does not exist insofar as the legal system is concerned. Legal reasoning, then, is essentially a process of attempting to predict the decision of a court.

. . . [L]awyers often cannot predict with certainty how a court will decide a dispute. In those cases, legal reasoning can do no more than identify some of the possible results, suggest the arguments that may lead a court to reach each of the possible results, and perhaps provide some indication of the relative probability that each possible result will occur.

. . . .

The reader may notice two conclusions in particular that emerge from the discussion of basic legal reasoning. First, although the legal reasoning process in form is structured as if it were based on mechanical logic, in reality, legal reasoning is impossible without reference to the policies underlying the law. Second, these policies are in conflict, and thus, legal reasoning requires a lawyer to make judgments about which policies are to prevail in particular circumstances.

. . . .

Identifying Applicable Law

The first step in legal reasoning is to identify the law that is potentially applicable to a particular situation. Law is generally of two types.

One type is case law or, as it is sometimes referred to in American courts, "common law." This is law created by a court for the purpose of deciding a specific dispute as well as future, similar cases. Case law is announced by a court in the written opinion in which it decides the dispute.

The other type is enacted law. This consists of laws adopted, usually by a legislature or other elected body, not to decide a single dispute, but to stand as general rules of conduct. Enacted law governs all persons subject to the power of the government in all future situations in which the rule by its terms applies. Enacted law includes constitutions, statutes, treaties, executive orders, and administrative regulations. For the sake of brevity, the different forms of enacted law are often referred to collectively here as statutes.

Two differences between case law and enacted law are of particular importance in this study. First, because of the doctrine of legislative supremacy, . . . enacted law binds the courts. Case law, however, may be changed by a court with sufficient justification. Second, enacted law is cast in authoritative language; that is, the precise words of an enacted law rule are clear and fixed until such time as the enacting body modifies them. Case law, by contrast, often cannot be captured by a single, authoritative, and uncontroversial formulation. Rather, lawyers are likely to disagree among themselves concerning the law that was established by a particular case. The result of these differences is that the application of case law is considerably more flexible than the application of enacted law. The court can manipulate the language of the case or even overrule the case entirely, whereas the language of enacted law is subject to judicial interpretation but cannot itself be manipulated or changed by the court. This means that the application of enacted law tends to involve principally the interpretation of the text of the statute, whereas the application of case law may involve subtle refinements of prior articulations of the law, the introduction of new qualifications or exceptions, or the outright rejection of a well-established body of law.

. . . .

Identifying Issues

Because there are only three things to be decided in a dispute, there are only three types of issues that can arise in legal reasoning. There are issues of fact, issues of law, and issues requiring application of law to fact.

Issues of fact all pose essentially the same basic question: What is the situation to which the law must be applied? In other words, what events have occurred to create the dispute?

Issues of law also pose essentially one basic question: What are the rules of law governing this situation?

Issues requiring the application of law to fact similarly pose one general question: What rights or duties exist between the parties under the governing law in this situation? These issues are sometimes called mixed questions of law and fact.

A single dispute may present all three types of issues or any combination of them. For example, assume that a man sues a female physician claiming that she was negligent in failing to administer a particular diagnostic test to him and that, as a result, he sustained injuries three years later that would have been preventable had his disease been diagnosed earlier.

The physician may put at issue some of the plaintiff's factual allegations. She may raise as issue of fact two questions: Would the diagnostic test actually have revealed that the patient was suffering from the disease? Would the disease have been less injurious had it been discovered earlier?

The parties may also disagree on the applicable law. For example, the physician may raise this question as an issue of law: Does the statute of limitations for negligence claims against a medical practitioner require the claims to be filed within two years of the time the negligence *occurred* or within two years of the time the negligence was *discovered*? If the law requires the claim to be filed within two years of the time the negligence occurred, then the patient would have no right to compensation from the physician.

In addition, the parties may disagree about the application of the law to the facts. For example, the parties may present another question to the court as a mixed issue of law and fact: In this situation, did the physician's failure to administer the test constitute negligence? This is a mixed question of law and fact because it requires the court to apply the legal definition of negligence to the facts to determine whether the physician's conduct constitute negligence. If the physician was not negligent, then the patient has no right to compensation.

Deciding Issues

Determining which category an issue falls into is critical because it determines who decides the issue at trial and the extent to which the issue can be reviewed on appeal. . . .

. . . . Issues of fact can be resolved only by a trial. . . .

Trials are of two types: bench trials and jury trials. . . .

In a bench trial, the judge decides all issues; that is, the judge determines what law applies to the dispute, resolves any factual questions necessary to decide the dispute, and applies the law to the facts. The court then records its decision by entering judgment, which generally entails signing a formal document. The judgment is accompanied by a written statement of the court's findings of facts and conclusions of law.

In a jury trial, the judge decides any issues of law and presides over the trial. After the parties have presented all the evidence, the judge instructs the jury on the laws applicable to the dispute. The jury then decides all issues of fact and applies the laws to the facts. At the conclusion of its deliberations, the jury announces its decision, known as a verdict.

. . . .

If there are no relevant issues of fact, then there is no need for a trial, and the case will be decided by the judge upon the motion of a party. . . .

IDENTIFYING APPLICABLE LAW

In this section, the process of identifying the law that potentially applies to a particular set of facts is examined. As the first section suggests, the lawyer confronts an array of case law and enacted law that could potentially apply to a given situation. The process of determining which law applies is really a process of winnowing out the law that could not plausibly apply.

A law may not apply to a given situation for any of three reasons: (1) the governmental entity that adopted the law does not have power to prescribe law applicable to the specific persons or transactions involved in the situation; (2) the law by its terms does not apply to the situation; or (3) although the governmental entity that adopted the law may have power as a general matter, another entity of greater power has enacted a contrary law that prevails in the situation. By applying these three criteria, the lawyer can eliminate the inapplicable law.

. . . .

Identifying Law by Subject Matter: An Introduction to Rule Analysis

Having narrowed the potentially applicable law to that of one or two sovereigns — one state, the federal government, or both — the lawyer must next winnow out those statutes or cases that, by their terms, do not apply to the subject matter of the situation under review. Lawyers do so by using the process of rule analysis. Let us discuss precisely what that entails.

Each statute or case contains one or more rules of law. . . . For now, the reader should simply assume that the lawyer, upon reading each statute or case, by its terms, is potentially applicable to the situation.

The Nature of Rules: Form

In general, rules of law have the form "if x, then y," meaning that if these facts occur, then this legal right or duty arise.

Rules of law thus have a factual predicate and a legal consequence. For example, a case may announce the rule that a physician performing medical services for a patient has a duty to exercise reasonable care to prevent injury to the patient. In other words, if these facts (a physician-patient relationship and the rendering of a medical service) occur, then this consequence (duty to exercise reasonable care) will result. The physician's performance of a medical service for a patient is the factual predicate, and the duty to exercise reasonable care is the legal consequence.

Usually the factual predicate requires some combination of facts. Each of these facts is referred to as an element. In the example above, the factual predicate has two elements: (1) the existence of a physician-patient relationship, and (2) the rendering of a medical service. When facts constituting all of the elements occur, then the legal consequence takes effect. The legal consequence is generally the creation of some right or duty between certain persons.

Identifying rules of law applicable to a particular situation means identifying those rules of law with factual predicates that accurately describe the situation. If one or more elements of the rule is not present in the situation under review, then the rule will not apply. For example, the rule above would not apply to a physician assisting his patient with the latter's income tax return because the second element, the rendering of a medical service, is absent.

As this suggests, the only way to determine whether a rule is applicable to a situation is actually to endeavor to apply it. Applying a rule to a situation is a potentially complex process . . . . Suffice it to say here that during the initial stage of identifying potentially applicable law, the lawyer looks for all laws that could plausibly apply. To put this another way, the lawyer searches for rules with factual predicates that could arguably be said to apply to the situation.

The Nature of Rules: Substance

Rules are presumed by the American legal system not to be mere arbitrary pronouncements but to be based on some underlying policy. That is, rules create a right or duty not for its own sake but in order to further a public policy.

When the rule is a statute, the underlying policy is generally that which the legislature intended to further when it enacted the statute. When the rule is a case law rule, the underlying policy is generally that which the court articulated as the justification for the rule at the time the rule was announced. Case law rules may also be based on the policies underlying legislative enactments, even in cases that do not involve a statute. For example, the court may adopt a rule favorable to consumers. In support, the court may cite recent legislation that may not be applicable to the case under consideration but nevertheless reflects a public policy of protecting the consumer against the superior bargaining power of merchants and manufacturers.

Rules, moreover, are usually not based on a single policy but represent compromises among sets of opposing policies. Typically, one set of policies favors creation of a broad right or duty, whereas an opposing set of policies favors restricting or elimination the same right or duty.

If the policies favoring the right or duty were to prevail all of the time, the right or duty would become absolute — with no exceptions or limitations. If the policies opposing the right or duty were to prevail all of the time, the right or duty would disappear.

In fact, however, both sets of policies are important, so neither can be permitted to prevail in every situation. Rather, policies supporting the right or duty will prevail in some situations, whereas the opposing policies will prevail in others.

The elements of the rule define exactly the situation in which the policies favoring the right or duty prevail. When the elements are satisfied, the right or duty exists; when they are not satisfied, the right or duty does not exist.

The policies underlying the rule are of great importance to the process of legal reasoning. If it would not further the underlying policies, then applying the rule to a particular situation would be undesirable and the court often will not apply it, especially if the rule is based on case law rather than enacted law. Further, at least where case law rules are concerned, even though the factual predicate of the rule may seem clearly not to apply, if the policy behind the rules would be furthered by finding the rule to be applicable, the court may nevertheless apply the case law rule by analogy, may synthesize a new case law rule to govern the situation, or may modify the rule so that it becomes applicable. Thus . . . the underlying policies provide much assistance in identifying those situations in which the rule will be applied.

The Problem of Generality

The elements of a rule are typically phrased in very general terms. This is especially true with respect to statutes and other forms of enacted law. Thus, for example, a rule does not usually refer to something as specific as a red Buick, or even an automobile, but refers more broadly to a motor vehicle. The elements, in other words, describe the facts in broad, generic terms.

The elements are phrased in general terms for reasons of both fairness and efficiency. If rules were written narrowly, legislatures and courts would need to adopt far more rules, which would be inefficient and would carry the risk that similar situations might not be treated the same way, which would be unfair.

. . . .

Analyzing Statutes and Cases

The second step in legal reasoning is to analyze the plausibly applicable statutes and cases to identify both the rules of law and the underlying polices contained therein. . . .

[The components of a case and the basic strategy for analyzing, understanding, and digesting cases will be discussed in Chapter 4. For now, just know that analyzing cases is a big part of what lawyers do and will require a basic knowledge of legal logic and a critical eye.]

ANALYZING RIGHTS AND DUTIES

In identifying rules of law, whether those rules are drawn from case law or from enacted law, the lawyer must be careful to characterize correctly the precise right or duty created. . . .

The Meaning of Right and Duty

As an initial matter, rights and duties should be understood as types of legal relationships among persons or entities. The law sometimes uses terms other than right or duty to identify a legal relationship. Other such terms include power, liability, privilege, and immunity.

. . . .

Most lawyers in practice tend to use the two terms "right" and "duty" in a sense broad enough to encompass nearly all legal relationships. The term "duty" generally refers to a legal relationship that requires a person to take some action, as in the case of the duty to exercise reasonable care in performing a surgical operation. The term "right" is often used in two different ways. First, it refers to a legal relationship that entitles a person or entity to take some action, as in the right to vote in an election. Second, it also refers to a legal relationship that entitles a person or entity to action from another, as in the right to receive payment of compensation.

. . . .

Three Characteristics of Rights and Duties

Describing a right or duty requires the lawyer to identify three characteristics of the legal relationship. . . .

First, the lawyer must identify the persons between whom the relationship exists. . . .

The second characteristic of a legal relationship that the lawyer must identify is its subject matter, that is, the type of conduct that the right or duty governs. For example, the duty to pay compensation requires one person to pay money to another. The right to exclude others from land may entitle the owner to build a fence but not to place land mines around the perimeter. Each of these rights or duties requires or permits only specified types of conduct.

The third characteristic that the lawyer must identify is the nature of the relationship, assessing whether the legal relationship is mandatory or permissive. Thus, the lawyer must be alert to whether a legal relationship *requires* or merely *permits* certain conduct. For example, the right to exclude others from one's land permits the owner to build a fence but does not require that the landowner to do so.

The Significance of the Three Characteristics

As has been demonstrated, legal reasoning is the process of using rules to draw conclusions about the existence of particular rights or duties in a given situation. More specifically, the lawyer must reach some conclusion about whether the right or duty described in the legal consequence of a rule also applies to the situation under review. In applying a rule to facts, the lawyer must be careful to ensure that the right or duty found to exist in the situation has the same characteristics as the right or duty described in the governing rule.

For example, returning to the illustration from the Introduction, the lawyer may conclude that the reporter has a contractual duty not to publish the informant's name. In analyzing the rules describing the legal consequence of a breach of a contract, the lawyer must be precise about whether the promisee's right as described in the rules is to obtain performance of the promise or compensation for the breach. That, in turn, will determine whether the informant's right is to obtain a court order prohibiting publication of the name or merely to obtain compensation after the name is published. Failure to be precise could result in reaching the wrong conclusion, such as a conclusion that the reporter's promise conferred on the informant the right to stop publication when it conferred only the right to obtain compensation in the event of publication.

One source of difficulty is that references to a right — such as the right of property, the right of privacy, or the right of free speech — can mean different things in different contexts. In each context, the term may have slightly different characteristics. It may be that in announcing the existence of a right or duty the court itself was not precise about the characteristics of the right or duty.

Another source of difficulty is that lawyers can manipulate the level of generality at which a case law rule is stated. In so doing, the lawyer changes the characteristics of the right or duty described in the legal consequence of the rule. The right or duty found to exist in the situation under review thus has different characteristics than the right or duty described in the governing rule.

As this suggests, in some cases, the lawyer in the course of applying a rule to a situation may deliberately change one or more of the characteristics of the right or duty described in the governing rule in order to change the result that the rule seems to require. For example, the lawyer may find a rule stating that a landowner has a right to build a fence around his land to exclude others but may restate the right more generally as a right to exclude other from the land. The lawyer now argues that the client has a right to plant land mines around the perimeter of the land. By manipulating levels of generality, the lawyer attempts to transform the right to build a fence into a right to plant mines.

Synthesizing the Law

The third step in legal reasoning is to synthesize the rules of law into a single, coherent framework that can be applied to the facts. This requires that the lawyer determine the relationship that each rule bears to the others.

In addition, legal reasoning at times requires that the lawyer construct a second, somewhat different typed of synthesis: the synthesis of a single rule from a number of holdings to govern a situation not within the confines of any prior rule or holding. Thus, in the second type of synthesis, the result is not a framework of rules, but a single rule. This rule, or course, once constructed, is integrated into the larger framework of rules.

. . . .

Synthesizing Rules: General to Specific

Synthesizing the rules into a coherent framework means, in effect, that the lawyer creates an outline of the applicable rules, with more specific rules categorized under more general rules. . . .

The Basic Organizing Principle

The key organizing principle in legal reasoning is to move from the general to the specific. For this reason, the lawyer usually begins with general rules of law, which direct the search to more specific rules, which then can be applied to specific facts to produce a conclusion.

. . . .

The categorization process is carried out by determining the type of relationship each rule bears to the others. The relationship between the rules determines the placement of each rule in the synthesis or outline.

. . . .

Researching the Facts

The fourth step in legal reasoning is to research the facts to which the law must be applied. In a real sense, it is misleading to suggest that factual research follows the process of analysis and synthesis described in the prior chapters. As should have been clear from the Introduction, the lawyer cannot even begin the legal reasoning process without a general idea of the circumstances to which the law is to be applied. Thus, a limited factual inquiry is, in fact, the first step of the legal reasoning process.

The Role of Factual Research

There is constant interplay between factual research and the other steps of legal reasoning. The lawyer uses the basic facts known at the beginning of the inquiry to identify the likely sources of applicable law. As potentially applicable general rules are identified, the lawyer may realize that additional facts are needed to determine the applicability of the more specific rule defining, applying, or limiting the general rule. Thus, the lawyer continues to alternate between legal and factual research until all of the plausibly applicable rules have been identified.

At some point, the lawyer believes that the governing rules have been identified and synthesized into a framework. It is at this point that the lawyer must complete the factual research to make certain that all the relevant facts have been discovered. Thus, the fourth step really marks not so much the beginning as the end of the lawyer's factual investigation.

. . . .

Applying the Law

The final step in the legal reasoning process is to apply the law to the facts to determine the rights and duties of the people involved in the situation. The law, as we have seen, consists of rules and the underlying policies.

A lawyer may attempt to use the rules to determine the rights or duties that exist in a particular situation. This requires the application of one of two methods: deduction or analogy. When using deduction, the lawyer determines whether the facts of the situation are or are not described by the factual predicate of a rule and thus whether the legal consequence imposed by the rule does or does not apply to the situation. When using analogy, the lawyer determines whether the facts of the situation are or are not like those described by the factual predicate of the rule and thus whether the legal consequence imposed by the rule does or does not apply to the situation. In applying either of these methods, the lawyer uses rules to determine the rights and duties that exist in the situation and thereby completes the legal reasoning process.

[The logic of deduction and analogy will be addressed at the end of this section in *Logic For Law Students: How to Think Like a Lawyer*.]

b.   Legal Logic: Analogy, Deduction and Induction

The next two articles focus on analogy, deduction and induction. For those unfamiliar with these terms, think of them in this way: analogy is about comparison, deduction is about going from general to specific (i.e. taking a general rule and applying it to specific facts), and induction is about going from specific to general (i.e. taking a set of similar specific facts and deriving a general rule). Through the application of these tools of logic, a good advocate capitalizes upon the similarities and differences between cases to make convincing arguments.

When using these tools, remember that law is not certain. Law is not certain in large part because every case contains a unique set of facts. Depending on the facts of the case on which you are working, you will want to compare or contrast the facts in a way that best supports your client. In order to compare and contrast effectively, however, the lawyer must become comfortable with analogy, deduction, and induction.

For example, if the law states that a person driving a car must wear a seatbelt, does this law apply to a person driving a truck? One argument might deduce that the law applies to all drivers because the law is focused on those who drive. Another argument might try to limit the deduction to drivers of cars only by analogizing to another case in which a court treated truck drivers and car drivers differently. Both arguments make sense and both lead to valid conclusions that can be derived from the current law. The effectiveness of the arguments, however, depends in part on the skillfulness with which the logic is used.

In the first article below, Levi will explore reasoning by analogy. He will talk about the process of legal reasoning as it relates to taking a general rule, or system of rules, and applying it to the specific set of facts presented. In the second article, Aldisert, Clowney, and Peterson continue the discussion on legal logic and delve into a detailed description and analysis of analogy, deduction, and induction.

EDWARD H. LEVI

AN INTRODUCTION TO LEGAL REASONING

1–9, 104 (University of Chicago 1948)[2]

I

This is an attempt to describe generally the process of legal reasoning in the field of case law and in the interpretation of statutes and of the Constitution. It is important that the mechanism of legal reasoning should not be concealed by its pretense. The pretense is that the law is a system of known rules applied by a judge; the pretense has long been under attack. In an important sense, legal rules are never clear, and, if a rule had to be clear before it could be imposed, society would be impossible. The mechanism accepts the differences of view and ambiguities of words. It provides for the participation of the community in resolving the ambiguity by providing a forum for the discussion of policy in the gap of ambiguity. On serious controversial questions, it makes

---

it possible to take the first step in the direction of what otherwise would be forbidden ends. The mechanism is indispensable to peace in a community.

The basic pattern of legal reasoning is reasoning by example. It is reasoning from case to case. It is a three-step process described by the doctrine of precedent in which a proposition descriptive of the first case is made into a rule of law and then applied to a next similar situation. The steps are these: similarity is seen between cases; next the rule of law inherent in the first case is announced; then the rule of law is made applicable to the second case. This is a method of reasoning necessary for the law, but it has characteristics which under other circumstances might be considered imperfections.

These characteristics become evident if the legal process is approached as though it were a method of applying general rules of law to diverse facts — in short, as though the doctrine of precedent meant that general rules, once properly determined, remained unchanged, and then were applied, albeit imperfectly, in later cases. If this were the doctrine, it would be disturbing to find that the rules change from case to case and are remade with each case. Yet this change in the rules is the indispensable dynamic quality of law. It occurs because the scope of a rule of law, and therefore its meaning, depends upon a determination of what facts will be considered similar to those present when the rule was first announced. The finding of similarity or difference is the key step in the legal process.

The determination of similarity or difference is the function of each judge. Where case law is considered, and there is no statute, he is not bound by the statement of the rule of law made by the prior judge even in the controlling case. The statement is mere dictum, and this means that the judge in the present case may find irrelevant the existence or absence of facts which prior judges thought important. It is not what the prior judge intended that is of any importance; rather it is what the present judge, attempting to see the law as a fairly consistent whole, thinks should be the determining classification. In arriving at his result he will ignore what the past thought important; he will emphasize facts which prior judges would have thought made no difference. It is not alone that he could not see the law through the eyes of another, for he could at least try to do so. It is rather that the doctrine of dictum forces him to make his own decision.

Thus, it cannot be said that the legal process is the application of known rules to diverse facts. Yet it is a system of rules; the rules are discovered in the process of determining similarity or difference. But if attention is directed toward the finding of similarity or difference, other peculiarities appear. The problem for the law is: When will it be just to treat different cases as though they were the same? A working legal system must therefore be willing to pick out key similarities and to reason from them to the justice of applying a common classification. The existence of some facts in common brings into play the general rule. If this is really reasoning, then by common standards, thought of in terms of closed systems, it is imperfect unless some overall rule has announced that this common and ascertainable similarity is to be decisive. But no such fixed prior rule exists. It could be suggested that reasoning is not involved at all; that is, that no new insight is arrived at through a comparison of cases. But reasoning appears to be involved; the conclusion is arrived at through a process and was not immediately apparent. It seems better to say there is reasoning, but it is imperfect.

Therefore it appears that the kind of reasoning involved in the legal process is one in which the classification changes as the classification is made. The rules change as the rules are applied. More important, the rules arise out of a process which, while comparing fact situations, creates the rules, and then applies them. But this kind of reasoning is open to the charge that it is classifying things as equal when they are somewhat different, justifying the classification by rules made up as the reasoning or classification proceeds. In a sense, all reasoning is of this type, but there is an additional requirement which compels the legal process to be this way. Not only do new situations arise, but in addition, peoples' wants change. The categories used in the legal process must be left ambiguous in order to permit the infusion of new ideas. And this is true even where legislation or a constitution is involved. The words used by the legislature or the constitutional convention must come to have new meanings. Furthermore, agreement on any other basis would be impossible. In this manner the laws come to express the ideas of the community and even when written in general terms, in statute or constitution, are molded for the specific case.

But attention must be paid to the process. A controversy as to whether the law is certain, unchanging, and expressed in rules, or uncertain, changing, and only a technique for deciding specific cases misses the point. It is both. Nor is it helpful to dispose of the process as a wonderful mystery possibly reflecting a higher law, by which the law can remain the same and yet change. The law forum is the most explicit demonstration of the mechanism required for a moving classification system. The folklore of law may choose to ignore the imperfections in legal reasoning, but the law forum itself has taken care of them.

What does the law forum require? It requires the presentation of competing examples. The forum protects the parties and the community by making sure that the competing analogies are before the court. The rule which will be created arises out of a process in which if different things are to be treated as similar, at least the differences have been urged. In this sense, the parties as well as the court participate in the law-making. In this sense, also, lawyers represent more than the litigants.

Reasoning by example in the law is a key to many things. It indicates in part the hold which the law process has over the litigants. They have participated in the lawmaking. They are bound by something they helped to make. Moreover, the examples or analogies urged by the parties bring into the law the common ideas of the society. The ideas have their day in court, and they will have their day again. This is what makes the hearing fair, rather than any idea that the judge is completely impartial, for of course he cannot be completely so. Moreover, the hearing in a sense compels at least vicarious participation by all the citizens, for the rule which is made, even though ambiguous, will be law as to them.

Reasoning by example shows the decisive role which the common ideas of the society and the distinctions made by experts can have in shaping the law. The movement of common or expert concepts into the law may be followed. The concept is suggested in arguing difference or similarity in a brief, but it wins no approval from the court. The idea achieves standing in the society. It is suggested again to a court. The court this time reinterprets the prior case and in doing so adopts the rejected idea. In subsequent cases, the idea is given further definition and is tied to other ideas which have been accepted by courts. It is now no longer the idea which was commonly held in the society. It becomes modified in subsequent cases. Ideas first rejected but which gradually have won acceptance now push what has become a legal category out of the system or convert it into something which may be its opposite. The process is one in which the ideas of the community and of the social sciences, whether correct or not, as they win acceptance in the community, control legal decisions. Erroneous ideas, of course, have played an enormous part in shaping the law. An idea, adopted by a court, is in a superior position to influence conduct and opinion in the community; judges, after all, are rulers. And the adoption of an idea by a court reflects the power structure in the community. But reasoning by example will operate to change the idea after it has been adopted.

Moreover, reasoning by example brings into focus important similarity and difference in the interpretation of case law, statutes, and the constitution of a nation. There is a striking similarity. It is only folklore which holds that a statute if clearly written can be completely unambiguous and applied as intended to a specific case. Fortunately or otherwise, ambiguity is inevitable in both statute and constitution as well as with case law. Hence, reasoning by example operates with all three. But there are important differences. What a court says is dictum, but what a legislature says is a statute. The reference of the reasoning changes. Interpretation of intention when dealing with a statute is the way of describing the attempt to compare cases on the basis of the standard thought to be common at the time the legislation was passed. While this is the attempt, it may not initially accomplish any different result than if the standard of the judge had been explicitly used. Nevertheless, the remarks of the judge are directed toward describing a category set up by the legislature. These remarks are different from ordinary dicta. They set the course of the statute, and later reasoning in subsequent cases is tied to them. As a consequence, courts are less free in applying a statute than in dealing with case law. The current rationale for this is the notion that the legislature has acquiesced by legislative silence in the prior, even though erroneous, interpretation of the court. But the change in reasoning where legislation is concerned seems an inevitable consequence of the division of function between court and legislature, and, paradoxically, a recognition also of the impossibility of determining legislative intent. The impairment of a court's freedom in interpreting legislation is reflected in frequent appeals to the constitution as a necessary justification for overruling cases even though these cases are thought to have interpreted the legislation erroneously.

Under the United States experience, contrary to what has sometimes been believed when a written constitution of a nation is involved, the court has greater freedom than it has with the application of a statute or case law. In case law, when a judge determines what the controlling similarity between the present and prior case is, the case is decided. The judge does not feel free to ignore the results of a great number of cases which he cannot explain under a remade rule. And in interpreting legislation, when the prior interpretation, even though erroneous, is determined after a comparison of facts to cover the case, the case is decided. But this is not true with a constitution. The constitution sets up the conflicting ideals of the community in certain ambiguous categories. These categories bring along with them satellite concepts covering the areas of ambiguity. It is with a set of these satellite concepts that reasoning by example must work. But no satellite concept, no matter how well developed, can prevent the court from shifting its course, not only by realigning cases which impose certain restrictions, but by going beyond realignment back to the over-all ambiguous category written into the document. The constitution, in other words, permits the court to be inconsistent. The freedom is concealed either as a search for the intention of the framers or as a proper understanding of a living instrument, and sometimes as both. But this does not mean that reasoning by example has any less validity in this field.

II

It may be objected that this analysis of legal reasoning places too much emphasis on the comparison of cases and too little on the legal concepts which are created. It is true that similarity is seen in terms of a word, and inability to find a ready word to express similarity or difference may prevent change in the law. The words which have been found in the past are much spoken of, have acquired a dignity of their own, and to a considerable measure control results. As Judge Cardozo suggested in speaking of metaphors, the word starts out to free thought and ends by enslaving it. The movement of concepts into and out of the law makes the point. If the society has begun to see certain significant similarities or differences, the comparison emerges with a word. When the word is finally accepted, it becomes a legal concept. Its meaning continues to change. But the comparison is not only between the instances which have been included under it and the actual case at hand, but also in terms of hypothetical instances which the word by itself suggests. Thus, the connotation of the word for a time has a limiting influence — so much so that the reasoning may even appear to be simply deductive.

But it is not simply deductive. In the long run, a circular motion can be seen. The first stage is the creation of the legal concept which is built up as cases are compared. The period is one in which the court fumbles for a phrase. Several phrases may be tried out; the misuse or misunderstanding of words itself may have an effect. The concept sounds like another, and the jump to the second is made. The second stage is the period when the concept is more or less fixed, although reasoning by example continues to classify items inside and out of the concept. The third stage is the breakdown of the concept, as reasoning by example has moved so far ahead as to make it clear that the suggestive influence of the word is no longer desired.

The process is likely to make judges and lawyers uncomfortable. It runs contrary to the pretense of the system. It seems inevitable, therefore, that as matters of kind vanish into matters of degree and then entirely new meanings turn up, there will be the attempt to escape to some overall rule which can be said to have always operated and which will make the reasoning look deductive. The rule will be useless. It will have to operate on a level where it has no meaning. Even when lip service is paid to it, care will be taken to say that it may be too wide or too narrow but that nevertheless it is a good rule. The statement of the rule is roughly analogous to the appeal to the meaning of a statute or of a constitution, but it has less of a function to perform. It is window dressing. Yet it can be very misleading. Particularly when a concept has broken down and reasoning by example is about to build another, textbook writers, well aware of the unreal aspect of old rules, will announce new ones, equally ambiguous and meaningless, forgetting that the legal process does not work with the rule but on a much lower level.

. . . .

The emphasis should be on the process. The contrast between logic and the actual legal method is a disservice to both. Legal reasoning has a logic of its own. Its structure fits it to give meaning to ambiguity and to test constantly whether the society has come to see new differences or similarities. Social theories and other changes in society will be relevant when the ambiguity has to be resolved for a particular case. Nor can it be said that the result of such a method is too uncertain to compel. The compulsion of the law is clear; the explanation is that the area of doubt is constantly set forth. The probable area of expansion or contraction is foreshadowed as the system works. This is the only kind of system which will work when people do not agree completely. The loyalty of the community is directed toward the institution in which it participates. The words change to receive the content which the community gives to them. The effort to find complete agreement before the institution goes to work is meaningless. It is to forget the very purpose for which the institution of legal reasoning has been fashioned. This should be remembered as a world community suffers in the absence of law.

Ruggero J. Aldisert, Stephen Clowney & Jeremy D. Peterson
Logic For Law Students: How to Think Like a Lawyer
69 U. Pitt. L. Rev. 1, 1–22 (2007)[3]

INTRODUCTION

Logic is the lifeblood of American law. In case after case, prosecutors, defense counsel, civil attorneys, and judges call upon the rules of logic to structure their arguments. Law professors, for their part, demand that students defend their comments with coherent, identifiable logic. By now we are all familiar with the great line spoken by Professor Kingsfield in *The Paper Chase:* "You come in here with a head full of mush and you leave thinking like a lawyer." What is thinking like a lawyer? It means employing logic to construct arguments.

Notwithstanding the emphasis on logical reasoning in the legal profession, our law schools do not give students an orientation in the principles of logic. Professor Jack L. Landau complained that "the idea of teaching traditional logic to law students does not seem to be very popular." Indeed, Professor Landau found that "[n]ot one current casebook on legal method, legal process, or the like contains a chapter on logic." In our view, this is tragic. The failure to ground legal education in principles of logic does violence to the essence of the law. Leaving students to distill the principles of logic on their own is like asking them to design a rocket without teaching them the rules of physics. Frustration reigns, and the resulting argument seems more mush-like than lawyerly. In these pages we make a small attempt to right the ship by offering a primer on the fundamentals of logical thinking.

Our goals are modest. At the risk of disappointing philosophers and mathematicians, we will not probe the depths of formal logic. Neither will we undertake to develop an abstract theory of legal thinking. This Article, rather, attempts something new: we endeavor to explain, in broad strokes, the core principles of logic and how they apply in the law school classroom. Our modest claim is that a person familiar with the basics of logical thinking is more likely to argue effectively than one who is not. We believe that students who master the logical tenets laid out in the following pages will be better lawyers and will feel more comfortable when they find themselves caught in the spotlight of a law professor on a Socratic binge.

Sifting through the dense jargon of logicians, we have identified a handful of ideas that are particularly relevant to the world of legal thinking. First, all prospective lawyers should make themselves intimately familiar with the fundamentals of deductive reasoning. Deductive reasoning, as Aristotle taught long ago, is based on the act of proving a conclusion by means of two other propositions. Perhaps 90 percent of legal issues can be resolved by deduction, so the importance of understanding this type of reasoning cannot be overstated. Second, students should acquaint themselves with the principles of inductive generalization. Inductive generalizations, used correctly, can help students resuscitate causes that seem hopeless. Third, reasoning by analogy — another form of inductive reasoning — is a powerful tool in a lawyer's arsenal. Analogies help lawyers and judges solve legal problems not controlled by precedent and help law students deflect the nasty hypotheticals that are the darlings of professors. Finally, we comment briefly on the limitations of logic.

It's Elementary: Deductive Reasoning & the Law

The Syllogism

Logic anchors the law. The law's insistence on sound, explicit reasoning keeps lawyers and judges from making arguments based on untethered, unprincipled, and undisciplined hunches. Traditionally, logicians separate the wider universe of logical reasoning into two general categories: inductive and deductive. As we will see, both branches of logic play important roles in our legal system. We begin with deductive reasoning because it is the driving force behind most judicial opinions. Defined broadly, deduction is reasoning in which a conclusion is *compelled* by known facts. For example, if we know that Earth is bigger than Mars, and that Jupiter is bigger than Earth, then we also know that Jupiter *must* be bigger than Mars. Or, imagine that you know your dog becomes deathly ill every time he eats chocolate. Using deduction we know that if Spike wolfs down a Snickers bar, a trip to the vet will be necessary. From these examples, we can get an idea of the basic structure of deductive arguments: If A and B are true, then C also must be true.

The specific form of deductive reasoning that you will find lurking below the surface of most judicial opinions and briefs is the "syllogism" a label logicians attach to any argument in which a conclusion is inferred from two premises. For example:

All men are mortal.

Socrates is a man.
Therefore, Socrates is mortal.

According to the traditional jargon, the syllogism's three parts are called the major premise, the minor premise, and the conclusion. The major premise states a broad and generally applicable truth: "All men are mortal." The minor premise states a specific and usually more narrowly applicable fact: "Socrates is a man." The conclusion then draws upon these premises and offers a new insight that is known to be true based on the premises: "Socrates is a mortal."

Gottfried Leibnitz expressed the significance of the syllogism three hundred years ago, calling its invention "one of the most beautiful, and also one of the most important, made by the human mind." For all its power, the basic principle of the syllogism is surprisingly straightforward: What is true of the universal is true of the particular. If we know that *all* cars have wheels, and that a Toyota is a car, then a Toyota must have wheels. The axiom may be stated this way: If we know that every member of a class has a certain characteristic, and that certain individuals are members of that class, then those individuals must have that characteristic.

It is no exaggeration to say that the syllogism lies at the heart of legal writing. Consider these examples taken from watershed Supreme Court opinions:

Marbury v. Madison
The Judicial Department's province and duty is to say what the law is.
The Supreme Court is the Judicial Department.
Therefore, the province and duty of the Supreme Court is to say what the law is.

Youngstown Sheet & Tube Co. v. Sawyer
The President's power to issue an order must stem from an act of Congress or the Constitution.
Neither an act of Congress nor the Constitution gives the President the power to issue the order
Therefore, the President does not have the power to issue the order.

Brown v. Board of Education
Unequal educational facilities are not permitted under the Constitution.
A separate educational facility for black children is inherently unequal.
Therefore, a separate educational facility for black children is not permitted under the Constitution.

We urge all law students to get in the habit of thinking in syllogisms. When briefing a case as you prepare a class assignment, the skeleton of the deductive syllogism should always poke through in your description of the case's rationale. Young attorneys should probably tattoo this on the back of their hands — or at least post it above their keyboards: Whenever possible, make the arguments in your briefs and memos in the form of syllogisms. A clear, well-constructed syllogism ensures each conclusion is well-supported with evidence and gives a judge recognizable guideposts to follow as he [shepherds] the law along his desired footpath.

But how, you might ask, does a new lawyer learn to construct valid syllogisms? Some people come to this ability instinctively. Just as some musicians naturally possess perfect pitch, some thinkers have logical instincts. Luckily for the rest of us, the skill can be learned through patience and practice. We start with the basics. To shape a legal issue in the form of a syllogism, begin by stating the general rule of law or widely-known legal rule that governs your case as your major premise. Then, in your next statement, the minor premise, describe the key facts of the legal problem at hand. Finally, draw your conclusion by examining how the major premise about the law applies to the minor premise about the facts. Like this:

Major Premise: Cruel and unusual punishment by a state violates the Eighth Amendment.

Minor Premise: Executing a minor is cruel and unusual punishment by a state.
Conclusion: Executing a minor is forbidden by the Eighth Amendment.

Although this might look simple, constructing logically-sound syllogisms requires a lot of grunt work. You must thoroughly research the law's nooks and crannies before you can confidently state your major premise. And you must become sufficiently knowledgeable about your case to reduce key facts to a brief yet accurate synopsis.

If you find yourself having trouble organizing a brief or memo, try shoehorning your argument into this generic model, which is based on the argument made by prosecutors in nearly every criminal case:

Major premise: **[Doing something]** [violates the law.]
Minor premise: [The defendant] **[did something.]**
Conclusion: [The defendant] [violated the law.]

The prosecutor's model can serve as a useful template for most legal problems. Using it will help you reduce your arguments to their most essential parts.

In addition to providing a useful template, the above example reflects the fact that the three parts of a syllogism — the two premises and the conclusion — are themselves built from three units. Logicians call these units "terms." Two terms appear in each statement: the "major term" in the major premise and conclusion, the "minor term" in the minor premise and conclusion, and the "middle term" in the major and minor premises but not in the conclusion. Notice that the middle term covers a broad range of facts, and that if the conclusion is to be valid, the minor term must be a fact that is included within the middle term. Although the jargon can get confusing, the basic idea isn't hard to grasp: Each statement in a syllogism must relate to the other two.

Finding Syllogisms in Legal Writing

But wait! — you might be thinking — this syllogism business is too simple; opinions and memos are never so straightforward. Well, yes and no. The syllogism is simple, and indeed it does undergird most legal arguments, but sometimes you have to dig a bit below the surface to excavate syllogisms. The fact that syllogisms aren't immediately evident doesn't mean that the writing is sloppy, or that it doesn't use syllogisms. But it does mean that you'll have to work a bit harder as a reader. One logician notes that "an argument's basic structure . . . may be obscured by an excess of verbiage . . . , but an argument's structure may also be obscured for us . . . because it is too sparse and has missing components. Such arguments may appear sounder than they are because we are unaware of important assumptions made by them. . . . "

Consider this one-sentence argument penned by Justice Blackmun in his *Roe v. Wade* opinion:

This right of privacy, whether it be founded in the Fourteenth Amendment's concept of personal liberty and restrictions upon state action, as we feel it is, or, as the District Court determined, in the Ninth Amendment's reservation of rights to the people, is broad enough to encompass a woman's decision whether or not to terminate her pregnancy.

Implicit within Justice Blackmun's statement is the following syllogism:

Major Premise: The right of privacy is guaranteed by the Fourteenth or Ninth Amendment.
Minor Premise: A woman's decision to terminate her pregnancy is protected by the right of privacy.
Conclusion: Therefore, a woman's decision whether to terminate her pregnancy is protected by the Fourteenth or Ninth Amendment.

The ideas are floating around in Judge Blackmun's sentence, but it requires some work on the reader's part to parse them into two premises and a conclusion.

Sometimes it's more than a matter of rearranging sentences and rephrasing statements to match up with the syllogistic form. Sometimes a legal writer doesn't mention all parts of the syllogism, leaving you to read between the lines. Logicians are certainly aware that an argument can be founded on a syllogism although not all parts of the syllogism are expressed. They even have a name for such an argument: an enthymeme. Often, enthymemes are used for efficiency's sake. If a premise or conclusion is obvious, then the writer can save her precious words to make less obvious points. Even a kindergarten teacher might find the full expression of a syllogism to be unnecessary. The teacher could say, "Good girls get stars on their foreheads; Lisa is a good girl; Lisa gets a star on her forehead." But she's more likely to say, "Lisa gets a star on her forehead because she is a good girl." In logic-speak, the teacher would be omitting the major premise because it is generally understood that good girls get stars on their foreheads.

Judges and lawyers write for more educated audiences — or so we hope — and so as a law student you had better be ready for hosts of enthymemes. The Third Circuit employed one in *Jones & Laughlin Steel, Inc. v. Mon River Towing, Inc.* That decision was founded on the following syllogism:

> **Major Premise:** Any federal procedural rule that conflicts with Rule 4 of the Federal Rules of Civil Procedure is superceded by Rule 4.
> **Minor Premise:** Section 2 of the Suits in Admiralty Act is a federal procedural rule that conflicts with Rule 4 of the Federal Rule of Civil Procedure.
> **Conclusion:** Rule 4 supersedes Section 2 of the Suits in Admiralty Act.

In the text of the opinion, however, the court left out a key part of the minor premise; it never stated that Section 2 of the Suits in Admiralty Act actually conflicts with Rule 4 of the Rules of Civil Procedure. The court can hardly be faulted for not explicitly stating the conflict. All parties involved recognized the conflict, and the court avoided needless words by leaving the conflict implicit. But an astute reader of the case should recognize that a bit of work on her part is necessary in order to develop the enthymeme into a full-fledged syllogism.

In addition to not handing the reader syllogisms on a platter, legal writers also have the tendency to pile one syllogism on top of another. Not surprisingly, logicians have a term for this too, but for once it is a term that makes sense and is easy to remember. A series of syllogisms in which the conclusion of one syllogism supplies a premise of the next syllogism is known as a polysyllogism. Typically, polysyllogisms are used because more than one logical step is needed to reach the desired conclusion. Be on the lookout for something like this as you pick apart a complex legal opinion:

> All men are mortal.
> Socrates is a man.
> Therefore Socrates is mortal.

> All mortals can die.
> Socrates is mortal.
> Therefore Socrates can die.

> People who can die are not gods.
> Socrates can die.
> Therefore Socrates is not a god.

You have been warned. Watch for enthymemes and polysyllogisms in every opinion or legal memo or brief that you read, and be aware of them in your own writing. Your arguments will be improved.

Watch Out!: Flawed Syllogisms

A syllogism is a powerful tool because of its rigid inflexibility. If the premises of a syllogism are properly constructed, the conclusion *must* follow. But beware of bogus arguments masquerading as syllogisms. For example, consider the following:

Some men are tall.
Socrates is a man.
Therefore Socrates is tall.

It looks something like a syllogism, but you have no doubt spotted the flaw: knowing that *some* men are tall isn't enough for you to conclude that a particular man is tall. He might fall into the group of other men about whom we know nothing, and who might be tall, but who also might be short. This type of non-syllogism got past the U.S. Supreme Court in the *Dred Scott* case, in which the Court held that people of African descent, whether or not they were slaves, could never be citizens of the United States. One dissenting opinion noted that the Court's ruling relied on a bad syllogism, simplified here:

Major Premise: At the time of the adoption of the Constitution, some states considered members of the black race to be inferior and incapable of citizenship and of suing in federal court.

Minor Premise: Dred Scott's ancestors at the time of the Constitution were members of the black race.

Conclusion: Therefore, Dred Scott's ancestors were considered to be inferior and incapable of citizenship and of suing in federal court.

Mistakes of this sort remain extremely common in legal writing. Certain buzzwords, however, can help distinguish valid syllogisms from fallacious ones. Alarm bells should sound immediately if you spot terms in the major premise like "some," "certain," "a," "one," "this," "that," "sometimes," "many," "occasionally," "once," or "somewhere." Remember at all costs that the principle behind the syllogism is that what's true of the universal is true of the specific. In deductive reasoning, you reason from the general to the particular. Accordingly, if you're unsure about the nature of the general, you can't draw proper conclusions about the particular.

Logical errors, unfortunately, are often tough to catch. Here is a different one:

Major Premise: All superheroes have special powers.
Minor Premise: Superman has special powers.
Conclusion: Superman is a superhero.

Unless you're an avid comic book reader, it might take a moment to spot the misstep. Knowing that every superhero has special powers doesn't allow you to conclude that everyone with special powers is a superhero. Recall again the golden rule of the syllogism: You can only draw a conclusion about the particular (Superman, in this case) after you demonstrate that it's part of the universal class. Thus, a correct syllogism would look like this:

Major Premise: All superheroes have special powers. [General statement about a class]
Minor Premise: Superman is a superhero. [Statement that an individual belongs to the class]
Conclusion: Superman has special powers. [Conclusion that the individual has properties common to other members of the class]

Remember this: Just because two things share a common property does not mean they also share a second property. Some other examples of this fallacy may help. Business executives read the *Wall Street Journal*, and Ludwig is a *Journal* reader, therefore Ludwig is a business executive — WRONG! All law students are smart, and John is smart, therefore John is a law student — WRONG AGAIN! You get the idea.

So far, we've considered only two logical fallacies. Logicians have many more. Although we cannot provide an exhaustive list of fallacies, here is a quick check you can run that often will uncover flaws in a deductive syllogism. Logicians have come up with a series of letters to identify different types of propositions. The letters "A" and "E" describe universal propositions, "A" being affirmative and "E" negative. Meanwhile, "I" and "O" describe particular propositions, "I" being affirmative and "O" negative. The letters come from two Latin words: Affirmo (I affirm) and Nego (I deny). Logicians would describe the three propositions in our friendly "All men are mortal" syllogism as

AII. Now for the check: For the major premise to be valid, it must be either "A" or "E." You can't make a major premise out of an "I" or an "O." The IAA form, for example, is not a valid syllogism. And your minor premise and conclusion must be either an "I" or an "O." If your tentative syllogism doesn't meet these requirements, you'll know something is wrong.

Certain logical errors crop up again and again, and so you should take particular care to avoid them. Don't cite inappropriate secondary authorities or cases from outside jurisdictions; logicians consider that an appeal to inappropriate authority. Don't rely on attacks on your opponent's character. Don't rely on appeals to emotion. Don't rely on fast talking or personal charm to carry the day. A cool head coupled with rigorous legal research, rather than rhetorical tricks, will turn a case in your favor.

It is critical to read every legal document you come across with care. Bad reasoning can seem persuasive at first glance. Logical fallacies are especially hard to spot in briefs, memos, and court opinions because of the dense writing and complex fact patterns. Yet the effort is worthwhile. The ability to detect and avoid logical missteps will improve your writing immensely and develop your ability to "think like a lawyer" — the skill that professors and partners so admire.

Inductive Reasoning: Generalizations

Deductive reasoning and its adherence to the "Socrates is Mortal" type of syllogism is the spine that holds our legal system together. Justice Cardozo estimated that at least nine-tenths of appellate cases "could not, with the semblance of reason, be decided in any way but one" because "the law and its application alike are plain," or "the rule of law is certain, and the application alone doubtful." After more than four decades on the bench, Judge Aldisert can confirm that Justice Cardozo's statement remains true today. In the language of logic, this means that practicing lawyers spend most of their time worrying about the minor premises of syllogisms (i.e., can the facts of the case be fit into the territory governed by a particular rule?).

In law school, however, you will be asked to concentrate on the ten percent (or less) of cases that can't be resolved so easily. In the classroom, knotty and unsettled questions of law predominate. Where an issue of law is unsettled, and there is no binding precedent to supply a major premise for your syllogism, deductive logic is of no use to you. By focusing on such cases, your professors will drag you kicking and screaming into the land of induction, the second category of logic.

Inductive generalization is a form of logic in which big, general principles are divined from observing the outcomes of many small events. In this form of inductive logic, you reason from multiple particulars to the general. To see how this works, suppose that you are asked to determine whether all men are mortal — the premise of the first syllogism we discussed. If nobody hands you the simple statement "All men are mortal," and you lack a way of deducing it, you have to turn to inductive reasoning. You might use what you know about particular men and their mortality as follows:

> Plato was a man, and Plato was mortal.
> Julius Caesar was a man, and Julius Caesar was mortal.
> George Washington was a man, and George Washington was mortal.
> John Marshall was a man, and John Marshall was mortal.
> Ronald Reagan was a man, and Ronald Reagan was mortal.
> Therefore, all men are mortal.

The principle underlying this way of thinking is that the world is sufficiently regular to permit the discovery of general rules. If what happened yesterday is likely to happen again today, we may use past experience to guide our future conduct. The contrast with deductive reasoning is stark. Whereas syllogisms are mechanical and exact — if the premises are true and properly assembled, the conclusion *must* be true — inductive logic is not so absolute. It does not produce conclusions *guaranteed* to be correct, no matter how many examples scholars assemble. Thousands of great men may live and die each year, but we will never know with absolute certainty whether every man is mortal. Thus, inductive reasoning is a logic of probabilities and generalities, not certainties. It yields workable rules, but not proven truths.

The absence of complete certainty, however, does not dilute the importance of induction in the law. As we stated at the outset, we look to inductive reasoning when our legal research fails to turn up a hefty, hearty precedent that controls the case. When there is no clear statute — no governing authority — to provide the major premise necessary for a syllogism, the law student must build the major premise himself. To use Lord Diplock's phrase, this requires him to draw upon "the cumulative experience of the judiciary" — the specific holdings of other cases. Once he has assembled enough case law, he tries to fashion a general rule that supports his position.

You might wonder how this works in the real world. Let's start with something mundane. Suppose a professor asks you to determine what happens to the contents of a jointly-leased safe deposit box if one of the lessees dies unexpectedly. Do all of the contents pass to the survivor, or does the dead man's estate claim his possessions? The Oklahoma Supreme Court faced this question in *Estate of Stinchcomb*. Finding that the state had no binding case law on point, the court turned to inductive reasoning. Its research demonstrated that judges in Illinois, Nevada, and Maryland had all ruled in favor of the dead man's estate. From these individual examples, the Oklahoma Supreme Court inferred the general rule that "a joint lease in and of itself alone, does not create a joint tenancy in the contents of the box."

Inductive generalizations, then, are easy enough to understand. You can get in trouble using them, however. Most importantly, you must be careful to assemble a sufficient number of examples before shaping a far-reaching rule, or you will be guilty of the fallacy of "hasty generalization." In logic-speak, this fallacy occurs when you construct a general rule from an inadequate number of particulars. It is the bugaboo of inductive reasoning and often surfaces in casebooks and classroom discussions, as well as on TV talk-shows and in newspaper editorials. Think about your overeager classmates who rely on nothing more than their personal life experiences to justify outlandish policy proposals. They're often guilty of creating bogus general rules from exceptional circumstances. Judges, lawyers, and law students all must be careful not to anoint isolated instances with the chrism of generality.

The difficulty comes in knowing how many instances are sufficient to make a generalization. Three? Ten? Forty thousand? This is where the art comes in. As a rule of thumb, the more examples you find, the stronger your argument becomes. In *O'Conner v. Commonwealth Edison Co.*, a federal judge in Illinois lambasted an expert witness for attempting to formulate a universal medical rule based on his observation of only five patients:

> Based on the five patients [Dr. Scheribel] has observed with cataracts induced by radiation therapy, he developed his "binding universal rule" that he applied to O'Conner, thus committing the logical fallacy known as Converse Accident (hasty generalization). . . . It occurs when a person erroneously creates a general rule from observing too few cases. Dr. Scheribel has illogically created a "binding universal rule" based upon insufficient data.

> For example, observing the value of opiates when administered by a physician to alleviate the pains of those who are seriously ill, one may be led to propose that narcotics be made available to everyone. Or considering the effect of alcohol only on those who indulge in it to excess, one may conclude that all liquor is harmful and urge that its sale and use should be forbidden by law. Such reasoning is erroneous . . . .

Don't let yourself make the same mistake.

Raw numbers are not enough to give you a reliable generalization, however. Consider this classic blunder: In 1936, *Literary Digest* magazine conducted a massive polling effort to predict the outcome of the Presidential election between Alf Landon and Franklin Roosevelt. The *Digest* polled well over two million people, and the vast majority indicated they would vote for Landon (keep in mind that modern news organizations base their polls on the responses of 1,000 people). In the actual election, however, Roosevelt won 523 electoral votes and Landon received only eight. How did *Literary Digest* get it so wrong when it had crafted its rule from a massive number of particular examples? It seems the *Digest* focused its polling efforts on car owners — an unrepresentative group of the American public in 1936. From this example, it should become clear that the strength of an inductive argument rests not only on the number of examples you turn up to support your generalization, but also on the representativeness of the sample size. Keep this in mind when your opponent makes an argument based solely on the use of statistics, as is the case in many antitrust, securities, and discrimination claims.

You will never completely escape the risks posed by the fallacy of hasty generalization. We can never know with certainty that an inductive generalization is true. The best that can be hoped for is that expert research and keen attention to statistics will divine workable rules that are grounded in the wisdom of human experience. If your professor demands absolute certainty of you, you'll have to explain to him that it cannot be achieved, at least not with an inductive generalization. Notwithstanding its shortcomings, inductive generalization remains a vital tool, because the ability to shape persuasive legal arguments when no clear precedent exists is often what separates a star attorney from your run-of-the-mill ambulance chaser.

Analogy

Anyone who has struggled through a first-year torts course knows that hypothetical questions play a central role in the law school classroom. Professors invent elaborate factual scenarios and ask students to distill the correct result from a handful of cases read the night before. Then they change the situation slightly; does the answer change? Now alter a different parameter; same result, or a different one? The imaginative fact patterns do not end with law school; judges, too, rely on outlandish hypotheticals to test the validity of a lawyer's argument. Yet, notwithstanding the importance of hypothetical questions in legal thinking, the ability to manage them remains poorly taught and rarely practiced. We believe that the careful use of analogy — a form of inductive reasoning — can get you past a nasty hypothetical. Analogy can help a budding lawyer advance untested legal arguments in the classroom and the courtroom. We stress that mastering the principles of analogy is not just another garden-variety lawyer's skill. Rather, it is one of the most crucial aspects of the study and practice of law.

Unlike most concepts employed by logicians, the use of "analogy" is not confined to the realms of higher mathematics and philosophy. Most law students, and even most laypersons, are familiar with formal analogies of the "Sun is to Day as Moon is to _ ?" variety. The use of informal, off-the-cuff analogies guides most of our own everyday decisionmaking. I own a Honda Civic that doesn't overheat, so I conclude that my friend's Honda Civic will never overheat. My eyes don't water when I cut an onion; I conclude that my brother's eyes won't water either. This type of reasoning has a simple structure: (1) A has characteristic Y; (2) B has characteristic Y; (3) A also has characteristic Z; (4) Because A and B both have Y, we conclude that B also shares characteristic Z. At base, analogy is a process of drawing similarities between things that appear different.

In the world of the law, analogies serve a very specific purpose. Attorneys use them to compare new legal issues to firmly established precedents. Typically, this means that a current case is compared to an older one, and the outcome of the new case is predicted on the basis of the other's outcome. Edward Levi, the foremost American authority on the role of analogy in the law, described analogical reasoning as a three step process: (1)

establish similarities between two cases, (2) announce the rule of law embedded in the first case, and (3) apply the rule of law to the second case. This form of reasoning is different from deductive logic or inductive generalization. Recall that deduction requires us to reason from universal principles to smaller, specific truths. The process of generalization asks us to craft larger rules from a number of specific examples. Analogy, in contrast, makes one-to-one comparisons that require no generalizations or reliance on universal rules. In the language of logicians, analogy is a process of reasoning from the particular to the particular.

An example might help to clarify the distinction. Imagine you are asked to defend a client who received a citation for driving a scooter without a helmet. After scouring Westlaw, you find there's no controlling statute. There are, however, two precedents that could influence the result. One opinion holds that motorcyclists must wear helmets; the other case says that a helmet is not required to operate a bicycle. Does either control the issue in your case? Without a clear universal rule or past cases on point, deductive logic and inductive generalizations are of little help. Instead, you must rely on the power of analogy to convince a judge that helmet laws don't apply. To defend your client, you must suggest that driving a scooter is similar to riding a "fast bicycle." You might argue that small scooters can't go faster than well-oiled road bikes. Thus, a scooter presents no more danger to its operator or other drivers than a bicycle. You could also argue that scooters, like bikes, can't be driven on highways. The process of drawing these comparisons and explaining why they are important is the heart of reasoning by analogy. The idea is to find enough similarities between the new case and old precedent to convince a judge that the outcomes must be the same.

A proper analogy should identify the respects in which the compared cases, or fact scenarios, resemble one another and the respects in which they differ. What matters is *relevancy* — whether the compared traits resemble, or differ from, one another in relevant respects. A single apt comparison can be worth more than a host of not-quite-right comparisons. You might be wondering how to tell whether a comparison is a fruitful one or whether it's not quite right. Well, that is where art once again enters the picture. As John Stuart Mill remarked:

> Why is a single instance, in some cases, sufficient for a complete induction, while in others myriads of concurring instances . . . go such a very little way towards establishing an universal proposition? Whoever can answer this question knows more of the philosophy of logic than the wisest of the ancients, and has solved the problem of Induction.

Notwithstanding the best efforts of logicians, no one has devised a mathematical equation for determining whether an analogy is strong or weak. "It is a matter of judgment, not mechanical application of a rule." Thinking back to our scooter example, your opponent will argue vigorously that a scooter resembles a motorcycle because both have quick-starting, gas-powered engines that are beyond human control. This comparison may strike the judge as more powerful than yours, convincing him to rule against your client.

The Court of Appeals for the Third Circuit discussed all of these principles in detail in an important class action antitrust case where the principal issue on appeal was whether the holding in a case called *Newton* applied to the case at bar:

> For Appellants' argument to prevail, therefore, they must demonstrate that the facts in *Newton* are substantially similar to the facts in the case at bar, what logicians call inductive reasoning by analogy, or reasoning from one particular case to another. To draw an analogy between two entities is to indicate one or more respects in which they are similar and thus argue that the legal consequence attached to one set of particular facts may apply to a different set of particular facts because of the similarities in the two sets. Because a successful analogy is drawn by demonstrating the resemblances or similarities

in the facts, the degree of similarity is always the crucial element. You may not conclude that only a partial resemblance between two entities is equal to a substantial or exact correspondence.

Logicians teach that one must always appraise an analogical argument very carefully. Several criteria may be used: (1) the acceptability of the analogy will vary proportionally with the number of circumstances that have been analyzed; (2) the acceptability will depend upon the number of positive resemblances (similarities) and negative resemblances (dissimilarities); or (3) the acceptability will be influenced by the relevance of the purported analogies. [Citing logicians].

For Appellants to draw a proper analogy, they had the burden in the district court, as they do here, of showing that the similarities in the facts of the two cases outweigh the differences. They cannot do so, for two significant reasons. First, in *Newton* it was clear that not all members of the putative class sustained injuries; here, all members sustained injuries because of the artificially increased prices. Secondly, in Newton there were hundreds of millions of stock transactions involved, thus making the putative class extremely unmanageable; here, an astronomical number of transactions is not present. [Thus, their argument fails.]

Let's turn to other examples of the process of analogy. Imagine you discover that Able Automobile Company is liable for violating the antitrust laws by requiring a tie-in purchase of a refrigerator manufactured by Mrs. Able with the purchase of any Able car. It is not difficult to see by analogy that liability also would follow from these facts: Baker Automobile Company requires a tie-in purchase of a refrigerator manufactured by Mrs. Baker if you want to buy a Baker Mustang.

But consider the following: State College had a championship basketball team last year. Team members came from high schools *A, B, C,* and *D.* State College has recruited new players from high schools *A, B, C,* and *D* for this year's team. Therefore, State College will have a championship basketball team this year. Is the resemblance relevant? We must ask if the resemblance — players from the same high schools — is meaningful. Does it help us get to the conclusion we seek to draw? If one good player came from a particular school, does that mean that another player is likely to be similarly good? Probably not, unless the high school is extremely unusual and has only good basketball players. More likely, what we have here is an analogy based on irrelevant similarities, and such an analogy is of no use at all.

As mentioned earlier, law professors love to test your ability to work with analogies by inventing grueling hypotheticals. They do this for a few reasons. First, as we've already discussed, the imagined fact patterns force you to grapple with questions of law that aren't amenable to syllogisms. Second, a professor can easily and repeatedly change the facts of a hypo, allowing him to ask questions of many students and to probe the boundaries of a particular legal issue. Finally, the fear of getting trapped in the tangle of a knotty question encourages students to study the law with care and to absorb its details. If you do find yourself in the Socratic spotlight, remember that the basic principles of analogy; they can be your lifeline. Begin by discussing the facts of a similar case that you are familiar with, and then lay out particulars of the hypothetical the professor has asked. Draw as many comparisons between the two cases as you can. If the relevant similarities outweigh the relevant differences, the outcomes of the cases should be the same. The more practice you get working with analogies, and the more adept you become at articulating why certain similarities or differences are relevant, the better you will fare when it's your turn to face the music.

LOGICAL LIMITS: WHEN THERE IS MORE TO THE STORY

We hope we have convinced you that logic is the lifeblood of the law, and that understanding basic logical forms will assist you both in law school and in your practice as a lawyer. We would be remiss, however, if we were to send you out into the world without acknowledging that there is more to the law than assembling logical expressions.

Consider the following:

> All federal judges are body builders.
> Judge Aldisert is a federal judge.
> Therefore, Judge Aldisert is a body builder.

What's wrong with this statement? It's a rock-solid syllogism, adhering to the blueprint of logical validity expressed by the "Socrates" syllogism. Just the same, Judge Aldisert does not spend much time pumping iron. You see the problem, of course: the major premise is false. Not all federal judges are body builders. In fact, we doubt any of them are. The point is an obvious but important one: make sure your premises are true. If you use an untrue premise as a lawyer, it's an invitation to the other side to pillory you. If you do so as a judge, you may fashion a dangerous precedent. Consider the infamous *Dred Scott* case. The crucial syllogism used by the majority was as follows:

> **Major Premise:** At the time of the adoption of the Constitution, *all* states considered members of the black race to be inferior and incapable of citizenship and of suing in federal court.
> **Minor Premise:** Dred Scott's ancestors at the time of the Constitution were members of the black race.
> **Conclusion:** Therefore, Dred Scott's ancestors were considered to be inferior and incapable of citizenship and of suing in federal court.

As discussed in Part I, the dissenting opinion pointed out that only some state legislatures labeled blacks inferior at the time of the adoption of the Constitution. Other states — namely New Hampshire, Massachusetts, New York, New Jersey, and North Carolina — maintained that all free-born inhabitants, even though descended from African slaves, possessed the right of franchise of electors on equal terms with other citizens. Once the "all" in the majority's major premise is replaced with "some," the syllogism fails to hold water.

Separately, logic is not the whole game. Even if your premises are true and your logical statements constructed properly, it is crucial to recognize that judges are motivated by more than the mandates of logic. As Judge Aldisert has said, "[w]e judges come to our robes bearing the stigmata of our respective experiences." Judges have notions of how things should be — of what is wrong and what is right — and often strive to do justice as much as to fulfill the mandates of precedent. They have biases, too. In reading cases, writing briefs, and arguing before a court, you will be more effective if you flesh out the logical bones of your arguments and attempt to appeal to the judge in other ways as well.

But always bear in mind: *An argument that is correctly reasoned may be wrong, but an argument that is incorrectly reasoned can never be right.* You may find the discipline of parsing legalese into logical forms to be time-consuming and arduous at first, but as you become more comfortable with logic's framework, you will find that the exercise helps you more efficiently peel a case back to its essence. A solid footing in logic will help you feel more secure when you find yourself in a complex doctrinal thicket. And while the fundamentals of logic laid out in this article will not give you a magic carpet on which you can float above the legal briar patch, we believe they will give you a machete that will help you start hacking your way through the tangle.

B.   LEGAL REASONING IN THE COURTS

This section continues the discussion on legal reasoning by taking a closer look at judicial decisionmaking. It will examine how a judge makes a decision, and what the judge considers when making a decision. Understanding the thoughts behind a judges decision will help you not only in the real world when you must refine your arguments to appeal towards a particular judge disposition towards the law, but also in law school when reading, understanding and digesting cases.

Benjamin Cardozo wrote the first selection from personal experience about how judges make their decisions. Although this writing comes from the early 20th century, his article continues to provide valuable insight into a judge's mind and the thought process he or she goes through when making decisions. The second selection by Neil MacCormick talks about the justifications that judges need in order to make sound decisions. The last selection departs from a focus on the judge, and concentrates on the case law itself, the impact (or lack therefore) that deduction and analogy have on a jury and describes how our common law changes.

BENJAMIN N. CARDOZO
THE NATURE OF THE JUDICIAL PROCESS
9–10, 14–15, 18–31 (Yale University Press reprint 1998) (1921)[4]

The work of deciding cases goes on every day in hundreds of courts throughout the land. Any judge, one might suppose, would find it easy to describe the process which he had followed a thousand times and more. Nothing could be farther from the truth. Let some intelligent layman ask him to explain: he will not go very far before taking refuge in the excuse that the language of craftsmen is unintelligible to those untutored in the craft. Such an excuse may cover with a semblance of respectability an otherwise ignominious retreat. It will hardly serve to still the pricks of curiosity and conscience. In moments of introspection, when there is no longer a necessity of putting off with a show of wisdom the uninitiated interlocutor, the troublesome problem will recur, and press for a solution. What is it that I do when I decide a case? To what sources of information do I appeal for guidance? In what proportions do I permit them to contribute to the result? In what proportions ought they to contribute? If a precedent is applicable, when do I refuse to follow it? If no precedent is applicable, how do I reach the rule that will make a precedent for the future? If I am seeking logical consistency, the symmetry of the legal structure, how far shall I seek it? At what point shall the quest be halted by some discrepant custom, by some consideration of the social welfare, by my own or the common standards of justice and morals? Into that strange compound which is brewed daily in the caldron of the courts, all these ingredients enter in varying proportions. . . .

Before we can determine the proportions of a blend, we must know the ingredients to be blended. Our first inquiry should therefore be: Where does the judge find the law which he embodies in his judgment? There are times when the source is obvious. The rule that fits the case may be supplied by the constitution or by statute. If that is so, the judge looks no farther. The correspondence ascertained, his duty is to obey. The constitution overrides a statute, but a statute, if consistent with the constitution, overrides the law of judges. In this sense, judge-made law is secondary and subordinate to the law that is made by legislators. It is true that codes and statutes do not render the judge superfluous, nor his work perfunctory and mechanical. There are gaps to be filled. There are doubts and ambiguities to be cleared. There are hardships and wrongs to be mitigated if not avoided. Interpretation is often spoken of as if it were nothing but the search and the discovery of a meaning which, however obscure and latent, had none the less a real and ascertainable pre-existence in the legislator's mind. The process is, indeed, that at times, but it is often something more. The ascertainment of intention may be the least of a judge's troubles in ascribing meaning to a statute. "The fact is," says Gray in his lectures on the "Nature and Sources of the Law," "that the difficulties of so-called interpretation arise when the legislature has had no meaning at all; when the question which is raised on the statute never occurred to it; when what the judges have to do is, not to determine what the legislature did mean on a point which was

---

present to its mind, but to guess what it would have intended on a point not present to its mind, if the point had been present." . . .

. . . . We reach the land of mystery when constitution and statute are silent, and the judge must look to the common law for the rule that fits the case. He is the "living oracle of the law" in Blackstone's vivid phrase. Looking at Sir Oracle in action, viewing his work in the dry light of realism, how does he set about his task?

The first thing he does is to compare the case before him with the precedents, whether stored in his mind or hidden in the books. I do not mean that precedents are ultimate sources of the law, supplying the sole equipment that is needed for the legal armory, the sole tools, to borrow Maitland's phrase, "in the legal smithy." Back of precedents are the basic juridical conceptions which are the postulates of judicial reasoning, and farther back are the habits of life, the institutions of society, in which those conceptions had their origin, and which, by a process of interaction, they have modified in turn. None the less, in a system so highly developed as our own, precedents have so covered the ground that they fix the point of departure from which the labor of the judge begins. Almost invariably, his first step is to examine and compare them. If they are plain and to the point, there may be need of nothing more. *Stare decisis* is at least the everyday working rule of our law. I shall have something to say later about the propriety of relaxing the rule in exceptional conditions. But unless those conditions are present, the work of deciding cases in accordance with precedents that plainly fit them is a process similar in its nature to that of deciding cases in accordance with a statute. It is a process of search, comparison, and little more. Some judges seldom get beyond that process in any case. Their notion of their duty is to match the colors of the case at hand against the colors of many sample cases spread out upon their desk. The sample nearest in shade supplies the applicable rule. But, of course, no system of living law can be evolved by such a process, and no judge of a high court, worthy of his office, views the function of his place so narrowly. If that were all there was to our calling, there would be little of intellectual interest about it. The man who had the best card index of the cases would also be the wisest judge. It is when the colors do not match, when the references in the index fail, when there is no decisive precedent, that the serious business of the judge begins. He must then fashion law for the litigants before him. In fashioning it for them, he will be fashioning it for others. The classic statement is Bacon's: "For many times, the things deduced to judgment may be meum and tuum, when the reason and consequence thereof may trench to point of estate." The sentence of today will make the right and wrong of tomorrow. If the judge is to pronounce it wisely, some principles of selection there must be to guide him among all the potential judgments that compete for recognition.

In the life of the mind as in life elsewhere, there is a tendency toward the reproduction of kind. Every judgment has a generative power. It begets in its own image. Every precedent, in the words of Redlich, has a "directive force for future cases of the same or similar nature." Until the sentence was pronounced, it was as yet in equilibrium. Its form and content were uncertain. Any one of many principles might lay hold of it and shape it. Once declared, it is a new stock of descent. It is charged with vital power. It is the source from which new principles or norms may spring to shape sentences thereafter. If we seek the psychological basis of this tendency, we shall find it, I suppose, in habit. Whatever its psychological basis, it is one of the living forces of our law. Not all the progeny of principles begotten of a judgment survive, however, to maturity. Those that cannot prove their worth and strength by the test of experience are sacrificed mercilessly and thrown into the void. The common law does not work from pre-established truths of universal and inflexible validity to conclusions derived from them deductively. Its method is inductive, and it draws its generalizations from particulars. The process has been admirably stated by Munroe Smith: "In their effort to give to the social sense of justice articulate expression in rules and in principles, the method of the lawfinding experts has always been experimental. The rules and principles of case law have never been treated as final truths, but as working hypotheses, continually retested in those great laboratories of the law, the courts of justice. Every new case is an experiment; and if the accepted rule which seems applicable yields a result which is felt to be unjust, the rule is reconsidered. It may not be modified at once, for the attempt to do absolute justice in every single case would make the development and maintenance of general rules impossible; but if a rule continues to work injustice, it will eventually be reformulated. The principles themselves are continually retested; for if the rules derived from a principle do not work well, the principle itself must ultimately be re-examined."

The way in which this process of retesting and reformulating works may be followed in an example. Fifty years ago, I think it would have been stated as a general principle that A. may conduct his business as he pleases, even though the purpose is to cause loss to B., unless the act involves the creation of a nuisance. Spite fences were the stock illustration, and the exemption from liability in such circumstances was supposed to illustrate not the exception, but the rule. Such a rule may have been an adequate working principle to regulate the relations between individuals or classes in a simple or homogeneous community. With the growing complexity of social relations, its inadequacy was revealed. As particular controversies multiplied and the attempt was made to test them by the old principle, it was found that there was something wrong in the results, and this led to a reformulation of the principle itself. Today, most judges are inclined to say that what was once thought to be the exception is the rule, and what was the rule is the exception. A. may never do anything in his business for the purpose of injuring another without reasonable and just excuse. There has been a new generalization which, applied to new particulars, yields results more in harmony with past particulars, and, what is still more important, more consistent with the social welfare This work of modification is gradual. It goes on inch by inch. Its effects must be measured by decades and even centuries. Thus measured, they are seen to have behind them the power and the pressure of the moving glacier.

We are not likely to underrate the force that has been exerted if we look back upon its work. "There is not a creed which is not shaken, not an accredited dogma which is not shown to be questionable, not a received tradition which does not threaten to dissolve." Those are the words of a critic of life and letters writing forty years ago, and watching the growing scepticism of his day. I am tempted to apply his words to the history of the law. Hardly a rule of today but may be matched by its opposite of yesterday. Absolute liability for one's acts is today the exception; there must commonly be some tinge of fault, whether willful or negligent. Time was, however, when absolute liability was the rule. Occasional reversions to the earlier type may be found in recent legislation. Mutual promises give rise to an obligation, and their breach to a right of action for damages. Time was when the obligation and the remedy were unknown unless the promise was under seal. Rights of action may be assigned, and the buyer prosecute them to judgment though he bought for purposes of suit. Time was when the assignment was impossible, and the maintenance of the suit a crime. It is no basis today for an action of deceit to show, without more, that there has been the breach of an executory promise; yet the breach of an executory promise came to have a remedy in our law because it was held to be a deceit. These changes or most of them have been wrought by judges. The men who wrought them used the same tools as the judges of today. The changes, as they were made in this case or that, may not have seemed momentous in the making. The result, however, when the process was prolonged throughout the years, has been not merely to supplement or modify; it has been to revolutionize and transform. For every tendency, one seems to see a counter-tendency; for every rule its antinomy. Nothing is stable. Nothing absolute. All is fluid and changeable. There is an endless "becoming." We are back with Heraclitus. That, I mean, is the average or aggregate impression which the picture leaves upon the mind. Doubtless in the last three centuries, some lines, once wavering, have become rigid. We leave more to legislatures today, and less perhaps to judges. Yet even now there is change from decade to decade. The glacier still moves.

In this perpetual flux, the problem which confronts the judge is in reality a twofold one: he must first extract from the precedents the underlying principle, the *ratio decidendi*; he must then determine the path or direction along which the principle is to move and develop, if it is not to wither and die.

The first branch of the problem is the one to which we are accustomed to address ourselves more consciously than to the other. Cases do not unfold their principles for the asking. They yield up their kernel slowly and painfully. The instance cannot lead to a generalization till we know it as it is. That in itself is no easy task. For the thing adjudged comes to us oftentimes swathed in obscuring dicta, which must be stripped off and cast aside. Judges differ greatly in their reverence for the illustrations and comments and side-remarks of their predecessors, to make no mention of their own. All agree that there may be dissent when the opinion is filed. Some would seem to hold that there must be none a moment thereafter. Plenary inspiration has then descended upon the work of the majority. No one, of course, avows such a belief, and yet sometimes there is an approach to it in conduct. I own that it is a good deal of a mystery to me how judges, of all persons in the world, should put their faith in dicta. A brief experience on the bench was enough to reveal to me all sorts of cracks and crevices and loopholes in my own opinions when picked up a few months after delivery, and reread with due contrition. The persuasion that one's own infallibility is a myth leads by easy stages and with somewhat greater satisfaction to a refusal to ascribe infallibility to others. But dicta are not always ticketed as such, and one does not recognize them always at a glance. There is the constant need, as every law student knows, to separate the accidental and the nonessential from the essential and inherent. Let us assume, however, that this task has been achieved, and that the precedent is known as it really is. Let us assume too that the principle, latent within it, has been skillfully extracted and accurately stated. Only half or less than half of the work has yet been done. The problem remains to fix the bounds and the tendencies of development and growth, to set the directive force in motion along the right path at the parting of the ways.

The directive force of a principle may be exerted along the line of logical progression; this I will call the rule of analogy or the method of philosophy; along the line of historical development; this I will call the method of evolution; along the line of the customs of the community; this I will call the method of tradition; along the lines of justice, morals and social welfare, the *mores* of the day; and this I will call the method of sociology.

NEIL MacCORMICK
LEGAL REASONING AND LEGAL THEORY
103–07, 126, 166, 192, 194 (reprint 2003) (1978)[5]

A legal system is not, and is in important ways fundamentally different from, a natural science. But from the point of view of the logic of justification there are two points of contact: that legal decisions deal with the 'real world' as do scientific hypotheses, and that they do so not *in vacuo* but in the context of a whole body of 'knowledge' — in this case, the whole corpus of the normative legal system, rather than a corpus of descriptive and explanatory theory.

To put it crudely, legal decisions must make sense in the world and they must also make sense in the context of the legal system. In our problem cases, they must be based on rulings which make sense in the context of the legal system. And just as scientific justification involves testing one hypothesis against another, and rejecting that which fails relevant tests, so (I shall argue) second-order justification in the law involves testing rival possible rulings against each other and rejecting those which do not satisfy relevant tests — the relevant tests being concerned with what makes sense in the world, and with what makes sense in the context of the system.

---

[5] Copyright ©1978 by Oxford University Press. All rights reserved. Reprinted by permission."

Of course we are not here using the idea of 'making sense' with any descriptive connotation. It cannot be in issue whether legal rulings describe the world accurately or ground true predictions about natural events. They do not describe it at all, nor are they predictions.

Legal rulings are normative — they do not report, they set patterns of behaviour; they do not discover the consequences of given conditions, they ordain what consequences *are to* follow upon given conditions. They do not present a model *of* the world, they present a model *for* it.

That in turn means that choosing between rival possible rulings in a given case involves choosing between what are to be conceived as rival models for, rival patterns of, human conduct in this society. Either manufacturers of consumer goods ought to take reasonable care in preparing and packaging them, and ought to be made liable in damages to anyone injured by their failure in that respect; or they are not required by law to take such care and not made by law liable for failure therein. To take that disjunction seriously as posing a real choice in a real society one must then ask what is the difference; and the answer is that the difference is determined by the differences which would follow from adopting and applying the one or the other of these rival rulings in an actual social situation.

Lord Macmillan in his speech in *Donoghue v. Stevenson* asked the question

> suppose that a baker through carelessness allows a large quantity of arsenic to be mixed with a batch of his bread, with the result that those who subsequently eat it are poisoned, could he be heard to say that he owed no duty to the consumers of his bread to take care that it was free from poison, and that, as he did not know that any poison had got into it, his only liability was for breach of warranty under his contract of sale to those who actually bought the poisoned bread from him? ([1932] A.C. at 620; 1932 S.C. (H.L.) at 71)

But what made that a relevant or significant question at all in a case involving the less desperate misfortune of one snail in one ginger-beer bottle? What made it relevant is precisely that the Lords had to test one against the other of two rival possible rulings on the question of manufacturer's liability versus manufacturers [sic] non-liability on grounds of negligence apart from contract.

If it is *unacceptable* that the baker whose carelessly made bread poisons those who eat it should be free from all liabilities save those arising from contract with some consumers, that is a ground for refusing to adopt a ruling whose application would yield that conclusion of non-liability in the event of an actual baker doing that actual deed. That means: a ground for refusing to rule — as the respondent's counsel urged — that a manufacturer of goods for consumption owes no duty to the ultimate consumer to take care in the process of manufacture.

Observe three points:

(i) This is a *consequentialist* mode of argument, albeit in a somewhat restricted sense. It considers the consequences of making a ruling one way or the other, to the extent at least of examining the types of decision which would have to be given in other hypothetical cases which might occur and which would come within the terms of the ruling.

(ii) It is intrinsically *evaluative*, in that it asks about the acceptability or unacceptability of such consequences. There is however no reason to assume that it involves evaluation in terms of a single scale, such as the Benthamite scale of supposedly measurable aggregates of pleasures and pains. Judges characteristically refer to criteria such as 'justice', 'common sense', 'public policy', and 'convenience' or 'expediency' in weighing the case for and against given rulings. It should not be assumed without proof that these really all boil down to the same thing. For that reason, we should be chary of calling it 'utilitarian' argumentation, although there is a marked resemblance to what is sometimes called 'ideal rule utilitarianism'.

(iii) It is in part at least *subjective*. Judges evaluating consequences of rival possible rulings may give different weight to different criteria of evaluation, differ as to the degree of perceived injustice, or of predicted inconvenience which will arise from adoption or rejection of a given ruling. Not surprisingly, they differ, sometimes sharply and even passionately in relation to their final judgement of the acceptability or unacceptability all things considered of a ruling under scrutiny. At this point we reach the bedrock of the value preferences which inform our reasoning but which are not demonstrable by it. At this level there can simply be irresoluble differences of opinion between people of goodwill and reason.

Taking these three points together, I suggest that second-order justification is concerned with 'what makes sense in the world' in that it involves *consequentialist* arguments which are essentially *evaluative* and therefore in some degree *subjective*. That is the first essential element of second-order justification; the second . . . concern[s] 'what makes sense in the system?' A few brief words will suffice by way of preliminary explanation of that notion.

The basic idea is of the legal system as a consistent and coherent body of norms whose observance secures certain valued goals which can intelligibly be pursued all together.

The idea of a 'consistent' body of norms I use in a strict sense: however desirable on consequentialist grounds a given ruling might be, it may not be adopted if it is contradictory of some valid and binding rule of the system. Of course, an ostensibly contradictory precedent may be 'explained' and 'distinguished' to avoid such a contradiction, or an ostensibly conflicting statute interpreted in a way which avoids such contradiction. But if such devices for reconciliation fail, the requirement of consistency would require rejection of an otherwise attractive ruling on the ground of its irresoluble conflict with (contradiction of) established valid rules.

'Coherence' is intended in a looser sense. One can imagine a random set of norms none of which contradict each other but which taken together involve the pursuit of no intelligible value or policy. A trivial example: a rule that all yellow motor cars must observe a maximum speed limit of 20 m.p.h. does not contradict or logically conflict with a rule that all red, green, or blue motor cars must observe a minimum speed limit of 25 m.p.h. and a maximum of 70 m.p.h. But on the face of it, no principled reason can be given for such a difference. If the goal of road safety is desired, and the speed restriction on yellow cars represented as essential to it, it is prima facie absurd to have a different rule for red, blue, and green cars. There appears to be no rational principle which could explain or justify differential treatment of two cases so essentially similar from a road-safety point of view.

The 'validity thesis' presents law as comprising or at least including a set of valid rules for the conduct of affairs: such rules must satisfy the requirement of consistency, at least by including procedures for resolving conflict. But rules can be consistent without the system being coherent as a means of social ordering, if 'order' involves organization in relation to intelligible and mutually compatible values. To the extent however that the rules are, or are treated as being, instances of more general principles the system acquires a degree of coherence. When problems of relevancy or of interpretation or of classification arise within the system, the requirement of coherence is satisfied only to the extent that novel rulings given can be brought within the ambit of the existing body of general legal principle.

Among reasons why this is a requirement of legal justification is that there are limits to the ambit of legitimate judicial activity: judges are to do justice according to law, not to legislate for what seems to them an ideally just form of society. Although this does not and cannot mean that they are only to give decisions directly authorized by deduction from established and valid rules of law, it does and must mean that in some sense and in some degree every decision, however acceptable or desirable on consequentialist grounds, must also be warranted by the law as it is. To the extent that the existing detailed rules are or can be rationalized in terms of more general principles, principles whose tenor goes beyond the ambit of already settled rules, a sufficient and sufficiently legal warrant exists to justify as a *legal* decision some novel ruling and the particular decision governed by it.

So much by way of introductory outline: second-order justification involves two elements, consequentialist argument and argument testing proposed rulings for consistency and coherence with the existing legal system. Because consequentialist argument is intrinsically evaluative, and because coherence as explained above involves reflection on the values of the system, the two interact and overlap as will appear; but they are not identical. . . .

. . . . A judge, by formulating a general principle as expressing the underlying common purpose of a set of specific rules at once rationalizes the existing law so as to reveal it in the light of a new understanding, and provides a sufficient ground for justifying a new development in the relevant field. He does not thereby show that the decision must be as he proposes to give it in the instant case; only that it may legitimately be so given. He does not simply find and state the rationale of the rules; to a greater or less degree, he makes them rational by stating a principle capable of embracing them, and he uses that as a necessary jumping-off point for a novel decision, which can now be represented as one already 'covered' by 'existing' law.

That this process should be possible depends in itself on the existence of analogous authorities brought before the Court through the researches and ingenuity of counsel. This is a point which need not be elaborated here. It is also essential that there should not be flatly contradictory authorities of binding character. . . .

. . . . Judges, let us say it again, must do justice indeed, but 'justice according to law'. That does not, indeed cannot, mean that judges are only to decide cases in a manner justifiable by simple deduction from mandatory legal rules; yet on the other hand, it cannot mean that they are left free to pursue their own intuitions of justice utility and common sense free of all limitations. The area of their freedom, power, and indeed duty to seek solutions justifiable by an evaluation in consequentialist terms of the needs of the generic case, is limited by the requirement that they show some legal warrant for what they do. The 'general principles' which provide this needed guidance on the one hand, but limitation on the other hand, express the underlying reasons for the specific rules which exist. As such, they are not found but made; to give principle p as the 'underlying reason' of rule r, or rules r, $r2$, $r3$ and so on, is to impute to those who first introduced it some general policy whose introduction it was supposed to promote, or alternatively to state what seems the best contemporary justification for maintaining it. The content of the rules partly determines the possible range of reasons which could conceivably be adduced as explanatory of them. The contemporary standards of received values (what judges call 'common sense') further limit the matter; only what is conceived good or desirable can count as a policy whose furtherance by the introduction or maintenance of legal rules can be propounded as the underlying justification and rationalization of the rules in question. Statements of 'legal principles' are normative expressions of such rationalizing or justifying policies. . . .

. . . . Those observations point to the conclusion that sufficiency of analogy depends on the existence of similarity between the facts of the novel case and the operative facts of reasonably specifically stated rules or principles embedded in precedents or statutes. That is not an exact test, admittedly, but it is a real and important one. 'Closeness' of analogy in this sense is indeed a requirement of the law, though within the range of sufficiently close analogies degrees of closeness are not in themselves decisive either way but must be tested by consequentialist arguments for and against competing rulings in law.

Lastly, the opinion is frequently expressed that argument by analogy is especially a feature of case law rather than of statute law. There is certainly a degree of truth in this, in so far as bodies of case law are regularly built up by the steady accretion of decisions gradually extending the concrete application of a principle from case to analogous case. . . .

. . . . From [the use of principles], we can infer the importance ascribed to coherence of values within the working of a legal system. The same goes for the closely related use of arguments by analogy. Both together help us to form some understanding of the limits of what is regarded as legitimate in the way of judicial law-making. But it would be unhelpful and misleading to take too seriously metaphorical notions of the 'weight', far less relative weight, of principles singly or in competition *inter se*. It is the interaction of arguments from principle and consequentialist arguments which fully justifies decisions in hard cases — and even at that we have yet to consider the important matter of 'consistency' mentioned earlier. A ruling in law may be shown to be supported by principles and to be desirable in its consequences. But still it must be shown not to conflict with established and binding rules of law.

KENNETH J. VANDEVELDE
THINKING LIKE A LAWYER: AN INTRODUCTION TO LEGAL REASONING
100–06 (1996)[6]

DEDUCTION AND ANALOGY IN A JURY SYSTEM

Although case law holdings are theoretically binding on subsequent cases, in a jury system a prior case often has little impact on subsequent, similar cases. This phenomenon occurs because a decision by one jury does not bind another jury. In other words, the jury's decision in the first case does not create a rule binding in the next case.

Assume that the jury in a case decides that a physician who failed to administer a particular diagnostic test was negligent. A jury in a later case involving identical facts would nevertheless be free to decide that the physician in that case was *not* negligent. The first jury's verdict does not bind the second jury, despite the similarity of the facts.

A jury verdict, however, can be "transformed" into a binding holding if the losing party challenges the verdict in some way, such as by moving for a new trial or for judgment as a matter of law, or by appealing. As a result of the challenge, the trial or appellate court reviews the jury verdict and renders a decision, perhaps set forth in a written opinion. Assuming that the opinion is published, its holding becomes a binding precedent in future similar cases.

For example, let us assume that the losing party appeals. . . . the appellate court does not decide the facts de novo. Rather, it merely considers whether the jury's verdict was supported by substantial evidence.

This inquiry produces one of two possible results. First, the appellate court may hold that the jury's verdict is supported by substantial evidence. For the first time in the case, there is a judicial holding — a rule binding in future cases.

Consider carefully, however, the exact nature of the holding. The appellate court did not hold that a physician who fails to administer the test is always negligent but only that the jury had before it sufficient evidence to conclude that the physician in that case was negligent.

This holding is that certain facts *may* constitute negligence, not that they necessarily do. The holding, nevertheless, can influence the resolution of future similar cases. For example, if a physician's lawyer in a later case involving similar facts moves for summary judgment on the ground that failure to administer the test cannot constitute negligence, the patient's lawyer may cite the earlier decision holding that failure to

---

[6] From Thinking Like a Lawyer by Kenneth Vandevelde ©1996. Reprinted by permission of Westview Press, a member of the Perseus Books Group.

administer the test may constitute negligence and thereby defeat the motion. When the later case goes to trial, however, the jury will be free to decide that the physician in the later case was not negligent. Thus, the appellate court's holding essentially does little more than assure that patents in later, similar cases are entitled to a trail on the issue of whether the physician was negligent.

Of course, the physician's lawyer in the later cases may attempt to defeat even that limited use of the earlier case. The lawyer may attempt to distinguish the earlier case or, failing that, argue that it was wrongly decided.

The other possible result on appeal is that the appellate court could hold that the failure to administer the test cannot be considered negligence. This holding can also influence the resolution of future similar cases. Another physician sued for failure to administer the test could argue that the prior case established as a matter of law that failure to administer the test does *not* constitute negligence. The patient, the plaintiff, can attempt to distinguish the prior case or to persuade a court that it was wrongly decided. Should the patient fail in that argument, the prior holding will become controlling.

This is not to suggest that a jury trial never has an impact on future cases unless the jury's verdict is challenged. In a jury trial, the judge decides all questions of law. The judge's decisions on these questions along with the decisions of the appellate court reviewing those decisions, if published, also constitute binding precedents.

Epilogue: Changing Case Law

The description of the legal reasoning process in the preceding chapters has assumed that the common law never changes, except by an act of legislature. If the law were subject to change at any time, then predicting the rights and duties of parties would be an impossibility. Further, conceding that a court is free to change the law at any time renders the principles of the rule of law and stare decisis meaningless.

Yet, the courts do have the power to modify the common law with sufficient justification. In this final section, the situations in which a court may be persuaded to modify case law rules and the techniques that the court may use are briefly discussed.

Flexibility Without Changing Case Law

As an initial matter, courts have considerable ability to reach the desired result without having to change the law. This flexibility exists because . . . common law rules are often indeterminate. First, prior cases applying the language are binding only to the extent of their narrow holdings, and thus the prior cases very often do not apply or can be distinguished. Second, even binding language may be too general to require only one result. Third, application of the policies may also support any of several results, depending upon the court's judgment about the relative weight of the policies and the relationship between the policies and the means used to further them.

Thus, except in the easy cases, the existing law does not really require a single result. Courts often have the ability to reach the result demanded by either party to a dispute. As long as the result can be reconciled with the language of the rules and any contrary precedents can plausibly be distinguished, the court has not "changed" the law. If anything, the court has merely created law where none existed.

Justifications for Changing Case Law

Occasionally, however, a situation arises in which the result the lawyer wishes to reach cannot plausibly be reconciled with the language of the existing rules. The rights or duties that the client wants to exist in some situation can arise only by changing one or more existing rules of case law.

The principle of stare decisis creates a strong presumption against overturning a prior decision but does not prohibit the practice. If the court is going to change the law, it will do so for reasons of policy.

Because the original rule was based on policy judgments, the lawyer must essentially persuade a court that the prior judgments can no longer be considered correct. Recall that applying policies to decide cases requires two types of judgments. The lawyer may argue that either or both of the judgments were wrong.

The first type of judgment pertains to the relative weight given to different policies. The prior court struck a balance between two policies, based on the perceived importance of each. The lawyer must now argue that the relative importance of the policies has changed. As a result, a new rule is necessary. Or, to put it another way, a new balance must be struck, a new line drawn.

For example, courts in the nineteenth century adopted a rule known as the "fellow servant rule," which held that an employee injured on the job could not sue his employer for negligence if the injury was caused by another employee. The courts essentially concluded that the policy of promoting economic development outweighed the policy of compensating the injured worker. In the twentieth century, however, courts began to create exceptions to the fellow servant rule, thereby allowing employees to sue their employers for injuries caused by the negligence of other employees. The courts had simply decided that the policy of compensating the injured was now entitled to greater weight.

The second type of judgment pertains to the relationship between ends and means. The prior court adopted a rule because it believed that such a rule would best promote certain policies. The lawyer now argues, without necessarily quarreling with the end sought by the prior court, that the rule adopted simply does not promote those policies any longer, if it ever did. The rule, in other words, has not worked in practice and must be changed.

For example, the traditional common law rules governing the duties that landowners owe those who come onto the land categorized those who entered the land as trespassers, licensees, or invitees. The landowners' duties varied, depending upon the category into which the entrant fell. Some courts, however, came to believe that the various categories were difficult to apply and that the underlying policies could best be effectuated by adopting a single duty requiring the landowner to exercise reasonable care under the circumstances.

Changes in the law of this type are perhaps easier for the court to adopt because, as noted above, the relationship between ends and means, in theory, is a matter that the court can decide empirically. Thus, in the example above, the court announced that the prior rule was "difficult to apply" — a conclusion that was ostensibly based on factual observation. By changing the law in this way, the court is not admitting that it has changed policies but only that it is "correcting" the law in light of new information. The underlying policies of the prior cases continue to receive the same weight.

Techniques for Changing Case Law

A court that has decided to change case law may use a variety of techniques, some of which may blunt the impression that it has departed from the principle of stare decisis. In this subsection, a few of these techniques are discussed.

Confining a Case to Its Facts

First, the court may confine a prior case to its facts. This is, in effect, a relatively weak form of overruling. The holding in the prior case is treated as correct, and yet the court refuses to generalize from that holding to any future case. The court has effectively repudiated any dictum in the prior case that suggested that the holding reflected a more broadly applicable rule.

For example, a case holding that to knock a cafeteria patron's dinner tray out of that person's hand is an offensive touching might be confined to its facts by a court. The court is now free to hold that it is not an offensive touching to knock a box of pizza, a deck of cards, a family heirloom, or anything else out of the hand. The holding in the prior case has been confined to the facts of the case. The court need not find some basis on which to distinguish later cases involving pizza or heirlooms. The law has changed, permitting the court to treat pizza and heirlooms differently from dinner trays, even though the court has not explicitly overruled the prior case.

Overruling Sub Silentio

Second, the court may overrule a prior case *sub silentio*. The court generally does this by articulating a set of policy judgments in a later case that, if applied to the earlier case, would have caused a different result. The court declines explicitly to overrule the prior case, and yet the lawyer understands that the prior case no longer controls future decisions.

For example, assume that a case holds that a court must give a consumer prior notice and an opportunity to be heard before authorizing the sheriff, who is acting on behalf of a store, to seize goods for which the consumer allegedly has failed to pay the store. Assume also that a later case permits seizure of the goods without prior notice and an opportunity to be heard, as long as the court at the time it authorizes seizure has adequate grounds to believe the store's claim to the goods is well founded and gives subsequent notice to the consumer. This may amount to a *sub silentio* overruling of the first case. Nothing in the first case suggested that the court there did not have adequate grounds to believe that the store's claim was well founded, and thus the first case is arguably indistinguishable from the second. The second case reached a different result because the court changed its policy. The first case is not explicitly overruled, but future cases will apparently be decided differently.

Creating Exceptions

Third, the court may create an exception. This is an explicit, but only partial, repudiation of the prior case. The prior case remains good law, but it no longer controls all of the situations it once did.

The last example could be used to illustrate this technique as well. Assume that, in the first case, there had *not* been adequate assurances that the store's claim was well founded. In that situation, the second case, rather than overruling the prior case *sub silentio*, might simply create an exception — holding that, although prior notice is generally required, subsequent notice is sufficient if the court has adequate assurances that the store's claim to a right of seizure is well founded.

Obviously, lawyers may differ at times over whether the second case represents an exception to the first case or an overruling of it *sub silentio*. To the extent that the two cases are truly different, the second case may well be carving out an exception to the general rule set forth in the first case. To the extent that the two cases seem indistinguishable, however, then the conclusion is almost inescapable that the first case has been overruled *sub silentio*. As has been seen, lawyers may differ over whether two cases are distinguishable, and thus they may differ over whether the second case created an exception to, or overruled *sub silentio*, the first case.

Any exception changes the law with respect to those situations embraced within the exception. Moreover, by defining the factual predicate of the exception broadly, the court can bring large numbers of cases within the exception. Eventually, the exception may become more widely applicable than the so-called general rule, with the result that the exception is said to "swallow the rule." At the time it was created, the exception seemed a minor change in the law, but over time it proved to be a virtually complete repudiation of the earlier rule.

Legal Fictions

Fourth, the court may use a legal fiction to change the law. A legal fiction, in effect, is a declaration that the law regards something as true even though it is not. Generally speaking, a legal fiction is used to supply a missing element in a rule. By declaring the element to be present, the court permits the rule to apply to facts where it would otherwise not apply. To all appearances, the law has not changed. In reality, however, the court has rewritten the rule so that the missing element is eliminated or replaced.

One of the most commonly used legal fictions is the technique of implication, in which a court declares that some element is implied to be present, even though in any meaningful sense it is not present.

For example, assume that a case holds that a corporation cannot be sued in a state unless that corporation consents to the jurisdiction of the courts. Assume now that a second case holds that a corporation, by doing business with a citizen of the state, implies consent to jurisdiction. Obviously, the corporation did not truly consent to jurisdiction, and yet it may now be sued. The law appears not to have changed because it still bases jurisdiction on consent. In effect, however, the element of consent has been replaced with the element of "doing business," which is converted to consent by a legal fiction.

Legal fictions can prepare the legal community for an explicit change in the law. Once the fiction has become well established, a court may decide to abandon the pretense and admit that the fiction is only that. By this point, however, the rule as modified by the use of the legal fiction is so sufficiently entrenched that the court will very likely not be criticized for having changed the law. If anything, it may be praised for condor in abandoning what had been an obvious fiction all along.

Explicit Overruling

Finally, a court may explicitly overrule a prior case. The policy justifications for changing the law are sufficiently compelling to override the presumption in favor of stare decisis, and the court simply changes the law.

C. THE NATURE OF LAW AND JUDICIAL DECISIONMAKING

The first section of this chapter described the basics of legal reasoning and logic, while the second section discussed the reasoning and logic behind judicial decisions and a changing common law. Departing slightly from a focus on reasoning, logic and decisionmaking, this last section will discuss the nature of law, attempt to answer the question "what is law," and examine how the particular perspectives of judges on the nature of law can impact their decisions.

Although a judge should be impartial to all parties before the court, all people have philosophies (whether or not they can articulate them) on which they rely to make decisions. Similarly, judges and lawyers also have particular philosophies about the nature of law on which they base their arguments and decisions. So why should this matter to you now, before you have even entered law school? One reason is that a basic understanding about the different theories on the nature of law and the impact they have on judicial decisionmaking will make the cases you read in law school easier to digest and understand. Also, identifying and critiquing the theories used in your assigned cases will become easier. Consequently, cases that might have seemed difficult to understand may begin to make more sense when you recognize the judge's philosophy on law, and realize that the judge is using that philosophy to craft the rationale of the case.

Before we examine how a theory on the nature of law can impact a decision, we will examine the nature of law in general and attempt to answer the question, "what is law." Black's Law Dictionary defines law as the following:

1. The regime that orders human activities and relations through systematic application of the force of politically organized society, or through social pressure, backed by force, in such a society; the legal system<respect and obey the law>.

2. The aggregate of legislation, judicial precedents, and accepted legal principles; the body of authoritative grounds of judicial and administrative action; esp., the body of rules, standards, and principles that the courts of a particular jurisdiction apply in deciding controversies brought before them <the law of the land>.

3. The set of rules or principles dealing with a specific area of a legal system <copyright law>.

4. The judicial and administrative process; legal action and proceedings <when settlement negotiations failed, they submitted their dispute to the law>.

5. A statute <Congress passed a law>. — Abbr. L.

6. Common Law <law but not equity>.

7. The legal profession <She spent her entire career in law>.[7]

Law is a complex concept with a wide range of different aspects. It is not simply a listing of rules and regulations but also embodies the practice of law, the process of exercising the rules, and an overall regime that orders our civilization and changes as society changes. The first selection from Berman, Greiner and Saliba continues the discussion on "what is law" and presents different philosophies, concepts and functions concerning the nature of law. It proposes that the nature of law can be more fully understood through a vision not only of what it is but also of what it does.

The last four articles in this section will build upon the basic theories discussed by Berman, Greiner and Saliba and will delve into how these different theories on the nature of law can impact judicial decisionmaking. Kelso and Kelso, in the second selection, will introduce you to different approaches to legal decisionmaking and how the different theories on the nature of law interact with these approaches and impact decisions. The third selection by Scordato describes the movement away from formalism in the early part of the 20th century towards the more realist and instrumentalist approach to legal decisionmaking that is common today. In the praise that Scordato gives to realism and instrumentalism you might get the impression that formalism is a dying concept. The fourth article by Bibas, however, describes a current Supreme Court justice's active use of formalism in conjunction with an originalist approach and its impact on the decisions of the Supreme Court as a whole. No single approach to law stands alone; rather, the various theories blend and at times even dovetail. Finally, the last selection, published by the Oregon State Bar, reviews a few high profile cases from 2005. These cases highlight the pragmatic way in which courts can make decisions, without regard to any one particular theory of law.

As you read the articles in this section, consider what one legal scholar wrote about one view of our legal system: "all canons of law are man-made and thus always subject to reinterpretation. . . . [T]he future of jurisprudence remains in our hands, [and] it is up to us to build the legal world we wish to inhabit."[8]

---

[7] Black's Law Dictionary 900 (8th ed. 2004). Reprinted by permission of the West Group.

[8] Gary Minda, *Jurisprudence at Century's End*, 43 J. Legal Educ. 27, 59 (1993).

HAROLD J. BERMAN, WILLIAM R. GREINER, SAMIR N. SALIBA
THE NATURE AND FUNCTIONS OF LAW
5–6, 14–21, 24–27, 29–30, 32, 34–35 (6th ed. 2004)[9]

Law is not *essentially* a body of rules at all. Rules are an important part of the tools which law uses. But it is foolish to approach law in the first instance through one of the devices which it employs. . . .

Law is an institution in the sense of an integrated pattern or process of social behavior and ideas. What goes on inside courts, legislatures, law offices, and other places in which law-making, law-enforcing, law-administering, and law-interpreting is carried on, together with what goes on inside the minds of people thinking with reference to what goes on in those places, forms a law way of acting and thinking, which overlaps but is not identical with economic, religious, political, and other social ways of acting and thinking. . . .

To speak of law as a "social institution" and as a "way of acting and thinking" invites us to take a further step toward a definition by adding the conception of "order." *Law is a form of social order; legal order is one important way of holding a society together.* . . .

The proposition has two aspects. First, legal order is a vital part of any social order. People cannot live together in society without law of some kind. There has never been a society without some type of legal order, however rudimentary. Second, the place of law in our society — that is, in the Western tradition of thought and action — is unique. The West has exalted law as a fundamental basis of unity in society. Belief in the existence of a "fundamental law," to which governments must adhere or risk overthrow as despotisms, has been characteristic of European thought at least since the eleventh century. This belief finds expression in the English concept of the Rule of Law as well as in the German idea of the *Rechtsstaat*, not to mention the American Constitutional requirement of due process of law. It is a belief which has been challenged in modern times most strikingly by totalitarian systems, but also by some currents of democratic jurisprudence.

Not only in Western political life but also in Western social and economic life generally, law plays a role far greater than in other major cultures. The law of Western nations (and of some nations that have taken over Western legal institutions) reaches into virtually every aspect of social relations. In business, in family life, in recreation, in religious affairs, and in many other types of activities, legal concepts and legal rights and duties play a far more important part than Westerners themselves generally realize. "In the West," the 19th century Russian Slavophile Ivan Kireevsky wrote scornfully, "brothers make contracts with brothers." But whether the relatively high degree of "legalization" of Western life is viewed unfavorably or favorably, it is a fact.

. . . .

What is Law?

Purposes of a definition. The German philosopher Immanuel Kant chided lawyers with the fact that although for centuries they had been searching for a definition of the subject matter of their profession, they still were unable to agree upon one. Kant proceeded to construct his own definition of law — which, however, has found no more universal acceptance than the others that have been offered before or since.

It may be asked, Why bother with a definition at all? May we not simply assume that the meaning of the term "law" will become clear to the student as he studies "legal" materials? This indeed is the assumption made in most American law schools today, where the question, "What is law?" is usually left to be considered in a course labeled

---

[9] Reprinted by permission of the West Group.

Jurisprudence, which is generally an elective course chosen by only a small proportion of the student body. The professional law student tends to define law subconsciously as what law professors teach, just as the professional lawyers tend to define law subconsciously as what they practice, namely what courts and legislatures do.

Lawyers are not necessarily handicapped — indeed they may sometimes be aided — by the lack of articulated definition of law. By immersing themselves in the tradition of their profession, they may acquire a sound feeling of what law is, just as a musician may acquire a sound feeling of what music is through he or she may be unable to put it in words. The tradition of law teaching and law practice embodies concepts which tend to become part of the lawyer's intellectual heritage even though they are not definitely formulated. . . .

. . . . The limiting effects of a definition are especially harmful to the professional lawyer, to whose practice nothing human should be alien. The professional lawyer should not be inhibited from making any investigation, or from thinking any thought, by a definition of law which categorically excludes certain materials or certain ideas as "non-legal."

. . . .

Traditional concepts of law. Although law has been defined in hundred of different ways, three general types of concepts have predominated. One type of concept emphasizes the relationship between law and moral justice; it sees both the ultimate origin of law and the ultimate sanction of law in "right reason." A second type of concept emphasizes the relationship between law and political power; it sees both the ultimate origin of law and the ultimate sanction of law in "the will of the state." A third type of concept emphasizes the relationship between law and the total historical development of the community; it sees both the ultimate origin of law and the ultimate sanction of law in "tradition," "custom" and "national character."

These types of concepts, and the social philosophies which they manifest, have vied with each other for ascendancy throughout the history of civilization, and continue to do so today. Nevertheless, in different periods of Western legal development particular stress has been laid on one or another of these concepts; they are not to be understood in isolation from the total social and historical context from which they derive.

Thus in the formative era of the development of Western legal systems, from the 11th through the 15th centuries, most concepts of law centered around its relationship to moral justice and right reason. Building on the 6th century Byzantine Emperor Justinian's definitions of law as "a theory of right and wrong" (*iusti atque iniusti scientia*) and "an art of the good and the equitable" (*ars boni et aequi*), and also on Aristotle's concept of law as "reason unaffected by desire" (that is, by the passions of the individual), jurists and theologians of medieval Christendom developed the theory that human law is based on the law of human nature, which in turn reflects divine law. Because "natural law" forbids unjustified killing, commands compensation for harm cause by wrongful acts, and so forth, therefore man, in order to realize natural justice, elaborates, by the exercise of reason, rules as to when homicide is justified, what kinds of acts are wrongful, and so forth. Thus St. Thomas Aquinas defined law as "nothing else than an ordinance of reason for the common good, made and promulgated by him who has care of the community" (**Summa Theologica**, Part II, First Part, Question 90).

The belief that law is founded essentially on right reason did not go unchallenged, however, even in the Catholic Middle Ages. In 1345 in a case reported in the English Year Books — which were notes on cases tried in the royal courts — the following interchange took place:

Hillary, J. Plaintiff, will you say anything else * * *?

R. Thorpe (who was lawyer for the plaintiff) * * * I think you will do as others have done in the same (kind of) case, or else we do not know what the law is.

Hillary, J. It is the will of the Justices.

Stonore, C.J. No; law is that which is right.

Thorpe takes a characteristically professional view of "what the law is." To the lawyer whose job it is to advise and represent clients, law is apt to appear as what the courts (or other officials with power of decision) do in particular cases. Five-and-one-half centuries after Thorpe, Oliver Wendell Holmes, Jr., then not yet a justice of the Supreme Court of the United States, wrote, "The prophecies of what the courts will do in fact, and nothing more pretentious, are what I mean by law."

Justice Hillary's definition, on the other hand, recalls the statement of Chief Justice of the United States Charles Evans Hughes, Jr., who shocked some people (though he was only restating in a blunt form the orthodox American constitutional doctrine of judicial supremacy) by writing that "The Constitution is what the judges say it is." To define law as the will of the justices, or what the judges say it is, suggests that what the courts will in fact do may differ from lawyers' or others' prophecies of what they will do based on past experiences. Holmes's definition is, after all, an impossible one for judges to adopt as a guide to their own decisions in cases, since it would place them in the position of predicting their own conduct. Thus while Thorpe urges the court to decide on the basis of what it had done in similar cases in the past, Hillary says, in effect, "We are not bound by what we did in the past; we can decide on any basis we please." The Chief Justice corrects both men in terms of a law of nature, saying, in effect, "It is true that we are not bound by past decisions, but neither can we decide the case on any basis we please. We must decide on the basis of what is right, on the basis of natural justice."

"Natural law theory" — the view that law has its origin and its ultimate sanction in the nature of man as a moral and rational creature — stresses the moral and rational elements in legal processes and in legal solutions to social problems. In contrast, "positivism" — the view that law has its origin and its sanction in the will of officials and ultimately of the state — stresses the political elements in laws, and especially the political authoritativeness of legal rules. With the rise of the secular national state in the 16th century, positivist definitions of law came to the fore and by the end of the 19th century came to predominate. "Law properly is the word of him, that by right hath command over others," wrote Thomas Hobbes. "Law is a command proceeding from the supreme political authority of a State, and addressed to the persons who are subject of that authority," wrote a leading English jurist in the early twentieth century. A statement of the circumstances under which the public force will be brought to bear on persons through the courts — is another definition of law by Holmes, in which the element of politics is put in the forefront.

The "imperative theory of law" — that law is essentially a general command of the highest political authority, backed by coercive sanctions — has usually been associated with the theory that law is distinct from morals, and that the law as it ought to be should not affect the *interpretation* of the law as it is. It is not argued by adherents of this view that moral principles do not play a part in bringing into being the law as it is, or in changing it; but at any given moment, they state, the existing law is analytically separate from any moral ideas of what that law should be. In that sense, law is morally neutral; it is essentially a body of technical rules and concepts to be analyzed. Hence the name "analytical jurisprudence" is often given to this school, as contrasted with the "philosophical school" which adheres to natural-law theory.

A third type of concept of law finds its origin and its sanction neither in reason and morals nor in political power but in the traditions, customs and character of the community. The so-called historical school of jurisprudence views law as having an organic connection with the mind and spirit of the people. Law "is developed first by custom and popular faith," wrote Savigny, "and only then by juristic activity — everywhere, therefore, by internal silently operating powers, not by the arbitrary will of the lawgiver." As people became more mature and complex, their law loses some of its simplicity and its symbolism and becomes more abstract, more technical. Hence it is a mistake to view law either as a body of ideal or "natural" propositions, or as a system of rules promulgated by the state; law is, rather, a particular expression of the common consciousness of a people at a given time and place.

Other adherents of the historical school went beyond the concept of the consciousness of the people, and sought to link the history of law with the social history of man conceived as an evolution from the primitive family group to the modern territorial state. Thus in the view of Sir Henry Maine, law has developed in all societies by certain stages, and its growth has followed certain patterns. By law, then, Maine meant a whole complex of ideas, institutions and techniques seen as a developing system. By adding a historical dimension to the concept of law, the historical school of jurisprudence challenged the analytical and philosophical schools to broaden their definition of law. At the same time historical jurisprudence laid the foundations for later sociological theories of law.

The foregoing sketch by no means lists all the various concepts of law of the various schools of legal philosophy; yet virtually all other concepts bear close enough affinity to natural-law theory, positivism, or historical jurisprudence to be considered as variations of one or more of them. Thus so-called "sociological jurisprudence," which developed at the end of the 19th and in the early 20th centuries, is an offspring of positivism and historical jurisprudence which seeks to interpret the rules of law of a given society as a balancing of various kinds of interest. Each legal decision is thus seen as the result of weighing of the social consequences of alternatives. Indeed, "sociological jurisprudence" is not a systematic theory of law but rather a classification of interests for the guidance of those who make and interpret law. Adherents of this school oppose the wooden application of rules according to the internal logic of their concepts, and urge their application according to their social functions.

Special mention should also be made of the so-called "legal realist" movement which obsessed much of American legal thinking in the 1920s and 1930s. The "legal realists" built on positivism in rejecting reason and nature as foundations of law, but departed from traditional positivism — as well as from "sociological jurisprudence" — in viewing legal realities not in terms of rules at all, but in terms of behavior, especially official behavior. "What there officials [judges, sheriffs, clerks, jailers, lawyers, *etc.*] do about disputes is, to my mind, the law itself," wrote Llewellyn, then a prominent spokesman of "realist" jurisprudence, in 1930. In searching for the underlying factors which determine official behavior various adherents of the approach turned to psychological factors, economic factors, ideological factors, and others.

"Legal realism" not only shook the legal academy of its time but also was a source of two important jurisprudential movements of the 1970s, 1980s, and 1990s, one called "critical legal studies" (CLS for short), the other called "law and economics." Like legal realists, the adherents of CLS assert the "indeterminancy" of all legal rules and the essentially political and ideological basis of all legal decisions. "Law and economics," on the other hand, though it has confidence in the potential objectivity of law, advocates that courts as well as legislatures should (1) analyze legal question in terms of the economic costs and benefits of alternative decisions, and (2) resolve them on the basis of economic efficiency. . . . Although the schools CLS and law and economics are in sharp conflict with each other, both rest (as Anthony Kronman has shown) on an "unspoken common ground," namely, the conception of law solely as an instrument of non-legal values. Various other schools of legal thought that arose in the late 1960s and thereafter share the instrumental concept of law, which treats law always as a means to other ends, never as an end in itself. They share also, by the same token, a positivist definition of law as a body of rules laid down by the lawmaker, rejecting both the moral dimension of law, whose source is reason and conscience, and the historical dimension of law, whose source is precedent and custom.

. . . .

A Functional Approach to Law

Once one juxtaposes the three schools of jurisprudence which have been described, it becomes apparent that what is needed is not a choice of one to the exclusion of the others but rather a syntheses which will build on what is valid in all three. Such a synthesis has been called an "integrative jurisprudence." The legal aspect of social order must be approached partly in terms of the particular moral principles which it embodies, partly in terms of the particular political authorities which shape it, and partly in terms of the particular historical experience and values which it expresses. Indeed, these are not three things but one thing viewed from three different angles.

A synthesis may be achieved, and the nature of law more fully clarified, if the distinctive features of law are sought not in its *origins* and *sanctions* but in its *functions*.

We have stressed earlier that law is a social institution, that is, an integrated pattern or process of behavior and ideas, which helps to restore, maintain and create social order. The act that law helps to give order to social life does not, of course, distinguish it from other social institutions. The factory, the market, the state, the family, the church, the school, the club — these too, each in its own fashion, are integrated ways of acting and thinking which contribute to the resolutions, prevention and control of social disorder. But we can best understand law, it is submitted, if we consider it primarily as one of the order-creating, or ordering, processes . . . .

If . . . a *legal* solution is sought to the problems that arise from breaches of etiquette or other disruptions of the patterns or norms of social behavior, then time must be taken for *deliberate* action, for *articulate definition* of the issues, for a decision which is subject to *public* scrutiny and which is *objective* in the sense that it reflects an explicitly community judgment and not merely an explicitly personal judgment. These qualities of legal activity may be summed up in the word *formality*; formality, in this particular sense, inheres in all kinds of legal activity, whether it be the making of laws (legislation), the issuing of regulations under law (administration), the applying of laws to disputes (adjudication), or the making of private arrangements intended to be legally binding (negotiation of contract, drawing a will, *etc.*). . . .

Law, then, is something that is done when things go wrong. Implicit in this usage is the concept that the way a society is organized and the way it functions normally is to be distinguished from the way it responds to challenge, to crisis, to disruption of the normal organization; and that law is invented to deal with actual or potential disruptions of patterns or norms of social behavior. The characteristics which we have assigned to it — its deliberateness, its expensiveness in time, its articulateness, its publicity, its objectivity, its generality — make it suitable as a solution for some, but not all, such disruptions. Others are resolved by more informal processes, whether of friendship or of force. Law is thus seen as a special kind of ordering process, a special type of process of restoring, maintaining or creating social order — a type of ordering which is primarily neither the way of friendship nor the way of force but something in between.

Such a definition of law focuses primarily on the nature of the legal response to social problems, rather than on its origin and its sanctions. Law may be imposed downward by omnipotent authority, or it may grow upward from tradition and the ethos of the culture, or it may grow outward, so to speak, from reason. Indeed, it probably must have its origin and its sanction in one or more of these aspects of social order. But what makes it law, as distinct from other social institutions and processes, is its formality — in the sense of that word specified above. It is the formality of legal processes which makes legal relations a special and unique type of social relations, distinct from informal (that is, undefined, spontaneous, intimate) relations.

To see law as a particular kind of institutional process is to lay the foundation for an analysis of the social functions of legal activity and legal relations. . . .

By social function of law is meant a tendency of law to contribute to the maintenance of social order. . . .

We may identify three general social functions of any system of law. The first is the function of restoring equilibrium to the social order (or to some part thereof) when that equilibrium has been seriously disrupted. . . .

A second general function of law in any society is that of enabling members of the society to calculate the consequences of their conduct, thereby securing and facilitating voluntary transactions and arrangements. . . .

A third general function of law in any society is to teach people right belief, right feeling, and right action — that is, to mold the moral and legal conceptions and attitudes of a society. . . .

In speaking of law, then, we have in mind a special type of process of restoring, maintaining or creating social order, characterized by formality (in the sense indicated: that is, by relative deliberateness, definiteness, etc.), whose main general functions are (1) to resolve disputes, (2) to facilitate and protect voluntary arrangements, (3) to mold and remold the moral and legal conceptions of a society and (d) in the Western tradition, at least, to maintain historical continuity and consistency of doctrine.

The foregoing discussion of the nature and functions of law is intended only as the barest introduction of a subject far too big and important to be exhausted in a few pages, or, for that matter, a few volumes. The student who comes to this discussion "cold" is bound to be confused and frustrated. "Why can't the experts agree?" "Each theory seems inadequate by itself: why not put them all together into one?" "How can a beginner answer questions which have tormented legal scholars for thousands of years?" "Must one make up his or her mind on this?" "Could not other qualities and functions of law be listed?" "What difference does it make?"

The answers to these questions are not difficult. Experts *seldom* agree. Each theory *is* inadequate by itself — and rarely, except for purposes of exposition, are they held in absolute isolation from each other. A beginner *cannot* answer these questions. It is *not* necessary to make up one's mind on this *right away, once and forever*. Other qualities and functions of law *could* be listed.

But it does make an enormous difference. What one stresses as fundamental to the nature and functions of law determines one's approach not only to the subject as a whole but also to particular legal problems. As United States Supreme Court Justice Felix Frankfurter once said, "every [legal] decision is a function of some juristic philosophy."

R. RANDALL KELSO & CHARLES D. KELSO
STUDYING LAW: AN INTRODUCTION
113–21 (1984)[10]

As described by Gilmore, two general types of judicial style have characterized American legal decisionmaking. The first type, the formalist or conceptualist style, is based on the assumption that law is composed of a system of rationally related rules, and that the judge's main or sole function is to apply those rules mechanically to the case at hand. It is a system of pure logical categorization and deduction. Judges do not need to inquire into the particular consequences of applying the rule in the case before them. The judge's duty is to apply the rule. Change in such a system comes not from the judicial branch, but from the legislature. Judges should not make rules; they should merely apply existing law.

The other approach has been characterized by Llewellyn as the Grand Style. It is also known as pragmatic instrumentalism or the realist approach. When deciding cases in the Grand Style, the judge must test the formulation and application of each rule by its purpose or policy. Where the reason for the rule stops there stops the rule. Rules are not to be tested merely by internal logical symmetry, as they might be tested by a

[10] Reprinted by permission of the West Group.

formalist, but rather should be tested by the social ends to which they are the means. The consequences of a rule are all important. Instrumentalist judges thus tend to be result-oriented. Judges must of course follow the law, and cannot make law whimsically. But there can be cases where the law does not command a particular result, either because no law exactly covers the situation or because each of two conflicting rules arguably applies. In such a case, a judge can and must make law interstitially.[11]

Between these two styles of judicial decisionmaking, however, two other styles exist. The adherents to formalism and pragmatic instrumentalism often overlook these other styles because they are intent on depicting a dichotomy of polar opposites in which formalism and instrumentalism are at different poles. There are, however, more than two relevant dimensions. Formalism and instrumentalism disagree on two basic propositions about law. The first concerns whether law is separable from moral or social value considerations (in the sense of law being solely a body of principles about which predictions can be made — law as science), or whether law is a body of rules testable by reference to some external standard of rightness (some social or moral value — law as normative or prescriptive, not descriptive). The second disagreement concerns whether law is ultimately capable of being represented as a set of logically consistent universal rules (what has been called the analytic assumption), or whether rules are ultimately to be judged not in terms of logical consistency but as means to an end (the functional attitude). Typically, those who think law and morals are separable think laws are ideally formulated as logically consistent universal rules. These are the formalists. Those who think law is testable by some external standard also tend to see law as a means to the end of that standard. These are the proponents of instrumentalism. The two sets of propositions do not necessarily have to co-exist, however, as is illustrated by the jurisprudence of Holmes and by the natural law philosophic tradition.

Holmes, as we have noted, thought that the life of the law was not logic, but experience, and that law therefore must be responsive to social conditions, as a means to that end. However, he also believed that law and morals were separable, that law was a science, and that the most important thing for any law was its certainty and predictability. This concern with certainty led Holmes to postulate that law should be guided by external, objective standards, about which individuals can more readily agree, than on internal, subjective standards, about which disagreement is more likely. Later instrumentalists often discount Holmes' belief that law and morals are separable, and implant into Holmes their own social value science, typically utilitarianism (in simple terms, the thesis that the end of law in society is to seek the greatest happiness for the greatest number). Holmes, however, was ultimately skeptical of the validity of any moral system. The role of the law, in Holmes' view, was to permit the majority to do whatever it wanted. Thus, he hoped, society could avoid violent confrontation. In this

---

[11]   There is perhaps a subtle difference between realism and instrumentalism. Some realists, like Llewellyn, claim that realism is not a theory, but rather a methodology. That is, realism represents only a methodological approach to investigation, consisting in focusing on what is actually happening in the world, rather than focusing solely on the logic of doctrinal analysis. Under this view, realism is not involved with any particular theoretical approach to judicial decisionmaking, but rather is concerned with studying how the law works in practice. Nevertheless, the realist and instrumentalist attitudes share many of the same attributes, in particular the fact that most "realists," in Llewellyn's narrower definition of the term, were instrumental-ists, that is, advocates of the Grand Style. What realists saw judges doing in the real world, and what realists said they had to do, was not pure logical, doctrinal analysis, but rather instrumental reaching of favored results. For the most part, therefore, we will use the terms interchangeably. (You should also note that some writers distinguish instrumentalism and realism in a different way. For these writers, realism represents a more extreme form of instrumentalism. It is an approach to judicial decisionmaking that takes the premises of instrumentalism to their extreme and typically, in such authors' views, bad conclusion. For example, an author might say that while the "instrumentalists" were right to reject Langdell's "formalist" conception that law could and should have an overall logical coherence, the "realists" go too far in asserting that there is no doctrinal unity to the law at all. Thus, when you come across the term realism in your readings, you must be careful to identify in what way the author is using the term.) [Footnote from Kelso & Kelso.]

sense, Holmes agreed with the formalist view that law cannot be tested by an external standard of moral rightness. Rather, law is merely a reflection of the outcome of the relevant political process. Under this view, legislatures, not courts, are the proper balancers of public policy. Holmes disagreed with the formalists, however, over whether legal rules were universally true, because he saw that the dominant group in society often changes. Thus law must change to reflect new power relationships and be a means to the end of facilitating that process.

Holmes' view on the nature of induction and deduction in legal analysis is typical of his jurisprudential views. The formalists, Holmes noted, typically took what is called in philosophy the rationalist view. They conceived of science and, by analogy, ideal legal decisionmaking, as categorical and deductive. One categorizes the facts into the appropriate legal category, then by deduction mechanically produces the end result.

Increasingly over the past three centuries, this rationalist view, associated most closely with Descartes, has been replaced by the view that scientific investigation is empirical. The emphasis of empiricists is on the need for experimental inquiry and induction from facts to reach conclusions. This is the view of scientific method that Holmes embraced. See the Introduction to O.W. Holmes, *The Common Law* xvi–xxi (1881) by Mark DeWolfe Howe. Thus, while Holmes felt that law ought to be a science, it was a science of experience, facts, and induction. It was not a science of categorization and deduction, as it was for the formalists.

A fourth type of judicial decisionmaking can be described as natural law or natural rights.[12] Natural law (or rights) theory agrees with the formalist proposition that law can ultimately be expressed as a system of logically related, universal rules. Law is not just a means to the end of some social value, regardless of what that does to the symmetry of rules. On the other hand, natural law theorists disagree with the formalist conclusion that law and morals are separable, believing that law can be tested by an external standard of rightness, the standard of natural law.

Recognizing that four main methods of legal decisionmaking exist, instead of two, helps clarify thinking about the stages of American law. Formalism is unquestionably the post-Civil War style, and instrumentalism is the post-World War I style. However, in the "formative era of American law" (the pre-Civil War period), judicial decisionmaking is more accurately characterized as reflecting natural law suppositions. It did not reflect instrumentalism, in our view, despite the claims of Llewellyn, Gilmore, and others to the contrary. In this early period, while the judges were sensitive to the consequences that adopting a particular rule would have and recognized that judges did, and needed, to make law (propositions that are consistent with both instrumentalist and natural law theories), judges resorted to the notion of natural law (or rights). Law, for them, could be systematized and organized around rational principles. As Gilmore notes . . . , "The post-Revolutionary generation of American lawyers approached the problem of providing a new law * * * as eighteenth century rationalists * * *"

Between formalism and instrumentalism, Holmesian jurisprudence was in vogue for

---

[12] Natural law and natural rights theories can be distinguished by their differing emphasis on religion as a source of moral guidance. Natural law theories ultimately appeal to God-given standards, though in such theories the dictates of human reason play a large part. The moral and legal theory of St. Thomas Aquinas is typical in this regard. In contrast, natural rights theories appeal to secular sources, like rights deriving from a rational inquiry into human nature. Because both theories appeal to human reason, however, and because both adopt the analytic view that rules are deontological pronouncements (i.e., they agree with the formalist view that if a rule or principle applies it should be followed according to its terms) as opposed to teleological pronouncements (the functional view of rules as relative and a means to other ends adopted by Holmes and the instrumentalists), from the standpoint of the analysis of judicial decisionmaking styles they are quite similar and will be so treated here. Whether one adds to the conclusion that certain rights are natural (because they are based on human reason's understanding of human nature), Aquinas' conclusion that God gave man reason to so use, makes little difference from the perspective of how rules are treated or what conclusions are reached. [Footnote from Kelso & Kelso.]

a time. Law was considered a means to an end, but far the most important end was certainty and predictability. The insistence by Holmes and Williston on external standards in the law of contracts to promote certainty and predictability is an example of this jurisprudence being applied to a field of law. There it reigned for a number of years until Corbin and Llewellyn pushed for a truly instrumentalist approach . . . .

A chart may help clarify these relationships:

STYLES OF JUDICIAL DECISIONMAKING

	Law and Morals Separate (Law as Science)	Law as Normative (or Prescriptive)
Law as Logical, Universal and Analytic	Formalism (1850–1920)	Natural Law (1776–1870)
Law as Means to Ends; Functional Attitude	Holmesian (1900–1950)	Instrumentalism (1930–Today)

Concerning the various "ages" of American law, under the hypothesis suggested here, styles of judicial decisionmaking have followed a counterclockwise pattern, from the formative era of natural law, to the post-Civil War era of formalism, to the early twentieth century transition to Holmesian jurisprudence, and, finally, to the realism or instrumentalism which started in the 1930's and continues today. The dates listed in the chart for each era of decisionmaking overlap in each case by twenty years in order to underscore the point that there was not a sudden transformation in judicial style, and that we are talking about tendencies and emphasis. Judge Hand and Justice Frankfurter, for example, were Holmesian enthusiasts, but they did not persuade a majority of the judges to follow that approach in every case.

Three major participants in this process of legal evolution deserve special mention: Blackstone, Holmes, and Cardozo. Each can be seen as a major force through which transformation from one stage to another was effectuated. As Gilmore notes, Blackstone, whose lectures at Oxford became the basis for his famous and influential *Commentaries on the Laws of England* (1764–69), proclaimed that the common law of England was based on reason (natural law). However, Blackstone concluded that by 1760 the common law had reached the stage of perfection (perfect reason), and thus no further development was needed. Judges could apply whatever law then existed (the formalist approach), confident that the precedents would lead to justice because they represented natural law. When thirty years later Blackstone's views triumphed in England, and a generation or so after that triumphed in the United States, the formalist style of judicial decisionmaking became dominant. (The cultural lag was due in part to England's advance through the Industrial Revolution a generation or so earlier than the United States, and in part to other social factors, such as our lag in developing the system of case reports that is necessary for a formalist approach to be practical).

Holmes' Lowell Lectures at the Harvard Law School in November and December of 1880 (the basis for Holmes' great work *The Common Law* (1881)), were the next landmark event. Between 1870 and 1873, Holmes had edited the 12th edition of Kent's *Commentaries on the Laws of the United States*. Kent's *Commentaries* had become one of the great formalist treatises of the 19th century. Holmes was thus quite familiar with the formalist tradition. He shared its concern with certainty and predictability in law. But he also saw that law must change to reflect the changing times, and said so in 1881. As in the case of Blackstone's work, it took twenty-five to thirty years before similar voices began to be heard. Dean Pound's speech in 1906, for example, entitled "The Causes of Popular Dissatisfaction with the Administration of Justice," reprinted in 40 Am. L. Rev. 729, is often credited with sparking the breakdown of formalism in the law and signaling the beginning of sociological jurisprudence and a theory of law based on social needs. During this period, it was predominantly to Holmes that writers and judges turned for their model of enlightened judicial decisionmaking and the right-minded statement of the judicial role. As Holmes' views were adopted, Holmesian jurisprudence replaced formalism as the dominant style of judicial decisionmaking in the first half of the twentieth century.

Benjamin Cardozo's series of lectures in the 1920's, particularly his Storrs lectures at Yale in 1920 (which formed the basis for his book *The Nature of the Judicial Process* (1921)), represent the third great event in American jurisprudence. Cardozo was known as a devout Holmesian. President Hoover picked Cardozo to replace Holmes on the Supreme Court (when Holmes retired at the age of 90 in 1932), primarily because of pressure from many sources who claimed that Cardozo was the only judge in the nation who could adequately replace Holmes, if indeed any judge could. Cardozo nevertheless went beyond Holmesian jurisprudence in his Storrs lectures and called for a more instrumentalist view of judicial decisionmaking. Sometimes cautious in his rhetoric, and the master at using old phrases in new settings to conceal judicial creativity, Cardozo, particularly during his years on New York's highest court (1914–1932), set the shining example for students to emulate of a result-oriented judge. Cardozo's opinions reveal a judge less concerned than was Holmes with certainty and predictability, and more concerned with achieving particular results in specific cases. Again, it would take twenty-five to thirty years (and much realist commentary in the meantime), before Cardozo's approach would enter the main-stream of American judicial thinking. But, after the Roosevelt Court broke with the philosophy of Holmes in the early 1940's (evidenced most clearly by Justices Black, Douglas, and Murphy's break with Justice Frankfurter during those years), the instrumentalism or realism of Cardozo became the dominant style of judicial decisionmaking. While Cardozo shared many of Holmes' views, his significantly different, and more activist, view on the role of the judge provided the bridge by which American thinking about law has moved in the past 50 years from Holmesian jurisprudence to instrumentalism.

. . . [T]he dynamic which motivated instrumentalism has lost much of its force. If the general pattern continues in the future as it has in the past, one would predict a return to natural law or rights theories of some kind. If the hallmark of natural law is concern with reason, as has been the case for most natural law theorists, such a revival, at least in scholarly writings, may be under way. Kant's commitment to reason and to the unity of law and morals through reason is the basis for many philosophical works of the past ten years, including John Rawls' *A Theory of Justice* (1971), Robert Nozick's *Anarchy, State, and Utopia* (1974), Ronald Dworkin's *Taking Rights Seriously* (1977), and Alan Gewirth's *Reason and Morality* (1978). If, as suggested by the above account, the writings of one generation tend to become the practical philosophy of the next, this may suggest the possible future direction of styles in judicial decisionmaking. What will be needed, though, if the past is any guide, is a Blackstone, Holmes or Cardozo of the revived natural law approach. He or she has yet to appear.

. . . . The reasons given for judicial decisions typically include both an explicit (or sometimes implicit) framework of logic and an explicit (or implicit) statement of the justifications for that logic. The logical framework is a syllogism or several linked syllogisms where the major premise usually is a rule of law, the minor premise is comprised of facts characterized in terms of the rule that forms the major premise, and the conclusion recites how the rule applies to the facts. The justification for a court's logic typically reflects both a technical and a justice aspect.

The technical aspect of a judge's decision is likely to reflect Holmesian or formalist premises, that is, is likely to adopt devices which help achieve certainty and predictability and help insure that similar cases are decided alike. These techniques include reasoning from the literal import of rules or reasoning from precedents (finding them analogous or distinguishable). They also include reasoning from a system of legal principles. The other kind of justification for a court's logic (the fairness or justice aspect of judicial reasoning) is more likely to reflect premises of natural law or instrumentalist decisionmaking philosophies. Thus, judicial decisions are often rooted in what Llewellyn called "Reasons," or what others from the natural law perspective might call principles. Judges also emphasize to varying extents the instrumental concern with the sense for, or perspectives on, the type of situation before the court or the particular facts of the case. Llewellyn called this "Situation Sense."

No matter what perspective or approach tends to dominate a judge's thinking, however, a thoroughly reasoned opinion typically is grounded in both technical and justice reasoning. As a law student, you should learn how to weave together technical and justice arguments for maximum argumentative effect. To repeat, what differentiates judges of the various decisionmaking styles are largely matters of degree and emphasis, not rigid categorical differences.

. . . .

It may help . . . to distinguish between rules, principles, and policies. These concepts tend to merge, but general differences nevertheless can be noted. Professor Ronald Dworkin, a well-known contemporary legal philosopher, has explained:

> I call a "policy" that kind of standard that sets out a goal to be reached, generally an improvement in some economic, political, or social feature of the community. * * * I call a "principle" a standard that is to be observed, not because it will advance or secure an economic, political, or social situation deemed desirable, but because it is a requirement of justice or fairness or some other dimension of morality. Thus the standard that automobile accidents are to be decreased is a policy, and the standard that no man may profit by his own wrong a principle. * * *
>
> The difference between legal principles and legal rules is [that r]ules are applicable in an all or nothing fashion. If the facts a rule stipulates are given, then either the rule is valid, in which case the answer it supplies must be accepted, or it is not, in which case it contributes nothing to the solution.
>
> * * *
>
> This first difference between rules and principles entails another. Principles have a dimension that rules do not — the dimension of weight or importance. When principles intersect * * * , one who must resolve the conflict has to take into account the relative weight of each. * * *
>
> Rules do not have this dimension. * * * If two rules conflict, one of them cannot be a valid rule. Dworkin, *The Model of Rules*, 35 U. Chi. L. Rev. 14 (1967).[13]

There are systematic relationships among the four ages of American law and Dworkin's definitions of rules, principles, and policies. In general, formalist legal decisionmaking concentrates on the application of rules. This concern with rule application leads formalist judging typically to be concerned with narrowly-defined precedents which embody the specific facts ("on all fours") that trigger a particular rule's application. Rejection of this formalist approach to rules is what Langdell's "inaugura[tion of] a new mode of envisaging American law" (p. 19) was all about.

Instrumentalist judging is more concerned with advancing the correct policies. For instrumentalists, the formalist concern with applying rules is mechanical and approaches fetishism. Instrumentalists need flexibility to reach results in each case that will advance the correct policies. Certainty and predictability in law are not the instrumentalist's main aim; rather adopting rules, principles, or policies to meet the needs of each particular situation is the concern of instrumentalist judging. Instrumen-

---

[13] Reprinted by permission of Ronald Dworkin.

talists prefer to formulate general standards that call for balancing and weighing many factors rather than to articulate rules or principles that draw bright lines.

Marin Roger Scordato
Post-Realist Blues: Formalism, Instrumentalism, and the Hybrid Nature of Common Law Jurisprudence
7 Nev. L.J. 263, 266, 271–78 (2007)[14]

FORMALISM AND INSTRUMENTALISM IN COMMON LAW JURISPRUDENCE

. . . .

The Shift from Formalism to Instrumentalism

This dominant formalist conception of common law jurisprudence eventually came under increasingly serious challenge. To more and more participants, as well as observers, the notion of trial courts as mere managers of the case and predictable administrators of existing doctrine failed to describe what was actually happening in the disposition of these cases. Similarly, the actual work of the appellate courts, and the opinions that they issued, did not seem to be captured in a satisfying way by the formalist narrative.

One powerful critique of the formalist account focused on the supposedly tight logical structure of induction and deduction that was said to characterize common law jurisprudence. From a formalist perspective, a common law doctrine begins as the concrete resolution of a dispute, or a series of similar disputes, that are rationalized by an articulated general principle of decision. This generalized principle of decision should, if designed correctly, harmonize and make consistent the varied results in specific cases from which it was induced. This principle of decision, once established, is then relied upon by courts later facing a similar dispute and is deductively applied to reach a disposition in the new case.

The general legal doctrine that is developed through this process of induction is, then, in a sense, tested to see if it produces an acceptable result each time it is deductively applied to a new case. Occasionally, on review, an appellate court will be unsatisfied with the operation of the doctrine and will tinker with it by amending it slightly or by recognizing an exception to it. In this way, much like the currently understood principles of science, the body of common law in a jurisdiction, continually tested by the results of empirical experiments, slowly evolves and improves. Just as we hope that our currently understood principles of science move closer and closer to being the actual laws of nature, so, too, we hope in a formalist world that our actual common law moves ever closer to an ideal set of legal principles, often referred to as natural law.

Starting most famously in the 1920s with writers like Karl Llewellyn and a movement that came to be known as legal realism, the formalist description of the work of the courts was challenged as being unsatisfying and insufficient. The realists claimed that the actual work of both the trial and appellate courts was far more expansive and value-laden than was captured by the tight process of logical induction and deduction and the strict discipline of prior precedent, holding, and dicta imposed by the doctrine of stare decisis that is so much a part of the formalist conception.

The legal realists offered a very different account of the structure and process of common law jurisprudence. As much as treatise writers and codifiers might have presented it in that way, the realists did not look at the common law and see a coherent, cohesive, relatively well-organized body of rules analogous to the current state of

---

understanding in a mature natural science like physics or chemistry. Instead, the realists saw the common law as more of a cloud of assorted principles, aphorisms, and maxims, some relatively tightly organized around particular topics and issues, and others not much integrated into a larger structure at all. To varying degrees, there existed support in the way of precedent for most all of the many tenets and precepts that constituted the common law. Thus, most all of it possessed formal status under the doctrine of stare decisis.

The critical feature of the common law that significantly distinguished it from the body of principles that made up a natural science, said the realists, was the fact that some, perhaps many, of the rules and maxims that were contained within the common law were potentially in direct contradiction with one another. A judge, faced with the task of resolving a particular legal issue in a case, could look to the existing common law in the relevant jurisdiction and likely find two or more honored principles, either of which could be logically applied to resolve the issue, and each of which, when deductively applied to the problem, would yield an opposite result.

For example, imagine the first time that a court had to deal with the problem of an inaccurate offer in contract law, made without the fault of the offering party. Suppose that B is a very successful retailer of clothes, currently quite fashionable and in vogue. In order to gain exposure and access to the large market that B currently enjoys, A, a manufacturer of clothing, sends to B an offer to sell certain clothing produced by A for "$1.50 a piece." Due to no mistake or carelessness on the part of A, the message that is received by B states "$1 a piece." B reads the offer, reasonably believes that it is a genuine offer from A, and promptly accepts. Is A bound by B's acceptance of the offer?

A court looking at this problem as an issue of first impression, long before the modern consensus on the issue had been formed, might reasonably determine that the well-accepted contract law maxim that an offeror is the master of his offer should appropriately apply, and therefore that A is bound to B. The same court could just as well determine that the appropriate principle to apply to this issue is the equally honored notion that a binding contract should only arise from an authentic meeting of the minds of the potentially contracting parties, and therefore because A never actually intended to make such an offer to B, A is not legally bound to B.

In a strictly formalist system, either decision is technically correct and ought to be upheld on appeal. Both approaches start with widely-recognized doctrines of the common law and apply them with deductive accuracy to reach their different results. Neither approach gets "the math" wrong in a way that should invoke an appellate reversal. And yet each approach leads to different resolutions of the exact same issue arising in the same case from a single set of facts.

The thrust of the realist critique on this point was that the formalist conception of common law adjudication was, in practice, largely indeterminate. Not just subtly indeterminate in cases of unusually difficult logical challenges or especially ambivalent facts, but profoundly indeterminate along a wide spectrum of potential issues. The source of this indeterminacy, said the realists, was the co-existence of equally established but potentially contradictory principles and maxims residing within the universe of principles and maxims that constituted the common law in a given jurisdiction at any given time.

The existence of equally authoritative principles that could result in importantly different outcomes when logically applied to the facts of a specific case meant that the real action in deciding these cases was not taking place in the deductive application of the common law to the facts of the case, as was supposed by the formalist model. Instead, it was occurring at the point of choosing which of the possible common law principles should be selected and applied to resolve the dispute. From this perspective, the ultimate resolution of most cases was decided and sealed once the court selected the legal principle that was to be applied. In practice, only rarely did a genuine and significant issue exist regarding the logical application of the selected principle to the facts of the specific case.

This characterization of the operation of the common law legal system can be seen as having its counterpart in the larger world as well. That is to say that a person trying to decide how to proceed in a given situation can reach for one or another of a variety of well-recognized and generally accepted maxims, or principles, of conventional wisdom and can end up deciding to act in either one or another of two polar opposite directions, depending upon the specific maxim that is selected.

For example, should I buy a new computer system for my business? Well, a penny saved is a penny earned; but, you've got to spend money to make money. . . . When I get back home, and the kids misbehave, should I respond with physical punishment? If I spare the rod, then I'll spoil the child; although, of course, violence teaches violence.

Regardless of the larger philosophical status of the conflict between formalism and realism, the legal realist critique of formalism and the realists' alternative account of common law jurisprudence resonated with large numbers of lawyers and legal academics. Before long, the realist conception of the work of the courts became the prevailing perspective. Fewer and fewer observers continued to believe that the primary work of the appellate courts was a more or less technical review of the deductive logic of the lower courts, with an occasional revision of the existing common law. Increasingly, both observers and participants came to view the work of the appellate courts as heavily value-laden, involving the selection of specific principles, and thus resultant specific outcomes, from a variety of nearly equal logical possibilities. The values and policies that guided these selections might be more or less explicit, or tacitly underlying, but in either case they were nevertheless operative in the process.

If the common law were no longer to be seen as analogous to the laws of nature, something that may not at present be in a completely satisfactory form but which we strive to improve upon over time as we test it against the constant flow of cases that are processed by the court systems, what then is a more acceptable concept of it? Why should the courts prefer one possible version of a common law doctrine to another? On what broader principled basis could an advocate try to convince a court to create a new exception to an existing common law rule or to recognize a new common law doctrine altogether? What is the reason for asking an advocate to place her preferred resolution of a case into the structure of a jurisdiction's existing precedent if we did not have faith that the existing precedents represent some settled understanding of the best treatment of a particular issue?

The Instrumentalist Approach to Common Law Jurisprudence

As the formalist paradigm waned under the continuing critical challenge of the realist movement, the emerging perspective that came to replace it viewed the common law not as the current product of a long-term search for the best, the ideal, the natural law, but instead as a social tool, one among many, that could be brought to bear to try to achieve particular social outcomes or solve particular social problems. From such a perspective the primary purpose of contract law, then, is not so much to discover the abstractly optimal set of rules governing the exchange of promises among members of society, but is instead to maximize beneficial reliance and to minimize friction in executory transactions. Similarly, the goal of tort law is much less to articulate the proper obligation owed by one who harms another than to fashion a set of rules that maximizes compensation to victims and deters future harm producing behavior.

Thus, tort law would be seen much less as a great social statement on the responsibility of citizens for harm caused to others or their property than as a particular social system, operating within a complicated complex of other social systems, such as criminal law, insurance, and government benefit programs, seeking to minimize injury and to provide adequate compensation to the injured. From this perspective, the common law generally is seen primarily as another tool, or an instrument, for attaining desired results in society. Thus this view of the law is often called instrumentalism.

From an instrumentalist perspective the practical force of precedent in the determination of the outcome of a given case is inevitably far less than it would be under a formalist conception. For the formalist, the existing common law represents the distillate of many decades of articulation, testing, tinkering, and improvement of the doctrine. It is our current best formulation of ideal regulation in the field, and it is not to be disregarded or tampered with lightly. In fact, a court operating within a formalist model would be required to meet a heavy burden before resolving a particular dispute in a manner that was not consistent with the existing pattern of precedent in the jurisdiction.

For an instrumentalist, adherence to the existing precedent in a jurisdiction may be valuable to the extent that it permits parties to anticipate accurately the outcome of disputes, thus reducing the volume of costly litigation brought into the system. It may also be valued because such adherence will result in a more consistent resolution of similar cases brought into the system at different times or decided by different courts within the same system, thus advancing a certain kind of fairness. On the other hand, adherence to an existing precedent from an instrumentalist perspective is a hindrance to the extent that it slows the alteration of the common law to achieve desired outcomes more effectively, or it makes more difficult the changing of existing common law to reflect new goals or to respond to new problems.

For the formalist, the existing common law is a carefully constructed social canon in which decades of painstaking thought and practical testing have been invested. To the instrumentalist, it is a tool, one whose primary value is its ability to be used at a given time and place to respond to the currently understood needs of the society. If the tool is no longer doing the job that is currently required, then the obligation of the user is to modify the instrument until it performs more effectively.

Stephanos Bibas

Originalism and Formalism in Criminal Procedure: The Triumph of Justice Scalia, the Unlikely Friend of Criminal Defendants?
94 GEO. L.J. 183, 184–88, 199–202, 204 (2005)[15]

INTRODUCTION

Though commentators frequently caricature Supreme Court decisions as a battle between the left and right wings, this neat, politicized diagram has always been too crude. In 2004, the Court outdid itself in defying stereotypes. Justice Scalia, long the darling of tough-on-crime conservatives, authored two sweeping majority opinions that vindicated criminal defendants' rights: *Crawford v. Washington* reinterpreted the Sixth Amendment's Confrontation Clause to exclude reliable testimonial hearsay unless the defendant has been able to cross-examine it. *Blakely v. Washington* required that juries — not judges — find, beyond a reasonable doubt, all facts that trigger sentences above ordinary sentencing-guidelines ranges. In both cases, conservative Justice Thomas and liberal Justices Stevens, Souter, and Ginsburg joined Justice Scalia's opinions. And in both, the pragmatic swing Justice who supposedly controlled the Court, Justice O'Connor, disagreed sharply with Justice Scalia's reasoning and approach.

Justice Scalia has occasionally shown a libertarian, pro-defendant streak in the past, but *Crawford* and *Blakely* mark the triumph of his approach. In each case, Justice Scalia had advocated an originalist, formalist rethinking of that area of law years

---

[15] Reprinted by permission of Stephanos Bibas ©2005. All rights reserved.

earlier. And, in each case, a majority of the Court eventually came around to his view. Even Justices Stevens, Souter, and Ginsburg, who are wedded to neither originalism nor formalism, embraced these principles in *Crawford* and *Blakely*. Why?

This Essay uses *Crawford* and *Blakely* as case studies to evaluate Justice Scalia's originalism and formalism in criminal procedure and their influence on the rest of the Supreme Court. Rather than surveying the vast literature on originalism and formalism, I will focus on Justice Scalia's own brands of each doctrine and how they have shaped two areas of criminal procedure. Part I briefly sets forth Justice Scalia's versions of originalism and formalism and explains the main virtues and vices that he sees in them.

. . . .

Part IV considers how compatible originalism and formalism are and what happens if they conflict. In many areas of criminal procedure, the text and historical record reveal a bright-line rule, in which case originalism promotes formalism. But often the text and historical record are unclear or point to a multi-factor balancing test rather than a formalistic rule. This is true, for example, in search-and-seizure law, where courts invented a warrant requirement more rigid than the Fourth Amendment's historic reasonableness standard. In *Crawford*, Justice Scalia suggested that originalism, not formalism, is the foundational principle. But in the *Blakely* line of cases, Justice Scalia reveals what I suspect are his true formalist colors; formalism, not originalism, was *Blakely*'s foundation. Indeed, at times Justice Scalia seems to embrace originalism precisely as a brand of formalism. To him, originalism is appealing as a bright-line way of resolving cases with a minimum of judicial discretion and unpredictability. But originalism cannot succeed in its aims when no majority of the Court consistently adheres to that approach. Nevertheless, originalism holds enough appeal that it often sways Justices who are not thoroughgoing originalists. Originalism, in short, is a powerful force in criminal procedure and often dovetails with formalism. But while formalism may drive Justice Scalia's criminal procedure jurisprudence, it has much less independent influence over other members of the Court.

. . . .

JUSTICE SCALIA'S VERSION OF ORIGINALISM AND FORMALISM

First, a few definitions are in order. Justice Scalia's originalism rests upon the original meaning of the Constitution's text. This inquiry is not a subjective quest for what particular Framers had in mind, but an objective understanding of what the words themselves meant at the time. In other words, Justice Scalia's jurisprudence emphasizes original understanding, not original intent. Justice Scalia treats his originalism as a species of textualism, because he reads texts reasonably and naturally for all that they fairly contain. Sometimes, people can disagree about what the original meaning was or how to apply it to a particular situation, but [quoting from Scalia] "[o]ften — indeed, I dare say usually — [original meaning] is easy to discern and simple to apply." Originalism also helps to preserve the separation of powers, by keeping courts from encroaching on the legislative role and democratic will.

Originalism likewise protects juries from judicial encroachment. The Founding generation trusted juries, and not judges, in part because King George III had pressured judges and used them to oppress the colonies. Thus, Article III and the Sixth Amendment guarantee criminal petit juries, the Fifth Amendment guarantees grand juries, and the Seventh Amendment guarantees civil juries. . . . The Framers prized the jury as the representative, democratic lower house of the bicameral judiciary, a populist check on arbitrary judges. The Framers also analogized juries to mini-legislatures. As quasi-legislators, jurors apply law to facts ex post and inject needed flexibility into a rule-bound system. They thus check the inevitable overinclusiveness of legislation, as well as executive decisions to charge and prosecute. Originalism therefore seeks to protect the jury's role as a check on all three branches of government. . . .

Though many people criticize his approach as formalistic, Justice Scalia embraces formalism as the point of the rule of law. As he has put it: "Long live formalism. It is what makes a government a government of laws and not of men." In a famous essay, he praised "the rule of law as a law of rules." While generalizations are bound to impose costs because they are always over- or under-inclusive, the benefits of clear, categorical rules outweigh these costs. Clear, general rules, he has argued, promote predictability and equal treatment, reduce judicial arbitrariness, and foster judicial courage to make unpopular decisions. By adopting general rules, judges constrain their discretion and minimize the role of their own policy preferences. Juries, he has suggested, are better suited than judges to exercise discretion and determine reasonableness, because these inquiries are not reducible to judicially administrable rules. . . . [W]hile originalism does not always lead to formalism, in Justice Scalia's view the former tends to produce the latter. . . .

Justice Scalia's formalism stands in stark contrast to the pragmatism of his jurisprudential arch rival, Justice Breyer. In Justice Breyer's "consequential[ist]" view, courts should look not only backward at text, history, and precedent, but also forward to the likely outcomes of various rulings. In other words, courts need to be practical and flexible enough to adapt their rulings to reality and necessity. Put another way, Justice Breyer values judicial flexibility, which leaves judges wiggle room to apply general rules to particular cases in a manner that seems fair. This forward-looking approach trusts judges' expertise and ability to forecast wise policy outcomes and to adjust the Constitution accordingly. It puts less faith in history and in particular legal texts, whose meaning may be indeterminate.

While Justice Scalia admits that flexibility is a countervailing value, he emphasizes the need for legislative rather than judicial flexibility. Non-originalism, he notes, usually leads to even less legislative flexibility. Judges who stray from originalism and formalism tend to constrict the ambit of democratic government, whereas originalism usually preserves a larger role for elected legislatures. In his view, legislatures — not judges — are primarily responsible for updating the law to fit changing times. . . .

ORIGINALISM VERSUS FORMALISM

Up until now, I have discussed originalism and formalism in tandem, as if they were natural bedfellows. But do the two really belong together? As I have suggested earlier, the two methodologies not only spring from different sources, but sometimes come into conflict. Subpart A below explores the compatibility of these two approaches. Subpart B considers which of the two is really driving the Court. Though he relies heavily on originalism, at root Justice Scalia's opinions rest more on formalism. Formalism, however, holds much less sway over other members of the Court, for whom originalism is the more powerful force.

A. COMPLEMENTARY OR CLASHING?

One might be tempted to lump originalism and formalism together, in part because the same jurists, notably Justices Scalia and Thomas, tend to embrace both. Sometimes the two dovetail neatly. Where the text and historical record disclose a bright-line rule, the originalist approach leads one to a formalistic rule. This is true, for example, of *Crawford*'s approach to the Confrontation Clause. The text and history of the clause say nothing about judicial balancing of a statement's reliability. They simply guarantee the right to confront and cross-examine any adverse witness, a historical bright-line rule. The same is true of the Double Jeopardy Clause's historical, bright-line limitation to criminal cases. The text of the Clause forbids twice placing a person in jeopardy of "life or limb" for the "same offence," meaning criminal punishment for a criminal offense.

Surrounding clauses of the Fifth Amendment guarantee the privilege against self-incrimination "in any criminal case" and grand jury indictments for any "capital, or otherwise infamous crime." Finally, history confirms that the purpose of the double-jeopardy protection was limited to criminal punishments. Though the Supreme Court tried extending double-jeopardy protection to civil fines, this extension proved to be unworkable and hard to administer. Ultimately, the Court limited the Clause's scope to criminal prosecutions, returning to a workable, clear, simple rule grounded in history.

Text and history, however, sometimes support a balancing test rather than a bright-line rule. A good example is the Fourth Amendment, which judges have interpreted to require warrants, probable cause, and the exclusionary rule. These bright-line rules are clear mandates that promise to guide and constrain police discretion. But when these rules proved to be rigid and overbroad, courts created a thicket of increasingly arcane exceptions to the warrant, probable cause, and exclusionary rules. As an originalist matter, however, the Fourth Amendment requires only that searches be reasonable, and reasonableness sounds much more like a multi-factor balancing test than a clear rule. Thus, one must distinguish originalism from formalism and, if the two clash, determine which should prevail.

B. AT ROOT, IS THE COURT ORIGINALIST OR FORMALIST?

Which of these two principles is ultimately driving the Court's criminal procedure jurisprudence? The Court's rhetoric on this point is mixed. In *Crawford*, Justice Scalia began his opinion for the Court with pages of historical and textual analysis. After discussing English and American colonial history, Justice Scalia concluded that the Clause was designed to prevent in-court use of ex parte out-of-court witness examinations. The history and text "do[] not suggest any open-ended exceptions from the confrontation requirement to be developed by the courts. . . . [They] admit[] only those exceptions established at the time of the founding." Justice Scalia then criticized *Roberts'* "malleable [reliability] standard" as "unpredictable [and] . . . amorphous, if not entirely subjective." This unpredictable standard afforded little safeguard against clear violations of the Clause and produced inconsistent and contradictory outcomes. Though this strand of argument is formalist, the Court ultimately rested its decision on originalism: "The unpardonable vice of the *Roberts* test, however, is not its unpredictability, but its demonstrated capacity to admit core testimonial statements that the Confrontation Clause plainly meant to exclude."

What is most impressive about *Crawford* is how its skillful blend of originalism and formalism persuaded seven members of the Court to throw out decades of precedent. *Crawford*'s formalism highlighted the inconsistent, unpredictable muddle that had emerged from a hopelessly vague test. And *Crawford*'s originalism was a compelling account of the Confrontation Clause's purpose and how ad hoc decisionmaking has drifted away from that aim. These powerful and coherent accounts persuaded even fair-weather originalists that originalism and formalism worked well here. Even a functionalist can see the strong functional value of originalism and formalism in this case, much as a utilitarian can sometimes see the value of following rules. Thus, liberal concern for criminal defendants' rights dovetailed with conservative reverence for the Founding and distrust of government and balancing tests.

In the *Apprendi-Blakely* line of cases, however, originalism was not the driving force. True, *Apprendi* cited much history in support of its jury-trial right. But the same members of the Court admitted in *Jones*, the precursor of *Apprendi*, that no history squarely supported this rule . . . .

Rather, the *Apprendi-Blakely* rule was motivated less by originalism than by formalism. *Apprendi* referred repeatedly to the fear of a slippery slope that would gradually erode the role of juries. Justice Scalia's concurrence in *Apprendi* rested explicitly on the need for a coherent bright line: "What ultimately demolishes the case for the dissenters is that they are unable to say what the right to trial by jury *does* guarantee if, as they assert, it does not guarantee [jury findings of facts that raise maximum sentences]. They provide no coherent alternative." In *Blakely*, Justice Scalia reiterated the importance of a coherent bright line, justifying *Apprendi*'s rule by "the need to give intelligible content to the right of jury trial." Clarity not only constrains judges, but also gives prospective criminals fair warning of the maximum sentences they may face. . . .

In sum, originalism is a powerful force in criminal procedure, and it often leads to formalism. At times, however, originalism seems to be a cloak for formalism, invoked (as in *Blakely*) even where there is no solid, workable originalist answer. Perhaps as a result of this sleight of hand, while Justice Scalia's originalist and formalist approach to criminal procedure periodically triumphs on the Court, it enjoys no consistent majority.

Jeff Bleich, Anne Voigts & Michelle Friedland
A Practical Era: The Beginning (or the End) of Pragmatism
65 OR. ST. B. BULL. 19, 19–20, 22–24, 26 (2005)[16]

In her final term on the Supreme Court, despite Justice Sandra Day O'Connor's issuing no landmark concurrences and losing some key 5-4 decisions, she demonstrated — perhaps more than ever before — the profound mark she has made on the Supreme Court's jurisprudence. Throughout her time on the Court, Justice O'Connor has defied easy labels, baffled pundits and either delighted or bedeviled her colleagues by deciding cases incrementally and pragmatically. While other justices' opinions invoked one particular judicial doctrine or another — judicial restraint, original intent, loose constructionism — Justice O'Connor's opinions appeared less concerned with allegiance to any of these sacred cows than with fairly deciding the case in front of her, using whatever tools seemed necessary. She has been the Court's pragmatist. And this term, even when she was not in the majority, pragmatism reigned supreme. In case after case — whether the question concerned a town taking private property for commercial development, the Ten Commandments being displayed in public spaces, states regulating the sale of medical marijuana, condemned people challenging application of the death penalty against them for crimes they'd committed as juveniles, or the United States balking at the effect of decisions of the International Court of Justice — the Court's debate was principally practical, not doctrinal. . . .

. . . . In addition to displaying pragmatism, four traits in particular help explain some of the Court's actions this term: namely, the Court's reluctance to take many cases, its tendency toward open disagreement; its aggressive policing of other branches' use of authority and its tendency to revisit and refine its own earlier decisions.

. . . .

Despite taking relatively few cases [this term], the Court managed to generate more than its share of opinions and to express sharp disagreements in more than 40 percent of those cases. This term 20 decisions were decided by a 5-4 vote on either the entire case or on a major issue. Another 15 cases were decided by margins of 5-3 or 6-3. This means that in a whopping two-fifths of the Court's cases, a change in one or two votes would have changed the outcome of the case. Interestingly, though, differences arose not from the usual philosophical disagreements, but based upon dueling visions of pragmatism. As a result, cases broke along relatively unpredictable lines. To put it in perspective, in the 2003 term, Justice O'Connor had been in the majority in 100 percent of the Court's 5-4 decisions. This past term, she and Justice Kennedy were in the majority in barely half of the 5-4 cases. Instead, participation in majorities was pretty evenly split among all of the nine justices, although the tone of the dissenting opinions was just as sharp.

. . . .

Ten Commandments

The Court's split rulings on the Ten Commandments epitomized the justices' heavy emphasis on pragmatism this term. In *McCreary County v. ACLU*, the Court considered the constitutionality of a six-year effort by two Kentucky county courthouses to hang the King James version of the Ten Commandments prominently in their hallways. After being sued for displaying the Ten Commandments by themselves, the counties clumsily added other historical documents such as the Declaration of Independence and the Mayflower Compact, but with their religious references highlighted, as a simultaneous tip-of-the-hat, and poke-in-the-eye to the original display's detractors. Writing for a 5-4 majority, Justice Souter noted that the counties' purpose of seeking to advance a religious purpose was obvious from the history of the case, and the Court simply could not swallow the counties' "implausible claim" that the displays were for a secular purpose of teaching history to visitors. Justice O'Conner concurred but added a broader practical concern: those who questioned the Court's current *Lemon* test for restricting state endorsement of religion should recognize that the test has been effective in preventing the nation from becoming a theistic society. "At a time when we see around the world the violent consequences of the assumption of religious authority by government, Americans may count themselves fortunate . . . Why would we trade a system that has served us so well for one that has served others so poorly."

In the companion case of *Van Orden*, the Court found that practical considerations took them in a different direction. In that case, the Court considered a much older display of the Ten Commandments that had been installed on the Texas statehouse grounds nearly 45 years earlier. The commandments had been donated by the Fraternal Order of Eagles, a benevolent society that sought to combat juvenile delinquency by giving these monuments to communities around the country. The Court found that, in this case, there was no religious endorsement — again 5-4 — but with no actual majority. The controlling fifth vote, a concurrence by Justice Breyer, offered an unbridled homage to pragmatism. Justice Breyer shrugged that this was one of those borderline cases for which there exists "no test-related substitute for the exercise of legal judgment." He found that as a practical matter, this just did not seem like an attempt to foist religion on people. In particular, he noted that: the Eagles had made special efforts to track down a non-sectarian version of the Ten Commandments; the monument had been placed innocuously in a large park with many other monuments; and the monument hadn't bothered anyone enough to cause them to complain for over 40 years.

A Controversial Take on Takings

One of the most controversial decisions of the term, *Kelo v. City of New London* also highlights the great extent to which questions of pragmatism shaped the debate. As set out in *Kelo*, the city of New London, Conn. had fallen on rough times. With an unemployment rate that was twice the state's average, and its lowest population since 1920, its listless economy earned it the dubious designation of a "distressed" community. Perhaps inspired by Super Bowl advertisements, the slumping city turned to Pfizer, the maker of Viagra, to help restore New London to its former vigor. Pfizer agreed to construct a $300 million research facility adjacent to a former naval base, Fort Trumbell. Seizing on this opportunity, New London adopted a comprehensive plan to attract other desirable economic partners such as Starbucks to what would be a newly revitalized water front area, built by private developers. Mr. Kelo, a local resident, refused to sell his home in this redevelopment area to those developers and he challenged the city's condemnation of his property as an unconstitutional taking, because it was not for a "public purpose." Instead, Mr. Kelo argued, the city was merely taking property from one private citizen (him) and giving it to a more attractive private citizen (a developer with big bucks). Justice Stevens, writing for the 5-4 majority, upheld the taking, finding that New London was entitled to condemn property for a private developer, as long as doing so was a rational means to achieve a legitimate "public purpose." The majority found that reviving New London's stalled economic engine and restoring its reputation satisfied that public purpose. The decision offered a practical standard for deciding if a taking was for a public purpose: as long as the purpose was to promote the community good and not to give economic or other benefit to another private entity, then the "public purpose" requirement was satisfied. In a stinging dissent, Justice O'Connor took that practical analysis to task and offered her own version of pragmatism. Writing for herself and Justices Rehnquist, Scalia and Thomas, Justice O'Connor criticized the majority for being naïve about the ways of small town government. She explained that a bright line was necessary to prevent city councils from using their power to condemn the private property of disenfranchised people in order to award lucrative property rights to their friends and supporters. Any squishy test, she explained, was destined to fail because a transfer of property to a commercial interest will almost always advance some economic development interest, but the backroom political influences that actually inspired the transfer will be almost impossible to detect. Justice Thomas, characteristically, proposed an even brighter, bright-line test that would require that the property be acquired not simply for a public purpose but for a public *use*, which is open to the entire public.

By contrast, in *Lingle v. Chevron USA Inc*, the Court was in heated agreement about the need for bright line rules in a different takings situation. The Court unanimously found that — for practical reasons — a bright line test was necessary to avoid confusion about whether a government burden was or was not a taking. The case concerned Hawaii's questionable attempt to keep gas prices low by adopting a statute that limits the rents that an oil company could charge for leasing its service stations. The Ninth Circuit, applying the Supreme Court's 1980 decision in *Agins v. City of Tiburon*, noted that the taking did not substantially advance a legitimate interest (because it was not at all clear that service station owners would pass on their savings to gas purchasers). For that reason, it invalidated the law. The Court reversed, concluding that its old *Agins* test had been "regrettable." As the Court explained, whether the government had burdened someone's property to the point of a "taking" should not depend upon whether there was a good reason for the government's action, but only on what effect that action had on the property. Again, the conclusion was practical. For purposes of determining whether a property owner is entitled to just compensation, it simply does not matter *why* property was taken, only *whether* it was taken. The Court thus overruled *Agins* and apologized to the lower courts for leading them astray.

The Commerce Clause Limits Weed, Not Wine

Although Mr. Kelo was not a party in *Gonzalez v. Raich*, he had the right moniker for a case that took the "high" out of the high court. In *Raich*, the Court considered whether a federal law prohibiting all use of marijuana was a valid exercise of Congress' commerce power that would prevent enforcement of California's Compassionate Use Act. The Compassionate Use Act permitted seriously ill individuals to purchase and use marijuana for medicinal purposes. The plaintiffs argued that under the Court's more recent Commerce Clause jurisprudence, the federal government exceeded its power by barring use of home-grown marijuana that had no effect on interstate commerce. By a 6-3 margin, the Court demonstrated that — regardless of whether marijuana has all of the healing properties that Californians attribute to it — it does have the remarkable capacity to make Justice Scalia vote with the anti-federalists.

Again, the divisions broke down along practical lines. Writing for the Court, Justice Stevens explained that allowing people to grow and use marijuana as a medical supply could, as a practical matter, affect the national market for marijuana and for other painkillers that these patients would use instead of marijuana. Carving out an exception for medicinal use would also make the enforcement of marijuana laws more difficult. As Justice Stevens noted, it would be difficult if not impossible for federal agents to distinguish home-grown California marijuana that had been cultivated for medicinal use from evil weed grown elsewhere or for illegitimate purposes such as "inspiring" Snoop Dogg. This, he explained, would leave a gaping hole in federal law enforcement efforts. Justice Scalia, who concurred in the judgment, stressed that in his view the purchase and sale of marijuana is an economic activity that can be regulated intrastate by the federal government as long as doing so is "necessary and proper" to accomplish a more comprehensive regulation of interstate commerce.

Justice O'Connor, joined by the Chief and Justice Thomas, dissented, on the ground that the Court's decision had, in their view, no practical, limiting principle. Congress had made no findings that marijuana use by seriously ill Californians who took marijuana for pain relief had any impact on interstate markets. Instead, under the Court's ruling, even if only a dozen people qualified for the right to grow and use their own marijuana for therapeutic purposes, it would still have an effect on interstate commerce sufficient to allow Congressional action. The dissent thus faulted the majority for adopting a rule by which virtually every human activity could be said to affect interstate commerce, and thus be subject to federal regulation.

Justice O'Connor's brand of practicality also lost out in this term's gift to the state of California, *Granholm v. Heald*. In *Granholm*, the Court broke down along unusual lines to invalidate state laws that prohibited the sale of wine from out-of-state retailers based on the Dormant Commerce Clause. The 5-4 majority relied on practical conclusions and (at least according to Justice Stevens' dissent), an apparent generation gap. *Granholm* concerned whether the 21st Amendment to the Constitution permits states to bar direct purchases of out-of-state wine. The amendment, which repealed prohibition, provided that "(t)he transportation or importation into any State . . . of intoxicating liquors, in violation of the laws thereof, is hereby prohibited." Although the majority and dissenting opinions sparred principally over matters of history (causing Justice Stevens to grumpily lament "the younger generations who make policy decisions"), the Court also made some practical judgments about wine use generally. In dealing with whether the regulations violated the Dormant Commerce Clause, the majority rejected New York's and Michigan's attempts to justify their laws as advancing legitimate local purposes that could not be achieved in a non-discriminatory way.

Invalidating the Juvenile Death Penalty

In *Roper v. Simmons*, a 5-4 majority found that offenders who commit capital offenses before they are 18 are not eligible for the death penalty. Simmons, who was 17 when he committed a capital murder, had his sentence commuted from death to life without parole by the Missouri Supreme Court based on the Eighth Amendment's prohibition on cruel and unusual punishment. In affirming that decision, Justice Kennedy applied the Court's "evolving standards of decency" test to conclude that there was now a national consensus against a juvenile death penalty. In particular, the Court noted that 30 states now bar application of the death penalty against juveniles, those that have such a penalty on the books rarely if ever enforce it, and virtually no other civilized nation permits it. But beyond that standard, the Court also considered practical concerns including the deficits of juveniles, the fact that public passion may cause juries to ignore those deficits and the need for a bright-line to police that tendency. In dissent, Justice O'Connor accepted the majority's framework but rejected its ideas about what was or was not practical. She concluded that state legislatures and juries were perfectly capable of distinguishing between mature and immature juveniles. Instead, the Court's bright-line would allow mature juveniles to automatically avoid the death penalty, but still leave in the hands of a jury the virtually identical issue of whether to execute an immature 18-year-old.

. . . .

The Future

With Justice O'Connor's departure, and an imminent change in the Court's composition, there is no way to know whether this term's pragmatism will continue. Given Justice O'Connor's pivotal role on the Court, it could well be that her colleagues adopted her approach as a way of seeking to gain her support. If that were the case, then when she leaves the Court, their interest in practical analysis may depart as well. On the other hand, if Justice O'Connor's approach has actually gained adherents among some other Court members, then this may be part of her enduring legacy. For all practical purposes, though, only time will tell.

Chapter 3
THE CASE METHOD OF STUDY

In this chapter we move from the level of abstract theorizing about the law and legal reasoning to the concrete mechanics of briefing a case. The first section discusses general approaches to reading and briefing cases in the context of the common law tradition of precedent and also explains the value and importance of the briefing process. The second section focuses more specifically on how to read a case and what to look for. Section three discusses how to create a useful brief. Finally, section four provides some tips on how to extract the relevant information from a case to use in a brief, with a focus on annotating and highlighting.

A. CASES, PRECEDENT, AND THE COMMON LAW SYSTEM

Before we get to the specifics on how to brief a case, it will help to know a few specifics about briefs themselves, case opinions, and how to approach both. The next selection by Karl Llewellyn addresses beginning law students and provides tremendous insight into how to approach cases, how to interpret cases, how to take notes, and how to deal with precedent. All of these skills together will aid in your ability to create useful briefs.

While nearly 50 years old, *The Bramble Bush* is as helpful and on-target as if it were written today. Because it was written so long ago, however, the text can be a bit cumbersome. As one reader commentated, "Professor Llewellyn's writing style is not easy. It's not an antiquated style, but rather the style of an obviously erudite man whose mind is very active . . . . To put it simply: either Llewellyn had a poor editor or his editor never heard of Strunk & White's Elements of Style."[1] Nonetheless, the commentator gave the book five stars, as did another reader who wrote, "This is perhaps the greatest book ever written about the law, aimed at law students."[2]

Fight through the language and dig into what Llewellyn has to say. You will find it extremely helpful not only in the ways described above but also in establishing a general mindset that will help you conquer some of the more difficult cases you read.

KARL N. LLEWELLYN
THE BRAMBLE BUSH: ON OUR LAW AND ITS STUDY
41–59, 60–62, 64–69, 76–78 (1960)[3]

III. THIS CASE SYSTEM: WHAT TO *DO* WITH THE CASES

. . . . It is a pity, but you must learn to *read*. To read each word. To understand *each* word. You are outlanders in this country of the law. You do not know the speech. It must be learned. Like any other foreign tongue, it must be learned: by seeing words, by using them until they are familiar; meantime, by constant reference to the dictionary. What, dictionary? Tort, trespass, trover, plea, assumpsit, nisi prius, venire de novo, demurrer, joinder, traverse, abatement, general issue, tender, mandamus, certiorari, adverse possession, dependent relative revocation, and the rest. Law Latin, law French, aye, or law English — what do these strange terms mean to you? Can you rely upon the crumbs of language that remain from school? Does *cattle levant and couchant* mean *cows getting up and lying down*? Does *nisi prius* mean *unless before*? Or *traverse* mean an upper gallery in a church? I fear a dictionary is your only hope — a law dictionary — the one-volume kind you can keep ready on your desk. Can you trust the

---

[1] Amazon.com: Bramble Bush: Customer Reviews, http://www.amazon.com/Bramble-Bush-Our-Law-Study/dp/0379000733 (last visited May 6, 2008).

[2] Id.

[3] Copyright ©1960 by Oxford University Press. All rights reserved. Reprinted by permission.

dictionary, is it accurate, does it give you what you want? Of course not. No dictionary does. The life of words is in the using of them, in the wide network of their long associations, in the intangible something we denominate their feel. But the bare bones to work with, the dictionary offers; and without those bare bones you may be sure the feel will never come.

The first thing to do with an opinion, then, is read it. The next thing is to get clear the actual decision, the judgment rendered. Who won, the plaintiff or defendant? And watch your step here. You are after in first instance the plaintiff and defendant *below*, in the trial court. In order to follow through what happened you must therefore first know the outcome *below*; else you do not see what was appealed from, nor by whom. You now follow through in order to see exactly what *further* judgment has been rendered on appeal. The stage is then cleared of form — although of course you do not yet know all that these forms mean, that they imply. You can turn now to what you want peculiarly to know. Given the actual judgments below and above as your indispensable framework — what has the case decided, and what can you derive from it as to what will be decided later?

You will be looking, in the opinion, or in the preliminary matter plus the opinion, for the following: a statement of the facts the court assumes; a statement of the precise way the question has come before the court — which includes what the plaintiff wanted below, and what the defendant did about it, the judgment below, and what the trial court did that is complained of; then the outcome on appeal, the judgment; and finally the reasons this court gives for doing what it did. This does not look so bad. But it is much worse than it looks.

For all our cases are decided, all our opinions are written, all our predictions, all our arguments are made, on certain four assumptions. They are the first presuppositions of our study. They must be rutted into you till you can juggle with them standing on your head and in your sleep.

1) *The court must decide the dispute that is before it.* It cannot refuse because the job is hard, or dubious, or dangerous.

2) *The court can decide* only *the particular dispute which is before it.* When it speaks to that question it speaks ex cathedra, with authority, with finality, with an almost magic power. When it speaks to the question before it, it announces *law*, and if what it announces is new, it legislates, it *makes* the law. But when it speaks to any other question at all, it says mere words, which no man needs to follow. Are such words worthless? They are not. We know them as judicial *dicta*; when they are wholly off the point at issue we call them *obiter dicta* — words dropped along the road, wayside remarks. Yet even wayside remarks shed light on the remarker. They may be very useful in the future to him, or to us. But he will not feel bound to them, as to his ex cathedra utterance. They came not hallowed by a Delphic frenzy. He may be slow to change them; but not so slow as in the other case.

3) *The court can decide the particular dispute only according to a* general *rule which covers a whole class of like disputes.* Our legal theory does not admit of single decisions standing on their own. If judges are free, are indeed forced, to decide new cases for which there is no rule, they must at least make a new rule as they decide. So far, good. But how wide, or how narrow, is the general rule in this particular case? That is a troublesome matter. The practice of our case-law, however, is I think fairly stated thus: it pays to be suspicious of general rules which look too wide; it pays to go slow in feeling *certain* that a wide rule has been laid down at all, or that, if seemingly laid down, it will be followed. For there is a fourth accepted canon:

4) *Everything, everything, everything, big or small, a judge may say in an opinion, is to be read with primary reference to the particular dispute, the particular question before him.* You are not to think that the words mean what they might if they stood alone. You are to have your eye on the case in hand, and to learn how to interpret all that has been said *merely* as a reason for deciding *that* case *that* way. At need.

Now why these canons? The first, I take it, goes back to the primary purpose of law. If the job is in first instance to settle disputes which do not otherwise get settled, then the only way to do it is to do it. And it will not matter so much *how* it is done, in a baffling instance, so long as it is done at all.

The third, that cases must be decided according to a general rule, goes back in origin less to purpose than to superstition. As long as law was felt as something ordained of God, or even as something inherently right in the order of nature, the judge was to be regarded as a mouthpiece, not as a creator; and a mouthpiece of the general, who but made clear an application to the particular. Else he broke faith, else he was arbitrary, and either biased or corrupt. Moreover, justice demands, wherever that concept is found, that like men be treated alike in like conditions. Why, I do not know; the fact is given. That calls for general rules, and for their even application. So, too, the "separation of powers" comes in powerfully to urge that general rules are made by the Legislature or the system, not the judges, and that the judge has but to act *according* to the general rules there are. . . .

Back, if I may now, to the why of the two canons I have left: that the court *can* decide only the particular dispute before it; that all that is said is to be read with eyes on that dispute. Why these? I do believe, gentlemen, that here we have as fine a deposit of slow-growing wisdom as ever has been laid down through the centuries by the unthinking social sea. Here, hardened into institutions, carved out and given line by rationale. What is this wisdom? Look to your own discussion, look to any argument. You know where you would go. You reach, at random if hurried, more carefully if not, for a foundation, for a major premise. But never for itself. Its interest lies in leading to the conclusion you are headed for. You shape its words, its content, to an end decreed. More, with your mind upon your object you use words, you bring in illustrations, you deploy and advance and concentrate again. When you have done, you have said much you did not mean. You did not mean, that is, *except* in reference to your point. You have brought generalization after generalization up, and discharged it at your goal; all, in the heat of argument, were over-stated. None would you stand to, if your opponent should urge them to *another* issue.

So with the judge. Nay, more so with the judge. He is not merely human, as are you. He is, as well, a lawyer; which you, yet, are not. A lawyer, and as such skilled in manipulating the resources of persuasion at his hand. A lawyer, and as such prone without thought to twist analogies, and rules, and instances, to his conclusion. A lawyer, and as such peculiarly prone to disregard the implications which do not bear directly on his case.

More, as a practiced campaigner in the art of exposition, he has learned that one must prepare the way for argument. You set the mood, the tone, you lay the intellectual foundation — all with the case in mind, with the conclusion — all, because those who hear you also have the case in mind, without the niggling criticism which may later follow. You wind up, as a pitcher will wind up — and as in the pitcher's case, the wind-up often is superfluous. As in the pitcher's case, it has been known to be intentionally misleading.

With this it should be clear, then, why our canons thunder. Why we create a class of dicta, of unnecessary words, which later readers, their minds now on quite other cases, can mark off as not quite essential to the argument. Why we create a class of *obiter dicta*, the wilder flailings of the pitcher's arms, the wilder motions of his gumruminant jaws. Why we set about, as our job, to crack the kernel from the nut, to find the true rule the case in fact decides: the *rule of the case*.

Now for a while I am going to risk confusion for the sake of talking simply. I am going to treat as the rule of the case the *ratio decidendi*, the rule *the court tells you* is the rule of the case, the ground, as the phrase goes, upon which the court itself has rested its decision. For there is where you must begin, and such refinements as are needed may come after.

The court, I will assume, has talked for five pages, only one of which portrayed the facts assumed. The rest has been discussion. And judgment has been given for the party who won below: judgment affirmed. We seek the rule.

The first thing to note is this: *no rule can be the ratio decidendi from which the actual judgment* (here: affirmance) *does not follow.* Unless affirmance follows from a rule, it *cannot* be the rule which produced an actual holding of affirmance. But the holding is the decision, and the court speaks ex cathedra only as to the dispute decided, and only as to the decision it has made. At this point, too, I think you begin to see the bearing of the *procedural* issue. There *can* be a decision (and so an ex cathedra ratio) *only* as to a point which is before the court. But points come before a court of review by way of specific complaint about specific action of the court below, and in no other way. Hence nothing can be *held* which is not thus brought up.

You will have noted that these two statements are not quite the same. For the losing party may have complained of five, or fourteen, different rulings by the court below, but the final judgment below is affirmed or reversed but once. If you see what is ahead you will see that — on my argument to date — I am about to be driven either into inconsistency or into an affront to common sense. For obviously the court will in many or most instances take up the objections made before it, one by one. Now in that event we shall meet either of two phenomena, and very likely both at once. I shall assume this time, to set my picture more neatly, that the court *reverses* the judgment below. Then *either* it will say that the court below was wrong *on all five points*, or it will say that although right on less than all, it was nonetheless wrong on *at least one*. Suppose, first, it says: wrong on all. It is clear that *any one* would be sufficient for reversal. It is more than likely that the court will not rest peculiarly on any of the five. Any one of the five rulings would then be enough to justify a reversal, and four of them are by consequence wholly unnecessary. Which, now, are which? Further, under the canon I so proudly wheeled before you, the court *can* decide only the particular dispute before it. Which was that particular dispute?

Again, take a case where the court rules on four points in favor of a man who won below, but reverses, for all that, on the fifth point. Of the four rulings, not a single one *can* be a premise for the actual holding. They are, then, dicta merely?

Here, I say, common sense and my canons seem to be at odds. The fact is, that they are both right, and yet both wrong. To that, as a phase of the doctrine of precedent, I shall return. Here merely the solution. One of the reasons, of the sound ones, often given for weighing dicta lightly, is that the background and consequences of the statement have not been illumined by the argument of counsel, have not received, as being matters to be weighed with brows a-wrinkle, the full consideration of the court. In the case put the first reason does not fit; the second, if it is to be put on at all, hangs loose and flaps. No one point being the only crucial point, and the points decided which do not lead to judgment not being absolutely necessary to decide, it may be the court has not sweated over them as it would had each stood alone. But sweated some, it has; and with due antecedent argument. Hence we have, in what we may call *the multi-point decision*, an intermediate type of authority. If a decision stands on two, or three, or five legs, any one of them is much more subject to challenge than it would be if the decision stood on it alone. Yet prima facie there remains "a decision" on each one of the points concerned. It is, as Morgan well says, within the province of a court to instruct the trial court how to act on points disputed and argued in the case in hand. The same reasoning in form, yet with distinctly lesser cogency in fact, applies to the multi-points ruled in favor of the party which ultimately loses the appeal. Authorities of a third water, these; and getting watery.

But our troubles with the ratio decidendi are not over. We meet forthwith a further formal one. Our judge states his facts, he argues his position, he announces his rule. And lo, he seems but to have begun. Once clean across the plate. But he begins again, winds up again and again he delivers his ratio — this time, to our puzzlement, the words are not the same. At this point it is broader than it was before, there it is narrower. And like as not he will warm up another time, and do the same job over — differently again. I have never made out quite why this happens. A little, it may be due to a lawyer's tendency to clinch an argument by summarizing its course, when he is through. A little, it may be due to mere sloppiness of composition, to the lack, typical of our law and all its work, of a developed sense for form, juristic or esthetic, for what the Romans knew as *elegantia*. Sometimes I get a wry suspicion that the judge repeats because he is uneasy on his ground, that he lifts up his voice, prays his conclusion over loud and louder, to gain and make conviction, much like an advertiser bare of arguments except his slogan. At other times I feel as I read opinions the thrill of adventure in an undiscovered country; the first and second statements of the ratio, with all that has led up to them, are like first and second reconnoiterings of strange hills; like first and second chartings of what has been found and what surmised — knowledge and insight growing as the opinion builds to its conclusion. But whatever the reason, recurrent almost-repetition faces us; also the worry that the repetition seldom is exact. Which phrasing are we then to tie to? Perhaps in this, as in judging how far to trust a broadly stated rule, we may find guidance in the facts the court assumes. Surely this much is certain: the actual dispute before the court is limited as straitly by the facts as by the form which the procedural issue has assumed. What is not in the facts cannot be present for decision. Rules which proceed an inch beyond the facts must be suspect.

But how far does that help us out? What are *the* facts? The plaintiff's name is Atkinson and the defendant's Walpole. The defendant, despite his name, is an Italian by extraction, but the plaintiff's ancestors came over with the Pilgrims. The defendant has a schnautzer-dog named Walter, red hair, and $30,000 worth of life insurance. All these are facts. The case, however, does not deal with life insurance. It is about an auto accident. The defendant's auto was a Buick painted pale magenta. He is married. His wife was in the back seat, an irritable, somewhat faded blonde. She was attempting back-seat driving when the accident occurred. He had turned around to make objection. In the process the car swerved and hit the plaintiff. The sun was shining; there was a rather lovely dappled sky low to the West. The time was late October on a Tuesday. The road was smooth, concrete. It had been put in by the McCarthy Road Work Company. How many of these facts are important to the decision? How many of these facts are, as we say, legally relevant? Is it relevant that the road was in the country or the city; that it was concrete or tarmac or of dirt; that it was a private or a public way? Is it relevant that the defendant was driving a Buick, or a motor car, or a vehicle? Is it important that he looked around as the car swerved? Is it crucial? Would it have been the same if he had been drunk, or had swerved for fun, to see how close he could run by the plaintiff, but had missed his guess?

It is not obvious that as soon as you pick up this statement of the facts to find its legal bearings you must discard some as of no interest whatsoever, discard others as dramatic but as legal nothings? And is it not clear, further, that when you pick up the facts which are left and which do seem relevant, you suddenly cease to deal with them in the concrete and deal with them instead in *categories* which you, for one reason or another, deem significant? It is not the road between Pottsville and Arlington; it is "a highway". It is not a particular pale magenta Buick eight, by number 732507, but "a motor car", and perhaps even "a vehicle". It is not a turning around to look at Adorée Walpole, but a lapse from the supposedly proper procedure of careful drivers, with which you are concerned. Each concrete fact of the case arranges itself, I say, as the *representative* of a much wider abstract *category* of facts, and it is not in itself but as a member of the category that you attribute significance to it. But what is to tell you whether to make your category "Buicks" or "motor cars" or "vehicles"? What is to tell you to make your category "road" or "public highway"? The court may tell you. But the precise point that you have up for study is how far it is safe to trust what the court says. The precise issue which you are attempting to solve is whether the court's language can be taken as it stands, or must be amplified, or must be whittled down.

This brings us at last to the case system. For the truth of the matter is a truth so obvious and trite that it is somewhat regularly overlooked by students. *That no case can have a meaning by itself!* Standing alone it gives you no guidance. It can give you no guidance as to how far it carries, as to how much of its language will hold water later. What counts, what gives you leads, what gives you sureness, *that is the background of the other cases* in relation to which you must read the one. They color the language, the technical terms, used in the opinion. But above all they give you the wherewithal to find which of the facts are significant, and in what aspect they are significant, and how far the rules laid down are to be trusted.

Here, I say, is the foundation of the case system. For what, in a case class, do we do? We have set before you, at either the editor's selection or our own, a *series* of opinions which in some manner are related. They may or may not be exactly alike in their outcome. They are always supposedly somewhat similar on their legally relevant facts. Indeed, it is *the aspects in which their facts are similar* which give you your first guidance as to what *classes* of fact will be found legally relevant, that is, will be found *to operate alike*, or to operate *at all*, upon the court. On the other hand, the states of fact are rarely, if ever, quite alike. And one of the most striking problems before you is: when you find two cases side by side which show a difference in result, then to determine *what* difference in their facts, or *what* difference in the procedural set-up, has produced that difference in result. Those are the two problems which must be in your mind as you examine the language of the opinions. I repeat them. First, what *are* the significant categories of facts, and what is their significance to the court? Second, what *differences* in facts or in procedural set-up produce differences in the court's action when the situations are otherwise alike?

This, then, is the case system game, the game of matching cases. We proceed by a rough application of the logical method of comparison and difference.

And here there are three things that need saying. The first is that by this matching of facts and issues in the different cases we get, to come back to where we started, some indication of when the court in a given case has over-generalized; of when, on the other hand, it has meant all the ratio decidendi that it said. "The Supreme Court of the United States", remarks the sage Professor T.R. Powell, "are by no means such fools as they talk, or as the people are who think them so". We go into the matter expecting a certain amount of inconsistency in the broader language of the cases. We go into the matter set in advance to find distinctions by means of which we can reconcile and harmonize the outcomes of the cases, even though the rules that the courts seem to lay down in their deciding may be inconsistent. We are prepared to whittle down the categories of the facts, to limit the rule of one case to its new whittled narrow category, to limit the rule of the other to its new other narrow category — and thus to make two cases stand together. The first case involves a man who makes an offer and gets in his revocation before his offer is accepted. The court decides that he cannot be sued upon his promise, and says that no contract can be made unless the minds of both parties are at one at once. The second case involves a man who has made a similar offer and has mailed a revocation, but to whom a letter of acceptance has been sent before his revocation was received. The court holds that he can be sued upon his promise, and says that his offer was being repeated every moment from the time that it arrived until the letter of acceptance was duly mailed. Here are two rules which are a little difficult to put together, and to square with sense, and which are, too, a little hard to square with the two holdings in the cases. We set to work to seek a way out which will do justice to the holdings. We arrive perhaps at this, that it is not necessary for the two minds to be at one at once, if the person who has received an offer thinks, and thinks reasonably, as he takes the last step of acceptance, that the offeror is standing by the offer. And to test the rule laid down in either case, as also to test our tentative formulation which we have built to cover both, we do two things. First and easiest is to play variations on the facts, making the case gradually more and more extreme until we find the place beyond which it does not seem sense to go. Suppose, for example, our man does think the offeror still stands to his offer, and thinks it reasonably, on all his information; but yet a revocation has arrived, which his own clerk has failed to bring to his attention? We may find the stopping-place much sooner than we had expected, and thus be forced to recast and narrow the generalization we have made, or to recast it even on wholly different lines. The second and more difficult way of testing is to go to the books and find further cases in which variations on the facts occur, and in which the importance of such variations has been put to the proof. The first way is the intuitional correction of hypothesis; the second way is the experimental test of whether an hypothesis is sound. Both are needed. The first, to save time. The second, to make sure. For you will remember that in your casebook you have only a sampling, a foundation for discussion, enough cases to set the problem and start you thinking. Before you can trust your results, either those which you achieve yourselves, or those which you take with you from the class, you must go to the writers who have read more cases and see what they have to say.

In all of this I have been proceeding upon the assumption — and this is the second further point about case method that I had in mind — that all the cases everywhere can stand together. It is unquestionably the assumption you must also make, at first. If they can be brought together you must bring them. At the same time you must not overlook that our law is built up statewise. It is not built up in one piece. With fifty supreme courts plus the federal courts at work, it is inevitable that from time to time conflicting rules emerge. The startling thing is that they have been so few. And where a given state, say Pennsylvania, has laid down one rule, but another state, New York, say, has laid down another, the mere fact that fifteen further states go with New York is unlikely in the extreme to change the Pennsylvania point of view. A *common* law in one sense is therefore non-existent on that point. What we have is fifteen states deciding one way, one state deciding another way *and thirty states whose law is still uncertain*. Yet in these circumstances, we do speak of "common law", and for this reason: True though it is that each state sticks, in the main, to its own authorities, when it has them, yet common to all the states is a large fundamental body of institutions which show at least a brother-and-sister type of likeness, which, to a surprising extent, as I have indicated, can even fairly be called identical. Furthermore, the *manner* of dealing with the legal authorities, the *way* of thinking, the *way* of working, the *way* of reading cases, the reasoning from them — or from statutes — these *common law techniques* are in all our courts in all our states substantially alike. And finally, if in a given state a point has not been settled, the court will turn to the decisions of the country as a whole as to a common reservoir of law. If there is but a single line of decision that court, although it never decided on the point before, is likely to lead off its argument: "It is well settled". If the decisions are divided on the point, the court is more likely than not to go with any substantial majority which may exist. But whether it goes with the majority or with the minority or picks a third variant of its own, it works with the materials from the other states almost as if they were its own, save that there is rarely any one of them which carries the sanction of transcendent authority.

Hence, in your matching of cases, you may, as a last resort when unable to make the cases fit together, fall back upon the answer: here is a conflict; these cases represent two different points of view.

You must, however, before you do that, make sure that they come from different jurisdictions, else one will have to be regarded as flatly overruling the other. Which brings me to the point of dates. Not the least important feature in the cases you are comparing will be their dates. For you must assume that the law, like any other human institution, has undergone, still undergoes development, clarification, change, as time goes on, as experience accumulates, as conditions vary. The earlier cases in a series, therefore, while they *may* stand unchanged today, are yet more likely to be forerunners, to be indications of the first gropings with a problem, rather than to present its final solution even in the state from which they come. That holds particularly for cases prior to 1800. It holds in many fields of law for cases of much more recent date. But in any event you will be concerned to place the case in time as well as in space, if putting it together with the others makes for difficulty.

The third thing that needs saying as you set to matching cases, is that on your materials, often indeed on all the materials that there are, a perfect working out of comparison and difference cannot be had. In the first case you have facts a and b and c, procedural set-up m, and outcome x. In the second case you have, *if* you are lucky, procedural set-up m again, but this time with facts a and b and d, and outcome y. How, now, are you to know with any certainty whether the changed result is due in the second instance to the absence of fact c or to the presence of the new fact d? The court may tell you. But I repeat: your object is to *test* the telling of the court. You turn to your third case. Here once more is the outcome x, and the facts are b and c and e; but fact a is missing, and the procedural set-up this time is not m but n. This strengthens somewhat your suspicion that fact c is the lad who works the changed result. But an experimentum crucis still is lacking. Cases in life are not made to our hand. A scientific *approach* to prediction we may have, and we may use it as far as our materials will permit. An exact science *in result* we have not now. Carry this in your minds: a scientific approach, no more. Onto the green, with luck, your science takes you. But when it comes to putting you will work by art and hunch.

Where are we now? We have seen the background of the cases. We have seen what they consist of. We have seen that they must be read and analyzed for their facts, for their procedural issue and for their decision. We have seen that they are to be matched together to see which are the facts which have the legal consequences, and in what categories we must class the facts with that in view. And out of this same matching process we can reach a judgment as to how much of the language, even in the ratio decidendi, the court has really meant.

But if you arrive at the conclusion that a given court did not mean all it said in the express ratio decidendi it laid down, that the case must really be confined to facts narrower than the court itself assumed to be its measure, then you are ready for the distinction that I hinted at earlier in this lecture, the distinction between the ratio decidendi, the court's own version of the rule of the case, and the *true* rule of the case, to wit, what *it will be made to stand for by another later court.* For one of the vital elements of our doctrine of precedent is this: that any later court can always reexamine a prior case, and under the principle that the court could decide only what was before it, and that the older case must now be read with that in view, can arrive at the conclusion that the dispute before the earlier court was much narrower than that court thought it was, called therefore for the application of a much narrower rule. Indeed, the argument goes further. It goes on to state that no broader rule *could* have been laid down ex-cathedra, because to do that would have transcended the powers of the earlier court.

You have seen further that out of the matching of a number of related cases it is your job to formulate a rule that covers them all in harmony, if that can be done, and to test your formulation against possible variants on the facts. Finally, to test it, if there is time, against what writers on the subject have to say, and against other cases.

It does not pay to go too early to the writers. To do so is to come under strong temptation to skip through the process of case matching on your own. If your chin is square enough, then you may risk it. If you can take what the writer says not as an answer, but as an hypothesis, if you have patience to test it against the cases in your book, and to read, too, some of those the writer cites to see how far they bear out his own conclusions, then you are better off when you consult the writer early. But otherwise, and if you try to use him as a trot, you court disaster.

Now you come into class. There you find the instructor carrying on the same process I have been describing, save that he is more skilful, that he has more knowledge and more insight. He points distinctions which had not yet occurred to you. He tries cases on you you had never thought about. He speaks from a background rich with knowledge of specific states of fact and of their background. Precisely for that reason it is necessary, it is vital, it is the very basic element of case law study, for you to have done your matching of the cases before you meet with his. For it is not by watching him juggle the balls that you will learn. It is by matching his results against your own, by criticizing the process you have gone through in the light of the process he is going through. Indeed if you have not tried the game yourself, *you will not follow him.* The man who sees line-play in the football game is the man who once tried playing on the line himself. . . . Let me repeat: you will get little out of your instruction unless daily, repeatedly, consistently, you try the game out to the end the weary night before. At the same time, with growing skill, you will bring criticism to bear on the man behind the desk as well. You will, if he is human, find inconsistencies between his work today and what he did or said five weeks ago. That will be useful for him. It will be infinitely more for you.

What now of preparation for your case class? Your cases are assigned. Before they can be used they have to be digested. Experience shows that it is well to brief them. Briefing is valuable if only for the impending discussion. Briefing is well nigh essential when it comes to the review. Make no mistake in this. Day to day, at ten or fifteen pages every day, it still is possible to keep your material well enough in mind to follow much that will go on in class. But when you come to attempting to review 300, 400, or 500 pages at once, you will find that your mind is blank as to most of the cases, and there is no time to fill that blank with meat. There is one answer and there is only one: your brief, or abstract, or digest.

There is another point at which the brief is valuable. You cannot take adequate notes on class discussion in your casebook, yet you need in one place the substance of a case and the notes on its discussion. The classic plan is briefing on gummed paper, and the pasting of the briefs into the relevant passages in your notes. At this point I would make one remark. The class discussion will show you often that your brief is bad. The thing to do before you paste it in is to make it over. *Before* you paste it, make it over right.

And one thing more. Briefing, I say, is valuable. Briefing, I say, is well nigh essential. Briefing is also the saddest trap that ever awaited a law student, if he does not watch his step. For the practice under pressure of time, as eyes grow tired in the evening, or the movies lure, is to brief cases *one by one*, and therefore blindly. Now if I have made one point in this discussion it should be this: that a case read by itself is meaningless, is nil, is blank, is blah. Briefing should begin *at the earliest* with the second case of an assignment. Only *after* you have read the second case have you any idea what to do with the first. Briefing, I say again, is a problem of putting down what in the one case bears upon the problem stated by the other cases. Each brief should be in terms of *what this case adds to what I already know about* this subject. Hence at least two cases must be read before any can be intelligently briefed. And as you pass to the third case and the fourth case, you have accomplished nothing unless both in your reading and your briefing of them you work at them with reference to the cases that have gone before. What does the case *add, what difference does it make*, to what I already know? This is the keynote of the brief. For this same reason, when you ever do any research in law, you must distrust your briefs, and distrust most the earliest ones you made. The earlier in the research the brief was made, the less you knew when you made it; hence, the more worthless it is. Read through the first-found case again, and see! The chances are the first half of the briefs made in any one job of research belong on the ash-heap. The cases blossom under further study, under new reading. They yield more wisdom as your wisdom grows.

. . . .

So much for the brief. And if you follow this advice you will discover that by the time the last brief is made the class is well prepared. For you cannot brief four cases each with reference to the other without having *already* put them together, without having *already* phrased the results that you have come to on them all. Your last brief will have incorporated, at least by implication, all the rest. And let me say once again, that till they all are put together, and some of the bearings of your phrasing thought over, you will not be prepared, you will not know what *any* of them is about.

IV. THIS CASE SYSTEM: PRECEDENT

There are psychologists who delight in talking of an apperceptive mass. I am not quite sure what such an apperceptive mass may be, nor of whether it is at all. But I am very sure that these psychologists have a strong truth by the tail. The only question, as A.G. Keller used to put it, is whether, for all our firm grip on the tail, we shall have skill and patience to work up over the rump.

The truth that we have seized upon is this: you see in your case almost exactly what you brought to it, and hardly more. If you bring much, you see much. If you bring nothing, that is what you see. A *little*, each case will add to what you knew. The measure of what it adds, again, is what you bring.

This point I dwelt on lovingly in the last lecture, in regard to briefing. I shall dwell on it now again, in reference to review. Case study progresses slowly. It works intensively. It works, because it must work intensively, upon a *tiny* body of material day by day. Hence you can *seem* to do the work, and *seem* to follow, although each day you have in mind the cases for the day, and nothing more. At this point, gentlemen, we meet the rump. You *seem* to do the work. But if you are to *do* it, you require, each day, each week, to build your new material together with your old. You require to enlarge, above all you require to consolidate, your apperceptive mass in law. You require to bring to each new case and each new briefing the *whole* of the body of the knowledge you have that far met. The crux of your briefing: "What does this case *add*"? develops value to you in exact proportion to the size and quality of the existing stock of skill to which the new addition will be made.

Now I know well that you have heard all this before. I know that you have met before our old familiar frog: three feet a day he climbs out of the slickery pit, two feet each night he slides down as he sleeps. The benighted frog does not dig in betweenwhiles. He takes no thought about his apperceptive mass. He does not, in the military jargon, consolidate his position. Having no tail he does not see the problem of surmounting rumps.

Yet you perhaps lay claim to being more than frogs. Presumably, at least in theory, you own intelligence. The Dean's office vouches that you have got by our private lunacy commission. You should thus *understand* me, when I tell you that the only road to making the slow-moving case instruction gain momentum is to *accelerate* the learning process day by day. The quantity of new material studied you will not much increase. The quantity and quality of what you *get out of* your new material you can jack up daily. But in one way only: by daily, by weekly, going over, arranging, consolidating what you have. Our class instruction is invaluable to you. But, I insisted yesterday, valuable only as you labor through the problems first yourself, as you prepare yourself to see what goes on in the class. And, I insist today, valuable only as you work through the problems *afterward* yourself (or in a group), build what you have seen into a *working* part of your equipment for tomorrow. Our class instruction, as a catalyzer, is all that you have hoped. But *by itself* it is a poorer show than Keith's, at higher prices.

Now I have told you. Before this lecture closes I shall hope to indicate enough niceties in the material, enough lines fine, yet profitable to follow, to stir in you some realization of the meaning of the telling. Just this last thing to end the exhortation: your instructors, many of them, have taught some cases ten or twenty times, and studied those cases over each time before they taught them. *Constantly*, they are finding new things, new light, new problems, in that same material. They have meanwhile increased their apperceptive mass. They sit triumphantly astride the beast!

One other point I wish to make in the same connection. Note-taking is well nigh essential. Writing helps memory. Writing records. What seems so easy to remember slips away. You need it, if you would consolidate. But note-taking, like briefing, is a treacherous tool. Notes that have any value are not *copied* down. Before the writing down goes a critique. Notes that have value are not what is said, they are a selection, a working over, a working up, of what is said — a preservation of the queries opened by the instructor, a preservation of the independent queries which occur to you. If you are actively — though silently — engaged in the discussion, your mind *must* open queries as the class proceeds. Those things belong in your notes. What the instructor gives as information then has some reference value. You can see its setting. You can judge whether it is holding or mere dictum.

It is much harder, it is much slower to take notes this way. It is much harder: reacting, rephrasing, you must *think* to take a note. Selecting in the light of the discussion the essential from the surrounding whirl of words, you have to give attention, to be using the stuff between your ears, throughout the whole discussion. So, too, it is much harder, much slower, to brief cases with intelligence. It is much harder, slower, to put in daily time upon consolidation of your notes. These things take guts, some mental and some moral. They are the conjugations and declensions and syntax of your study of the law; they are your plant, your engine, your machine. If they are grubbed through once, and grubbed through hard, if they are once put together and set moving — then you have them. The outlay on investment is complete. Within a month or two they pay out dividends. Within six months you find them a bonanza. Then your machine is oiled and running smoothly, while your neighbor who speeded blithely through the football season knocks and stalls. This is a wisdom hidden from the frog.

So, I have said my piece. Let us get on to something interesting.

We looked yesterday at the art of matching cases to extract the rules from them. Today we go further. We take up what can be done with such an extract when you have it. We take up also some of the less systematized lore which lies in the cases if you have the wit to find it. The two types of study interlock. Both take us back to the cases themselves as the ore which we are to refine.

. . . . Each case now which is not one purely pathological is an experiment in this great laboratory, and the problem is how to milk that experiment for your training.

The first thing, not only for this purpose, but indeed for any, is to *visualize* the initial transaction between the parties. Who were they? What did they look like? Above all, what did each one want, and why did he want it? If you can see the facts in their chronological order, one by one; if you can see them occurring one by one as particular people (be they well or ill advised) were moving to the accomplishment of their desires — if you can see these desires and feel them in the light of who the parties were and of their situation — then and then only will the case become real to you, will it stick in your head, will the words speak and set your mind to working. Call this, if you will, dramatizing. Call it, if you will, the writing of fiction. It resembles them at least in this: that to do it will require you to loose your imagination — but with discipline; will require you first to feel yourself into the situation as depicted and then to see, to feel the texture and the rough knobs of each fact.

So equally when the case arises out of an event. You will, I may say, find it very useful to take this distinction between *transaction* and *event*, to keep it in mind. We have a *transaction* when two or more parties get together to accomplish something. They bargain, they sell, they lease, they write insurance. Here, before the dispute, there is a deal. Here the possibility offers always of shaping the transaction in advance and with design to the ends of the two parties or of one. Here, therefore, there is room for all kinds of legal safeguard, room for the work of counsel in the office. But what I am calling *events* will rarely be intended by both parties, if by either. A man is killed. It may be purpose in the killer; it rarely is in the deceased. There is a brawl. True, in a sense, the two parties deal together, and now that the brawl is on they may be dealing with intent. Still, it is rare to have the brawl in mind beforehand. With events, equally, however, visualization helps. But their dramatic character leads commonly of itself to your doing what visualization you may need. Hence the facts of tort cases commonly are "easy". But in the facts of contract cases, or of property cases, you are more likely to have to drive yourself to the work. Drive, then, for it is needed.

There is more, however, to dramatize than merely what the parties wanted, or what they did. Especially in the transaction. There you have eternally the question, *what would you, had you been counsel, have advised* this man on this point, at each stage of the negotiation? How do you analyze the facts thus far? What is their legal meaning? How will that legal meaning bear on this party's proper course?

If you can read facts thus the case is no longer flat. It foams as golden as Toronto ale. Fine bubbles rise: did the court read the facts as did the parties? Did the court see what the parties were driving at? To put the question in legal phrasing, was the court's interpretation of the facts sound?

This leads us into one of the most striking and useful discriminations that in your reading of the cases you must make, to wit, the difference between the *rule of law* laid down on a set of facts assumed, on the one hand, and on the other, the *way the court interpreted the facts* before it. I like to call these the two levels of the decision. In logic you will observe the interpretation of the facts comes first. There are some statements in the record as to evidence. You give a meaning to these statements. You decide precisely what they mean. Your application of a rule of law bears then on what you have already decided to be the meaning of the facts. It does not touch the raw evidence at all. It touches only the final product that remains after the evidence has been worked over.

Yet in life the operation may be the reverse; rule and decision may dictate the interpretation of the facts. For it is clear that if a later court, in pondering a case substantially equivalent, does not like the results achieved by the earlier court, then it may reach a contrary decision in either of two ways. Either it may reject the rule laid down by court number one; and this is not so likely. Or it may accept that rule as a verbal formula, may cite the prior case as authority, and yet interpret the raw evidence before it differently, saying that due to the difference in the facts, the rule does not apply. . . . . [U]ntil you study the first level of decision, the interpretation of the facts at hand, you do not *know* the rule. I do not care what you may know about its words, until you know what the words *stand for*. This is important in putting your cases together. It is important, too, in saving time. For it does not pay to quarrel with the rule of law laid down by a court because you just do not like its way of interpreting the evidence. You can see and approve the rule of law announced and still reserve your quarrel upon the evidence. But to quarrel intelligently you must clarify the issues. On the other hand, when it comes to seeing the bearing of the rule on life, on actual disputes, on actual transactions, it is clear that the first level moves into the limelight of your mind.

This brings me now to a further point about the courts. Some courts in their work of interpretation you will discover very eager to find what the parties' situation really was; to read their words, to interpret the bits of evidence as the parties themselves would have regarded them. Such courts feel their way into the situation as you ought to. They take you with them. Other courts sit in what seems to be sublime indifference. They act not only in their laying down of rules of law, but even in their interpretation of the facts, as if life had been made for law. We find, I say, in the interpretation of the evidence divergencies in *attitude* among the courts.

. . . .

I think we are now ready to lock horns with the problem of *precedent* and make something out of it. I fear that I am going to have to be as unorthodox in what I say about this as in what I said about law. The one vagary is indeed a corollary of the other. For, whereas much or most of what is commonly written about precedent takes as its raw material what judges have *said* about precedent, I propose to take as mine, not so much what they have said as what they have *done* about it.

First, what is precedent? In the large, disregarding for the moment peculiarities of our law and of legal doctrine — in the large, precedent consists in an official doing over again under similar circumstances substantially what has been done by him or his predecessor before. The foundation, then, of precedent is the official analogue of what, in society at large, we know as folkways, or as institutions, and of what, in the individual, we know as habit. And the things which make for precedent in this broad sense are the same which make for habit and for institutions. It takes time and effort to solve problems. Once you have solved one it seems foolish to reopen it. Indeed, you are likely to be quite impatient with the notion of reopening it. Both inertia and convenience speak for building further on what you have already built; for incorporating the decision once made, *the solution once worked out*, into your operating technique *without reexamination* of what *earlier went into* reaching your solution. . . .

At this point there enters into the picture an ethical element, the argument that courts (and other officials) not only do, but *should* continue what they have been doing. Here, again, the first analogue is in the folkway or the individual habit. I do not know why, nor do I know how, but I observe the fact that what one has been doing acquires in due course another flavor, another level of value than mere practice; a flavor on the level of policy, or ethics, or morality. What one has been doing becomes the "right" thing to do; not only the expected thing but the thing whose happening will be welcomed and whose failure to happen will be resented. This is true in individuals whose habits are interrupted; this is true in social intercourse when the expected event, when the expectation based upon the knowledge of other people's habits, materializes or fails to materialize. Indeed, in social matters in the large, there develops distinct group pressure to *force conformity* with the existing and expected social ways.

. . . .

But it will have occurred to you that despite all that I have said in favor of precedent, there are objections. It may be the ignorance or folly, or idleness, or bias of the predecessor which chains a new strong judge. It may be, too, that conditions have changed, and that the precedent, good when it was made, has since become outworn. The rule laid down the first time that a case came up may have been badly phrased, may have failed to foresee the types of dispute which later came to plague the court. Our society is changing, and law, if it is to fit society, must also change. Our society is stable else it would not be a society, and law which is to fit it must stay fixed. Both truths are true at once. Perhaps some reconciliation lies along this line; that the stability is needed most greatly in large things, that the change is needed most in matters of detail. At any rate, it now becomes our task to inquire into how the system of precedent which we actually have works out in fact, accomplishing at once stability and change.

We turn first to what I may call the orthodox doctrine of precedent, with which, in its essence, you are already familiar. Every case lays down a rule, the rule of the case. The express ratio decidendi is prima facie the rule of the case, since it is the ground upon which the court chose to rest its decision. But a later court can reexamine the case and can invoke the canon that no judge has power to decide what is not before him, can, through examination of the facts or of the procedural issue, narrow the picture of what was actually before the court and can hold that the ruling made requires to be understood as thus restricted. In the extreme form this results in what is known as expressly "confining the case to its particular facts". This rule holds only of redheaded Walpoles in pale magenta Buick cars. And when you find this said of a past case you know that in effect it has been overruled. Only a convention, a somewhat absurd convention, prevents flat overruling in such instances. It seems to be felt as definitely improper to state that the court in a prior case was wrong, peculiarly so if that case was in the same court which is speaking now. It seems to be felt that this would undermine the dogma of the infallibility of courts. So lip service is done to that dogma, while the rule which the prior court laid down is disembowelled. The execution proceeds with due respect, with mandarin courtesy.

Now this orthodox view of the authority of precedent — which I shall call the *strict* view — is but *one of two views* which seem to me wholly contradictory to each other. It is in practice the dogma which is applied to *unwelcome* precedents. It is the recognized, legitimate, honorable technique for whittling precedents away, for making the lawyer, in his argument, and the court, in its decision, free of them. It is a surgeon's knife.

It is orthodox, I think, because it has been more discussed than is the other. Consider the situation. It is not easy thus to carve a case to pieces. It takes thought, it takes conscious thought, it takes analysis. There is no great art and no great difficulty in merely looking at a case, reading its language, and then applying some sentence which is there expressly stated. But there is difficulty in going underneath what is said, in making a keen reexamination of the case that stood before the court, in showing that the language used was quite beside the point, as the point is revealed under the lens of leisured microscopic refinement. Hence the technique of distinguishing cases has given rise to the closest of scrutiny. The technique of arguing for a distinction has become systematized. And when men start talking of authority, or of the doctrine of precedent, they turn naturally to that part of their minds which has been *consciously* devoted to the problem; they call up the cases, the analyses, the arguments, which have been made under such conditions. They put this together, and call this *"the* doctrine". I suspect there is still another reason for the orthodoxy. That is that only finer minds, minds with sharp mental scalpels, can do this work, and that it is the finer minds — the minds with sharp cutting edge — which write about it and which thus set up the tradition of the books. To them it must seem that what blunt minds can do as well as they is poor; but that which they alone can do is good. They hit in this on a truth in part: you can pass with ease from this strict doctrine of precedent to the other. If you can handle this, then you can handle both. Not vice versa. The strict doctrine, then, is the technique to be learned. *But not to be mistaken for the whole.*

For when you turn to the actual operations of the courts, or, indeed, to the arguments of lawyers, you will find a totally different view of precedent at work beside this first one. That I shall call, to give it a name, the *loose view* of precedent. That is the view that a court has decided, and decided authoritatively, *any* point or all points on which it chose to rest a case, or on which it chose, after due argument, to pass. No matter how broad the statement, no matter how unnecessary on the facts or the procedural issues, if that was the rule the court laid down, then that the court has held. Indeed, this view carries over often into dicta, and even into dicta which are grandly obiter. In its extreme form this results in thinking and arguing exclusively from *language* that is found in past opinions, and in citing and working with that language wholly without reference to the facts of the case which called the language forth.

Now it is obvious that this is a device not for cutting past opinions away from judges' feet, but for using them as a springboard when they are found convenient. This is a device for *capitalizing welcome precedents*. And both the lawyers and the judges use it so. And judged by the *practice* of the most respected courts, as of the courts of ordinary stature, this doctrine of precedent is like the other, recognized, legitimate, honorable.

What I wish to sink deep into your minds about the doctrine of precedent, therefore, is that it is two-headed. It is Janus-faced. That it is not one doctrine, nor one line of doctrine, but two, and two which, *applied at the same time to the same precedent, are contradictory of each other*. That there is one doctrine for getting rid of precedents deemed troublesome and one doctrine for making use of precedents that seem helpful. That these two doctrines exist side by side. That the same lawyer in the same brief, the same judge in the same opinion, may be using the one doctrine, the technically strict one, to cut down half the older cases that he deals with, and using the other doctrine, the loose one, for building with the other half. Until you realize this you do not see how it is possible for law to change and to develop, and yet to stand on the past. You do not see how it is possible to avoid the past mistakes of courts, and yet to make use of every happy insight for which a judge in writing may have found expression. Indeed it seems to me that here we may have part of the answer to the problem as to whether precedent is not as bad as good — supporting a weak judge with the labors of strong predecessors, but binding a strong judge by the errors of the weak. For look again at this matter of the *difficulty* of the doctrine. The strict view — that view that cuts the past away — is *hard* to use. An ignorant, an unskilful judge will find it hard to use: the past will bind him. But the skilful judge — he whom we would make free — *is* thus made free. He has the knife in hand; and he can free himself.

Nor, until you see this double aspect of the doctrine-in-action, do you appreciate how little, in detail, you can predict *out of the rules alone*; how much you must turn, for purposes of prediction, to the reactions of the judges to the facts and to the life around them. Think again in this connection of an English court, all the judges unanimous upon the conclusion, all the judges in disagreement as to what rule the outcome should be rested on.

Applying this two-faced doctrine of precedent to your work in a case class you get, it seems to me, some such result as this: You read each case from the angle of its *maximum* value as a precedent, at least from the angle of its maximum value as a precedent *of the first water*. You will recall that I recommended taking down the ratio decidendi in substantially the court's own words. You see now what I had in mind. Contrariwise, you will also read each case for its *minimum* value as a precedent, to set against the maximum. In doing this you have your eyes out for the narrow issue in the case, the narrower the better. The first question is, how much can this case fairly be made to stand for by a later court to whom the precedent is welcome? You may well add — though this will be slightly flawed authority — the dicta which appear to have been well considered. The second question is, how much is there in this case that cannot be got around, even by a later court that wishes to avoid it?

You have now the tools for arguing from that case as counsel on *either* side of a new case. You turn them to the problem of prediction. Which view will this same court, on a later case on slightly different facts, take: will it choose the narrow or the loose? Which use will be made of this case by one of the other courts whose opinions are before you? Here you will call to your aid the matter of attitude that I have been discussing. Here you will use all that you know of individual judges, or of the trends in specific courts, or, indeed, of the trend in the line of business, or in the situation, or in the times at large — in anything which you may expect to become apparent and important to the court in later cases. But always and always, you will bear in mind that each precedent has not one value, but two, and that the two are wide apart, and that whichever value a later court assigns to it, such assignment will be respectable, traditionally sound, dogmatically correct. Above all, as you turn this information to your own training you will, I hope, come to see that in most doubtful cases the precedents *must* speak ambiguously until the court has made up its mind whether each one of them is welcome or unwelcome. And that the job of persuasion which falls upon you will call, therefore, not only for providing a technical ladder to reach on authority the result that you contend for, but even more, if you are to have *your* use of the precedents made as *you* propose it, the job calls for you, on the facts, to persuade the court your case is sound.

People — and they are curiously many — who think that precedent produces or ever did produce a certainty that did not involve matters of judgment and of persuasion, or who think that what I have described involves improper equivocation by the courts or departure from the court-ways of some golden age — such people simply do not know our system of precedent in which they live.

. . . .

It will pay you to observe here and to sever off one by one what we may call the *levels of discussion* about law, especially in a case class. Cross-level discussion is *never* profitable. One must be conscious, always, of which level he is talking on, and which level the other person is talking on, and see to it that differences in level are corrected. One must, moreover, know and signal his shifting from one level to another. Else false issues, cross-purposes, and general footlessness ensue.

1) (a) There is first the question of what the court *actually decided* in a given case: judgment reversed, and new trial ordered. And the question of what express ratio decidendi it announced. These are facts of observation. They are the starting point of all discussion. Until you have them there is no use doing any arguing about anything.

1) (b) There is the question of *what the rule of the case is*, as derived from its comparison with a number of other cases. This is not so simple, but the technical procedures for determining it are clear. Skilled observers should rather regularly be able to agree on two points: (i) the reasonably safe maximum rule the case can be used for; (ii) the reasonably certain minimum rule the case must be admitted to contain.

2) As against both of these, there is the question of the manner, attitude and accuracy of the court's *interpretation* or transformation of the raw evidence. Here judgment factors enter, and you and I may not agree about it. But at least we can keep the level of discussion separate from the levels just above. There we *presuppose* facts as they *result* from this interpretation we are here discussing; and we look to the rule laid down upon the facts already transformed.

3) There is the question of what the *probable* precedent value of the case is, in a given court or in general. Here, too, judgment factors enter very largely, and objective agreement is not to be expected; for we must draw into our thinking the results of our work on the second level, and must draw further things as well. Yet here, too, as to the *level* of discourse all can agree: it is a question of predicting what some court will in fact do. You can phrase this, if you will, in terms of Ought: what some court will understand this case to tell it to do. I think this latter phrasing slightly misleading, and certainly cumbersome; but defensible it surely is.

4) There is the question of *estimating what consequences the case* (and its effects on other cases) will have to laymen: the relation between the *ways* of the court and the *ways* of those affected by the court. This I take again to be purely on the level of description or prediction, but to be a very complicated matter, and one which involves even more information from outside the cases than does problem 3. The consequences may turn, for instance, on the persons concerned making quite inaccurate prediction of how later cases will eventuate — on their quite misinterpreting the case, on their readjusting their own ways not to their actual environment, but to an *imaginary* environment of court ways.

5) (a) There is the question of *evaluating* the court's action in the case — of concluding how desirable it is. And this is of course the most complicated of all, because it includes all the foregoing, and various premises also as to what values are to be taken as the baseline and the goal. What is utterly vital to see at least is that you cannot begin on this *until you have settled* the matters in the first and second problems, and grappled with those in the third and fourth. And, finally, that this matter of evaluation, while it presupposes the others, in no way touches the *level* on which they are discussed.

5) (b) There is the evaluation of the court's decision or ratio from the angle of *doctrine*. Here some premise or concept is *assumed*, as authoritatively given, and the court's action is tested for whether it is or is not dogmatically *correct*, when compared with that premise. Less dogmatically minded thinkers use the same technique, on the same *logical* level, to see not whether the case is "correct", but whether it *squares* with a given hypothesis (either of doctrine or of prediction) — i.e., to test its consistency with some formulation of a "rule" derived inductively from other cases. It should be clear that this touches neither 3, nor 4, nor (really) even 5a.

Now it would be a case-hardened theorist who proposed to exclude any of these problems from the field law. Yet I think it equally clear that central to them all is the question of what the courts will do. I think it also clear that after study of a group of cases and estimates of just how far courts do follow what prior courts have done, one can set about constructing generalized statements, generalized predictions of their action. I have no hesitancy in calling these predictions rules; they are, however, thus far only rules *of* the court's action; they are statements of the practices of the court. Thanks to the doctrine of precedent the courts themselves regard them also and simultaneously as rules *for* the court's action, *precepts* for the court. So far, the two phases of prediction and of Ought cover identical territory. Yet the moment that you forsake the relatively solid rock of attempted prediction, you run into difficulty, and for this reason: that when you are told by anyone that a given rule is *the proper rule* (not "an accurate prediction") you are dealing with his value judgment, based on no man knows what. *If* you will keep that fact in mind, and your own feet on the cases, and *if* you will remember especially that the only test of whether and how far a rule *authoritatively prevails as a rule of Ought* is: how far will courts follow it — then you will be safe, whatever language is employed.

B. HOW TO READ A CASE

As Llewellyn stated in the first line of the last selection, "you must learn to *read.*" If you made it to law school, there is no doubt that you know how, and in fact most of you probably read more quickly than the average person. Reading case law, however, is not like reading a novel from beginning to end. Reading in the legal sense of the term requires that you read not only for the overall story but also for crucial details. Some of these details may be obvious on a first read, but others may be buried in a foggy haze of citations, dicta, facts, rationale, and even superfluous explanation. Therefore, case decisions almost always require multiple reads.

The first read should be in its entirety to get the story. The story is incredibly important because without a story, the law is almost meaningless. The facts of a case comprise the story, case decisions rest on an application of the law to the facts, and each case may be distinguished on the basis of its facts. Law is useless unless it can be applied to facts, and the story puts facts into perspective. Furthermore, cases are decided by people, who take into consideration the policy and particular set of circumstances that come to them in the context of that particular story. As either a lawyer or a law student attempting to digest a case, your understanding of the story (facts) is the first step in finding the crucial details of the case such as the controversy (the issue) and the resolution of that controversy (the rationale and holding of the case). If you read a case only once, however, you are likely to miss this critical information especially during long or complicated cases.

The second read should be more directed in order to target specific critical information. Therefore, during the second read you need to read proactively. Skim over the information that appears from your first read to be less pertinent and target and highlight the parts of the case that contain the information you need. The specific information that warrants the majority of your attention will become more obvious during the second read because you will have already obtained a basic understanding of the story.

Reading in the legal sense requires you to read for multiple purposes. Remember, you must read almost every case more than once; sometimes twice, sometimes five times. The better you become at reading a case and spotting the important information, the fewer times you will need to read cases. Think of driving into a foggy city in the middle of rush hour. You have never been to this city before and are not sure exactly where to go. You look for the road signs, but with the necessity to pay attention to traffic, you miss some of them, are forced to go in circles, or, worse yet, you find yourself lost. The more you drive, however, the fog seems to thin, and familiar guideposts begin to take form. Eventually you notice patterns that allow you to navigate even when the fog is thick. So too is it with reading cases. The more you read them, the easier it will become to distinguish the facts from the procedural history, the dicta from the basis for the decision, and the holding from the judgment. Eventually the foggy haze of words and endless analysis will start to form familiar patterns.

The following selection from Vandevelde begins to clear the fog by describing the basic components of a typical case.

KENNETH J. VANDEVELDE
THINKING LIKE A LAWYER: AN INTRODUCTION TO LEGAL REASONING
27–32 (1996)[4]

The Components of a Case

. . . . Discussion in this section covers the various components that may be found in a well-written judicial opinion, the significance of each, and how each should be analyzed. Because the overwhelming majority of published judicial opinions are appellate decisions, this discussion assumes that the case under analysis is an appellate decision.

Facts

A judicial opinion usually begins with a description of the facts. This is a narrative of the events that gave rise to the dispute submitted to the court for decision.

Many of the facts in the opinion are of meager significance but are there merely to provide a context for the facts that do matter. Without them, the rest would not make sense. On a first reading, however, the lawyer generally does not know which of the facts are significant. As will be seen, determining which facts are significant requires first identifying the rules of law and the underlying policies that govern the case.

Procedural History

Next, the procedural history is summarized. This portion of the opinion sets forth a description of the events that occurred in the trial or lower appellate court during the course of the litigation, beginning with the filing of a complaint.

Like the factual recitation, much of the procedural history is of minimal importance in itself but provides context. The procedural history generally indicates one detail that is of fundamental importance: the precise nature of the decision in the lower court from which one or both parties are appealing.

The nature of the decision from which the appeal is taken is critical because, as noted in Chapter 1, it determines the standard of review that the court of appeals applies to a trial court's decision. The standard of review, in turn, determines that the appellate court must decide and the effect that the appellate court's decision will have on future cases.

For example, if a physician is appealing a jury verdict that he was negligent in providing medical care, the appellate court reviews the verdict only to determine whether it was supported by substantial evidence. To affirm the judgment against the physician, the appellate court need not decide that the physician was negligent but only that there was substantial evidence to that effect, which is a much different determination. As long as there is substantial evidence that supports the verdict, however, the verdict will stand.

Moreover, because the appellate court is not deciding whether the physician was negligent but only whether there was substantial evidence that he was, the appellate

---

[4] From Thinking Like a Lawyer by Kenneth Vandevelde ©1996. Reprinted by permission of Westview Press, a member of Perseus Books Group.

court's opinion upholding the jury's verdict against the physician cannot be sited by lawyers in future cases as deciding that such conduct by the physician *was* negligent. Rather, the appellate court's opinion can be cited only as establishing that such conduct *could be* negligent. . . .

Questions Presented

At the end of the procedural history, the opinion states the questions presented. These are simply the questions that the appellant has asked the court to decide. In other words, they are the issues on appeal.

Each question asks, in effect, whether some decision made in the trial or lower appellate court was erroneous, requiring reversal of the judgment. The entire rest of the opinion is devoted to deciding the questions presented.

Rules of Law

To decide the questions presented, the opinion begins by announcing rules of law. There are general principles of law that state that, under a particular set of circumstances, a certain right or duty exists.

The court announces these rules because it believes they govern the questions that it must decide. In effect, the rules establish the parties' rights and duties in this case as well as in all similar cases. Usually, most or all of the rules have been announced in prior cases, and the court cites the earlier cases from which each rule is taken.

The rules of law are of great importance. Much of the factual and procedural history is significant because it provides the context for some other part of the opinion, but the rules of law are important simply in themselves. Because they are thought to govern the reported case as well as similar cases, these rules may ultimately determine the results of the situation that the lawyer has been asked to review. The lawyer must carefully read and extract from the opinion each of the rules of law announced.

Identifying the rules of law can be difficult because they may not be stated in a clear, concise fashion. The elements may be scattered throughout a lengthy discussion, requiring the lawyer to construct the rules form a series of statements. The same rule may be stated more than once, in slightly different form, requiring the lawyer to choose the version that best explains the result reached.

As this suggests, extraction of the rule from a judicial opinion is not a mechanical process. Two lawyers reading the same opinion may well disagree on the rule of the case. And, because of the need at times to construct rules, the rule extracted by the lawyer may be phrased in the lawyer's own words rather than in the words of the court.

A case law rule thus differs from an exacted rule. Less importance is attached to the literal language of a case law rule simply because often there is not a single, authoritative version of the case law rule. The indeterminacy of the language of a case law rule, of course, provides the lawyer with opportunity to articulate the rule in the form most favorable to the client's position.

Application of Law to Fact

The next position of the opinion applies the law to the facts. This is a discussion of how the court has decided whether each element of each rule was satisfied by the facts before it.

. . . [T]he elements of a rule are typically phrased in very general terms. When writing an opinion, the court must decide whether the specific facts of the dispute before it fall within the meaning of the broad, generic facts set forth in the rule. In some cases, the court finds the language of the rule of law so clear that it believes only one result is possible. For example, a court would certainly hold that a red Buick is a motor vehicle.

In other cases, the court may decide that the language of the rule is too general to dictate a single result and that the policy behind the rule must be examined. The court would then be attempting to decide which result would best further the policies underlying the particular rule.

For example, if the rule to be applied prohibits the use of a "motor vehicle" in a park, the court may have to decide whether a remote-controlled toy operated by a child falls within the definition of a motor vehicle. The court may decide that the purposes underlying the rule are to promote the recreational use of the park and to ensure the safety of pedestrians. Because a remote-controlled toy presents relatively little danger to pedestrians, ensuring pedestrian safety probably does not require that the toy be considered a motor vehicle. Moreover, promoting the recreational use of the park would require that the toy *not* be considered a motor vehicle. Thus, the court would further the policies underlying the rule by deciding that the toy does not fall within the meaning of the term "motor vehicle."

These discussions of policy are of considerable importance. They reveal the policies behind the rules and . . . they provide a basis for deciding whether the elements of the rules are satisfied in future cases or even whether the rules should be changed.

Paradoxically, despite its importance, the policy discussion may be the portion of the opinion that is the least structured or methodical. The court may simply announce that public policy favors a particular result, without attempting to explain how the court knew there was such a policy.

It is almost always the case, moreover, that a judicial decision, rather than being based on a single policy, reflects a balance between at least two competing policies, one of which supported creation of the right or duty and the other of which opposed it. In the example above, the motor vehicle rule was based on policies of promoting the recreational use of a park and protecting pedestrians. On the one hand, the policy of ensuring pedestrian safety, taken to extremes, would have required banning the toy, since a pedestrian could trip over it or be startled by it. On the other hand, promoting the recreational use of the park, as noted, required that the toy be allowed.

The court has to decide, under the circumstances of the case before it, how to resolve the conflict. Explanations of how such conflicts are resolved are very often brief and conclusory. The court may note that there are conflicting policies and that one policy outweighs the other, without any real discussion of how the court determined the relative weights of the policies. The court may decide that the result is necessary to further a particular policy, ignoring competing policies altogether.

Courts are sometimes not explicit about the policies that underlie their decisions, and thus it is left to lawyers and judges in later cases to infer those policies — in effect to explain the basis for the decision after the fact. A creative lawyer litigating subsequent cases can attribute policy judgments to the court that plausibly explain the earlier decision and simultaneously support the client's position in the later case.

In any event, it is the completion of this analysis that permits the lawyer to ascertain which were the dispositive facts in the opinion. The dispositive facts were those on which the court relied in deciding whether the elements of the rule were satisfied. Perhaps the court decided that the toy was a motor vehicle because it was motorized, even though minuscule. The lawyer would infer from this that the existence of a motor is a dispositive fact.

Or, perhaps the court decided that the toy was not a motor vehicle because, even though it had a motor, it could not carry a driver or passengers. The lawyer would infer that the inability to carry people was a dispositive fact. Although other details, such as the shape, color, or price of the toy may have been mentioned in the opinion, the court did not rely upon them in deciding whether the element of a motor vehicle was met, and thus they were not dispositive facts.

In identifying the dispositive facts, the lawyer must distinguish between necessary and sufficient facts. Necessary facts are those that *must* be present for the element to be satisfied. If a necessary fact is not present, the element cannot be satisfied and the rule cannot apply. The absence of a necessary fact means that the element is not met. The presence of a necessary fact, on the other hand, does not mean that the element *is* met. The fact may be necessary, but not sufficient, to establish the element.

For example, if a device is deemed a motor vehicle only if it has a motor and is capable of carrying passengers, then the presence of a motor is a necessary fact, but it is not sufficient. The device must also be capable of carrying passengers.

Sufficient facts are those whose presence establishes the element but which need not be present for it to be satisfied. If a sufficient fact is present, then the element is satisfied. At the same time, its absence does not mean that the element is not satisfied, because some other sufficient fact may be present. The fact is sufficient to establish the element but is not necessary.

The discussion that follows draws a distinction between the holding in a case and dictum. The holding essentially is the decision in the case, whereas dictum consists of statements made by the court that were not strictly necessary to the decision and will not be binding in future cases. In a technical sense, no court can ever hold that a particular fact was necessary to the result. To hold that the fact was necessary would be to hold, in effect, that any situation where the fact is not present the result would be different. Such a situation, however, is not before the court and thus the court's statement concerning the result that would occur in the absence of the fact is dictum. For this reason, a court, strictly speaking, can hold only that a fact is sufficient for the result, not that it is necessary. This point is of limited importance, however, given that dictum, very often, *is* followed in subsequent cases and thus the fact will be treated in future cases as if it were necessary.

Holding

The decision of the court with respect to a question presented is called the holding. This is the most important part of the decision. In some cases, the court announces the holding with an expression such as "we hold." In other cases, it leaves to the lawyer the task of identifying the holding.

All of the problems attendant on identifying rules may exist in equal or greater measure in identifying the holding. When the court does not clearly state the holding, the lawyer may have to construct it from scattered statements. This process can be an indeterminate one, which may leave lawyers in disagreement about what the case actually held and which may present a lawyer with the opportunity to articulate the holding in the terms most favorable to the client.

Disposition

Finally, the opinion contains the disposition. A disposition is essentially a procedural directive of some kind that gives effect to the court's decision. Typically, the disposition is either that the trial court's judgment be affirmed or that it be reversed. In some cases, in addition to reversing the judgment of the trial court, the appellate court remands the case to the trial court for additional proceedings, such as a new trial. Although the disposition is critical to the parties to the case, it is of relatively little interest to a lawyer analyzing the case for purposes of identifying applicable law for future situations.

C. HOW TO BRIEF

The previous section described the parts of a case in order to make it easier to read and identify the pertinent information that you will use to create your briefs. This section will describe the parts of a brief in order to give you an idea about what a brief is, what is helpful to include in a brief, and what purpose it serves. Case briefs are a necessary study aid in law school that helps to encapsulate and analyze the mountainous mass of material that law students must digest. The case brief represents a final product after reading a case, rereading it, taking it apart, and putting it back together again. In addition to its function as a tool for self-instruction and referencing, the case brief also provides a valuable "cheat sheet" for class participation.

Who will read your brief? Most professors will espouse the value of briefing but will never ask to see that you have, in fact, briefed. As a practicing lawyer, your client doesn't care if you brief, so long as you win the case. The judges certainly don't care if you brief, so long as you competently practice the law. You are the person that the brief will serve! Keep this in mind when deciding what elements to include as part of your brief and when deciding what information to include under those elements.

What are the elements of a brief? Different people will tell you to include different things in your brief. Most likely, upon entering law school, this will happen with one or more of your instructors. While opinions may vary, four elements that are essential to any useful brief are the following:

(a)   Facts (name of the case and its parties, what happened factually and procedurally, and the judgment)

(b)   Issues (what is in dispute)

(c)   Holding (the applied rule of law)

(d)   Rationale (reasons for the holding)

If you include nothing but these four elements, you should have everything you need in order to recall effectively the information from the case during class or several months later when studying for exams. Because briefs are made for yourself, you may want to include other elements that expand the four elements listed above. Depending on the case, the inclusion of additional elements may be useful. For example, a case that has a long and important section expounding dicta might call for a separate section in your brief labeled: Dicta. Whatever elements you decide to include, however, remember that the brief is a tool intended for personal use. To the extent that more elements will help with organization and use of the brief, include them. On the other hand, if you find that having more elements makes your brief cumbersome and hard to use, cut back on the number of elements. At a minimum, however, make sure you include the four elements listed above.

Elements that you may want to consider including in addition to the four basic elements are:

(e)   Dicta (commentary about the decision that was not the basis for the decision)

(f)   Dissent (if a valuable dissenting opinion exits, the dissent's opinion)

(g)   Party's Arguments (each party's opposing argument concerning the ultimate issue)

(h)   Comments (personal commentary)

Personal comments can be useful if you have a thought that does not fit elsewhere. In the personal experience of one of the authors, this element was used to label cases as specific kinds (e.g., as a case of vicarious liability) or make mental notes about what he found peculiar or puzzling about cases. This element allowed him to release his thoughts (without losing them) so that he could move on to other cases.

In addition to these elements, it may help you to organize your thoughts, as some people do, by dividing Facts into separate elements:

(1)   Facts of the case (what actually happened, the controversy)

(2)   Procedural History (what events within the court system led to the present case)

(3)   Judgment (what the court actually decided)

Procedural History is usually minimal and most of the time irrelevant to the ultimate importance of a case; however, this is not always true. One subject in which Procedure History is virtually always relevant is Civil Procedure.

When describing the Judgment of the case, distinguish it from the Holding. The Judgment is the factual determination by the court, in favor of one party, such as "affirmed," "reversed," or "remanded." In contrast, the Holding is the applied rule of law that serves as the basis for the ultimate judgment.

Remember that the purpose of a brief is to remind you of the important details that make the case significant in terms of the law. It will be a reference tool when you are drilled by a professor and will be a study aid when you prepare for exams. A brief is also like a puzzle piece. The elements of the brief create the unique shape and colors of the piece, and, when combined with other pieces, the picture of the common law takes form. A well-constructed brief will save you lots of time by removing the need to return to the case to remember the important details and also by making it easier to put together the pieces of the common law puzzle.

D.   EXTRACTING THE RELEVANT INFORMATION: ANNOTATING AND HIGHLIGHTING

So now that you know the basic elements of a brief, what information is important to include under each element? The simple answer is: whatever is relevant. But what parts of a case are relevant? When you read your first few cases, you may think that everything that the judge said was relevant to his ultimate conclusion. Even if this were true, what is relevant for the judge to make his decision is not always relevant for you to include in your brief. Remember, the reason to make a brief is not to persuade the world that the ultimate decision in the case is a sound one, but rather to aid in refreshing your memory concerning the most important parts of the case.

What facts are relevant to include in a brief? You should include the facts that are necessary to remind you of the story. If you forget the story, you will not remember how the law in the case was applied. You should also include the facts that are dispositive to the decision in the case. For instance, if the fact that a car is white is a determining factor in the case, the brief should note that the case involves a white car and not simply a car. To the extent that the procedural history either helps you to remember the case or plays an important role in the ultimate outcome, you should include these facts as well.

What issues and conclusions are relevant to include in a brief? There is usually one main issue on which the court rests its decision. This may seem simple, but the court may talk about multiple issues, and may discuss multiple arguments from both sides of the case. Be sure to distinguish the issues from the arguments made by the parties. The relevant issue or issues, and corresponding conclusions, are the ones for which the court made a final decision and which are binding. The court may discuss intermediate conclusions or issues, but stay focused on the main issue and conclusion which binds future courts.

What rationale is important to include in a brief? This is probably the most difficult aspect of the case to determine. Remember that everything that is discussed may have been relevant to the judge, but it is not necessarily relevant to the rationale of the decision. The goal is to remind yourself of the basic reasoning that the court used to come to its decision and the key factors that made the decision favor one side or the other.

A brief should be brief! Overly long or cumbersome briefs are not very helpful because you will not be able to skim them easily when you review your notes or when the professor drills you. On the other hand, a brief that is too short will be equally unhelpful because it lacks sufficient information to refresh your memory. Try to keep your briefs to one page in length. This will make it easy for you to organize and reference them.

Do not get discouraged. Learning to brief and figuring out exactly what to include will take time and practice. The more you brief, the easier it will become to extract the relevant information.

While a brief is an extremely helpful and important study aid, annotating and highlighting are other tools for breaking down the mass of material in your casebook. The remainder of this section will discuss these different techniques and show how they complement and enhance the briefing process.

Annotating Cases

Many of you probably already read with a pencil or pen, but if you do not, now is the time to get in the habit. Cases are so dense and full of information that you will find yourself spending considerable amounts of time rereading cases to find what you need. An effective way to reduce this time is to annotate the margins of the casebook. Your pencil (or pen) will be one of your best friends while reading a case. It will allow you to mark off the different sections (such as facts, procedural history, or conclusions), thus allowing you to clear your mind of thoughts and providing an invaluable resource when briefing and reviewing.

You might be wondering why annotating is important if you make an adequate, well constructed brief. By their very nature briefs cannot cover everything in a case. Even with a thorough, well constructed brief you may want to reference the original case in order to reread dicta that might not have seemed important at the time, to review the complete procedural history or set of facts, or to scour the rationale for a better understanding of the case; annotating makes these tasks easier. Whether you return to a case after a few hours or a few months, annotations will swiftly guide you to the pertinent parts of the case by providing a roadmap of the important sections. Your textual markings and margin notes will refresh your memory and restore specific thoughts you might have had about either the case in general or an individual passage. Annotations will also remind you of forgotten thoughts and random ideas by providing a medium for personal comments.

In addition to making it easier to review an original case, annotating cases during the first review of a case makes the briefing process easier. With adequate annotations, the important details needed for your brief will be much easier to retrieve. Without annotations, you will likely have difficulty locating the information you seek even in the short cases. It might seem strange that it would be hard to reference a short case, but even a short case will likely take you at least fifteen to twenty-five minutes to read, while longer cases may take as much as thirty minutes to an hour to complete. No matter how long it takes, the dense material of all cases makes it difficult to remember all your thoughts, and trying to locate specific sections of the analysis may feel like you are trying to locate a needle in a haystack. An annotation in the margin, however, will not only swiftly guide you to a pertinent section, but will also refresh the thoughts that you had while reading that section.

When you read a case for the first time, read for the story and for a basic understanding of the dispute, the issues, the rationale, and the decision. As you hit these elements (or what you think are these elements) make a mark in the margins. Your markings can be as simple as "facts" (with a bracket that indicates the relevant part of the paragraph). When you spot an issue, you may simply mark "issue" or instead provide a synopsis in your own words. When a case sparks an idea — write that idea in the margin as well — you never know when a seemingly irrelevant idea might turn into something more. Finally, when you spot a particularly important part of the text, underline it (or highlight it as described below).

With a basic understanding of the case, and with annotations in the margin, the second read-through of the case should be much easier. You can direct your reading to the most important sections and will have an easier time identifying what is and is not important. Continue rereading the case until you have identified all the relevant information that you need to make your brief, including the issue(s), the facts, the holding, and the relevant parts of the analysis.

Pencil or pen — which is better to use when annotating? Our recommendation is a mechanical pencil. Mechanical pencils make finer markings than regular pencils, and also than ballpoint pens. Although you might think a pencil might smear more than a pen, with its sharp point a mechanical pencil uses very little excess lead and will not smear as much as you might imagine. A mechanical pencil will also give you the freedom to make mistakes without consequences. When you first start annotating, you may think that some passages are more important than they really are, and therefore you may resist the urge to make a mark in order to preserve your book and prevent false guideposts. With a pencil, however, the ability to erase and rewrite removes this problem.

Highlighting

Why highlight? Like annotating, highlighting may seem unimportant if you create thorough, well constructed briefs, but highlighting directly helps you to brief. It makes cases, especially the more complicated ones, easy to digest, review and use to extract information. Highlighting takes advantage of colors to provide a uniquely effective method for reviewing and referencing a case. If you prefer a visual approach to learning, you may find highlighting to be a very effective tool.

If annotating and highlighting are so effective, why brief? Because the process of summarizing a case and putting it into your own words within a brief provides an understanding of the law and of the case that you cannot gain through the process of highlighting or annotating. The process of putting the case into your own words forces you to digest the material, while annotating and highlighting can be accomplished in a much more passive manner.

What should you highlight? Similar to annotating, the best parts of the case to highlight are those that represent the needed information for your brief such as the facts, the issue, the holding and the rationale. Unlike annotating, highlighting provides an effective way to color code, which makes referring to the case even easier. In addition, Highlighters are particularly useful in marking off entire sections by using brackets. These brackets will allow you to color-code the case without highlighting all the text, leaving the most important phrases untouched for a more detailed highlight marking or underlining.

Highlighting is a personal tool, and therefore should be used to the extent that highlighting helps, but should be modified in a way that makes it personally time-efficient and beneficial. For instance, you might combine the use of annotations in the margins with the visual benefit of highlighting the relevant text. You may prefer to underline the relevant text with a pencil, but to use a highlighter to bracket off the different sections of a case. Whatever you choose to do, make sure that it works for you, regardless of what others recommend. The techniques in the remainder of this section will describe ways to make full use of your highlighters.

First, buy yourself a set of multi-colored highlighters, with at least four, or perhaps five or six different colors. Yellow, pink, and orange are usually the brightest. Depending on the brand, purple and green can be dark, but still work well. Although blue is a beautiful color, it tends to darken and hide the text. Therefore we recommend that you save blue for the elements that you rarely highlight.

For each different section of the case, choose a color, and use that color only when highlighting the section of the case designated for that color. Consider using yellow for the text that you tend to highlight most frequently. Because yellow is the brightest, you may be inclined to use yellow for the Conclusions in order to make them stand out the most. If you do this, however, you will exhaust your other colors much faster than yellow and this will require that you purchase an entire set of new highlighters when a single color runs out because colors such as green are not sold separately. If instead you choose to use yellow on a more frequently highlighted section such as the Analysis, when it comes time to replace your yellow marker, you will need only to replace your yellow highlighter individually. In the personal experience on one of the authors, the sections of cases that seemed to demand the most highlighter attention were the Facts and the Analysis, while the Issues and Holdings demanded the least. Other Considerations and Procedural History required lots of highlighting in particular cases although not in every case.

Experiment if you must, but try to choose a color scheme early on in the semester and stick with it. That way, when you come back to the first cases of the semester, you will not be confused with multiple color schemes. The basic sections of a case for which you should consider giving a different color are:

- Facts
- Procedural History
- Issue (and questions presented)
- Holding (and conclusions)
- Analysis (rationale)
- Other Considerations (such as dicta)

Not all of these sections demand a separate color. You may find that combining Facts and Procedural History or Issues and Holdings works best. Furthermore, as mentioned above, some sections may not warrant highlighting in every case (e.g., dicta probably do not need to be highlighted unless they are particularly important). If you decide that a single color is all that you need, then stick to one, but if you find yourself highlighting lots of text from many different sections, reconsider the use of at least a few different colors. Highlighters make text stand out, but only when used appropriately. The use of many colors enables you to highlight more text without reducing the highlighter's effectiveness. Three to four colors provides decent color variation without the cumbersomeness of handling too many markers.

Once you are comfortable with your color scheme, determining exactly what to highlight still may be difficult. Similar to knowing what to annotate, experience will perfect your highlighting skills. Be careful not to highlight everything, thus ruining your highlighters' effectiveness; at the same time, do not be afraid to make mistakes.

Now that we have covered the basics of reading, annotating, highlighting, and briefing a case, you are ready to start practicing. Keep the tips and techniques mentioned in this chapter in mind when you tackle the four topics in the remainder of this book. If you have difficultly, refer back to this chapter to help guide you as you master the case method of study and the art of using the common law.

Topic I
LANDLORD'S DUTY TO PROTECT A TENANT
(3 Assignments)

To get some idea of what the general law is in a particular area, it is often helpful to read the relevant passages from a hornbook or treatise on the subject. Because it is a new subject, do not expect to absorb everything. Read the introductory material to gain a basic understanding so that you have something on which to build when you read the first case in that area of law. Since the assignments here focus on a landlord's duty to protect a tenant, the following excerpt from one of the most widely noted hornbooks on the subject will introduce you to the concept of duty, especially as it relates to the landlord-tenant relationship. In addition, a few definitions from Black's Law Dictionary on licensee, trespasser, and invitee, followed by an excerpt from a treatise discussing the relevant duties owed to each, will be helpful as you read the first case.

W. Keeton, D. Dobbs, R. Keeton & D. Owen
Prosser and Keeton on the Law of Torts
356–59, 373–75, 434–35, 440–42 (5th ed. 1984)[1]

Duty

. . . It is quite possible, and not at all uncommon, to deal with most of the questions which arise in a negligence case in terms of "duty." Thus, the standard of conduct required of the individual may be expressed by saying that the driver of an automobile approaching an intersection is under a duty to moderate his speed, to keep a proper lookout, or to blow his horn, but that he is not under a duty to take precautions against an unexpected explosion of a manhole cover in the street. But the problems of "duty" are sufficiently complex without subdividing it in this manner to cover an endless series of details of conduct. It is better to reserve "duty" for the problem of the relation between individuals which imposes upon one a legal obligation for the benefit of the other, and to deal with particular conduct in terms of a legal standard of what is required to meet the obligation. In other words, "duty" is a question of whether the defendant is under any obligation for the benefit of the particular plaintiff; and in negligence cases, the duty is always the same — to conform to the legal standard of reasonable conduct in the light of the apparent risk. What the defendant must do, or must not do, is a question of the standard of conduct required to satisfy the duty. The distinction is one of convenience only, and it must be remembered that the two are correlative, and one cannot exist without the other.

A duty, in negligence cases, may be defined as an obligation, to which the law will give recognition and effect, to conform to a particular standard of conduct toward another. In the early English law, there was virtually no consideration of duty. Liability was imposed with no great regard even for the fault of the defendant. The requirements as to conduct were absolute, and once the act was found to be wrongful, the actor was liable for the damage that might result. Such few limitations upon his responsibility as are found in the earlier cases are stated, not in any terms of duty, but of remoteness of the damage, or what we now call "proximate cause." Certainly there is little trace of any notion of a relation between the parties, or an obligation to any one individual, as essential to the tort. The defendant's obligation to behave properly apparently was owed to all the world, and he was liable to any person whom he might injure by his misconduct.

The conception of an absolute wrong remains in the criminal law, and in the field of

---

[1] Reprinted from W. Keeton, D. Dobbs, R. Keeton & D. Owen, Prosser and Keeton on the Law of Torts (5th ed. 1984) with permission of the West Group.

intentional torts, where the doctrine of "transferred intent" makes any one who attempts to injure another liable to any stranger whom he may injure instead. But when negligence began to take form as a separate basis of tort liability, the courts developed the idea of duty, as a matter of some specific relation between the plaintiff and the defendant, without which there could be no liability. We owe this to three English cases, decided between 1837 and 1842. The rule which developed out of them was that no action could be founded upon the breach of a duty owed only to some person other than the plaintiff. He must bring himself within the scope of a definite legal obligation, so that it might be regarded as personal to him. "Negligence in the air, so to speak, will not do." The first cases in which this idea was stated held only that the obligation of a contract could give no right of action to one who was not a contracting party; but it was soon extended to the whole field of negligence. The period during which it developed was that of the industrial revolution, and there is good reason to believe that it was a means by which the courts sought, perhaps more or less unconsciously, to limit the responsibilities of growing industry within some reasonable bounds.

This concept of a relative duty is not regarded as essential by the continental law, and it has been assailed as serving no useful purpose, and producing only confusion in ours. Its artificial character is readily apparent; in the ordinary case, if the court should desire to find liability, it would be quite as easy to find the necessary "relation" in the position of the parties toward one another, and hence to extend the defendant's duty to the plaintiff. The statement that there is or is not a duty begs the essential question — whether the plaintiff's interests are entitled to legal protection against the defendant's conduct. It is therefore not surprising to find that the problem of duty is as broad as the whole law of negligence, and that no universal test for it ever has been formulated. It is a shorthand statement of a conclusion, rather than an aid to analysis in itself. Yet it is embedded far too firmly in our law to be discarded, and no satisfactory substitute for it, by which the defendant's responsibility may be limited, has been devised. But it should be recognized that "duty" is not sacrosanct in itself, but is only an expression of the sum total of those considerations of policy which lead the law to say that the plaintiff is entitled to protection.

There is little analysis of the problem of duty in the courts. Frequently it is dealt with in terms of what is called "proximate cause," usually with resulting confusion. In such cases, the question of what is "proximate" and that of duty are fundamentally the same: whether the interests of the plaintiff are to be protected against the particular invasion by the defendant's conduct.

Scope of Duty

In *Heaven v. Pender*, Brett, M.R., afterwards Lord Esher, made the first attempt to state a formula of duty. "Whenever one person," he said, "is by circumstances placed in such a position with regard to another that every one of ordinary sense who did think would at once recognize that if he did not use ordinary care and skill in his own conduct with regard to those circumstances he would cause danger of injury to the person or property of the other, a duty arises to use ordinary care and skill to avoid such danger." But this formula, which afterwards was rejected by Lord Esher himself, was soon recognized as far too broad. As a general proposition to be applied in the ordinary negligence case, where the defendant has taken some affirmative action such as driving an automobile, it holds good. That is to say, that whenever the automobile driver should, as a reasonable person, foresee that his conduct will involve an unreasonable risk of harm to other drivers or to pedestrians, he is then under a duty to them to exercise the care of a reasonable person as to what he does or does not do. There are, however, a good many defendants, and a good many situations, as to which there is no such duty. In other words, the defendant is under no legal obligation toward the particular plaintiff to act with the care of a reasonable man, and he is not liable even though his conduct falls short of that standard, and the other is injured as a result.

A later attempt at a formula for duty was that of Lord Atkin in *Donoghue v. Stevenson*:

> "The rule that you are to love your neighbor becomes in law, you must not injure your neighbor; and the lawyer's question, Who is my neighbor? receives a restricted reply. You must take reasonable care to avoid acts or omissions which you can reasonably foresee would be likely to injure your neighbor. Who, then, in law is my neighbor? The answer seems to be — persons who are so closely and directly affected by my act that I ought reasonably to have them in contemplation as being so affected when I am directing my mind to the acts or omissions which are called in question."

As a formula this dictum is so vague as to have little meaning, and as a guide to decision it has had no value at all. Within some such undefined general limits, it may be said that the courts have merely "reacted to the situation in the way in which the great mass of mankind customarily react," and that as our ideas of human relations change the law as to duties changes with them. Various factors undoubtedly have been given conscious or unconscious weight, including convenience of administration, capacity of the parties to bear the loss, a policy of preventing future injuries, the moral blame attached to the wrongdoer, and many others. Changing social conditions lead constantly to the recognition of new duties. No better general statement can be made than that the courts will find a duty where, in general, reasonable persons would recognize it and agree that it exists.

. . . .

Acts and Omissions

In the determination of the existence of a duty, there runs through much of the law a distinction between action and inaction. In the early common law one who injured another by a positive, affirmative act, was held liable without any great regard even for his fault. But the courts were far too much occupied with the more flagrant forms of misbehavior to be greatly concerned with one who merely did nothing, even though another might suffer harm because of his omission to act. Hence there arose very early a difference, still deeply rooted in the law of negligence, between "misfeasance" and "nonfeasance" — that is to say, between active misconduct working positive injury to others and passive inaction or a failure to take steps to protect them from harm. The reason for the distinction may be said to lie in the fact that by "misfeasance" the defendant has created a new risk of harm to the plaintiff, while by "nonfeasance" he has at least made his situation no worse, and has merely failed to benefit him by interfering in his affairs. The highly individualistic philosophy of the older common law had no great difficulty in working out restraints upon the commission of affirmative acts of harm, but shrank from converting the courts into an agency for forcing men to help one another.

. . . . During the last century, liability for "nonfeasance" has been extended still further to a limited group of relations, in which custom, public sentiment and views of social policy have led the courts to find a duty of affirmative action. In such relationships the plaintiff is typically in some respect particularly vulnerable and dependent upon the defendant who, correspondingly, holds considerable power over the plaintiff's welfare. In addition, such relations have often involved some existing or potential economic advantage to the defendant. Fairness in such cases thus may require the defendant to use his power to help the plaintiff, based upon the plaintiff's expectation of protection, which itself may be based upon the defendant's expectation of financial gain. The largest single group upon whom the duty of affirmative conduct has been imposed are the owners and occupiers of land. . . .

Lessor and Lessee

When land is leased to a tenant, the law of property regards the lease as equivalent to a sale of the premises for the term. The lessee acquires an estate in the land, and becomes for the time being both owner and occupier, subject to all of the responsibilities of one in possession, to those who enter upon the land and those outside of its boundaries.

In the absence of agreement to the contrary, the lessor surrenders both possession and control of the land to the lessee, retaining only a reversionary interest; and he has no right even to enter without the permission of the lessee. Consequently, the traditional common law rule has been that he is under no obligation to anyone to look after the premises or to keep them in repair, and is not responsible, either to persons injured on or off the land for conditions which develop or are created by the tenant after possession has been transferred. Neither is he held responsible, in general, for activities which the tenant carries on upon the land after such transfer, even when they create a nuisance. Furthermore, the doctrine of *caveat emptor* has traditionally been applied to the lessee, quite as much as to a vendee, so that a tenant who has not exacted an express warranty is left to inspect the land for himself, and ordinarily at common law must take it as he finds it, for better or for worse. There is therefore, as a general rule, no liability upon the landlord, either to the tenant or to others entering the land for defective conditions existing at the time of the lease.

Modern ideas of social policy have given rise to a number of exceptions to these general rules of nonliability of the lessor, which to a large extent swallow up the general no-duty rule. There is increasing recognition of the fact that the tenant who leases defective premises is likely to be impecunious and unable to make the necessary repairs, and that sometimes the financial burden is best placed upon the landlord, who receives a benefit from the transaction in the form of rent. This policy is expressed by statutes in a number of states which require the landlord to put and keep certain types of premises, such as tenement houses, in good condition and repair, the breach of which may be evidence of negligence or even negligence per se. It is also expressed by statutes and judicial opinions in a growing minority of states holding exculpatory clauses in residential leases void and unenforceable, at least in certain contexts. The shifting responsibility from tenant to landlord for defects in the premises has been perhaps most significantly expressed in the recent surge of statutes and decisions implying a warranty of habitability into residential leases.

. . . .

Common Areas Retained Under Landlord's Control

When different parts of a building, such as an office building or an apartment house, are leased to several tenants, the approaches and common passageways normally do not pass to the tenant, but remain in the possession and control of the landlord. The tenants are permitted to make use of them but do not occupy them, and the responsibility for their condition remains upon the lessor. His position is closely analogous to that of a possessor who permits visitors to enter for a purpose of his own; and those who come in the course of the expected use may be considered his invitees, as a good many courts have held. He is therefore under an affirmative obligation to exercise reasonable care to inspect and repair such parts of the premises for the protection of the lessee; and the duty extends also to members of the tenant's family, his employees, his invitees, his guests, and others on the land in the right of the tenant, since their presence is a part of the normal use of the premises for which the lessor holds them open. It extends also to those outside of the premises who may be injured as a result of their condition. It is entirely possible that as to any of these plaintiffs the landlord may be liable where the tenant is not. The duty does not extend to intruders who come for a purpose for which the building is not open and provided, and such individuals are at best licensees.

The obligation is one of reasonable care only, and the lessor is not liable where no injury to anyone was reasonably to be anticipated, or the condition was not discoverable by reasonable inspection, unless it is shown to have been of such duration as to permit the conclusion that due care would have discovered it. The prevailing view is that the duty extends to conditions of purely natural origin, such as ice and snow on the steps, although the rule is to the contrary in a number of jurisdictions.

The lessor's obligation extends to hallways, stairs, elevators, approaches and entrances, yards, basements, bathrooms, common rooms, porches, the roof of the building, and any other parts of the premises maintained for the benefit of the tenants within the purposes of the lease. It extends also to any appliances, such as a heating plant, water system, or washing machine, over which the lessor retains control, and which he furnishes for common use by the tenants. It may even extend into the portion of the premises leased to the tenant, provided that the landlord has retained control over that aspect of the premises responsible for the injury. It does not extend, however, to parts of the premises where the tenant or his visitors may not reasonably be expected to go, or to their use for an unintended purpose. If the lessee discovers the dangerous condition, he may, but does not necessarily, assume the risk or become contributorily negligent in dealing with it; but his knowledge will not prevent recovery by a third party who is himself ignorant of the danger.

BLACK'S LAW DICTIONARY [2]

trespasser. One who commits a trespass; one who intentionally and without consent or privilege enters another's property.

licensee. 1. One to whom a license is granted. **2.** One who has permission to enter or use another's premises, but only for one's own purposes and not for the occupier's benefit.

> *bare licensee.* A licensee whose presence on the premises the occupier tolerates but does not necessarily approve, such as one who takes a shortcut across another's land.

> *licensee by invitation.* One who is expressly or impliedly permitted to enter another's premises to transact business with the owner or occupant or to perform an act benefiting the owner or occupant.

> *licensee by permission.* One who has the owner's permission or passive consent to enter the owner's premises for one's own convenience, curiosity, or entertainment.

invitee. A person who has an express or implied invitation to enter or use another's premises, such as a business visitor or a member of the public to whom the premises are held open.

Corpus Juris Secundum
Care Required and Liability for Injuries to Licensees
65A C.J.S. NEGLIGENCE § 440 (Thomson Reuters/West 2008)[3]

The owner or occupant of premises owes a duty to licensees to abstain from injuring them willfully or wantonly and, under many authorities, additional duties are placed on him to avoid injury to them.

One who goes on the premises of another as a mere licensee is in the same attitude as a trespasser, and the duties of the owner or occupant are substantially the same as with respect to a trespasser. The only essential difference arises out of the duty of

---

[2] BLACK'S LAW DICTIONARY 1543, 939, 846 (8th ed. 2004). Reprinted by permission of the West Group.

[3] Reprinted by permission of the West Group.

anticipating the presence of a licensee. The owner's or occupant's duty also depends, to some extent, on whether the licensee is such by permission or passive acquiescence only, or whether he is a licensee by the owner's or occupant's express or implied inducement or invitation.

It has been stated that generally there is no affirmative duty of care with respect to a mere licensee and no duty to protect him from injury, or, as has been stated, only a limited duty of care is due to a licensee, or gratuitous or bare licensee. Accordingly, a mere licensee generally has no cause of action because of an injury received through the negligence of the owner or occupant of the premises to which the license extends. A property owner is not an insurer of the safety of licensees. An iron-clad guarantee of safety against all hazards is not due a licensee, and the duty owed to a licensee is less than the duty owed to an invitee, at least in those jurisdictions which have not abrogated the common-law distinctions between the duties owed to licensees and invitees. However, since a licensee has some rights and the owner of the premises has some duties toward him, statements of the rule are usually accompanied by statements of some of the exceptions thereto.

The most usual statement of the general rule, sometimes expressed by statute, is that no duty exists toward a mere, bare, or gratuitous licensee, or licensee by permission, except to refrain from willfully or wantonly injuring him, or, as otherwise stated, not to injure the licensee willfully, wantonly, or through gross negligence, or to refrain from injuring the licensee through such gross negligence as is equivalent to willfulness or wantonness. To constitute "willful or wanton conduct," for purposes of a landowner's duty to a licensee to refrain from injuring him through willful or wanton conduct, there must be a course of action which shows a deliberate intention to harm or utter indifference to, or conscious disregard of, the safety of others. "Willful and wanton conduct" exceeds mere inadvertence or lack of attention characteristic of ordinary negligence, and means that the possessor consciously disregards a known, serious danger. It has also been stated that the duty owed to a licensee is to refrain from willful, wanton, or reckless conduct which will or is likely to injure the licensee, or to abstain from the doing of any intentional, willful, or wanton acts or misconduct, endangering the safety of the licensee. Similar expressions are to be found in the cases. While there is not uniformity of opinion among the authorities as to the extent of the duty which an owner or occupant owes to a licensee, many courts have expanded the duties owed to a licensee beyond the mere duty to refrain from willful and wanton injury. Indeed, in those jurisdictions which have abrogated the common-law distinctions between the duties owed to licensees and invitees, the rule, except as to trespassers, is reasonable care under the circumstances. Under some authorities a licensee may recover only where there is something on the premises in the nature of a trap or where the owner or occupant of the premises is guilty of active negligence.

Some courts have recognized a marked difference between a trespasser and a licensee with respect to the liability of a landowner for injury occurring on his property, and are committed to the rule that, under some circumstances, an owner or proprietor is charged with the duty of exercising ordinary care to avoid injuring a licensee. It has been observed that in modern times the immunities of landowners based on the status of the person entering on premises as licensees or trespassers have rightfully, although gradually, been giving way to the overriding social view that where there is foreseeability of substantial harm landowners should generally be subjected to a reasonable duty to avoid it. It has also been held that there is a duty to exercise reasonable care to avoid unnecessary injury to a licensee, and that the owner or occupant may be held liable for unreasonable risks incident to his activities.

The duty of the owner or occupant may extend to the employees of a licensee on the premises. On the other hand, it has been held that the affirmative duty of an owner or occupant to a licensee is distinct from any duty to employees of the licensee.

ASSIGNMENT 1
Briefing: Examples in Tort Law

Having developed a feel for the black-letter law in this area, we now turn to the first assignment and our first three cases. These cases in the area of tort law discuss the concept of duty in the context of negligence — a concept that has just been discussed by scholars on the subject in the hornbook selection above. Why read the cases when the scholars have already read the cases and digested the material for us in a hornbook? Four reasons: cases provide a sharper picture of the law; cases can be interpreted in different ways that may not be caught by a hornbook; cases are constantly being decided with new law not covered by a dated hornbook; and perhaps most importantly, judges and lawyers rely on cases, not hornbooks or black letter law, so it is important to know how to read a case and how to extract the law and its rationale. Therefore, cases are used to teach the student not only substantive law but also the methodology of how to read a case and interpret it.

Read the first case through two or three times and then try briefing it on your own before proceeding with the notes that follow. The notes will help you retrace your steps in writing the brief and provide a sample brief in conclusion.

LEVINE v. KATZ
407 F.2d 303 (D.C. Cir. 1968)

PRETTYMAN, Senior Circuit Judge:

This is a civil action for damages by reason of negligence. Appellant-plaintiff slipped on a small strawlike mat, lying without adhesive undercoating on a highly polished floor, while entering the lobby of a multi-family apartment house. In leasing, the landlord had reserved to his own control the halls and other parts of the premises designed for the common use and convenience of all of the tenants. Plaintiff and her husband were on a visit to their grandchildren (granddaughter and husband), tenants in the apartment house. This was a customary Saturday afternoon family occurrence and followed some telephone conversation between the ladies. Before plaintiff completed her evidence, the trial court directed a verdict for defendants upon the ground that plaintiff was a mere licensee and consequently the landlord was under no duty to exercise reasonable care for her safety. We think the court erred in that determination, and accordingly we vacate the judgment and remand.

It has long been well settled in this jurisdiction that, where a landlord leases separate portions of property to different tenants and reserves under his own control the halls, stairs, or other parts of the property for use in common by all tenants, he has a duty to all those on the premises of legal right to use ordinary care and diligence to maintain the retained parts in a reasonably safe condition. The apartment house in the case at bar was across the line in suburban Maryland, and the rule of law in that jurisdiction has long been the same as in the District. The Court of Appeals of Maryland in 1959, in a unanimous opinion written by Judge Hammond, carefully stated the matter with succinct explanation and extended citations. [Landay v. Cohn, 220 Md. 24 (1959).] He said in part:

> "Where a landlord leases separate portions of a property to different tenants and reserves under his control halls, stairways or other parts of the property for use in common by all the tenants, he must use ordinary care and diligence to maintain the retained parts in reasonably safe condition. [Citing cases.] The duty stems from the responsibility engendered in the landlord by his having extended an invitation, express or implied, to use the portions of the property retained by him [Citations.] Such an invitation extended to a tenant includes the members of his family, his guests, his invitees and others on the land in the right of the tenant. [Citations.]"

In 1964 the Maryland court unanimously iterated the rule, saying, "There is no doubt in Maryland that [the landlord reserving control over parts of the property] must then exercise ordinary care and diligence to maintain the retained portions in a reasonably safe condition."

In the case before us the trial court cited, quoted, and expressly relied upon the Maryland case of Levine v. Miller [218 Md. 74 (1958), written by the same judge who wrote *Landay* and stating, "The Maryland law is firmly established that the owner of land owes no duty to a trespasser or licensee, even one of tender years, except to abstain from wilful or wanton misconduct and entrapment."]. The record there disclosed that the landlord maintained an empty and locked recreation room, the key to which was given to the tenants upon request. On the occasion in question a little girl, having been granted permission to use the room, left the door open, returned the key, and thereafter returned to the room without permission and was injured. We think that case is inapposite. The child in that case was on the premises at the time without permission. The case at bar falls within the ambit of the long line of cases which have repeatedly held that the landlord owes a duty of due care to all those on the premises of legal right.

Reversed and remanded.

BAZELON, Chief Judge (concurring in the result):

The rule developed in the cases cited by the majority is often explained on the theoretical basis that all persons lawfully on the premises are the landlord's invitees. But in my view our decision does not depend upon adherence to the out-moded "invitee-licensee-trespasser trinity." The Supreme Court, several states, and England have all recognized that the common-law classifications and their progeny of sub-classifications are discordant with the realities of modern living. In admiralty law the Supreme Court has replaced the trinity with a flexible standard based on the ordinary rule of negligence requiring due care under all the circumstances — a concept which this court had previously adopted to replace conceptual distinctions between "degrees of care." Here, in accordance with this modern authority, the landlord's duty to entrants upon common-use areas reserved to his control is better expressed in terms of "due care under all the circumstances."

DISCUSSION

The first aspect of importance in this case is the rule that appears in the first sentence of the second paragraph as well as in the quoted section of Judge Hammond's opinion: The landlord "has a duty to all those on the premises of legal right to use ordinary care and diligence to maintain the retained parts [common areas under the control of the landlord] in a reasonably safe condition." The quote from *Landay* explains that this duty, which applies to "all those on the premises of legal right," includes not only a tenant but also "the members of his family, his guests, his invitees, and others." *Landay* expressly includes certain people who have an express or implied permission by the landlord to be on the premises (including a tenant's family members, guests and invitees) and appears to exclude trespassers and people whose presence on the premises is merely tolerated (bare licensees). What is unclear is who are "others on the land in the right of the tenant" beyond family members, guests, and invitees.

The plaintiff is a grandmother visiting her grandchildren. To be clear, the grand-mother here is a licensee of the landlord. She is not an invitee because she was not in the building for a business purpose and the lobby of the apartment building was not held out to the public for a public purpose. The grandmother is also not a trespasser. She received her licensee status through an invitation (express or implied) by the landlord that extends to all family members and guests of the tenant, and she appears to fall within the protection of the landlord's duty according to *Landay*.

The trial court directed a verdict against the grandmother based on the rule in *Levine v. Miller*, which states that a landowner is under no duty to exercise reasonable care for the safety of a licensee. A directed verdict is a verdict that the jury returns as directed by the court; basically, the judge determines the case for the jury because only one decision could reasonably follow from the evidence. Although we do not have the trial court's opinion, it appears to have found that the landlord did not owe a duty to exercise reasonable care for the grandmother's safety based on its classification of the grandmother as a licensee within the context of the *Miller* rule. The appellate court felt that the lower court was wrong and therefore reversed the decision.

So what did the lower court do wrong? In the *Miller* case, a little girl was apparently granted permission to use a room to which she later returned without permission and in which she was injured on that later occasion. The trial court in the instant case apparently did not see any difference between the girl's status as a licensee and the status of the grandmother. The trial court therefore applied the *Miller* holding to the present case by analogy. The appellate court disagreed with the way in which the trial court drew this analogy, especially in light of the *Landay* decision (written by the same judge who wrote the *Miller* decision). The appellate court distinguished the *Miller* case from the instant case by noting that the child in the *Miller* case was in the room without permission while the grandmother of the tenant in the instant case was in a common area with permission. Thus, the child in the *Miller* case, even if a mere licensee, was not the type of guest who would be protected by the landlord's duty to those in the right of the tenant to maintain the premises in a reasonably safe condition, whereas the grandmother was.

Be careful not to jump to the conclusion that this court overruled *Miller*, which it did not do. The appellate court merely qualified the *Miller* court's general rule that the owner of land owes no duty of due care to a licensee. In fact this general rule appears to have been qualified a year after *Miller* by the same judge who wrote the *Miller* decision. He stated in *Landay* that landlord owes a duty of due care to people in the common areas in the right of the tenant. These people include the tenant's guests and family members. Therefore, the general rule (concerning licensees in general as described in the C.J.S. excerpt above) may continue to deny a landowner's duty of due care to a bare licensee and even to a licensee of the landlord who is not in the right of the tenant, but will not apply to people in common areas in the right of the tenant (who now have a right to protection). What is crucial to understand is that this modified rule does not overrule *Miller* because the rule can still be applied to the facts in *Miller* to reach the same result (denial of the right of protection to the little girl as a trespasser or bare licensee).

Although the appellate court's decision ruled in favor of the grandmother, it did not provide her relief. It remanded the case, i.e. sent it back to the trial court for the purpose of deciding the outcome. Why did the court send the case back for a new trial? Was the finding that the landlord owed a duty to the grandmother not enough? The grandmother slipped on a small strawlike mat without adhesive undercoating on a highly polished floor in the lobby. Was this not a breach of duty on the part of the landlord for permitting it to happen? In the middle of the first paragraph, the appellate court noted that the trial court did not allow the plaintiff to complete her evidence. There may have been facts that were not produced but which might have had a bearing on the question of damages. Therefore, the appellate court did not have sufficient evidence before it to determine the outcome of the case. The appellate court only found that the duty existed and left the question of breach and proof of damages to the trial court to be decided after a proper review of the facts.

With this general understanding of the case, we are now ready to brief it:

Levine v. Katz
407 F.2d 303 (D.C. Cir. 1968)

FACTS:	A visiting grandmother, P, slips on a mat, which was laid over the polished floor in the lobby (common area) of her granddaughter's apartment building. P sues the landlord, D, for negligence, and the lower court directed a verdict for D. This court reverses and remands.
ISSUE:	Does a landlord owe a duty to licensees to maintain common areas in a reasonably safe condition?
HOLDING:	The landlord owes a duty to licensees to maintain common areas in a reasonably safe condition if the licensee's permission to be in the common areas is derived from the right of the tenant.
RATIONALE:	Although *Miller* states the common law rule (on which the lower court in the instant case appears to have relied) that a landowner does not owe a licensee a duty of due care, this court qualifies (without overruling *Miller*) the rule to apply only to licensees who do not have the benefit of being in the right of the tenant. In accord with *Landay*, licensees whose permission stems from the right of the tenant are protected by the landlord's duty to maintain the premises.

The concurrence by Chief Judge Bazelon suggests that a more flexible standard requiring due care of the landlord under all the circumstances, even in the case of trespassers, should be applied. Given Judge Bazelon's stature as a distinguished judge, his concurrence is an important indicator of possible changes that may be made to the law in the future. As an interesting note, both the Maryland and Federal jurisdictions maintain the distinctions between trespasser, licensee, and invitee, but other jurisdictions, such as Colorado, California, and New York have done away with the distinctions, in favor of a duty of ordinary care under all circumstances.[4]

Prosser, in the hornbook selection above, states that the landlord's duty "to exercise reasonable care to inspect and repair such parts of the premises for the protection of the lessee . . . extends also to members of the tenant's family, his employees, his invitees, his guests, and others on the land in the right of the tenant. . . . The duty does not extend to intruders who come for a purpose for which the building is not open and provided, and such individuals are at best licensees." It is from cases such as *Levine v. Katz* that this black-letter hornbook law is established.

Having started the briefing process with a relatively short and simple case, we shall now proceed to a much longer and more complex one. Again, read the entire case through and over again until you have a good grasp of the facts and the holding and then brief it. Avoid turning to the discussion following the case until after you have completed your brief.

KENDALL v. GORE PROPERTIES, INC.
236 F.2d 673 (D.C. Cir. 1956)

DANAHER, Circuit Judge.

Appellant is administratrix of the Estate of Miss Codie A. Whitman, deceased, on account of whose wrongful death this action had been brought. Decedent, on July 12, 1952, then 39 years of age, was strangled to death with a painter's towel in apartment 201 of which she was a tenant in the Ritz Apartments at 1631 Euclid Street, N.W., District of Columbia. Appellee Gore Properties, Inc., was the owner of the Ritz, appellee William F. Hickey was resident manager. . . . Perpetrator of the murder was one Harry Clifford Porter who had been engaged by Hickey to paint the interior of Miss Whitman's apartment. At the close of appellant's case, the trial judge directed a verdict in favor of all appellees. . . . The principal question presented may be stated as follows:

---

[4] Vitauts M. Gulbis, J.D., *Modern status of rules conditioning landowner's liability upon status of injured party as invitee, licensee, or trespasser*, 22 A.L.R. 4th 294 (1983).

"Did the Court err in directing a verdict for the appellees (defendants) at the close of appellant's evidence where the evidence showed (1) that the appellant's decedent, Codie A. Whitman, occupied as a tenant an apartment in an apartment house owned by one of the appellees and managed by the other two appellees, (2) that on Saturday afternoon, July 12, 1952, in her apartment, Miss Whitman was strangled and choked to death by an agent of the appellees, Harry Clifford Porter, (3) that on Friday night, July 11, 1952, immediately upon being employed by the appellees, Porter had been assigned by them to Miss Whitman's apartment to paint the interior of it, (4) that when the appellees employed Porter, they did not know him, made no investigation of him, obtained no references from him, and without any previous experience with him, assigned him to paint the interior of the apartment occupied by Miss Whitman, who was known by the appellees to be a single girl living alone and unprotected in her apartment, (5) that the appellees did not in any manner supervise or control Porter while he was painting Miss Whitman's apartment and gave him a key and unrestricted access to her and her apartment, and (6) that Porter was a person of unsound mind, dangerous and irresponsible and was adjudicated so and committed to the ward for insane criminals in St. Elizabeth's Hospital?"

Appellant took the pretrial deposition of Hickey, read it at the trial, and also called Hickey as an adverse witness. It was thus developed that on one or two occasions, perhaps two weeks before the murder, Hickey saw Porter outside an Air Force building near the National Airport wearing fatigue clothes such as are worn by enlisted men in the Air Force. Porter was cleaning brushes at the time. Although Hickey did not know Porter and knew nothing about him, he asked Porter if he would like to make some extra money. When Porter replied affirmatively Hickey invited him to call at the apartment house to give him a price for painting the interiors of various apartments. On Wednesday evening, July 9, or the following evening, Porter and Hickey agreed upon a price, and Hickey put Porter to work on the evening of Friday, July 11, painting Miss Whitman's apartment. Appellees knew Miss Whitman was single, living alone and unprotected in her apartment. At the time Hickey made arrangements with Porter he also employed through Porter two other men to do painting. Hickey knew none of them, had no knowledge of where they had worked, what kind of work they had done, by whom they had been employed, had no references concerning them, and made no investigation of any of them. On the day Miss Whitman met her death there had been employed at the apartment, a hall man, one Keyes, who some six months to twelve months earlier had been engaged by Hickey. Hickey had made an investigation of Keyes before hiring him, discovered he had been convicted of robbery and had recently been released from the penitentiary and was on parole. When Hickey first talked to Porter about taking the painting job the evidence runs:

"Q. At the time you asked him that, what did you know about him? A. Just that he worked, he was in the service and he was working over there at the Air Force.

"Q. Did you know where he was from? A. No, sir.

"Q. Did you know who his parents were? A. No, sir.

"Q. Did you know where he was employed before he came in the service? A. No, sir, I did not.

"Q. Did you know how long he had been in the service? A. No.

"Q. Did you know anyone for whom he had worked? A. No.

"Q. Did you know anything about his work? A. No.

"Q. Did you know anything about his habits? A. No, sir.

"Q. Did you know anything about his past record in any connection? A. No, sir, not at that time."

Under these circumstances, between 6 and 7 P.M. on the evening of Friday, July 11,

Hickey, Porter and Miss Whitman went to her apartment. Hickey started Porter painting in the kitchen, could not say how long he remained there but Hickey left. He had no recollection of returning to Miss Whitman's apartment that evening, did not know when Porter stopped working that night, did not see Miss Whitman again that evening, and had no recollection of seeing Porter leave. The following morning Hickey took Porter again to Miss Whitman's apartment around 8 A.M. He looked at the painting which had been done in the kitchen, did not see Miss Whitman in the apartment and Hickey left. Although he saw Miss Whitman downstairs in the lobby around 3:30 P.M. on the afternoon of July 12, 1952, Hickey did not remember about going to the apartment during the day, did not see Porter leave the building at any time that day, had no knowledge when Porter quit working on Saturday, did not know whether anyone else was working in the apartment with Porter, but certainly paid no one else for doing so, and did not at any time on Saturday send anyone to the apartment to see Porter. Hickey next saw Porter in the basement of the apartment Sunday around mid-day, when he again admitted Porter to Miss Whitman's apartment. Although Hickey visited the apartment two or three or four times Sunday afternoon, and at no time saw Miss Whitman there, he made no inquiry as to her whereabouts. Although he testified in his deposition he had given Porter no keys to Miss Whitman's apartment, he was examined by appellant's counsel concerning his testimony at the coroner's inquest on July 15, 1952, as follows:

"Q. And then were you asked this question, following those that I have just asked you:

" 'Q. At any time had you given Mr. Porter the key to this apartment?'

"And didn't you answer: 'I maybe gave it to him Saturday morning. I am not sure, sir, that I did. I can't think of any reason why I should.' "Were you asked that question and did you make that answer?

"A. Well, whatever is there, sir, is the answers I made to it."

When ruling on appellees' motion for directed verdict the trial judge said:

"Unless the employer is put upon notice by some fact which would cause him to make an inquiry as to the mentality, mental health or habits of the proposed employee, then, in the Court's opinion, no burden rests upon a proposed employer to make an examination as to such phases of the proposed employee's life, habits and activities."

After further recapitulation of various aspects of the problem, the trial judge said:

"Now, the question arises under that state of facts, standing alone, is it incumbent upon the defendant in order to discharge his obligation, to free himself from negligence, to make an independent inquiry *as to the sanity* of the individual who later is shown to have been a person of unsound mind? * * *" (Emphasis added.)

It is true that appellant's complaint had alleged that Porter "was then and there a person of unsound mind and dangerous and irresponsible," but the question was not as narrowly to be stated as the trial judge put it. It was not merely that the defendants might be called upon "to make an independent inquiry as to the sanity of the individual who later is shown to have been a person of unsound mind. * * *" The allegation upon which the plaintiff's case must rest, taken as a whole, charges that the appellees negligently employed Porter, that they negligently provided him with a key to Miss Whitman's apartment, and that they "negligently allowed him to go in and out of and remain in the said apartment without proper supervision or proper control." As is to be deduced from the evidence previously summarized, it was not simply a matter of whether or not Porter was insane. It *was* a matter of whether or not, *in the absence of any investigation whatever*, any man, Porter or anyone else, sane or insane, should have been employed as here, or without any supervision whatever, or the attempted exercise of any control over his conduct, should have been permitted by the landlord to have access to the apartment of this woman tenant, living alone and unprotected. This was the gravamen of the case.

A reading of the entire record discloses a repeated series of colloquies between counsel and trial judge concerning Porter's insanity and the appellees' knowledge thereof. Seemingly overlooked was the alleged negligence of the appellees. If a reasonable investigation had been made as to Porter's background which disclosed no basis for a conclusion of lack of competency, if he had been sufficiently long employed to have established himself as entitled to trust, if the landlord or the tenants had had adequate opportunity to scrutinize him and his conduct and had found a basis upon which confidence could be reposed in him, and if, thereafter, he had suddenly gone berserk, a jury, we may suppose, would scarcely have deemed the landlord liable. But that is not this case. Here the appellees exercised no care whatever, either in the selection of Porter or the workers hired with him or at his instance. The latter were assigned to paint the apartments of people who were away. But Porter was assigned to after-hours employment, without supervision, in the apartment of a tenant living alone. No one asked where he had last been employed as a basis for a check on his work performance. No one so much as telephoned to his commanding officer to ascertain what information he would be able to supply. No one called his wife. Although he was not even a resident of Washington, no one asked that he produce references or recommendations. In such failure to act, in almost purposeful refusal to find out anything about the man, and thereafter in the failure to supervise this stranger, lay the basis for the claimed breach of duty by the appellees. Appellees knew full well, or are charged with knowing, that no reasonable steps had been taken with reference to the employment of Porter, and thus that a risk was created, the extent of which depended upon the circumstances of the employment which followed. Slight care might be expected as to the employment of a yard man, not ordinarily to be sent into a tenant's apartment. But a very different series of steps are justified if an employee is to be sent, after hours, to work for protracted periods in the apartment of a young woman tenant, living alone.

Much of what has been said applies equally to another aspect of the case. Here Miss Whitman had two locks on her door, an upper and a lower lock, working independently of each other. The locks were obviously for the protection of the tenant, living alone, that she might be as secure against intruders as reasonable precautions made possible. She had a lease pursuant to which she paid for shelter and protection. She had one set of keys for herself; another set was retained by the landlord. She was entitled to assume that appellees would introduce no intruder into her apartment. She had a right to expect that the landlord would not give up his set of keys to a stranger or so negligently fail to guard them that they might fall into the hands of one bent on mischief. Miss Whitman had no voice in the selection of the landlord's employee. She was entitled to assume that appellees would assign no person without supervision to work after hours in her apartment, when they had failed to exercise any care in ascertaining the trustworthiness of such person. Here, however, appellant claims, in breach of their clear duty to their tenant, appellees sent Porter to work after hours. The only instructions given to Porter and Prince were that Hickey "would have no drinking at any time or any visiting in apartments, I told them that. Of course, with Prince I knew there wouldn't be because he was a colored man."

To say that appellees may fail to make even the most cursory inquiry concerning Porter and then be allowed to excuse themselves in their ignorance is to say that their recklessness will be exalted. A premium thus would be placed even upon a wilful refusal to make an elementary inquiry into the habits and tendencies and work experience of employees of landlords who choose to disregard the possibilities of harm to a trusting woman, living alone where she had a right to expect inviolability of her person, even more than her property, at the hands of an unknown stranger brought there by her landlord. In this compact land area of only 60 square miles known as the District of Columbia, more than 828,000 people dwell. Thousands of them are government women employees, like Miss Whitman, living, often alone, in small apartments where they have a right to think they are not to be molested as a result of the reckless ignorance of their landlords in the selection of apartment employees.

We have never said that a landlord may, with impunity, disregard elemental precautions and make no inquiry whatever concerning an employee who is to work in his apartments or, without supervision to be sent to accomplish the landlord's objectives, into the leased premises of an unprotected tenant, living alone. Here, the jury could have found there was no care whatever in either respect. Accordingly, on this aspect of the case, the appellant made out, at the very least, a prima facie case of negligence. Thus, it was error for the trial judge to direct a verdict for the appellees.

Whatever the law may be elsewhere, in the District of Columbia, to govern the usual complex of human relationships, we apply the standard of ordinary care. Thus, *particular* conduct, *depending upon circumstances*, can raise an issue for the jury to decide in terms of negligence and proximate cause.

Appellee cites such cases as Bradley v. Stevens and Longo v. Tabasso and similar cases involving business invitees, but our Municipal Court of Appeals, correctly recognizing the policy of this Circuit observed in Fleming v. Bronfin:

> "* * * [W]e think there was a clear duty on defendants to use reasonable care in the selection of a delivery man. The duties of such employee carried him into homes where likely there would be women and children alone and unprotected and it was defendants' duty to use reasonable care to select one reasonably fit to perform such duties."

The court recited a series of facts from which it was unanimously concluded that a reasonable inquiry had been made as to the suitability of the employee before he was hired. In Argonne Apartment House Co. v. Garrison the treasurer of the apartment house company interviewed one Johnson as well as other prospective employees and required them to exhibit written references. Johnson furnished at least two or three such references which were written on business letterheads and which appeared to the company treasurer to be satisfactory. Johnson was put to work under the observation of the resident manager who, after some four or five days, assigned Johnson to be helper to the electrician, one Jackson. We there pointed out: "It cannot be inferred or assumed that these recommendations were not bona fide or that they were bogus." Recognizing fully the duty of the owner of the apartment house to exercise reasonable care in the employment of his employee, the court nonetheless concluded that "there was no proof of negligence on the part of the defendant in employing Johnson * * *." In that case the tenant had asked the apartment manager to install an electric socket in her bedroom. Jackson, an old and trusted employee of the defendant whom the plaintiff had often seen around the apartment and knew to be trustworthy, brought with him the new employee Johnson, and after getting him started on the work, left the apartment. A guest of the tenant had left jewelry on top of a bureau near where the employee was working. Johnson stole the jewelry. Yet other valuable jewelry in unlocked drawers was untouched. Our records show that the appellant there urged us to rule that the plaintiff had been guilty of contributory negligence. It was argued that, had she not exposed her jewelry to an obvious peril when she left it in full view of a strange colored man, it would not have been touched. Appellee here urges upon us as controlling, a dictum to be found in the Argonne case which reads: "There was no evidence to show that a further investigation would have disclosed sufficient facts to put the defendant on notice as to the dishonesty of Johnson." The fact had been developed that Johnson, some four years earlier, had been convicted of intoxication. The dictum must be understood to mean that a conviction of intoxication does not suggest that a person so convicted was dishonest. We continued: "* * * even though the employer had knowledge that an employee had been convicted of such a charge, that would not in itself put the employer on notice as to the dishonesty of such employee." In any event, in the instant case the evidence is uncontradicted that the appellees made no investigation whatever. As we have already remarked, *particular conduct*, depending upon circumstances, gives rise to the duty, just as in Medes v. Hornbach where we said:

> "It is the duty in general of one operating a garage in which automobiles are kept in storage for pay to exercise ordinary care by the employment of trustworthy servants and otherwise for the safe-keeping of the cars in his charge."

We have heretofore made clear as to apartment houses, the reasons which underlie the landlord's duty under modern conditions and which, as to various hazards, call for at least "reasonable or ordinary care, which means reasonably safe conduct, but there is no sufficient reason for requiring less." True, the landlord does not become a guarantor of the safety of his tenant. But, if he knows, or in the exercise of ordinary care ought to know, of a possibly dangerous situation and fails to take such steps as an ordinarily prudent person, in view of existing circumstances, would have exercised to avoid injury to his tenant, he may be liable. So if he negligently takes such steps as he did take, he may be liable. "The landlord was * * * under a duty not to *create* an unsafe condition in the premises either permanent or temporary by any *affirmative* action on his part." (Emphasis supplied.) Thus, the landlord would be liable if Miss Whitman without fault on her part, had met her death due to the fault of Porter: by electrocution as, if without notice to Miss Whitman, he had left the light switch open and exposed; by suffering a fractured skull, due to plaster falling from the ceiling defectively loosened through means adopted by Porter; by suffering a fractured skull because without knowledge to Miss Whitman a window had been left in such condition, with window chains out of the pulleys, that it fell on her as she tried to close the window; or by breaking her neck because Porter's ladders had negligently been so placed as to occasion her fall.

In short, in the usual landlord-tenant relationships, under the circumstances supposed, the landlord's liability may be established.

> "Independent of the ordinary legal relations of landlord and tenant, the former owes a duty to the latter that is imposed by a general principle of the common law. He must neither misrepresent the condition of the premises, nor conceal from the tenant knowledge of defects attended with danger to the occupants. Where he has knowledge of such defects which are not open to the observation of his lessee, it is his duty to reveal them in order that the latter may be able to guard against injury from them."

Here, Miss Whitman had no knowledge of the negligent circumstances attendant upon the selection of Porter. Certainly such circumstances were not open to her observation, and she clearly had a right to assume that the landlord neither would create a risk nor expose her to possible danger through his introduction into her apartment of the man Porter.

. . . .

Reversed.

DISCUSSION

In this case a tenant was strangled to death by an employee of the landlord. What is the main issue? Is it whether the landlord had a duty to exercise reasonable care in the selection of his employee? In the preceding case, *Levine v. Katz*, the court raised the question whether a duty existed, but this case starts from the premise that a duty exists. Therefore, the court is looking to determine something other than the existence of a duty. The court does explore in detail several of the facts surrounding the strangulation almost as if to determine whether reasonable care itself has been exercised, but this determination is traditionally within the province of the jury to decide as a question of fact (leaving the court to decide questions of law such as whether a duty exists). Then is this court usurping the function of the jury?

To understand what the court is doing, it is important to know a little procedure. An appellate court cannot sit as a factfinder to determine the merits of a case, but it can review the evidence in the record to determine whether the trial judge had sufficient grounds to remove the case from the jury's consideration by directing a verdict for the defendant. A "directed verdict" is "[a] judgment entered on the order of a trial judge who takes over the factfinding role of the jury because the evidence is so compelling that only one decision can reasonably follow or because it fails to establish a prima facie case."[5]A "prima facie case" is defined as "[a] party's production of enough evidence to allow the fact-trier to infer the fact at issue and rule in the party's favor."[6]Therefore, the appellate court is examining the facts in this case, not to make a determination whether the landlord satisfied his duty of due care, but rather whether, contrary to the finding of the court below, there was sufficient evidence to make a prima facie case of negligence that should go to the jury for their consideration. The court determined that there was a prima facie case and reversed the judgment of the court below.

Why did the lower court direct the verdict in the first place? The quoted sections of the trial judge's ruling indicate that the judge felt that no inquiry by a landlord concerning an employee was necessary unless he was "put upon notice by some fact which would cause him to make an inquiry." The appellate court disagreed with the trial court over what was "reasonable" here and found that, in the particular circumstances of this case, the conduct of the landlord raised a prima facie case of negligence. Therefore, it would be up to the landlord to provide sufficient evidence to convince a jury to the contrary if liability was to be avoided.

The issue for the court was to define the meaning of "reasonable inquiry." In so doing, the court was addressing an issue of law (what is the standard of due care required of the landlord) with a detailed exposition of the facts in order to define it. It was important in this case, as opposed to the previous one, to lay out the facts in detail. These facts helped define the requirements of the standard of due care which the landlord had to follow to protect a tenant. We may start the brief with this in mind, i.e., that the trial court and the appellate court were not in disagreement over the issue whether a duty existed, but rather over the issue of how that duty was defined.

Kendall v. Gore Properties, Inc.
236 F.2d 673 (D.C. Cir. 1956)

FACTS:	Wrongful death action. T was strangled by employee (E) of landlord (L) who is being sued by administratrix (A) of T's estate. At the close of appellant's (A's) case, trial court directed verdict for appellees (L).
	T was single, female, living alone in apartment. L hired E, without any investigation or inquiry, on the street in fatigues and cleaning brushes at the time. L assigned E to paint T's apartment and left him alone there after hours for long periods of time with practically no supervision and possibly with a key. E turned out to be insane and dangerous.
	Trial court's ruling: No burden on employer to investigate employee unless put on notice by some fact which would cause him to make an inquiry, and, under the facts, L did not have to inquire about sanity of E. Appellate court's decision: reversed. It was error for trial judge to direct a verdict.
ISSUE:	What is the standard of care that L must follow in order to satisfy his duty of protection for T? (Negligence means failure to satisfy duty of care.)
HOLDING:	Amount of care depends on risk created for T by employment of E. (Slight care may be expected for employment of yard man. This is dictum.)

---

[5] Black's Law Dictionary 1555 (7th ed. 1999).

[6] Black's Law Dictionary 1228 (8th ed. 2004).

<table>
<tbody>
<tr>
<td></td>
<td>Ordinary care is required for employment of interior painter for single woman's apartment after hours and for long periods of time. No care existed here where there was no investigation and no supervision or attempted exercise of control over E's conduct. Facts show prima facie evidence of negligence.</td>
</tr>
<tr>
<td>RATIONALE:</td>
<td>Authority for duty of care by employer in selection of employees: Fleming (delivery man) and Medes (garage man). Argonne distinguished: Investigation and observation of employee made in that case, and further investigation may not have disclosed potential dishonesty of employee who stole jewelry. Analogy to L's duty not to create an unsafe condition by affirmative action: e.g., electrocution through leaving wires exposed, injury from falling plaster defectively loosened by L's E, etc. Analogy to the duty of L to inform T of latent defects (here no knowledge by T of negligent circumstances in selection of E).</td>
</tr>
</tbody>
</table>

The next case raises the question whether a landlord has a duty to provide protection from the acts of third parties who are strangers to the landlord. No brief is provided for the *Goldberg* case. Brief the case on your own and be prepared to discuss it in class.

GOLDBERG v. HOUSING AUTHORITY OF THE CITY OF NEWARK
38 N.J. 578, 186 A.2d 291 (1962)

WEINTRAUB, C.J. While delivering milk to a tenant at defendant's housing project, plaintiff was beaten and robbed by two men. The attack occurred at about 1:30 P.M. in a self-service passenger elevator. Whether the assailants were tenants, guests of tenants, or intruders, is not known. The jury found for plaintiff and the Appellate Division affirmed. We granted certification.

Plaintiff prevailed upon the single thesis that defendant had a duty to provide police protection.

Defendant is a public corporation created by the City of Newark under the Local Housing Authorities Law. It developed a number of projects. The one here involved embraces 19.15 acres, with 10 apartment houses, each of 12 stories, offering accommodations for 1,458 families. The residents at the time here involved numbered between 5,300 and 6,000. The Appellate Division said:

> "We hold that defendant, since it created and maintained a housing project which, because of its size, physical composition and method of operation, was beyond the pale of regular municipal police surveillance, and yet because of these same factors was susceptible to criminal activities, was under a duty to provide such protection in the Hayes project as was necessary under the circumstances, and that a question of fact was presented for jury consideration as to whether the provisions made by defendant for private police guards were adequate. As to whether defendant's dereliction, if any, was the proximate cause of plaintiff's injuries and the damage he suffered, again it was for the jury to decide from the evidence whether the assault and robbery was a result of defendant's negligence. Plaintiff was not required to prove that the assault and robbery would not have taken place had defendant supplied additional protection. It is axiomatic that better policing would have acted as a deterrent."

. . . .

I

The question whether a private party must provide protection for another is not solved merely by recourse to "forseeability." Everyone can foresee the commission of crime virtually anywhere and at any time. If foreseeability itself gave rise to a duty to provide "police" protection for others, every residential curtilage, every shop, every store, every manufacturing plant would have to be patrolled by the private arms of the owner. And since hijacking and attack upon occupants of motor vehicles are also foreseeable, it would be the duty of every motorist to provide armed protection for his passengers and the property of others. Of course, none of this is at all palatable.

The question is not simply whether a criminal event is foreseeable, but whether a *duty* exists to take measures to guard against it. Whether a *duty* exists is ultimately a question of fairness. The inquiry involves a weighing of the relationship of the parties, the nature of the risk, and the public interest in the proposed solution.

We are not aware of any decision which even approaches the result reached below. A brief review of the cases to which our attention has been drawn reveals they involved different risks or different relationships.

Common carriers have a duty to use a high degree of care to protect the persons of their patrons. [Cases cited with holdings.] In each of these cases the hazard was specific, localized, and known to the defendant.

Another group of cases relates to the duty of the proprietor of a business operation open to the public to protect his guest from the predictable behavior of other guests.

[Cases cited with holdings.]

In the following cases a triable issue was found with respect to criminal assaults but in each the basis of liability is foreign to the case before us. [Cases cited with holdings.]

Finally we come to a group of cases dealing with responsibility of the owner of housing projects. In *Da Rocha v. New York City Housing Authority*, defendant, in a play area it provided, turned on a water outlet for the refreshment of children on a hot day, thereby attracting a large number who ran in and out of the spray. A child was struck by a cyclist, riding in violation of a posted regulation. Liability was grounded upon defendant's failure to enforce its own rules and failure to protect children in an activity it set in motion. In *Geigel v. New York City Housing Authority*, children laid out a baseball diamond utilizing the regular walks upon which they painted bases. Defendant, knowing this, did nothing to remove the bases or to stop the practice. A child using the walk was injured by a player. The court found defendant's failure in the circumstances constituted an invitation to ball games, an activity dangerous to others in that specific setting. In *Hansen v. New York City Housing Authority*, a child was struck by a swing on a playground provided by defendant. The court left open the question whether defendant had a duty to supervise the playground, but found a triable question of fact with respect to the physical conditions. Finally, in *Kendall v. Gore Properties*, a tenant was strangled by an insane employee of the landlord. The basis of liability was not a failure to provide police protection but rather negligence in hiring an unknown, without investigation or references, and sending him on the first day of employment to paint after hours in the apartment of a woman who lived alone.

The duty to provide police protection is foreign to the history of the landlord-tenant relationship. By the common law there was neither an implied covenant by the landlord of the fitness of the premises for the intended use nor responsibility in him to maintain the leased premises. With respect to the common areas in his control, his duty was to keep them in a reasonably safe condition. The landlord's obligation was indirectly affected by building codes and was modified by legislation relating to tenement houses.

Subject to modifying legislation, a landlord offers to lease accommodations which a prospective tenant may take or not as he chooses. The landlord may offer sundry services, which of course will be reflected in the rental charge, but in the absence of statute, there is no duty to furnish them. Thus a landlord may offer to provide a doorman during the day or around the clock, but he need not, and we know that such services are available only in the more luxurious apartment houses, beyond the reach of the average citizen. The sole statutory mandate with respect to attending personnel appears to be R.S. 55:6-13 of the Tenement House Act, which provides that if there are more than six families, "there shall be a janitor, housekeeper or other responsible person, who shall reside in said house, and who shall have charge of the same, if the board shall so require."

There are cases dealing with the liability of a landlord for theft of property of his tenants. Liability may exist if there is a failure to secure such property placed within the control of the landlord. And the landlord may be liable for theft if he carelessly enables a thief to gain entrance to the apartment of the tenant. But no case holds a landlord is under a duty to provide police protection.

II

We come then to the question whether as an original proposition the owner of multi-family structures should have the duty to provide police protection. As we have said, the question is one of fairness in the light of the nature of the relationship, the nature of the hazard, and the impact of such a duty on the public interest. We think the duty should not be imposed, for a number of reasons.

The first reason is that we should not find the owner of property is liable for not furnishing police protection to deter invading criminals unless we also find he has the right to provide a police force to that end. We do not see how we can find that right in view of the statutes which vest in government the power to constitute police forces, with certain exceptions, referred to above, which do not include the owner of residential property. But if the statutes were not in the way, we would nonetheless find a barrier in the public welfare. The police function is highly specialized, involving skills and training which government alone can provide. There is no room for the private devices of the frontier days. The proper approach is to state, if there be any doubt upon the subject, the duty of the constituted police forces to move wherever they need to go, not only to detect crime but also to prevent it.

This is not to say that a private person may shut his eyes to the fact of crime and indulge in conduct which aids or invites it. So a bailee of an automobile who leaves the car on a public street with motor running or key in the switch may indeed be liable to the owner if the vehicle is stolen. But it is something else to say that if he turns off the motor and removes the key, he must provide police protection for the vehicle because it may nonetheless be stolen.

The second consideration is the inevitable vagueness of the proposed duty. Fairness ordinarily requires that a man be able to ascertain in advance of a jury's verdict whether the duty is his and whether he has performed it. To which multi-family houses would the duty apply? Would it depend upon the number of tenancies? If so, can we now fix the number? And if the duty springs from a combination of tenancies and prior unlawful events, what kind of offenses will suffice, and in what number, and will crimes next door or around the corner or in the neighborhood, raise the obligation? And if a prescient owner concludes the duty is his, what measures will discharge it? It is an easy matter to know whether a stairway is defective and what repairs will put it in order. Again, it is fairly simple to decide how many ushers or guards suffice at a skating rink or a railroad platform to deal with the crush of a crowd and the risks of unintentional injury which the nature of the business creates, but how can one know what measures will protect against the thug, the narcotic addict. the degenerate, the psychopath and the psychotic? Must the owner prevent *all* crime? We doubt that any police force in the friendliest community has achieved that end. How then can the owner know what is enough to protect the tenants in their persons and property? (We add parenthetically that if the duty were found, there would be no rational basis to confine liability to crimes committed in a common hallway as distinguished from the tenant's apartment.) Here, a city policeman patrolled the interior walks from 8 A.M. to 4 P.M. and in addition two maintenance men were assigned to each building during that period. From 4 P.M. to 8 A.M. there were three special policemen working in shifts, and the record indicates the incidents of unlawful conduct were more numerous then than in the daytime. We assume that advocates of liability do not intend an absolute obligation to prevent all crime, but rather have in mind some unarticulated level of effectiveness short of that goal. Whatever may be that degree of safety, is there any standard of performance to which the owner may look for guidance? We know of none, and the record does not suggest one, and we are at a loss to understand what standard the jurors here employed. The charge to the jury was unrevealing; it simply left to 12 men and women the task of deciding whether a prudent owner would have done more, and whether, if defendant had, the robbers here would likely have been deterred. That of course was also the view of the Appellate Division.

Not only would there be uncertainty as to *when* the duty to furnish police protection arises and as to *what* measures will discharge the duty, there would also be exceptional uncertainty with respect to the issue of causation. This is so because of the extraordinary speculation inherent in the subject of deterrence of men bent upon criminal ventures. It would be quite a guessing game to determine whether some unknown thug of unknowable character and mentality would have been deterred if the owner had furnished some or some additional policemen. It must be remembered that police protection does not, and cannot, provide assurance against all criminal attacks, and so the topic presupposes that inevitably crimes will be committed notwithstanding the sufficiency of the force. Hence the question of proximate cause is bound to be of exceptional difficulty.

Thus vagueness would here be conspicuous in all facets of the issue of negligence and causation. Perhaps this is one of the considerations which underlie the refusal in New York, where sovereign immunity was withdrawn by statute, to permit actions against a municipality for negligent failure to provide police protection, as distinguished, for example, from the failure to provide a bodyguard for an individual who, because of his aid to law enforcement, is threatened with criminal retaliation.

Finally, we should not let our understandable concern for the unfortunate plaintiff obscure the fact that the burden of this duty would fall upon citizens who can hardly afford it. We are not dealing with a risk which can be passed along in an increase in liability insurance premiums. We are talking of the employment of men, perhaps the employment, if something like effective assurance is to be realized, of doormen around the clock to cover each of the entrances to the buildings, here a total of 20 entrances. If the owner must provide that service, every insurance carrier will insist that he do it. The bill will be paid, not by the owner, but by the tenants. And if, as we apprehend, the incidence of crime is greatest in the areas in which the poor must live, they, and they alone, will be singled out to pay for their own police protection. The burden should be upon the whole community and not upon the segment of the citizenry which is least able to bear it.

Hence we believe this most troublesome problem must be left with the duly constituted police forces. The job is theirs to prevent crime and to go wherever need be to that end. It may well be that the owner of multi-family housing may refuse to permit patrol of the common areas by the public police, and if the owner should thus assert his property right, it would indeed be appropriate to visit upon him the losses sustained by those to whom he denied the protection the public authorities were willing to provide. But the duty to provide police protection is and should remain the duty of government and not of the owner of a housing project.

We do not mean that the owner may not seek authorization from appropriate public officials to provide further armed protection at his own cost. It may be in his interest to do so. That is a budgetary problem for him alone. It is for him to decide whether he can furnish such protection within the rental income he can obtain from his tenants, or, in the case of a public housing project, from such subsidy as the federal authorities may be able and willing to give. But it is something else to say that the owner *must* take such steps, indeed at the tenants' ultimate cost, on the pain of liability for damages.

The judgments of the Appellate Division and of the trial court are accordingly reversed.

JACOBS, J., joined by PROCTOR and SCHETTINO, JJ. (dissenting). . . .

. . . .

At the trial the plaintiff introduced evidence indicating that during the course of 1957 and prior to the assault upon him, the defendant had received many reports from its special policemen of crimes and acts of violence at the Hayes project; some of these reports related to daytime occurrences and many more bore on nighttime events. The daytime occurrences included several incidents involving armed intruders in parking lots at the project, a mugging in a hallway of a residential building, the arrest of a hallway loiterer who offered forceful resistance, and the molesting of a girl in the elevator of one of the residential buildings. A former special policeman at the Hayes project testified that during many monthly meetings prior to December 24, 1957 he had discussed the need for additional policing with Mr. Bland, who was employed by the defendant as manager of the Hayes project, and that he had recommended the employment of a special policeman for assignment between the hours of 8:00 A.M. and 4:00 P.M. In his testimony when called as a witness for the defendant, Mr. Bland acknowledged that he, in turn, had recommended to the defendant at or prior to December 1957 that another special policeman be employed at the project.

. . . .

In its attack on the action of the Appellate Division, the defendant relied primarily on its position that it was under no duty to furnish any special "police protection" to guard against assaults. It did not deny that, as landlord. it retained possession and control of the hallways, elevators, and other common facilities, and owed a duty to keep them in reasonably safe condition. It contended, however, that that duty related to the safety of the physical structure and did not extend to the furnishing of protection against crimes. [I]t relied on its stated proposition that "generally a property owner is not obliged to anticipate and guard against the criminal acts of others." Assuming that to be so, courts have nonetheless repeatedly held that where there are special conditions from which the owner or operator of the premises should recognize and foresee an unreasonable risk or likelihood of harm or danger to invitees from criminal or wrongful acts of others, he must take reasonable precautions which may, under the circumstances, fairly and justly entail the employment of special guards or police.

[Precedents cited and discussed.]

It must be borne in mind that in the instant matter the court is not at all concerned with the ordinary private multi-dwelling or apartment house. There the owner's customary reliance on the measure of protection afforded by the public police force against criminal acts by intruders may perhaps be viewed, as a matter of law, as not unreasonable in relation to the nature of the risk involved. Here, the court is concerned with a special situation in which the defendant has built a high-rise multi-unit housing project which, by virtue of its size, composition and mode of operation, presents special dangers requiring special precautions. Such patrol and surveillance activities as were engaged in by the Newark police officers were confined strictly to the streets and walks. They were not permitted to enter the buildings and the Housing Authority relied entirely on its own employees for supervision in the buildings. It engaged special policemen between the hours of 4:00 P.M. and 8:00 A.M. but decided, for obscure reasons of its own, not to engage any special policemen between the daytime hours of 8:00 A.M. and 4:00 P.M. It took no action to alter its decision, notwithstanding specific recommendations from one of its special officers and its project manager at Hayes, notwithstanding its awareness of the daytime crimes and acts of violence at Hayes, and notwithstanding the repeated expressions by individual housing commissioners of the need for additional policing at Hayes and elsewhere. Nor did it take any action to alter its policy of permitting the entrances to the residential buildings at Hayes to remain always unlocked and unattended. Indeed, the record indicates that, though the daytime special dangers were evident, the defendant took no special precautions at all with respect to them. Under the circumstances it seems clear to me that a jury could readily find, that a reasonably prudent person, situated as was the defendant, would have foreseen and recognized an unreasonable risk or likelihood of harm or danger to invitees such as the plaintiff, from criminal or wrongful acts of others, and would have taken reasonable protective precautions through the enlargement of its own special police force or in other appropriate manner.

The defendant has advanced the contention that, assuming dereliction of duty on its part in failing to take precautions such as the employment of a daytime special policeman, there is nothing to indicate that his presence would have prevented the assault. It is, of course, true that no one knows for certain what the effect of a daytime policeman would have been; nor does anyone know whether the employment of additional guards would have prevented the injuries in *Crammer, Geigel*, or in the many other cases where recovery was allowed. Nevertheless, it is likely that the daytime policeman would have served as a deterrent and it could reasonably be found that his absence was, in a legal sense, the proximate cause of the plaintiff's injuries. In the *Lee* case, a spectator at a ball game was injured when other spectators stampeded to recover a foul ball. The plaintiff recovered a judgment for money damages against the ball club and this was sustained by the Supreme Court of Wisconsin in an opinion which held that the jury was properly permitted to find that the defendant was negligent in failing to have an usher at his assigned position in the area. In response to the defendant's contention that even the presence of the usher would not have prevented the injury, the court pointed out that the jury could reasonably have inferred that the usher's presence "might have been effective" and that his absence constituted a "substantial factor" in the ultimate event. A comparably broad approach may be found in recent cases in New Jersey where the court held that it is sufficient if the defendant's negligence constituted a substantial factor in the occurrence; within wide outer limits, the issue of proximate cause is justly left to the jury.

The cited precedents overwhelmingly support the plaintiff's cause of action. They may, of course, be differentiated factually since none of them involved a negligence action for injuries suffered in the elevator of a Newark housing project. But they may not be differentiated legally since all of them involved soundly grounded principles which are patently applicable; indeed, most of them involved circumstances far less compelling than those presented here. High-rise housing projects have brought with them problems which have caused serious concern throughout the nation. Jane Jacobs has referred specially to the dangers of violence in corridors and elevators of the projects and has suggested that the reasonably safe way of dealing with them is to provide full-time attendants; and others have suggested the possibility of suitable alarm or "video guard" systems. When an act of violence occurred recently at a New York City housing project, locks were changed and additional private guards were engaged. Here the Newark Housing Authority had recognized some dangers and the need for taking precautions by engaging special policemen who were presumably employed in accordance with *N.J.S.A.* 40:47–19 and the Civil Service specifications relating to housing guards. But it neglected to engage any for assignment during the daytime hours or to take any other suitable precautions though it was fully aware of the serious daytime as well as nighttime dangers. That this amounts to actionable negligence finds ample support not only in the precedents but also in the strong underlying considerations of fairness and justice.

The defendant's duty was to take reasonable precautions; that duty was no more vague than is the test of reasonableness throughout our law generally. In *Nash v. United States*, Justice Holmes noted that even in the field of criminal law a test comparable to reasonableness may be applied without infringing any principles of fairness or due process. Similarly in *United States v. Ragen*, the Supreme Court, through Justice Black, pointed out that the fact that a penal statute is so framed as to require a jury to determine the question of reasonableness "is not sufficient to make it too vague to afford a practical guide to permissible conduct." Here there was no issue as to how many daytime guards would have been sufficient. The fact was that the defendant failed to engage even a single daytime guard or to take any other protective precautions insofar as daytime dangers were concerned. When the very serious nature of the dangers is considered, the cost of a daytime guard or other reasonable precaution fades into insignificance. Any suggestion that the defendant may fairly be entitled to an immunity because of the high-minded purposes of its facilities is readily dissipated by reference to judicial opinions such as *Collopy v. Newark Eye and Ear Infirmary*, where the court set forth fully the compelling reasons for discarding the common law immunity of charitable institutions. Furthermore, the pertinent legislation itself may properly be said to have rejected any notion that the Housing Authority was to be immunized from ordinary tort responsibility.

. . . .

After a full trial which was free of any prejudicial error, the jury found that the defendant had acted unreasonably in failing to take protective precautions despite notice of the serious dangers and that it should compensate the plaintiff for his resulting injury. Its verdict was firmly based on the evidence and on established principles of negligence law and the record presents no rational ground for upsetting it. Indeed, as I view the matter, the upsetting of the verdict not only operates unjustly to the plaintiff but also disserves the strong policy considerations which dictate that, in the maintenance and operation of its project, the defendant be placed under the traditional duty of due care and be justly accountable to those injured as the result of its breach. I vote to affirm.

For reversal — Chief Justice WEINTRAUB, and Justices FRANCIS, HALL and HANEMAN — 4.

For affirmance — Justices JACOBS, PROCTOR and SCHETTINO — 3.

ASSIGNMENT 2
Answering Questions: Examples in Contract Law

Read the following three cases and brief them. A thorough knowledge of each case, obtained by doing the brief, will provide the requisite foundation to respond effectively to questions in class. Questions are then provided at the end of the cases to give a sample of what may be asked in class. Responses are provided for some of the questions and hints at responses to others. These questions are basic inquiries concerning the cases themselves and their effects. The next assignment will continue to look at these questions and then move beyond this direct case analysis into questions raised by a synthesis of the material in the first two assignments.

PINES v. PERSSION
111 N.W.2d 409 (1961)

Action by plaintiffs Burton Pines, Gary Weissman, David Klingenstein, and William Eaglestein, lessees, against defendant Leon Perssion, lessor, to recover the sum of $699.99, which was deposited by plaintiffs with defendant for the fulfilment of a lease, plus the sum of $137.76 for the labor plaintiffs performed on the leased premises. After a trial to the court, findings of fact and conclusions of law were filed which determined that plaintiffs could recover the lease deposit plus $62 for their labor, but less one month's rent of $175. From a judgment to this effect defendant appeals. Plaintiffs have filed a motion for review of that part of the judgment entitling defendant to withhold the sum of $175.

At the time this action was commenced the plaintiffs were students at the University of Wisconsin in Madison. Defendant was engaged in the business of real-estate development and ownership. During the 1958–1959 school year plaintiffs were tenants of the defendant in a student rooming house. In May of 1959 they asked the defendant if he had a house they could rent for the 1959–1960 school year. Defendant told them he was thinking of buying a house on the east side of Madison which they might be interested in renting. This was the house involved in the lease and is located at 1144 East Johnson Street. The house had in fact been owned and lived in by the defendant since 1951, but he testified he misstated the facts because he was embarrassed about its condition.

Three of the plaintiffs looked at the house in June, 1959, and found it in a filthy condition. Pines testified the defendant stated he would clean and fix up the house, paint it, provide the necessary furnishings, and have the house in suitable condition by the start of the school year in the fall. Defendant testified he told plaintiffs he would not do any work on the house until he received a signed lease and a deposit. Pines denied this.

The parties agreed that defendant would lease the house to plaintiffs commencing September 1, 1959, at a monthly rental of $175 prorated over the first nine months of the lease term, or $233.33 per month for September through May. Defendant was to have a lease drawn and mail it to plaintiffs. It was to be signed by the plaintiffs' parents as guarantors and a deposit of three months' rent was to be made.

Defendant mailed the lease to Pines in Chicago in the latter part of July. Because the plaintiffs were scattered around the country, Pines had some difficulty in securing the necessary signatures. Pines and the defendant kept in touch by letter and telephone concerning the execution of the lease, and Pines came to Madison in August to see the defendant and the house. Pines testified the house was still in terrible condition and defendant again promised him it would be ready for occupancy on September 1st. Defendant testified he said he had to receive the lease and the deposit before he would do any work on the house, but Pines could not remember his making such a statement.

On August 28th Pines mailed defendant a check for $175 as his share of the deposit and on September 1st he sent the lease and the balance due. Defendant received the signed lease and the deposit about September 3rd.

Plaintiffs began arriving at the house about September 6th. It was still in a filthy condition and there was a lack of student furnishings. Plaintiffs began to clean the house themselves, providing some cleaning materials of their own, and did some painting with paint purchased by defendant. They became discouraged with their progress and contacted an attorney with reference to their status under the lease. The attorney advised them to request the Madison building department to inspect the premises. This was done on September 9th and several building-code violations were found. They included inadequate electrical wiring, kitchen sink and toilet in disrepair, furnace in disrepair, handrail on stairs in disrepair, screens on windows and doors lacking. The city inspector gave defendant until September 21st to correct the violations, and in the meantime plaintiffs were permitted to occupy the house. They vacated the premises on or about September 11th.

. . . .

The trial court concluded that defendant represented to the plaintiffs that the house would be in a habitable condition by September 1, 1959; it was not in such condition and could not be made so before October 1, 1959; that sec. 234.17, Stats., applied and under its provisions plaintiffs were entitled to surrender possession of the premises; that they were not liable for rent for the time subsequent to the surrender date, which was found to be September 30, 1959.

MARTIN, C.J. We have doubt that sec. 234.17, Stats., applies under the facts of this case. In our opinion, there was an implied warranty of habitability in the lease and that warranty was breached by the appellant.

There is no express provision in the lease that the house was to be in habitable condition by September 1st. We cannot agree with respondents' contention that the provision for "including furniture to furnish the said house suitable for student housing" constitutes an express covenant that the house would be in habitable condition. The phrase "suitable for student housing" refers to the "furniture" to be furnished and not to the general condition of the house.

Parol evidence is inadmissible to vary the terms of a written contract which is complete and unambiguous on its face.

The general rule is that there are no implied warranties to the effect that at the time a lease term commences the premises are in a tenantable condition or adapted to the purposes for which leased. A tenant is a purchaser of an estate in land, and is subject to the doctrine of *caveat emptor*. His remedy is to inspect the premises before taking them or to secure an express warranty. Thus, a tenant is not entitled to abandon the premises on the ground of uninhabitability.

There is an exception to this rule, some courts holding that there is an implied warranty of habitability and fitness of the premises where the subject of the lease is a furnished house. This is based on an intention inferred from the fact that under the circumstances the lessee does not have an adequate opportunity to inspect the premises at the time he accepts the lease. In the *Collins Case* the English court said:

> "Not only is the implied warranty on the letting of a furnished house one which, in my own view, springs by just and necessary implication from the contract, but it is a warranty which tends in the most-striking fashion to the public good and the preservation of public health. *It is a warranty to be extended rather than restricted.* [Emphasis supplied.]"

We have not previously considered this exception to the general rule. Obviously, however, the frame of reference in which the old common-law rule operated has changed.

Legislation and administrative rules, such as the safe place statute, building codes, and health regulations, all impose certain duties on a property owner with respect to the condition of his premises. Thus, the legislature has made a policy judgment — that it is socially (and politically) desirable to impose these duties on a property owner — which has rendered the old common-law rule obsolete. To follow the old rule of no implied warranty of habitability in leases would, in our opinion, be inconsistent with the current legislative policy concerning housing standards. The need and social desirability of adequate housing for people in this era of rapid population increases is too important to be rebuffed by that obnoxious legal cliché, *caveat emptor*. Permitting landlords to rent "tumble-down" houses is at least a contributing cause of such problems as urban blight, juvenile delinquency, and high property taxes for conscientious landowners.

There is no question in this case but that the house was not in a condition reasonably and decently fit for occupation when the lease term commenced. Appellant himself admitted it was "filthy," so much so that he lied about owning it in the first instance, and he testified that no cleaning or other work was done in the house before the boys moved in. The filth, of course, was seen by the respondents when they inspected the premises prior to signing the lease. They had no way of knowing, however, that the plumbing, heating, and wiring systems were defective. Moreover, on the testimony of the building inspector, it was unfit for occupancy, and:

> "The state law provides that if the building is not in immediate danger of collapse the owner may board it up so that people cannot enter the building. His second choice is to bring the building up to comply with the safety standards of the code. And his third choice is to tear it down."

The evidence clearly showed that the implied warranty of habitability was breached. Respondents' covenant to pay rent and appellant's covenant to provide a habitable house were mutually dependent, and thus a breach of the latter by appellant relieved respondents of any liability under the former.

Since there was a failure of consideration, respondents are absolved from any liability for rent under the lease and their only liability is for the reasonable rental value of the premises during the time of actual occupancy. That period of time was determined by the trial court in its finding No. 9, which is supported by the evidence. Granting respondents' motion for review, we direct the trial court to find what a reasonable rental for that period would be and enter judgment for the respondents in the amount of their deposit plus the amount recoverable for their labor, less the rent so determined by the court.

By the Court. — Cause remanded with instructions to enter judgment for the respondents consistent with this opinion.

QUESTIONS

1. Why did the oral statement by the landlord to the tenants not constitute an express covenant/warranty that the house would be in habitable condition?

The answer necessitates looking up the term "parol evidence." BLACK'S LAW DICTIONARY at 598 (8th ed. 2004) defines the term as "Evidence of oral statements." The term "parol-evidence rule" is also defined at p.1149:

> The common-law principle that a writing intended by the parties to be a final embodiment of their agreement cannot be modified by evidence of earlier or contemporaneous agreements that might add to, vary, or contradict the writing.
> • This rule usu. operates to prevent a party from introducing extrinsic evidence of negotiations that occurred before or while the agreement was being reduced to its final written form.

From this inquiry it is clear in the third paragraph of the decision that the parol evidence rule is used to exclude the landlord's statement from the contract.

2. The court mentions an exception to the *caveat emptor* rule: there is an implied warranty of habitability and fitness of the premises where the subject of the lease is a furnished house. Does the court use this exception to find that the landlord in this case had a duty under an implied warranty of habitability? If so, why does the court go into an extended discussion about social and political changes which make the old common law rule of *caveat emptor* obsolete?

The court appears to use the exception for a furnished house. (The house in this lease was supposed to be furnished.) The court states that they had "not previously considered this exception to the general rule." It was an exception appearing in England and other state jurisdictions. In adopting it in Wisconsin for the first time, the court felt obliged to justify its action through a discussion of the reasons in favor of adopting the exception: e.g., legislative and administrative rules in accord, need for adequate housing in an era of rapid population increases, etc.

The court may be reaching beyond the exception for a furnished house, however, in order to pave the way for a new general rule of implied warranty of habitability. This may account for the extended policy discussion in which the court does not mention the house furnishings.

3. Would it be desirable to extend the exception for a furnished house to a new general rule of implied warranty?

In *Green v. Superior Court of the City and County of San Francisco*, 10 Cal. 3d 616, 517 P.2d 1168 (1974), the California Supreme Court adopted such a rule. A subsequent article discussing the case had this to say:

> More particularly the issue can be framed in these terms: should a tenant who presumably knew of and accepted defects existing at the outset be allowed to use the implied warranty subsequently as a defense to eviction based on nonpayment of rent? The answer requires responses to several intermediate questions. What are the underlying purposes of the implied warranty doctrine pertinent to this issue? What troubling consequences might result from the doctrine's use, without modification, for premises defective at the inception of the tenancy? And how can one prevent such threatened consequences short of abandoning the doctrine altogether?
>
> Housing codes, and the public policy behind them, have played a vital role in developing the doctrine. Accordingly, they offer insight into the purposes underlying the implied warranty and supply the foundation for analyzing this issue. *Green* and the cases on which it relied based their adoption of the implied warranty doctrine partly on the fact that legislatures, in enacting housing codes, have expressed a public policy that certain housing standards must be maintained. Thus, reasoned the cases, giving tenants the implied warranty doctrine and its attendant remedies will encourage landlords to obey these housing standards. It follows that removing any dwelling units in violation of these standards from the scope of the doctrine would diminish the effectiveness of this purpose of the implied warranty doctrine. Therefore, the doctrine should apply to premises defective at the outset. Indeed, it should be noted that none of the out-of-state cases which adopted the implied warranty doctrine has held that the warranty does not apply to premises defective at the outset, and in fact several have held, expressly or impliedly, that it does so apply.
>
> In *Green*, however, although it was not required to (and in fact did not) rule directly on this issue, the court expressed some desire to limit the doctrine's application where premises are uninhabitable at the inception of the tenancy. The court's concern, it appears, is that allowing use of the doctrine in such circumstances might enable or even encourage scheming tenants to set up a landlord for rent withholding. In sidestepping the issue the court suggested that a lease executed under such conditions might be an illegal contract or, that the tenant might have assumed the risk of uninhabitable premises.
>
> The California Supreme Court's concern over the scheming tenant seems exaggerated. It would be a rare tenant who would combine all the attributes

which the court fears: the prerequisite evil motive, a need sufficiently great to warrant the legal and personal struggles which must result, and the knowledge, sophistication and skill necessary for successfully commencing and maintaining a rent withholding plan. Still, it is conceivable that the doctrine could be abused, as for instance where a tenant who can clearly afford decent housing deliberately seeks out substandard housing with a plan of later asserting the implied warranty doctrine to withhold rent or sue the landlord. Solutions for such abuses, superior to those suggested by the court, however, are available. The theories of estoppel and unclean hands, for example, seem better tailored to the court's concern than either illegal contract or assumption of risk. Using these equitable theories the court can remedy the abuses without depriving the great bulk of innocent tenants of the benefits of the doctrine.

The court's possible adoption of assumption of risk, as modifying the doctrine's application to premises defective at the outset, may in any event pose few problems for the typical tenant. Conceivably the court, on more thorough analysis, may find the assumption of risk theory inapplicable to this setting, since it would intrude on the two apparent purposes of the housing codes: to protect the tenant from his inability to protect himself through bargaining, and to protect the community from the social and health dangers from substandard housing. As to the first purpose, Prosser notes that the assumption of risk doctrine is not applicable to statutes "intended to protect the plaintiff against his own inability to protect himself, including his own lack of judgment or inability to resist various pressures." As to the second purpose, the Washington Supreme Court recently held that the implied warranty applied at the inception of the tenancy, even where the tenant then knew of the defects and in fact bargained for a lower rent because of them. Indeed, the rationale of *Green* itself supports such a finding of inapplicability. *Green* and the cases on which it relied adopted the implied warranty doctrine at least partly to encourage landlords to maintain those housing standards embodied in housing codes. Application of assumption of risk rules could remove from the scope of the doctrine at least some premises which violate these standards at the inception of the tenancy, and could thus diminish the effectiveness of this purpose of the implied warranty doctrine.

Moreover, even if found applicable, there still remain several reasons why standard assumption of risk rules will seldom, if ever, bar the tenant from using the implied warranty doctrine at the outset of the tenancy. First, in order for the doctrine to be applicable a tenant "must know and understand the risk he is incurring." Since it is unlikely that a prospective tenant will discover major, latent defects in wiring and plumbing and the like on a brief initial inspection, this limitation probably removes from the grasp of the assumed risk doctrine the great majority of cases where defects exist at the outset. Second, even with known defects the tenant does not assume the risk unless his choice of renting the dwelling is "a free and voluntary one." In the present rental market, such free and voluntary choices are rare. As the court in *Green* observed, "[t]he severe shortage of low and moderate cost housing has left tenants with little bargaining power. . . . [E]ven when defects are apparent the low income tenant frequently has no realistic alternative but to accept such housing with the expectation that the landlord will make the necessary repairs."

Treating the lease as an illegal contract, on the other hand, would appear completely to avoid the assumption of risk theory, since illegal contract doctrine is based not on an attempt to achieve justice between the parties, but on the court's policy of refusing to encourage the making of such contracts by enforcing them. Therefore, a tenant's conduct is irrelevant if the contract is otherwise illegal. Using the illegal contract theory, one may argue that, on either of two grounds, a lease is void where executed for premises defective at the outset. First, where the housing code specifically prohibits the rental of a dwelling with code violations, the contract is illegal. Such prohibitions are common, and have been present in most of the cases that have applied the illegal contract theory to residential tenancies. Indeed, California has such a provision in its state housing law. Second, even without such a specific regulatory prohibition, a contract is illegal it it contemplates performance in an illegal manner. Therefore, the contract is void if the landlord knows that the premises he will supply the tenant under the agreement are presently in violation of the housing code.

While the above authorities show that the implied warranty of habitability and the illegal contract doctrine should each apply to premises which violate the housing codes at the inception of the tenancy, it might appear that the latter logically precludes the former. If the contract is illegal, how can the tenant claim benefits under an implied warranty arising from that contract? The question seems academic unless the *consequences* of adopting one theory differ from those flowing from the other. So far, however, the few courts adopting the illegal contract approach have found ways to achieve the same results as those reached by courts using the implied warranty doctrine. For example, some courts have reasoned that since the tenant "had no real choice but to acquiesce in the illegality," and because the housing codes were adopted for his protection, the tenant is not *in pari delicto* with the landlord and can claim recovery of rents paid under the lease. But even though the lease is illegal, the reasoning has continued, the tenant took possession of the premises with the landlord's consent, thereby becoming a tenant at sufferance, and therefore he owes the landlord a reasonable rent for the premises in the condition in which they were occupied. Thus, the tenant's ability to defend or sue using the illegal contract theory and his measure of damages appear identical to those under the implied warranty theory. Moreover, it seems likely that the same standards used for ascertaining whether the warranty is breached will also be applied to determine whether code violations are serious enough to consider the lease an illegal contract.

Despite the similarity between the results obtained through use of the illegal contract theory and those achieved by using the implied warranty doctrine, there are reasons why implied warranty should nonetheless be preferred. The development of the law concerning tenant's rights to habitable premises has been confused and perhaps retarded by courts' attempts to apply various legal theories not specially suited to the problem. Since the implied warranty theory has been accepted, however, the courts have been able to put aside as judicial fictions such theories as constructive eviction and partial actual eviction, for they are unnecessary when the implied warranty doctrine is available. Because use of the illegal contract theory may cause similar problems, without any apparent offsetting benefits, it too should be put aside, making way for the development of a doctrine whose parameters are difficult enough to set without the added complexities caused by a competing legal theory.[7]

Certainly an extended and informed answer such as this is not expected of a student in class. But it raises some of the considerations which a student should reflect on generally in her answer.

4. Why didn't the court use a tort approach to solve the students' problems in this case?

---

[7] Myron Moskovitz, *The Implied Warranty of Habitability: A New Doctrine Raising New Issues*, 62 CAL. L. REV. 1444, 1449–54 (1974). Reprinted with permission of the California Law Review, Inc. ©1974. All rights reserved.

The answer to this question is to be found in the nature of the injury. What do you think?

5. How does the concept of duty differ from the concept of covenant?

Check your dictionary.

6. What social effect do you think the implied warranty of habitability will have on housing?

A survey of the reactions to *Green* describes three different points of view:

The adoption of the warranty of habitability has been hailed as a victory for tenants and low-income housing and cursed as another contributor to housing decline. Proponents of the adoption of the warranty have claimed that the reform will help preserve low-cost private housing, improve the legal status of tenants, broaden code enforcement, induce landlords to make repairs, and reduce the number of unlawful detainer actions. They believe that the law will result in some housing improvements without rent increases, increase the tenant's leverage in out-of-court settlements and lead to the creation of tenant unions.

Opponents of the warranty anticipate that it will diminish the landlord's return from the leased property and subsequently make repairs impossible. In this view, the warranty will lead to higher rents, overcrowding, abandonment, less investment in low-rent housing, and constriction of the supply of low-cost housing. Critics also believe that tenants will use the warranty to harass landlords or that lawyers will abuse the opportunity to conduct protracted litigation.

A third group, citing a recent study of the unlawful detainer process in San Francisco, argues that the warranty of habitability will have little positive or negative effect on housing or landlord-tenant relationships. The authors of the San Francisco study interviewed landlord and tenant attorneys in the Bay Area and examined the San Francisco Municipal Court docket for six months of 1974. They concluded that low-income tenants do not receive the legal advice necessary for them to make use of the warranty: *Green* appeared to be "a classic example of a 'progressive' judicial move remaining unknown and inaccessible to the very people it was intended to assist."

Each of these three positions makes untested assumptions about the condition of housing, the vitality of the real estate market, the situation of low-income tenants and their landlords, the diffusion of law reform, and the roles of lawyers and courts. The proponents of *Green* believe that the warranty can be effective because they assume that low-income housing is economically repairable. They anticipate few problems in the diffusion of law reform and great potential in tenant initiative. Critics of the warranty assume a non-renewable housing stock and a fragile real estate market like the model derived from studies of central cities in the Northeast. They also assume tenants and lawyers will exploit the law toward their short term interests, to the detriment of the landlord and the future of low-income housing. Those who believe that the warranty will have little practical impact either way assume that in-court activity is a good indicator of knowledge and use of the warranty. They also assume that low income housing is in such disrepair that most tenants who are evicted could legitimately plead the warranty in defense of their case.[8]

---

[8] Allan D. Heskin, *The Warranty of Habitability Debate: A California Case Study*, 66 CAL. L. REV. 37, 38–39 (1978). Reprinted with permission of the California Law Review, Inc. ©1978. All rights reserved.

SAUNDERS v. FIRST NATIONAL REALTY CORPORATION
245 A.2d 836 (D.C. Ct. App. 1968)

HOOD, Chief Judge:

Appellants were tenants in a large apartment complex known as Clifton Terrace. Their landlord, the appellee, filed separate actions against them for possession because of nonpayment of rent. Represented by the same counsel, appellants demanded trial by jury and presented identical defenses. At trial appellants offered to prove:

> That there are approximately 1500 violations of the Housing Regulations of the District of Columbia in the building at Clifton Terrace, where Defendant resides some affecting the premises of this Defendant directly, others, indirectly, and all tending to establish a course of conduct of violation of the Housing Regulations to the damage of Defendants and of others similarly situated.

This offer of proof was rejected by the trial court, and counsel for appellants then advised the court that without such evidence there were no issues to be tried. Accordingly the court entered judgment for possession in each of the cases.

. . . .

Two arguments are advanced by appellants. The first, made at oral argument, is that under our ruling in *Brown v. Southall Realty Co.*, if violations of the Housing Regulations occur during the tenancy (appellants conceded they could not prove the existence of any of the alleged violations at the commencement of the tenancies) and the landlord failed to correct them, the lease becomes illegal and void. Our holding in *Southall* was that where the owner of dwelling property, knowing that Housing Code violations exist on the property which render it unsafe and unsanitary, executes a lease for the property, such lease is void and cannot be enforced. We did not hold and we now refuse to hold that violations occurring after the tenancy is created void the lease.

Appellants' main argument, advanced in their brief, is that the Housing Regulations have abrogated the common law relation between landlord and tenant and have created a contractual duty on the landlord to comply with the Regulations. From this premise appellants argue that if the landlord fails to comply, the tenant, in an action for possession for nonpayment of rent, may use such failure as "an equitable defense or claim by way of recoupment or set-off in an amount equal to the rent claim" under Rule 4(c) of the Landlord and Tenant Branch of the trial court. This rule limits the landlord's basis for recovery of possession where the consideration for the rent has failed wholly or in part because of the landlord's breach of an express or implied lease obligation, and modifies the common law rule of independent covenants in the lease. Therefore, if appellee had a contractual duty to maintain the premises in compliance with the Housing Regulations, appellants may properly defend by way of set-off against the rent owed.

The long established rule in this jurisdiction, following the common law, is that, in the absence of statute or express covenant in the lease, a landlord does not impliedly covenant or warrant that the leased premises are in habitable condition and the landlord is not obligated to make ordinary repairs to the leased premises in the exclusive control of the tenant. The question here presented is whether the Housing Regulations impose upon the landlord a contractual duty to maintain the premises in compliance with the Regulations.

In both Edwards v. Habib and Whetzel v. Jess Fisher Management Co., the court implied that the Housing Regulations have the force and effect of statute, and for present purposes we will so treat the Regulations. Assuming, but not deciding, that in enacting the Regulations the Commissioners of the District of Columbia had the power to impose upon landlords a contractual duty, enforceable by tenants, to comply with the Regulations, the question is did they intend to do so and bring about a drastic change in the landlord and tenant law of this jurisdiction.

"No statute is to be construed as altering the common law, farther than its words import. It is not to be construed as making any innovation upon the common law which it does not fairly express." We find nothing in the Housing Regulations expressly or necessarily implying that a contractual duty is imposed on the landlords to comply with the Regulations. There are express provisions for punishment by fine or imprisonment, or suspension or revocation of a landlord's housing business license, as sanctions for violation of the Regulations. In some jurisdictions where similar penalties have been imposed, the enacting body has gone farther and provided a variety of tenant remedies, but we have no such provision here. Where, as here, the regulations or statute merely impose a penalty for failure to repair and maintain the leased premises in a habitable condition the courts have refused to enlarge the scope of the landlord-tenant relation by subjecting the landlord to implied contractual obligations.

Had the Commissioners intended that the Regulations impose a contractual duty on landlords enforceable by tenants (again we assume but do not decide that the Commissioners had the power to do so), we think they would have made such intention clear and not left it to conjecture. We see some very practical reasons why the Commissioners may have felt that enforcement of the Regulations should be left to the trained personnel authorized to administer the Regulations. The Regulations are broad in scope and in many instances are expressed in general language, leaving room for the exercise of judgment by those enforcing the Regulations. For example, we find scattered throughout the Regulations expressions such as "good repair," "good condition," "clean," "kept painted," "properly connected," "normal occupancy," "normal demands," "wide cracks," "adequate," etc. These and other like expressions in the Regulations do not state exact standards but leave considerable margin to the judgment of the enforcing authorities.

We cannot believe that the Commissioners intended that the single violation of any of the Regulations for any length of time would give ground for defending against payment of rent in whole or in part. And if a minor infraction of the Regulations for a brief period gives rise to no defense to a claim for rent, neither will a more serious violation for a greater length of time, because the Regulations furnish no standard for differentiating between consequential and inconsequential violations.

Appellants argue that Whetzel v. Jess Fisher Management Co. supports their contention. We do not so read that case. We understand it to hold that where a landlord negligently fails to comply with the Housing Regulations and as a result the tenant is injured, the tenant may sue the landlord in tort. This was simply an application of the rule that a private action for negligence may be based upon violation of a penal statute where the injured party is within the class of persons the statute intended to protect and the injury was of the type the statute intended to prevent. *Whetzel* did not hold that the Housing Regulations enlarge the contractual duties of a landlord.

Our conclusion is that under the established law of this jurisdiction the landlord's violations of the Housing Regulations is not a defense to his action for possession based on nonpayment of rent.

Affirmed.

QUESTIONS

1. Why is the lease in *Saunders* not illegal under the holding in *Brown v. Southall Realty Co.*?

2. What is the main issue in *Saunders*?

3. How does *Saunders* differ from *Pines* in its consideration of housing regulations as a basis for the implied warranty of habitability?

4. Do you agree with the court's decision in *Saunders*?

5. Does it make a difference that the conditions making premises uninhabitable were not proved to exist at the beginning of the lease?

One commentator has remarked:

The courts, however, when confronted with applying the principle of the implied warranty of habitability, have almost uniformly held that the condition of uninhabitability must be present at the beginning of the term in order for the landlord to have been in breach of the warranty. This, at least for policy reasons, makes good sense. Just as constructive eviction requires an act on the part of the landlord, it stands to reason that he should be held liable for a condition in or about the premises which was present when they were let. However, once the lessee is given exclusive possession, an argument might be made that any condition of uninhabitability arising thereafter would be more likely to be caused by him alone than by the landlord.[9]

Does this comment justify the finding of the court in *Saunders*?

LEMLE v. BREEDEN
462 P.2d 470 (Haw. 1969)

LEVINSON, Justice.

This case of first impression in Hawaii involves the doctrine of implied warranty of habitability and fitness for use of a leased dwelling. The plaintiff-lessee (Lemle) sued to recover the deposit and rent payment totalling $1,190.00. Constructive eviction and breach of an implied warranty of habitability and fitness for use were alleged as the basis for recovery. The defendant-lessor (Mrs. Breeden) counterclaimed for damages for breach of the rental agreement. The trial court, sitting without a jury, held for the plaintiff and the case comes to us on appeal from that judgment.

The facts in this case are relatively simple and without substantial conflict. The rented premises involved are owned by the defendant, Mrs. Breeden, and are located in the Diamond Head area of Honolulu. The house fronts on the water with the surrounding grounds attractively landscaped with lauhala trees and other shrubbery. The dwelling consists of several structures containing six bedrooms, six baths, a living room, kitchen, dining room, garage, and salt water swimming pool. The main dwelling house is constructed in "Tahitian" style with a corrugated metal roof over which coconut leaves have been woven together to give it a "grass shack" effect. The house is relatively open without screening on windows or doorways.

The defendant herself occupied the premises until sometime between September 14 and September 17, 1964, when she returned to the continental United States, having authorized a local realtor to rent the house for her. On September 21, 1964, during the daylight hours, the realtor showed the home to the plaintiff and his wife, newcomers to Hawaii from New York City, and told them that it was available for immediate occupancy. The plaintiff saw no evidence of rodent infestation during the one-half hour inspection.

That evening the rental agreement was executed. It was for the periods September 22, 1964 to March 20, 1965, and April 17, 1965 to June 12, 1965. The rental was $800.00 per month fully furnished. Mrs. Breeden reserved the right to occupy the premises between March 20 and April 17, 1965. The plaintiff tendered a check to the defendant's agent for $1,190.00 at that time.

The very next day, September 22, 1964, the plaintiff, his wife and their four children, who had been staying in a Waikiki hotel, took possession of the premises. That evening it became abundantly evident to the plaintiff that there were rats within the main dwelling and on the corrugated iron roof. It was not clear whether the rats came from within the house or from the rocky area next to the water. During that night and for the next two nights the plaintiff and his family were sufficiently apprehensive of the rats that they slept together in the downstairs living room of the main house, thereby

---

[9] Robert F. Klimek, *Landlord and Tenant — Implied Warranty of Habitability — How "Constructive" is "Eviction"?*, 19 DePaul L. Rev. 619, 627–28 (1970).

vacating their individual bedrooms. Rats were seen and heard during those three nights.

On September 23, 1964, the day after occupancy, the defendant's agent was informed of the rats' presence and she procured extermination services from a local firm. The plaintiff himself also bought traps to supplement the traps and bait set by the exterminators. These attempts to alleviate the rat problem were only partially successful and the succeeding two nights were equally sleepless and uncomfortable for the family.

On September 25, 1964, three days after occupying the dwelling, the plaintiff and his family vacated the premises after notifying the defendant's agent of his intention to do so and demanding the return of the money which he had previously paid. Subsequently this suit was brought.

The trial judge ruled that there was an implied warranty of habitability and fitness in the lease of a dwelling house, that there was a breach of warranty, that the plaintiff was constructively evicted, and that the plaintiff was entitled to recover $1,110.00 plus interest.

We affirm.

A. THE IMPLIED WARRANTY OF HABITABILITY AND FITNESS OF LEASED PREMISES.

It is important in a case of this type to separate carefully two very distinct doctrines: (1) that of implied warranty of habitability and fitness for the use intended, and (2) that of constructive eviction. The origin, history, and theoretical justification for these legal doctrines are quite different and are not to be confused.

At common law when land was leased to a tenant, the law of property regarded the lease as equivalent to a sale of the premises for a term. The lessee acquired an estate in land and became both owner and occupier for that term subject to the ancient doctrine of *caveat emptor*. Since rules of property law solidified before the development of mutually dependent covenants in contract law, theoretically once an estate was leased, there were no further unexecuted acts to be performed by the landlord and there could be no failure of consideration. Predictably enough, this concept of the lessee's interest has led to many troublesome rules of law which have endured far beyond their historical justifications.

Given the finality of a lease transaction and the legal effect of *caveat emptor* which placed the burden of inspection on the tenant, the actual moment of the conveyance was subject to an untoward amount of legal focus. Only if there were fraud or mistake in the initial transaction would the lessee have a remedy. "[F]raud apart, there is no law against letting a tumble-down house." In the absence of statute it was generally held that there was no implied warranty of habitability and fitness.

The rule of *caveat emptor* in lease transactions at one time may have had some basis in social practice as well as in historical doctrine. At common law leases were customarily lengthy documents embodying the full expectations of the parties. There was generally equal knowledge of the condition of the land by both landlord and tenant. The land itself would often yield the rents and the buildings were constructed simply, without modern conveniences like wiring or plumbing. Yet in an urban society where the vast majority of tenants do not reap the rent directly from the land but bargain primarily for the right to enjoy the premises for living purposes, often signing standardized leases as in this case, common law conceptions of a lease and the tenant's liability for rent are no longer viable. As one authority in the field of Landlord-Tenant law has said:

> Obviously, the ordinary lease is in part a bilateral contract, and it is so regarded by the civil law. There is no reason why it could not be recognized for what it is, both a conveyance and a contract. But the doctrine that a lease is a conveyance

and the rules based thereon were established before the development of the concept of mutual dependency in contracts, and the Anglo-American courts have been slow to apply the doctrine to the contractual provisions of leases.

American and English courts have attempted to circumvent this historical rigidity by the use of the doctrine of constructive eviction which serves as a substitute for the dependency of covenants in a large class of cases involving the enjoyment of the premises. Furthermore, limited exceptions to the general rule of no implied warranty of habitability and fitness are also widely recognized. The exception raised in this case applies when a furnished dwelling is rented for a short period of time. This exception has been justified on the ground that there is no opportunity to inspect, therefore the rule of *caveat emptor* does not apply. Nevertheless, some courts have strictly construed this exception limiting it to only "temporary" rentals, defects existing at the time of rental, and defects in furnishings.

While the inability to inspect is the avowed justification for the exception, it is more soundly supported by the obvious fact that the tenant is implicitly or expressly bargaining for immediate possession of the premises in a suitable condition. The fact that a home or apartment is furnished merely demonstrates the desire for immediate inhabitability as does the brevity of the lease. The exception was plainly a method of keeping the rule of *caveat emptor* from working an injustice in those special circumstances.

Yet it is clear that if the expectations of the tenant were the operative test, the exception would soon swallow up the general rule. "It is fair to presume that no individual would voluntarily choose to live in a dwelling that had become unsafe for human habitation." We think that the exception itself is artificial and that it is the general rule of *caveat emptor* which must be re-examined.

In the law of sales of chattels, the trend is markedly in favor of implying warranties of fitness and merchantability. The reasoning has been (1) that the public interest in safety and consumer protection requires it, and (2) that the burden ought to be shifted to the manufacturer who, by placing the goods on the market, represents their suitability and fitness. The manufacturer is also the one who knows more about the product and is in a better position to alleviate any problems or bear the brunt of any losses. This reasoning has also been accepted by a growing number of courts in cases involving sales of new homes. The same reasoning is equally persuasive in leases of real property.

The Supreme Court of New Jersey recently re-examined the doctrine of *caveat emptor* in a case involving a tenant who vacated leased business premises after being consistently flooded during every rain. In assessing the relative positions of the parties, that court said:

> It has come to be recognized that ordinarily the lessee does not have as much knowledge of the condition of the premises as the lessor. Building code requirements and violations are known or made known to the lessor, not the lessee. He is in a better position to know of latent defects, structural and otherwise, in a building which might go unnoticed by a lessee who rarely has sufficient knowledge or expertise to see or to discover them. A prospective lessee, such as a small businessman, cannot be expected to know if the plumbing or wiring systems are adequate or conform to local codes. Nor should he be expected to hire experts to advise him. Ordinarily all this information should be considered readily available to the lessor who in turn can inform the prospective lessee. These factors have produced persuasive arguments for re-evaluation of the *caveat emptor* doctrine and, for imposition of an implied warranty that the premises are suitable for the leased purposes and conform to local codes and zoning laws.

The application of an implied warranty of habitability in leases gives recognition to the changes in leasing transactions today. It affirms the fact that a lease is, in essence, a sale as well as a transfer of an estate in land and is, more importantly, a contractual relationship. From that contractual relationship an implied warranty of habitability and fitness for the purposes intended is a just and necessary implication. It is a doctrine which has its counterparts in the law of sales and torts and one which when candidly countenanced is impelled by the nature of the transaction and contemporary housing realities. Legal fictions and artificial exceptions to wooden rules of property law aside, we hold that in the lease of a dwelling house, such as in this case, there is an implied warranty of habitability and fitness for the use intended.

Here the facts demonstrate the uninhabitability and unfitness of the premises for residential purposes. For three sleepless nights the plaintiff and his family literally camped in the living room. They were unable to sleep in the proper quarters or make use of the other facilities in the house due to natural apprehension of the rats which made noise scurrying about on the roof and invaded the house through the unscreened openings.

The defendant makes much of the point that the source of the rats was the beach rocks and surrounding foliage. She contends that this exonerated her from the duty to keep the house free of rats. While it is not clear where the rats came from, assuming that they did originate from outside of the premises, the defendant had it within her power to keep them out by proper and timely screening and extermination procedures. Indeed this was done before the next tenant moved in. But to begin such procedures after the plaintiff had occupied the dwelling and to expect that he have the requisite patience and fortitude in the face of trial and error methods of extermination was too much to ask.

We need not consider the ruling of the trial court that the plaintiff was constructively evicted in light of the decision of this court that there was an implied warranty of habitability in this case. The doctrine of constructive eviction, as an admitted judicial fiction designed to operate as though there were a substantial breach of a material covenant in a bilateral contract, no longer serves its purpose when the more flexible concept of implied warranty of habitability is legally available.

B. CHOICE OF REMEDIES.

It is a decided advantage of the implied warranty doctrine that there are a number of remedies available. The doctrine of constructive eviction, on the other hand, requires that the tenant abandon the premises within a reasonable time after giving notice that the premises are uninhabitable or unfit for his purposes. This is based on the absurd proposition, contrary to modern urban realities, that "[a] tenant cannot claim uninhabitability, and at the same time continue to inhabit." Abandonment is always at the risk of establishing sufficient facts to constitute constructive eviction or the tenant will be liable for breach of the rental agreement. Also the tenant is forced to gamble on the time factor as he must abandon within a "reasonable" time or be deemed to have "waived" the defects.

Some courts have creatively allowed for alternatives to the abandonment requirement by allowing for a declaration of constructive eviction in equity without forcing abandonment. Other courts have found *partial* constructive eviction where alternative housing was scarce, thus allowing the tenant to remain in at least part of the premises. In spite of such imaginative remedies, it appears to us that to search for gaps and exceptions in a legal doctrine such as constructive eviction which exists only because of the somnolence of the common law and the courts is to perpetuate further judicial fictions when preferable alternatives exist. We do not agree with Blackstone that "[t]he law of real property * * * is formed into a fine artificial system, full of unseen connections and nice dependencies, and he that breaks one link of the chain endangers the dissolution of the whole." The law of landlord-tenant relations cannot be so frail as to shatter when confronted with modern urban realities and a frank appraisal of the underlying issues.

By adopting the view that a lease is essentially a contractual relationship with an implied warranty of habitability and fitness, a more consistent and responsive set of remedies are available for a tenant. They are the basic contract remedies of damages, reformation, and rescission. These remedies would give the tenant a wide range of alternatives in seeking to resolve his alleged grievance.

In considering the materiality of an alleged breach, both the seriousness of the claimed defect and the length of time for which it persists are relevant factors. Each case must turn on its own facts. Here there was sufficient evidence for the trier of fact to conclude that the breach was material and that the plaintiff's action in rescinding the rental agreement was justifiable. The plaintiff gave notice of rescission and vacated the premises after the landlord's early attempts to get rid of the rats failed. When the premises were vacated, they were not fit for use as a residence. Nor was there any assurance that the residence would become habitable within a reasonable time. We affirm the judgment for the plaintiff on the ground that there was a material breach of the implied warranty of habitability and fitness for the use intended which justified the plaintiff's rescinding the rental agreement and vacating the premises.

Affirmed.

QUESTIONS

1. If we are going to apply the implied warranty of habitability doctrine, what type of defect constitutes a breach? And how serious must the defect be before it reaches the level of breach?

What constitutes a breach of the implied warranty of habitability depends, first, on what constitutes "habitable" premises. Habitable must mean something more than merely a dwelling in which the tenant can survive, for otherwise the mere fact that the tenant inhabited the premises would prove their habitability. Beyond this, however, the courts have so far found it difficult to articulate a precise test; they have stressed that "each case must turn on its own facts" in determining whether the premises were rendered "uninhabitable in the eyes of a reasonable person." Nevertheless, several of the cases read together offer some guidance as to how the courts will apply the doctrine in terms of what facilities of the premises are covered by the warranty and how serious defects in these facilities must be in order for there to be a breach of the warranty.

A. Facilities Covered by the Warranty

In deciding which facilities are covered by the warranty, courts are agreed at least as to the location of such facilities. Facilities located within the tenant's apartment are of course covered. Moreover, since the tenant's health and safety might be seriously threatened by defects in such common areas as stairs, hallways and yards, the warranty should include, under this reasoning, facilities within the common areas he uses. Indeed, in some instances defective facilities even beyond the tenant's apartment and the common areas he uses might endanger his health and safety, as, for example, where serious fire hazards or defective main water pipes or central heating systems exist in areas controlled by the landlord and not open to the tenant.

The *types* of facilities covered by the implied warranty are those affected by "applicable building and housing code standards which materially affect health and safety." Of course, not every facility in a residence has the requisite material effect on health and safety, but many do. For example, health and safety certainly are affected materially by insect or rodent infestation, hazardous common areas, inadequate room size, light, or ventilation, defective bathroom fixtures or kitchen facilities, insufficient or nonexistent hot and cold running water, insubstantial weather protection or heating, dangerous electrical outlets, light fixtures, or wiring, or inadequate emergency exits, fire-resistant materials or fire-extinguishing systems. Accordingly, a tenant threatened by such defects could offer as evidence of the landlord's breach the applicable housing code standards regulating the facilities in question.

Housing code standards should not, however, be viewed as an exhaustive list of which facilities are includable. Admittedly, including within the purview of the implied warranty doctrine certain facilities *not* covered by the codes may appear to go beyond one of the bases for court decisions adopting the implied warranty doctrine: the public policy expressed in a legislature's decision to enact housing codes. Other landlord-tenant legal theories, however, are not limited to facilities covered by the codes. For example, the tenant may claim constructive eviction for serious defects in facilities outside the codes or may in some circumstances sue in negligence for personal injuries resulting from such defects. It would seem anomalous, therefore, to exclude from the implied warranty doctrine facilities which the courts have already decided may bring about the possibly more serious consequences of constructive eviction and personal injury suits. Moreover, there is case support for the proposition that the housing codes serve not as an outer boundary of which facilities are includable, but rather as a starting point in that determination. Some cases hold, for instance, that the codes provide merely threshold requirements or minimal standards, while others apparently have applied the implied warranty doctrine in situations where there was no indication that the defective facilities were covered by any code provisions.

In short, the housing codes should be viewed as a floor and not a ceiling. Threats to a tenant's health and safety, not simply or solely violations of the codes, should determine whether certain facilities are includable. Surely in most instances the housing codes will support this determination. But in some instances no statutory support will be available. In such cases the courts should nonetheless include under the implied warranty doctrine any facilities which, if defective, would threaten a tenant's health or safety.

B. Seriousness of Defects Constituting a Breach

Determining includable facilities is just one step. There remains the more difficult question of how serious a defect to that facility must be to constitute a breach of the warranty. Drawing once again on the housing code as a guide, some courts, including the California Supreme Court in *Green*, have held that substantial compliance is sufficient and that minor violations may be considered *de minimis*. Others have indicated that the warranty requires defects serious enough to have constituted a constructive eviction if the tenant had vacated, a test which appears to differ only slightly, if at all, from one requiring substantial compliance. But on the whole the courts have noticeably failed to provide much guidance. Certain general principles, however, seem to emerge from the cases. From the concern that the tenant be protected from threats to his safety or health, the courts appear to have derived two concerns: that the tenant not be deprived of those essential functions which a residence is expected to provide; and that the tenant not be subjected to the fear of injury of a kind which, were the injury to occur, would impose tort liability on some responsible party. Many factors must be considered in resolving these concerns. Foremost among them are the effect of any defect on safety or sanitation and the length of time such defects have persisted.

Deprivation of essential residential functions is a theme, never fully articulated, which runs through many of the decisions. Courts have apparently decided that certain elements of that "package of goods and services" which constitutes the modern urban dwelling unit are vital. One must be able to sleep, to eat, to use a bathroom. If, in the eyes of a normal person, defects in the dwelling preclude the tenant from these essential functions, a breach of the warranty has occurred.

Deprivation, of course, can occur for any number of reasons. A bathroom may become useless due to the collapse of its ceiling or a hole in its floor caused by dry rot. Toilet facilities may fall into disrepair, cease to function, or simply not be present. Indeed, while use may still be possible for the desperate or insensitive, a bathroom may be so unpleasant or so burdensome of upkeep that in any real sense an ordinary person is deprived of its function.

Similarly, kitchen facilities can be in such disrepair as to constitute a breach of the warranty. Plumbing, of course — both for the supply of water, hot and cold, and for the disposal of waste and sewage — is as necessary to kitchens as to bathrooms. Any sustained disruption in this service goes beyond inconvenience to become a deprivation of essential residential functions. Despite some similarities, however, kitchen facilities differ in a quite significant way from bathroom facilities. If they are faulty, stoves, ovens, and to a lesser degree refrigerators, freezers, and other electrical or gas appliances threaten not only deprivation, but physical harm as well. Such a dual threat to health and safety clearly is sufficiently serious to breach the warranty.

Sleep is very special. Dwellings can and do exist without bathrooms or kitchens; that courts have included deprivation of these latter facilities under the implied warranty doctrine appears an accommodation to a modern perception of society. But if a dwelling does not at least provide sleep, what does it provide other than storage of personal belongings? Moreover, sleep is essential to health, and it can be disrupted not only by inadequate sleeping facilities themselves, but also by encroachments upon sleep such as rat infestation or the fear that a wiring defect will lead to fire. Where sleep is deprived unnecessarily, even for relatively short periods, a breach of the warranty has occurred.

Certain defects may affect several or all of these functions, causing deprivation. Thus, drafts from faulty doors or from broken or missing windows, or inadequate heating or ventilation can cause general deprivation of use, and as such constitute breaches of the warranty. More than this, however, these defects, especially an absence of heat, pose threats to health quite apart from depriving a tenant of certain vital residential functions.

Subjecting a tenant to the fear that he may suffer injury or deterioration in health due to an unrepaired defect is best viewed as an independent basis for breach of the warranty — although such fear can also be expressed in the deprivation of sleep. Inadequate heating and dangerous wiring, offer some illustration. It is not so much that stairs in disrepair make mobility inconvenient, that faulty wiring makes using certain kitchen appliances problematical, or that insufficient heat makes sleeping difficult that deprivation occurs. Rather it is that each threatens direct physical injury: faulty stairs or handrails collapse while people are using them; exposed or overloaded wiring causes fire; no heat in winter leads to colds, pneumonia, or worse. Thus, the principle that appears to have evolved is this: If the defect is such that tort liability would be imposed on the landlord were the harm that is feared actually to occur, the defect constitutes a breach of the implied warranty of habitability despite the absence of injury.

C. Other Factors in the Definition

Having a sufficiently serious defect to an includable facility, however, does not end the inquiry, since, primarily in dicta, several courts have indicated that certain other factors may be relevant as well. Some courts, for instance, have stated that there can be no breach of the implied warranty if the defects were caused by the tenant's wrongful action or abnormal use of the premises, since it would be unfair to permit the tenant to benefit from his own wrong. Beyond this, the language of a few cases appears to state a flat rule that the tenant must give *notice* of the defects to the landlord in order later to claim a breach of the implied warranty. There would seem, however, to be no need for such notice where the landlord already knows of the defects. Several cases, therefore, have limited the notice requirement to defects not known to the landlord. Indeed, where defects exist in common areas under the landlord's control, even the landlord's lack of actual knowledge of these defects should not excuse him, since he has a duty to inspect those areas. Some cases which impose a notice requirement also state that the landlord must be given *reasonable time* to make the repairs.

Thus if one considers, along with the above discussion of what constitutes a sufficiently serious defect, the requirements that the tenant not be at fault in the defect's causation, that he give the landlord notice, and that he allow reasonable time for repair, a new definition emerges of what constitutes breach. Depriving a tenant of an essential residential function or subjecting him to fear of injury or deterioration in health, when caused by a defect in the dwelling, is a potential breach of the implied warranty so long as the tenant is not at fault for the defect's existence. The deprivation or subjection becomes an actual breach once the landlord has been notified or otherwise has actual or constructive knowledge of the defect and has had reasonable time to repair.[10]

2. Does *Lemle* add any weight to the argument in favor of the implied warranty of habitability? In what way?

Consider the historical discussion in *Lemle* and the changes in society it mentions. This discussion focuses on policy considerations as opposed to the authority of precedent or other prior decisions.

3. What arguments can you make now for an opposite ruling in *Saunders*?

Note that *Saunders* was decided by the D.C. Court of Appeals in 1968. *Lemle* was decided in Hawaii in 1969 and does not have the force of precedent in Washington D.C.

---

[10] Myron Moskovitz, *The Implied Warranty of Habitability: A New Doctrine Raising New Issues*, 62 Calif. L. Rev. 1444, 1455–63 (1974). Reprinted with permission of the California Law Review, Inc. ©1974. All rights reserved.

ASSIGNMENT 3
A Synthesis in Property Law

The next case, *Javins*, continues the materials in Assignment 2 with a further discussion of questions asked in the classroom. Note that *Javins* is the result of an appeal from the *Saunders* case in Assignment 2. The last case, *Kline*, is presented to demonstrate how a court may develop a trend in the law by its creative use of precedents to establish a new rule without the aid of the legislature.

JAVINS v. FIRST NATIONAL REALTY CORPORATION
428 F.2d 1071 (D.C. Cir. 1970)

J. SKELLY WRIGHT, Circuit Judge:

These cases present the question whether housing code violations which arise during the term of a lease have any effect upon the tenant's obligation to pay rent. The Landlord and Tenant Branch of the District of Columbia Court of General Sessions ruled proof of such violations inadmissible when proffered as a defense to an eviction action for nonpayment of rent. The District of Columbia Court of Appeals upheld this ruling. Saunders v. First National Realty Corp., 245 A.2d 836 (1968).

Because of the importance of the question presented, we granted appellants' petitions for leave to appeal. We now reverse and hold that a warranty of habitability, measured by the standards set out in the Housing Regulations for the District of Columbia, is implied by operation of law into leases of urban dwelling units covered by those Regulations and that breach of this warranty gives rise to the usual remedies for breach of contract.

I

The facts revealed by the record are simple. By separate written leases, each of the appellants rented an apartment in a three-building apartment complex in Northwest Washington known as Clifton Terrace. The landlord, First National Realty Corporation, filed separate actions in the Landlord and Tenant Branch of the Court of General Sessions on April 8, 1966, seeking possession on the ground that each of the appellants had defaulted in the payment of rent due for the month of April. The tenants, appellants here, admitted that they had not paid the landlord any rent for April. However, they alleged numerous violations of the Housing Regulations as "an equitable defense or [a] claim by way of recoupment or set-off in an amount equal to the rent claim," as provided in the rules of the Court of General Sessions. They offered to prove

> "[t]hat there are approximately 1500 violations of the Housing Regulations of the District of Columbia in the building at Clifton Terrace, where Defendant resides some affecting the premises of this Defendant directly, others indirectly, and all tending to establish a course of conduct of violation of the Housing Regulations to the damage of Defendants * * *."

Appellants conceded at trial, however, that this offer of proof reached only violations which had arisen since the term of the lease had commenced. The Court of General Sessions refused appellants' offer of proof and entered judgment for the landlord. The District of Columbia Court of Appeals affirmed, rejecting the argument made by appellants that the landlord was under a contractual duty to maintain the premises in compliance with the Housing Regulations. Saunders v. First National Realty Corp., *supra*, 245 A.2d at 838.

II

Since, in traditional analysis, a lease was the conveyance of an interest in land, courts have usually utilized the special rules governing real property transactions to resolve controversies involving leases. However, as the Supreme Court has noted in another context, "the body of private property law * * *, more than almost any other branch of law, has been shaped by distinctions whose validity is largely historical." Courts have a duty to reappraise old doctrines in the light of the facts and values of contemporary life — particularly old common law doctrines which the courts themselves created and developed. As we have said before, "[T]he continued vitality of the common law * * * depends upon its ability to reflect contemporary community values and ethics."

The assumption of landlord-tenant law, derived from feudal property law, that a lease primarily conveyed to the tenant an interest in land may have been reasonable in a rural, agrarian society; it may continue to be reasonable in some leases involving farming or commercial land. In these cases, the value of the lease to the tenant is the land itself. But in the case of the modern apartment dweller, the value of the lease is that it gives him a place to live. The city dweller who seeks to lease an apartment on the third floor of a tenement has little interest in the land 30 or 40 feet below, or even in the bare right to possession within the four walls of his apartment. When American city dwellers, both rich and poor, seek "shelter" today, they seek a well known package of goods and services — a package which includes not merely walls and ceilings, but also adequate heat, light and ventilation, serviceable plumbing facilities, secure windows and doors, proper sanitation, and proper maintenance. Professor Powell summarizes the present state of the law:

> "* * * The complexities of city life, and the proliferated problems of modern society in general, have created new problems for lessors and lessees and these have been commonly handled by specific clauses inserted in leases. This growth in the number and detail of specific lease covenants has reintroduced into the law of estates for years a predominantly contractual ingredient. In practice, the law today concerning estates for years consists chiefly of rules determining the construction and effect of lease covenants.* * *"

Ironically, however, the rules governing the construction and interpretation of "predominantly contractual" obligations in leases have too often remained rooted in old property law.

Some courts have realized that certain of the old rules of property law governing leases are inappropriate for today's transactions. In order to reach results more in accord with the legitimate expectations of the parties and the standards of the community, courts have been gradually introducing more modern precepts of contract law in interpreting leases. Proceeding piecemeal has, however, led to confusion where "decisions are frequently conflicting, not because of a healthy disagreement on social policy, but because of the lingering impact of rules whose policies are long since dead."

In our judgment the trend toward treating leases as contracts is wise and well considered. Our holding in this case reflects a belief that leases of urban dwelling units should be interpreted and construed like any other contract.

III

Modern contract law has recognized that the buyer of goods and services in an industrialized society must rely upon the skill and honesty of the supplier to assure that goods and services purchased are of adequate quality. In interpreting most contracts, courts have sought to protect the legitimate expectations of the buyer and have steadily widened the seller's responsibility for the quality of goods and services through implied warranties of fitness and merchantability. Thus without any special agreement a merchant will be held to warrant that his goods are fit for the ordinary purposes for which such goods are used and that they are at least of reasonably average quality. Moreover, if the supplier has been notified that goods are required for a specific purpose, he will be held to warrant that any goods sold are fit for that purpose. These implied warranties have become widely accepted and well established features of the common law, supported by the overwhelming body of case law. Today most states as well as the District of Columbia have codified and enacted these warranties into statute, as to the sale of goods, in the Uniform Commercial Code.

Implied warranties of quality have not been limited to cases involving sales. The consumer renting a chattel, paying for services, or buying a combination of goods and services must rely upon the skill and honesty of the supplier to at least the same extent as a purchaser of goods. Courts have not hesitated to find implied warranties of fitness and merchantability in such situations. In most areas product liability law has moved far beyond "mere" implied warranties running between two parties in privity with each other.

The rigid doctrines of real property law have tended to inhibit the application of implied warranties to transactions involving real estate. Now, however, courts have begun to hold sellers and developers of real property responsible for the quality of their product. For example, builders of new homes have recently been held liable to purchasers for improper construction on the ground that the builders had breached an implied warranty of fitness. In other cases courts have held builders of new homes liable for breach of an implied warranty that all local building regulations had been complied with. And following the developments in other areas, very recent decisions and commentary suggest the possible extension of liability to parties other than the immediate seller for improper construction of residential real estate.

Despite this trend in the sale of real estate, many courts have been unwilling to imply warranties of quality, specifically a warranty of habitability, into leases of apartments. Recent decisions have offered no convincing explanation for their refusal; rather they have relied without discussion upon the old common law rule that the lessor is not obligated to repair unless he covenants to do so in the written lease contract. However, the Supreme Courts of at least two states, in recent and well reasoned opinions, have held landlords to implied warranties of quality in housing leases. Lemle v. Breeden; Reste Realty Corp. v. Cooper. *See also* Pines v. Perssion. In our judgment, the old no-repair rule cannot coexist with the obligations imposed on the landlord by a typical modern housing code, and must be abandoned in favor of an implied warranty of habitability. In the District of Columbia, the standards of this warranty are set out in the Housing Regulations.

IV

A. In our judgment the common law itself must recognize the landlord's obligation to keep his premises in a habitable condition. This conclusion is compelled by three separate considerations. First, we believe that the old rule was based on certain factual assumptions which are no longer true; on its own terms, it can no longer be justified. Second, we believe that the consumer protection cases discussed above require that the old rule be abandoned in order to bring residential landlord-tenant law into harmony with the principles on which those cases rest. Third, we think that the nature of today's urban housing market also dictates abandonment of the old rule.

The common law rule absolving the lessor of all obligation to repair originated in the early Middle Ages. Such a rule was perhaps well suited to an agrarian economy; the land was more important than whatever small living structure was included in the leasehold, and the tenant farmer was fully capable of making repairs himself. These historical facts were the basis on which the common law constructed its rule; they also provided the necessary prerequisites for its application.

Court decisions in the late 1800's began to recognize that the factual assumptions of the common law were no longer accurate in some cases. For example, the common law, since it assumed that the land was the most important part of the leasehold, required a tenant to pay rent even if any building on the land was destroyed. Faced with such a rule and the ludicrous results it produced, in 1863 the New York Court of Appeals declined to hold that an upper story tenant was obliged to continue paying rent after his apartment building burned down. The court simply pointed out that the urban tenant had no interest in the land, only in the attached building. Another line of cases created an exception to the no-repair rule for short term leases of furnished dwellings. The Massachusetts Supreme Judicial Court, a court not known for its willingness to depart from the common law, supported this exception, pointing out:

> "* * * [A] different rule should apply to one who hires a furnished room, or a furnished house, for a few days, or a few weeks or months. Its fitness for immediate use of a particular kind, as indicated by its appointments, is a far more important element entering into the contract than when there is a mere lease of real estate. One who lets for a short term a house provided with all furnishings and appointments for immediate residence may be supposed to contract in reference to a well-understood purpose of the hirer to use it as a habitation. * * * It would be unreasonable to hold, under such circumstances, that the landlord does not impliedly agree that what he is letting is a house suitable for occupation in its condition at the time. * * *"

These as well as other similar cases demonstrate that some courts began some time ago to question the common law's assumptions that the land was the most important feature of a leasehold and that the tenant could feasibly make any necessary repairs himself. Where those assumptions no longer reflect contemporary housing patterns, the courts have created exceptions to the general rule that landlords have no duty to keep their premises in repair.

It is overdue for courts to admit that these assumptions are no longer true with regard to all urban housing. Today's urban tenants, the vast majority of whom live in multiple dwelling houses, are interested, not in the land, but solely in "a house suitable for occupation." Furthermore, today's city dweller usually has a single, specialized skill unrelated to maintenance work; he is unable to make repairs like the "jack-of-alltrades" farmer who was the common law's model of the lessee. Further, unlike his agrarian predecessor who often remained on one piece of land for his entire life, urban tenants today are more mobile than ever before. Atenant's tenure in a specific apartment will often not be sufficient to justify efforts at repairs. In addition, the increasing complexity of today's dwellings renders them much more difficult to repair than the structures of earlier times. In a multiple dwelling repair may require access to equipment and areas in the control of the landlord. Low and middle income tenants, even if they were interested in making repairs, would be unable to obtain any financing for major repairs since they have no long-term interest in the property.

Our approach to the common law of landlord and tenant ought to be aided by principles derived from the consumer protection cases referred to above. In a lease contract, a tenant seeks to purchase from his landlord shelter for a specified period of time. The landlord sells housing as a commercial businessman and has much greater opportunity, incentive and capacity to inspect and maintain the condition of his building. Moreover, the tenant must rely upon the skill and *bona fides* of his landlord at least as much as a car buyer must rely upon the car manufacturer. In dealing with major problems, such as heating, plumbing, electrical or structural defects, the tenant's position corresponds precisely with "the ordinary consumer who cannot be expected to have the knowledge or capacity or even the opportunity to make adequate inspection of mechanical instrumentalities, like automobiles, and to decide for himself whether they are reasonably fit for the designed purpose."

Since a lease contract specifies a particular period of time during which the tenant has a right to use his apartment for shelter, he may legitimately expect that the apartment will be fit for habitation for the time period for which it is rented. We point out that in the present cases there is no allegation that appellants' apartments were in poor condition or in violation of the housing code at the commencement of the leases. Since the lessees continue to pay the same rent, they were entitled to expect that the landlord would continue to keep the premises in their beginning condition during the lease term. It is precisely such expectations that the law now recognizes as deserving of formal, legal protection.

Even beyond the rationale of traditional products liability law, the relationship of landlord and tenant suggests further compelling reasons for the law's protection of the tenants' legitimate expectations of quality. The inequality in bargaining power between landlord and tenant has been well documented. Tenants have very little leverage to enforce demands for better housing. Various impediments to competition in the rental housing market, such as racial and class discrimination and standardized form leases, mean that landlords place tenants in a take it or leave it situation. The increasingly severe shortage of adequate housing further increases the landlord's bargaining power and escalates the need for maintaining and improving the existing stock. Finally, the findings by various studies of the social impact of bad housing has led to the realization that poor housing is detrimental to the whole society, not merely to the unlucky ones who must suffer the daily indignity of living in a slum.

Thus we are led by our inspection of the relevant legal principles and precedents to the conclusion that the old common law rule imposing an obligation upon the lessee to repair during the lease term was really never intended to apply to residential urban leaseholds. Contract principles established in other areas of the law provide a more rational framework for the apportionment of landlord-tenant responsibilities; they strongly suggest that a warranty of habitability be implied into all contracts for urban dwellings.

B. We believe, in any event, that the District's housing code requires that a warranty of habitability be implied in the leases of all housing that it covers. The housing code — formally designated the Housing Regulations of the District of Columbia — was established and authorized by the Commissioners of the District of Columbia on August 11, 1955. Since that time, the code has been updated by numerous orders of the Commissioners. The 75 pages of the Regulations provide a comprehensive regulatory scheme setting forth in some detail: (a) the standards which housing in the District of Columbia must meet; (b) which party, the lessor or the lessee, must meet each standard;and (c) a system of inspections, notifications and criminal penalties. The Regulations themselves are silent on the question of private remedies.

Two previous decisions of this court, however, have held that the Housing Regulations create legal rights and duties enforceable in tort by private parties. In Whetzel v. Jess Fisher Management Co., we followed the leading case of Altz v. Lieberson in holding (1) that the housing code altered the common law rule and imposed a duty to repair upon the landlord, and (2) that a right of action accrued to a tenant injured by the landlord's breach of this duty. As Judge Cardozo wrote in *Lieberson*:

> "* * * We may be sure that the framers of this statute, when regulating tenement life, had uppermost in thought the care of those who are unable to care for themselves. The Legislature must have known that unless repairs in the rooms of the poor were made by the landlord, they would not be made by any one. The duty imposed became commensurate with the need. The right to seek redress is not limited to the city or its officers. The right extends to all whom there was a purpose to protect. * * *"

Recently, in Kanelos v. Kettler, we reaffirmed our position in *Whetzel*, holding that "the Housing Regulations did impose maintenance obligations upon appellee [landlord] which he was not free to ignore."

The District of Columbia Court of Appeals gave further effect to the Housing Regulations in Brown v. Southall Realty Co. There the landlord knew at the time the lease was signed that housing code violations existed which rendered the apartment "unsafe and unsanitary." Viewing the lease as a contract, the District of Columbia Court of Appeals held that the premises were let in violation of Sections 2304 and 2501 of the

Regulations and that the lease, therefore, was void as an illegal contract. In the light of *Brown*, it is clear not only that the housing code creates privately enforceable duties as held in *Whetzel*, but that the basic validity of every housing contract depends upon substantial compliance with the housing code at the beginning of the lease term. The *Brown* court relied particularly upon Section 2501 of the Regulations which provides:

> "Every premises accommodating one or more habitations shall be maintained and kept in repair so as to provide decent living accommodations for the occupants. This part of this Code contemplates more than mere basic repairs and maintenance to keep out the elements; its purpose is to include repairs and maintenance designed to make a premises or neighborhood healthy and safe."

By its terms, this section applies to maintenance and repair during the lease term. Under the *Brown* holding, serious failure to comply with this section before the lease term begins renders the contract void. We think it untenable to find that this section has no effect on the contract after it has been signed. To the contrary, by signing the lease the landlord has undertaken a continuing obligation to the tenant to maintain the premises in accordance with all applicable law.

This principle of implied warranty is well established. Courts often imply relevant law into contracts to provide a remedy for any damage caused by one party's illegal conduct. In a case closely analogous to the present ones, the Illinois Supreme Court held that a builder who constructed a house in violation of the Chicago building code had breached his contract with the buyer:

> "* * * [T]he law existing at the time and place of the making of the contract is deemed a part of the contract, as though expressly referred to or incorporated in it. * * *

> "The rationale for this rule is that the parties to the contract would have expressed that which the law implies 'had they not supposed that it was unnecessary to speak of it because the law provided for it.' * * * Consequently, the courts, in construing the existing law as part of the express contract, are not reading into the contract provisions different from those expressed and intended by the parties, as defendants contend, but are merely construing the contract in accordance with the intent of the parties."

We follow the Illinois court in holding that the housing code must be read into housing contracts — a holding also required by the purposes and the structure of the code itself. The duties imposed by the Housing Regulations may not be waived or shifted by agreement if the Regulations specifically place the duty upon the lessor. Criminal penalties are provided if these duties are ignored. This regulatory structure was established by the Commissioners because, in their judgment, the grave conditions in the housing market required serious action. Yet official enforcement of the housing code has been far from uniformly effective. Innumerable studies have documented the desperate condition of rental housing in the District of Columbia and in the nation. In view of these circumstances, we think the conclusion reached by the Supreme Court of Wisconsin as to the effect of a housing code on the old common law rule cannot be avoided:

> "* * * [T]he legislature has made a policy judgment — that it is socially (and politically) desirable to impose these duties on a property owner — which has rendered the old common law rule obsolete. To follow the old rule of no implied warranty of habitability in leases would, in our opinion, be inconsistent with the current legislative policy concerning housing standards. * * *"

We therefore hold that the Housing Regulations imply a warranty of habitability, measured by the standards which they set out, into leases of all housing that they cover.

V

In the present cases, the landlord sued for possession for nonpayment of rent. Under contract principles, however, the tenant's obligation to pay rent is dependent upon the landlord's performance of his obligations, including his warranty to maintain the premises in habitable condition. In order to determine whether any rent is owed to the landlord, the tenants must be given an opportunity to prove the housing code violations alleged as breach of the landlord's warranty.

At trial, the finder of fact must make two findings: (1) whether the alleged violations existed during the period for which past due rent is claimed, and (2) what portion, if any or all, of the tenant's obligation to pay rent was suspended by the landlord's breach. If no part of the tenant's rental obligation is found to have been suspended, then a judgment for possession may issue forthwith. On the other hand, if the jury determines that the entire rental obligation has been extinguished by the landlord's total breach, then the action for possession on the ground of nonpayment must fail.

The jury may find that part of the tenant's rental obligation has been suspended but that part of the unpaid back rent is indeed owed to the landlord. In these circumstances, no judgment for possession should issue if the tenant agrees to pay the partial rent found to be due. If the tenant refuses to pay the partial amount, a judgment for possession may then be entered.

The judgment of the District of Columbia Court of Appeals is reversed and the cases are remanded for further proceedings consistent with this opinion.

So ordered.

Circuit Judge ROBB concurs in the result and in Parts IV-B and V of the opinion.

QUESTIONS

1. Under *Javins*, the traditional landlord-tenant relationship, which favored the landlord, has been modified to give tenants a better quality of housing. It must be recognized, however, that this places additional burdens on landlords in the form of increased maintenance and operating costs, taxes, insurance, and risks of litigation.

How might a landlord respond to such increased costs?

A number of possibilities exist:

(a) Absorb the costs and operate at a lower profit.

(b) Pass on the costs in the form of higher rents.

(c) Abandon the building (selling the building is infrequent because most of the buildings with major housing code violations have little marketability).

As for what is likely to happen, consider the following excerpt from an economic study:

First, except under the most unlikely circumstances, housing rents must increase if a law is implemented and enforced so as to impose additional costs on landlords. Second, if tenants feel that they derive no benefit from the law, price increases will be less than the additional costs imposed on landlords. Third, if the tenants do place some positive evaluation on the law, price increases will be larger — perhaps large enough to offset completely the additional costs associated with the provision of the new, higher level of services.

. . . .

With the aid of economic theory, we have shown that given certain housing market conditions, the increased costs associated with habitability laws must, to some extent, be passed on. On an empirical basis, we found the presence of receivership laws to be significantly associated with higher rents. But the presence of repair and deduct and rent withholding remedies were not significantly related to rent levels. It was hypothesized that the lack of a statistically significant relationship between rent levels and these two remedies was due to the non-use of these tenant remedies. Alternatively, it was suggested that the costs associated with habitability laws may be passed on to some tenants more than others. For example, a statistically significant relationship between the rent level and the presence of habitability laws was found for the subcategory of elderly low-income tenants.[11]

2. What remedies are available for tenants who initiate code enforcement proceedings?

(a) Repair and deduct

(b) Rent withholding

    — escrow method

    — rent abatement

(c) Receivership

3. If such enforcement does indeed lead to rent increases, are the rent increases smaller than the accompanying benefits obtained by low-income tenants?

Consider the following opinion:

This question was not answered herein. However, what sketchy evidence exists on this issue indicates that habitability laws are unlikely to effect a redistribution of wealth in favor of indigent tenants. Landlords alone cannot be expected to finance the achievement of this country's goal of a "decent home and suitable living environment for every American family." In addition, retaliatory eviction laws cannot permanently insulate tenants from the economic effects of exercising their rights. Thus, unless some supplemental action is taken by federal or state government, low-income tenants may be worse off in some ways with habitability laws than they would be without such laws.[12]

4. In addition to housing code enforcement what other tools can be employed by municipalities to ensure safe and sanitary housing?

(a) Urban renewal

(b) Neighborhood rehabilitation

(c) Public housing programs

5. Why has the use of criminal sanctions proved to be an inadequate method of enforcing housing regulations?

Consider the following:

There are several basic reasons proffered for this inadequacy. First, enforcement agencies lack sufficient administrative machinery and resources, and are plagued by an insufficient number of personnel and inept organization. Since the demands on a large urban criminal enforcement system are considerable, these agencies are forced to utilize a screening process; minor violations are disregarded and only cases involving extreme violations are investigated. Second, the high incidence of adjournments and delays in housing code violation cases favor the landlord, generally enabling him to postpone making repairs without incurring additional penalties. Third, courts have been hesitant to consider code violations authentic criminal offenses warranting jail sentences and heavy fines. Thus, fines have been minimal, and landlords often find it less expensive to pay

---

[11] Werner Hirsch, Joel Hirsch & Stephen Margolis, *Regression Analysis of the Effects of Habitability Laws Upon Rent: An Empirical Observation on the Ackerman-Komesar Debate*, 63 CAL. L. REV. 1098, 1119, 1139 (1975). Reprinted with permission of the California Law Review, Inc. ©1975. All rights reserved.

[12] *Id.* at 1139–40. Reprinted with permission of the California Law Review, Inc. ©1975. All rights reserved.

these fines than repair the premises. Finally, political realities have been offered to explain the reluctance of city officials to enforce housing regulations. Conscientious enforcement may involve the danger of alienating property-owners. Moreover, completion of a new housing project provides visual evidence of a housing administration's achievements, whereas the results of continuous code enforcement are not as visible to the entire community.[13]

6. According to *Javins*, what constitutes a breach of the implied warranty of habitability?

The court stated that in order to constitute breach, the housing code violations must affect the tenant's apartment or the common areas he uses, must not be caused by his own wrongful action, and need not be discovered by city inspectors. The core problem of how substantial, in terms of severity and number, the violations must be in order to justify rent withholding, however, is dealt with in little detail. In stating that "one or two minor violations standing alone which do not affect habitability are *de minimis* and would not entitle the tenant to a reduction in rent," the court seems to indicate that any violations which affect habitability would justify the withholding of *some* amount of rent. But the opinion does not attempt to establish the factors which would constitute "habitability," nor does it indicate which types of violations would incur what percentages of rental reduction.

Tenants and landlords, in addition to the lower courts, will find themselves without adequate guidance in the application of the *Javins* decision. When a tenant makes the decision to withhold rent, he risks eviction for nonpayment since the court's conception of rent-impairing violations may differ from his own. This uncertainty may also encourage landlords to delay repairs, believing that a court will be reluctant to find the violations substantial enough to justify rent withholding. If a list of rent-impairing code violations could be compiled and made readily available to the public, this problem could be substantially alleviated, and a uniform application of the *Javins* decision would be possible.[14]

7. If the landlord does not repair, how long may a tenant remain in possession without paying?

8. If the landlord makes repairs, can he demand the back rent at that time or is there a permanent extinguishment of the rental obligation for the period of the violations?

Having discussed the landlord's duty of care under tort law in the first assignment and contract law in the second assignment and the *Javins* case above, we now turn to the *Kline* case which increases the landlord's duty to provide tenants with a safe and secure place to live. The court in this case uses both tort and contract law to support its decision, and, in so doing, provides a good example of how prior law can be synthesized to apply to new situations. If one envisions the fact pattern in *Kline* to be a hypothetical case thrown out in the classroom for discussion and debate, the court's opinion and the materials following the case indicate what a student should be thinking about in order to answer the question: How and why would you decide to extend a landlord's duty of protection to include prevention of criminal attacks by strangers?

KLINE v. 1500 MASSACHUSETTS AVENUE APARTMENT CORP.
439 F.2d 477 (D.C. Cir. 1970)

WILKEY, Circuit Judge:

The appellee apartment corporation states that there is "only one issue presented for review * * * whether a duty should be placed on a landlord to take steps to protect

---

[13] Sharon Cohen & Jay Cooke, *Landlord-Tenant Law*, 39 GEO. WASH. L. REV. 152, 156–57 (1970). Reprinted with the permission of the George Washington Law Review © 1970.

[14] *Id.* at 163. Reprinted with the permission of the George Washington Law Review ©1970.

tenants from foreseeable criminal acts committed by third parties." The District Court as a matter of law held that there is no such duty. We find that there is, and that in the circumstances here the applicable standard of care was breached. We therefore reverse and remand to the District Court for the determination of damages for the appellant.

I

The appellant, Sarah B. Kline, sustained serious injuries when she was criminally assaulted and robbed at approximately 10:15 in the evening by an intruder in the common hallway of an apartment house at 1500 Massachusetts Avenue. This facility, into which the appellant Kline moved in October 1959, is a large apartment building with approximately 585 individual apartment units. It has a main entrance on Massachusetts Avenue, with side entrances on both 15th and 16th Streets. At the time the appellant first signed a lease a doorman was on duty at the main entrance twenty-four hours a day, and at least one employee at all times manned a desk in the lobby from which all persons using the elevators could be observed. The 15th Street door adjoined the entrance to a parking garage used by both the tenants and the public. Two garage attendants were stationed at this dual entranceway; the duties of each being arranged so that one of them always was in position to observe those entering either the apartment building or the garage. The 16th Street entrance was unattended during the day but was locked after 9:00 P.M.

By mid-1966, however, the main entrance had no doorman, the desk in the lobby was left unattended much of the time, the 15th Street entrance was generally unguarded due to a decrease in garage personnel, and the 16th Street entrance was often left unlocked all night. The entrances were allowed to be thus unguarded in the face of an increasing number of assaults, larcenies, and robberies being perpetrated against the tenants in and from the common hallways of the apartment building. These facts were undisputed, and were supported by a detailed chronological listing of offenses admitted into evidence. The landlord had notice of these crimes and had in fact been urged by appellant Kline herself prior to the events leading to the instant appeal to take steps to secure the building.

Shortly after 10:00 P.M. on November 17, 1966, Miss Kline was assaulted and robbed just outside her apartment on the first floor above the street level of this 585 unit apartment building. This occurred only two months after Leona Sullivan, another female tenant, had been similarly attacked in the same common way.

II

At the outset we note that of the crimes of violence, robbery, and assault which had been occurring with mounting frequency on the premises at 1500 Massachusetts Avenue, the assaults on Miss Kline and Miss Sullivan took place in the hallways of the building, which were under the exclusive control of the appellee landlord. Even in those crimes of robbery or assault committed in individual apartments, the intruders of necessity had to gain entrance through the common entry and passageways. These premises fronted on three heavily traveled streets, and had multiple entrances. The risk to be guarded against therefore was the risk of unauthorized entrance into the apartment house by intruders bent upon some crime of violence or theft.

While the apartment lessees themselves could take some steps to guard against this risk by installing extra heavy locks and other security devices on the doors and windows of their respective apartments, yet this risk in the greater part could only be guarded against by the landlord. No individual tenant had it within his power to take measures to guard the garage entranceways, to provide scrutiny at the main entrance of the building, to patrol the common hallways and elevators, to set up any kind of a security alarm system in the building, to provide additional locking devices on the main doors, to provide a system of announcement for authorized visitors only, to close the garage doors at appropriate hours, and to see that the entrance was manned at all times.

The risk of criminal assault and robbery on a tenant in the common hallways of the building was thus entirely predictable; that same risk had been occurring with increasing frequency over a period of several months immediately prior to the incident giving rise to this case; it was a risk whose prevention or minimization was almost entirely within the power of the landlord; and the risk materialized in the assault and robbery of appellant on November 17, 1966.

III

In this jurisdiction, certain duties have been assigned to the landlord because of his *control* of common hallways, lobbies, stairwells, etc., used by all tenants in multiple dwelling units. This Court in Levine v. Katz pointed out that:

> It has long been well settled in this jurisdiction that, where a landlord leases separate portions of property and reserves under his own control the halls, stairs, or other parts of the property for use in common by all tenants, he has a duty to all those on the premises of legal right to use ordinary care and diligence to maintain the retained parts in a reasonably safe condition.

While Levine v. Katz dealt with a physical defect in the building leading to plaintiff's injury, the rationale as applied to predictable criminal acts by third parties is the same. The duty is the landlord's because by his control of the areas of common use and common danger he is the only party who has the *power* to make the necessary repairs or to provide the necessary protection.

As a general rule, a private person does not have a duty to protect another from a criminal attack by a third person. We recognize that this rule has sometimes in the past been applied in landlord-tenant law, even by this court. Among the reasons for the application of this rule to landlords are: judicial reluctance to tamper with the traditional common law concept of the landlord-tenant relationship; the notion that the act of a third person in committing an intentional tort or crime is a superseding cause of the harm to another resulting therefrom; the oftentimes difficult problem of determining foreseeability of criminal acts; the vagueness of the standard which the landlord must meet; the economic consequences of the imposition of the duty; and conflict with the public policy allocating the duty of protecting citizens from criminal acts to the government rather than the private sector.

But the rationale of this very broad general rule falters when it is applied to the conditions of modern day urban apartment living, particularly in the circumstances of this case. The rationale of the general rule exonerating a third party from any duty to protect another from a criminal attack has no applicability to the landlord-tenant relationship in multiple dwelling houses. The landlord is no insurer of his tenants' safety, but he certainly is no bystander. And where, as here, the landlord has notice of repeated criminal assaults and robberies, has notice that these crimes occurred in the portion of the premises exclusively within his control, has every reason to expect like crimes to happen again, and has the exclusive power to take preventive action, it does not seem unfair to place upon the landlord a duty to take those steps which are within his power to minimize the predictable risk to his tenants.

This court has recently had occasion to review landlord-tenant law as applied to multiple family urban dwellings. In Javins v. First National Realty Corporation, the traditional analysis of a lease as being a conveyance of an interest in land — with all the medieval connotations this often brings — was reappraised, and found lacking in several respects. This court noted that the value of the lease to the modern apartment dweller is that it gives him "a well known package of goods and services — a package which includes not merely walls and ceilings, but also adequate heat, light and ventilation, serviceable plumbing facilities, *secure windows and doors*, proper sanitation, and proper maintenance." It does not give him the land itself, and to the tenant as a practical matter this is supremely unimportant. Speaking for the court, Judge Wright then went on to state, "In our judgment the trend toward treating leases as contracts is wise and well considered. Our holding in this case reflects a belief that leases of urban dwelling units should be interpreted and construed like any other contract."

Treating the modern day urban lease as a contract, this court in *Javins, supra,* recognized, among other things, that repair of the leased premises in a multiple dwelling unit may require access to equipment in areas in the control of the landlord, and skills which no urban tenant possesses. Accordingly, this court delineated the landlord's duty to repair as including continued maintenance of the rented apartment throughout the term of the lease, rightfully placing the duty to maintain the premises upon the party to the lease contract having the capacity to do so, based upon an implied warranty of habitability.

In the case at bar we place the duty of taking protective measures guarding the entire premises and the areas peculiarly under the landlord's control against the perpetration of criminal acts upon the landlord, the party to the lease contract who has the effective capacity to perform these necessary acts.

As a footnote to *Javins, supra,* Judge Wright, in clearing away some of the legal underbrush from medieval common law obscuring the modern landlord-tenant relationship, referred to an innkeeper's liability in comparison with that of the landlord to his tenant. "Even the old common law courts responded with a different rule for a landlord-tenant relationship which did not conform to the model of the usual agrarian lease. Much more substantial obligations were placed upon the keepers of inns (the only multiple dwelling houses known to the common law)."

Specifically, innkeepers have been held liable for assaults which have been committed upon their guests by third parties, if they have breached a duty which is imposed by reason of the innkeeper-guest relationship. By this duty, the innkeeper is generally bound to exercise reasonable care to protect the guest from abuse or molestation from third parties, be they innkeeper's employees, fellow guests, or intruders, if the attack could, or in the exercise of reasonable care, should have been anticipated.

Liability in the innkeeper-guest relationship is based as a matter of law either upon the innkeeper's supervision, care, or control of the premises, or by reason of a contract which some courts have implied from the entrustment by the guest of his personal comfort and safety to the innkeeper. In the latter analysis, the contract is held to give the guest the right to expect a standard of treatment at the hands of the innkeeper which includes an obligation on the part of the latter to exercise reasonable care in protecting the guest.

Other relationships in which similar duties have been imposed include landowner-invitee, businessman-patron, employer-employee, school district-pupil, hospital-patient, and carrier-passenger. In all, the theory of liability is essentially the same: that since the ability of one of the parties to provide for his own protection has been limited in some way by his submission to the control of the other, a duty should be imposed upon the one possessing control (and thus the power to act) to take reasonable precautions to protect the other one from assaults by third parties which, at least, could reasonably have been anticipated. However, there is no liability normally imposed upon the one having the power to act if the violence is sudden and unexpected provided that the source of the violence is not an employee of the one in control.

We are aware of various cases in other jurisdictions following a different line of reasoning, conceiving of the landlord and tenant relationship along more traditional common law lines, and on varying fact situations reaching a different result from that we reach here. Typical of these is a much cited (although only a 4-3) decision of the Supreme Court of New Jersey, Goldberg v. Housing Authority of Newark, *supra* relied on by appellee landlord here. There the court said:

Everyone can foresee the commission of crime virtually anywhere and at any time. If foreseeability itself gave rise to a duty to provide "police" protection for others, every residential curtilage, every shop, every store, every manufacturing plant would have to be patrolled by the private arm of the owner. And since hijacking and attack upon occupants of motor vehicles are also foreseeable, it would be the duty of every motorist to provide armed protection for his passengers and the property of others. Of course, none of this is at all palatable.

This language seems to indicate that the court was using the word *foreseeable* interchangeably with the word *possible*. In that context, the statement is quite correct. It would be folly to impose liability for mere possibilities. But we must reach the question of liability for attacks which are foreseeable in the sense that they are *probable* and *predictable*. Thus, the United States Supreme Court, in Lillie v. Thompson encountered no difficulty in finding that the defendant-employer was liable to the employee because it "was aware of conditions which created a likelihood" of criminal attack.

In the instant case, the landlord had notice, both actual and constructive, that the tenants were being subjected to crimes against their persons and their property in and from the common hallways. For the period just prior to the time of the assault upon appellant Kline the record contains unrefuted evidence that the apartment building was undergoing a rising wave of crime. Under these conditions, we can only conclude that the landlord here "was aware of conditions which created a likelihood" (actually, almost a certainty) that further criminal attacks upon tenants would occur.

Upon consideration of all pertinent factors, we find that there is a duty of protection owed by the landlord to the tenant in an urban multiple unit apartment dwelling.

Summarizing our analysis, we find that this duty of protection arises, first of all, from the logic of the situation itself. If we were answering without the benefit of any prior precedent the issue as posed by the appellee landlord here, "whether a duty should be placed on a landlord to take steps to protect tenants from foreseeable criminal acts committed by third parties," we should have no hesitancy in answering it affirmatively, at least on the basis of the facts of this case.

As between tenant and landlord, the landlord is the only one in the position to take the necessary acts of protection required. He is not an insurer, but he is obligated to minimize the risk to his tenants. Not only as between landlord and tenant is the landlord best equipped to guard against the predictable risk of intruders, but even as between landlord and the police power of government, the landlord is in the best position to take the necessary protective measures. Municipal police cannot patrol the entryways and the hallways, the garages and the basements of private multiple unit apartment dwellings. They are neither equipped, manned, nor empowered to do so. In the area of the predictable risk which materialized in this case, only the landlord could have taken measures which might have prevented the injuries suffered by appellant.

We note that in the fight against crime the police are not expected to do it all; every segment of society has obligations to aid in law enforcement and to minimize the opportunities for crime. The average citizen is ceaselessly warned to remove keys from automobiles and, in this jurisdiction, may be liable in tort for any injury caused in the operation of his car by a thief if he fails to do so, notwithstanding the intervening criminal act of the thief, a third party. In addition, auto manufacturers are persuaded to install special locking devices and buzzer alarms, and real estate developers, residential communities, and industrial areas are asked to install especially bright lights to deter the criminally inclined. It is only just that the obligations of landlords in their sphere be acknowledged and enforced.

Secondly, on the rationale of this court in Levine v. Katz, Kendall v. Gore Properties, and Javins v. First National Realty Corporation, *supra*, there is implied in the contract between landlord and tenant an obligation on the landlord to provide those protective measures which are within his reasonable capacity. Here the protective measures which were in effect in October 1959 when appellant first signed a lease were drastically reduced. She continued after the expiration of the first term of the lease on a month to month tenancy. As this court pointed out in *Javins, supra,* "Since the lessees continue to pay the same rent, they were entitled to expect that the landlord would continue to keep the premises in their beginning condition during the lease term. It is precisely such expectations that the law now recognizes as deserving of formal, legal protection."

Thirdly, if we reach back to seek the precedents of common law, on the question of whether there exists or does not exist a duty on the owner of the premises to provide protection against criminal acts by third parties, the most analogous relationship to that of the modern day urban apartment house dweller is not that of a landlord and tenant, but that of innkeeper and guest. We can also consider other relationships, cited above, in which an analogous duty has been found to exist.

IV

We now turn to the standard of care which should be applied in judging if the landlord has fulfilled his duty of protection to the tenant. Although in many cases the language speaks as if the standard of care itself varies, in the last analysis the standard of care is the same — reasonable care in all the circumstances. The specific measures to achieve this standard vary with the individual circumstances. It may be impossible to describe in detail for all situations of landlord-tenant relationships, and evidence of custom amongst landlords of the same class of building may play a significant role in determining if the standard has been met.

In the case at bar, appellant's repeated efforts to introduce evidence as to the standard of protection commonly provided in apartment buildings of the same character and class as 1500 Massachusetts Avenue at the time of the assault upon Miss Kline were invariably frustrated by the objections of opposing counsel and the impatience of the trial judge. . . .

. . . .

We therefore hold in this case that the applicable standard of care in providing protection for the tenant is that standard which this landlord himself was employing in October 1959 when the appellant became a resident on the premises at 1500 Massachusetts Avenue. The tenant was led to expect that she could rely upon this degree of protection. While we do not say that the precise measures for security which were then in vogue should have been kept up (e.g., the number of people at the main entrances might have been reduced if a tenant-controlled intercom-automatic latch system had been installed in the common entryways), we do hold that the same relative degree of security should have been maintained.

The appellant tenant was entitled to performance by the landlord measured by this standard of protection whether the landlord's obligation be viewed as grounded in contract or in tort. As we have pointed out, this standard of protection was implied as an obligation of the lease contract from the beginning. Likewise, on a tort basis, this standard of protection may be taken as that commonly provided in apartments of this character and type in this community, and this is a reasonable standard of care on which to judge the conduct of the landlord here.

V

Given this duty of protection, and the standard of care as defined, it is clear that the appellee landlord breached its duty toward the appellant tenant here. The risk of criminal assault and robbery on any tenant was clearly predictable, a risk of which the appellee landlord had specific notice, a risk which became reality with increasing frequency, and this risk materialized on the very premises peculiarly under the control, and therefore the protection, of the landlord to the injury of the appellant tenant. The question then for the District Court becomes one of damages only. To us the liability is clear.

Having said this, it would be well to state what is *not* said by this decision. We do not hold that the landlord is by any means an insurer of the safety of his tenants. His duty is to take those measures of protection which are within his power and capacity to take, and which can reasonably be expected to mitigate the risk of intruders assaulting and robbing tenants. The landlord is not expected to provide protection commonly owed by a municipal police department; but as illustrated in this case, he is obligated to protect those parts of his premises which are not usually subject to periodic patrol and inspection by the municipal police. We do not say that every multiple unit apartment house in the District of Columbia should have those same measures of protection which 1500 Massachusetts Avenue enjoyed in 1959, nor do we say that 1500 Massachusetts Avenue should have precisely those same measures in effect at the present time. Alternative and more up-to-date methods may be equally or even more effective.

Granted, the discharge of this duty of protection by landlords will cause, in many instances, the expenditure of large sums for additional equipment and services, and granted, the cost will be ultimately passed on to the tenant in the form of increased rents. This prospect, in itself, however, is no deterrent to our acknowledging and giving force to the duty, since without protection the tenant already pays in losses from theft, physical assault and increased insurance premiums.

The landlord is entirely justified in passing on the cost of increased protective measures to his tenants, but the rationale of compelling the landlord to do it in the first place is that he is the only one who is in a position to take the necessary protective measures for overall protection of the premises, which he owns in whole and rents in part to individual tenants.

Reversed and remanded to the District Court for the determination of damages.

QUESTIONS

1. What are the reasons for and against extending the landlord's duty of care in *Kline*?

For:

The existing relationship between modern landlords and tenants is the product of several centuries of legal evolution. Under the common law, the sole duty placed upon the landlord was the delivery of possession of the land to his lessee. All responsibility for maintenance, repairs, and protection of the premises fell upon the tenant. In the traditional agrarian economy, where a tenant was assumed to be a virtual "jack-of-all-trades" capable of maintaining the premises with little difficulty, this favorable attitude toward the landlord was understandable. Today, in the modern urban environment, where tenants, rather than renting large parcels of land, usually lease only single units in multiunit dwellings, the premise underlying the landlord-tenant relationship in times past has lost much of its validity.

The modern urban tenant rarely possesses the mechanical and tectonic talents of the traditional agrarian land dweller, and has come to depend increasingly upon his landlord for such basic services as light, heat, and maintenance. Today's tenants are seeking a "well-known package of goods and services" and expect from landlords basic necessities as part of their lease agreement. In a housing market based upon the law of supply and demand, modern urban landlords, though limited by their capacity and willingness to spend, seek to offer a commodity which will best satisfy the wants and needs of their prospective tenants.

An evolution in the legal concepts governing the landlord-tenant relationship, making it more truly reflective of modern urban conditions, is occurring because of several different factors. Initially, some impetus for change has come from the severe housing shortage in large metropolitan areas. Many tenants have been forced to accept unsuitable housing with substandard conditions because of the lack of a viable alternative.[15]

Against:

The rule that the landlord does not have a duty to protect tenants from the criminal acts of third parties has received almost universal acceptance. Several reasons have been cited for this, including (1) traditional refusal to breach the common law concepts of the landlord-tenant relationship; (2) the inherent obfuscation of the standard of care which must guide the landlord; (3) the difficulty in determining forseeability of criminal acts; (4) the inability to establish the causal relation between the landlord's breach of duty and the harm to his tenant resulting from the criminal acts of a third person; (5) the economic ramifications of such a duty; and (6) reluctance to transfer the duty of protection from the government to private persons.[16]

2. How is the landlord's duty towards the tenant extended in *Kline* beyond that which appears in the previous cases?

The following excerpt provides an explanation.

The majority, while discussing the case before it as though it were one sounding solely in tort, derived from *Levine v. Katz* the concept that a landlord owes a duty to exercise reasonable care over the common facilities. From *Kendall v. Gore Properties, Inc.* it extracted the duty of protection against foreseeable criminal acts, despite the fact that in *Kendall* the perpetrator of the crime was an employee of the lessor. The *Kline* court found that this duty "arises, first of all, from the logic of the situation itself." Intervening criminal acts should not cut off the landlord's duty to protect in modern urban multiple dwellings, because he "is the only one in the position to take the necessary acts of protection required."

The court alternatively posited a contract rationale for its holding. As *Javins* and kindred cases indicate, the lease of an urban dwelling has come to be viewed increasingly as a contract; this focus enables courts more readily to find obligations in the lease by implication. In *Javins*, the court found an implied duty to repair based on an implied warranty of habitability; in *Kline*, the court placed

the duty of taking protective measures guarding the entire premises and the areas peculiarly under the landlord's control against the perpetration of criminal acts upon the landlord, the party to the lease contract who has the effective capacity to perform these necessary acts.

The language seems to suggest an implied contractual obligation the scope of which is delineated by the tort standard of reasonable protection for areas under the landlord's control. Here we find tort law defining the scope of a contract duty. The court later justified its holding on the contract ground that there had been a decrease in services during the term of the lease.

If the court in *Kline* had limited its rationale either to a distinct tort or to a distinct contract notion, the case would be but a slight extension of the decision in *Ramsay.* But the court did not choose to remand for a determination of whether there had been a breach of either a tort standard of reasonable care or a contract standard to be found in the lease. Instead, it held that, as a matter of law, the landlord owed a specific duty to the tenant, whether grounded in tort or contract. . . .

---

[15] Note, *Landlord's Duty to Protect Tenants from Criminal Acts of Third Parties: The View from 1500 Massachusetts Avenue,* 59 Geo. L.J. 1153, 1155–57 (1971). Reprinted with permission of the publisher, Georgetown University ©1971.

[16] *Id.* at 1163.

In short, the court looked to tort law to determine the breadth of the lessor's duty, to contract law to avoid the problem of proximate cause, and to the statutory duty to repair to find a model for the interaction of the other two bodies of law.[17]

---

[17] Comment, *The Landlord's Emerging Responsibility for Tenant Security*, 71 COLUM. L. REV. 275, 284–86 (1971). Reprinted by permission of the Columbia Law Review ©1971. All rights reserved

Topic II
MITIGATION OF DAMAGES
(1 Assignment)

ASSIGNMENT 1
Briefing: Examples in Contract, Tort, and Property Law

In order to prevent waste, the doctrine of avoidable consequences requires that the harmed party do what he or she reasonably can to mitigate the effects of the harm. *Rockingham County* discusses the need to abandon work on a contract once it is repudiated. *Roy* discusses the need to seek medical treatment following an injury in tort. Mitigation is not always required. In the property area there still exists a trend of decisions that do not require a landlord to mitigate damages by rerenting an abandoned apartment. *Wright* discusses one technique for getting around this property exception. *Lefrak* discusses the abandonment of this property exception.

Let us begin by reading the *Rockingham* decision. Do not try to remember everything that it says. Read it the first time for its story. Once you have that, you can go back to do a more careful reading with specific questions in mind.

ROCKINGHAM COUNTY v. LUTEN BRIDGE CO.
35 F.2d 301 (4th Cir. 1929)

PARKER, Circuit Judge.

This was an action at law instituted in the court below by the Luten Bridge Company, as plaintiff, to recover of Rockingham county, North Carolina, an amount alleged to be due under a contract for the construction of a bridge. The county admits the execution and breach of the contract, but contends that notice of cancellation was given the bridge company before the erection of the bridge was commenced, and that it is liable only for the damages which the company would have sustained, if it had abandoned construction at that time. The judge below . . . excluded evidence offered by the county in support of its contentions as to notice of cancellation and damages, and instructed a verdict for plaintiff for the full amount of its claim. From the judgment on this verdict the county has appealed.

The facts out of which the case arises, as shown by the affidavits and offers of proof appearing in the record, are as follows: On January 7, 1924, the board of commissioners of Rockingham county voted to award to plaintiff a contract for the construction of the bridge in controversy. . . .

. . . .

At one of [the] meetings [of the board of commissioners], a regularly advertised called meeting held on February 21st, a resolution was unanimously adopted declaring that the contract for the building of the bridge was not legal and valid, and directing the clerk of the board to notify plaintiff that it refused to recognize same as a valid contract, and that plaintiff should proceed no further thereunder. This resolution also rescinded action of the board theretofore taken looking to the construction of a hard-surfaced road, in which the bridge was to be a mere connecting link. The clerk duly sent a certified copy of this resolution to plaintiff.

At the regular monthly meeting of the board on March 3d, a resolution was passed directing that plaintiff be notified that any work done on the bridge would be done by it at its own risk and hazard, that the board was of the opinion that the contract for the construction of the bridge was not valid and legal, and that, even if the board were mistaken as to this, it did not desire to construct the bridge, and would contest payment for same if constructed. A copy of this resolution was also sent to plaintiff. At the regular monthly meeting on April 7th, a resolution was passed, reciting that the board had been informed that one of its members was privately insisting that the bridge be constructed. It repudiated this action on the part of the member and gave notice that it would not be recognized. At the September meeting, a resolution was passed to the effect that the board would pay no bills presented by plaintiff or any one connected with the bridge. At the time of the passage of the first resolution, very little work toward the construction of the bridge had been done, it being estimated that the total cost of labor done and material on the ground was around $1,900; but, notwithstanding the repudiation of the contract by the county, the bridge company continued with the work of construction.

On November 24, 1924, plaintiff instituted this action against Rockingham county, and against Pruitt, Pratt, McCollum, Martin, and Barber, as constituting its board of commissioners. Complaint was filed, setting forth the execution of the contract and the doing of work by plaintiff thereunder, and alleging that for work done up until November 3, 1924, the county was indebted in the sum of $18,301.07. . . .

. . . .

As the county now admits the execution and validity of the contract, and the breach on its part, the ultimate question in the case is one as to the measure of plaintiff's recovery, and the exceptions must be considered with this in mind. Upon these exceptions, three principal questions arise for our consideration, viz.: (1) . . . . (2) . . . . And (3) whether plaintiff . . . can recover under the contract for work done after [the notices] were received, or is limited to the recovery of damages for breach of contract as of that date.

. . . .

Coming, then, to the third question — i.e., as to the measure of plaintiff's recovery — we do not think that, after the county had given notice, while the contract was still executory, that it did not desire the bridge built and would not pay for it, plaintiff could proceed to build it and recover the contract price. It is true that the county had no right to rescind the contract, and the notice given plaintiff amounted to a breach on its part; but, after plaintiff had received notice of the breach, it was its duty to do nothing to increase the damages flowing therefrom. If A enters into a binding contract to build a house for B, B, of course, has no right to rescind the contract without A's consent. But if, before the house is built, he decides that he does not want it, and notifies A to that effect, A has no right to proceed with the building and thus pile up damages. His remedy is to treat the contract as broken when he receives the notice, and sue for the recovery of such damages as he may have sustained from the breach, including any profit which he would have realized upon performance, as well as any other losses which may have resulted to him. In the case at bar, the county decided not to build the road of which the bridge was to be a part, and did not build it. The bridge, built in the midst of the forest, is of no value to the county because of this change of circumstances. When, therefore, the county gave notice to the plaintiff that it would not proceed with the project, plaintiff should have desisted from further work. It had no right thus to pile up damages by proceeding with the erection of a useless bridge.

The contrary view was expressed by Lord Cockburn in Frost v. Knight, but, as pointed out by Prof. Williston, it is not in harmony with the decisions in this country. The American rule and the reasons supporting it are well stated by Prof. Williston as follows:

"There is a line of cases running back to 1845 which holds that, after an absolute repudiation or refusal to perform by one party to a contract, the other party cannot continue to perform and recover damages based on full performance. This rule is only a particular application of the general rule of damages that a plaintiff cannot hold a defendant liable for damages which need not have been incurred; or, as it is often stated, the plaintiff must, so far as he can without loss to himself, mitigate the damages caused by the defendant's wrongful act. The application of this rule to the matter in question is obvious. If a man engages to have work done, and afterwards repudiates his contract before the work has been begun or when it has been only partially done, it is inflicting damage on the defendant without benefit to the plaintiff to allow the latter to insist on proceeding with the contract. The work may be useless to the defendant, and yet he would be forced to pay the full contract price. On the other hand, the plaintiff is interested only in the profit he will make out of the contract. If he receives this it is equally advantageous for him to use his time otherwise."

The leading case on the subject in this country is the New York case of Clark v. Marsiglia. In that case defendant had employed plaintiff to paint certain pictures for him, but countermanded the order before the work was finished. Plaintiff, however, went on and completed the work and sued for the contract price. In reversing a judgment for plaintiff, the court said:

"The plaintiff was allowed to recover as though there had been no countermand of the order; and in this the court erred. The defendant, by requiring the plaintiff to stop work upon the paintings, violated his contract, and thereby incurred a liability to pay such damages as the plaintiff should sustain. Such damages would include a recompense for the labor done and materials used, and such further sum in damages as might, upon legal principles, be assessed for the breach of the contract; but the plaintiff had no right, by obstinately persisting in the work, to make the penalty upon the defendant greater than it would otherwise have been."

And the rule as established by the great weight of authority in America is summed up in the following statement in 6 R.C.L. 1029, which is quoted with approval by the Supreme Court of North Carolina in the recent case of Novelty Advertising Co. v. Farmers' Mut. Tobacco Warehouse Co.:

"While a contract is executory a party has the power to stop performance on the other side by an explicit direction to that effect, subjecting himself to such damages as will compensate the other party for being stopped in the performance on his part at that stage in the execution of the contract. The party thus forbidden cannot afterwards go on, and thereby increase the damages, and then recover such damages from the other party. The legal right of either party to violate, abandon, or renounce his contract, on the usual terms of compensation to the other for the damages which the law recognizes and allows, subject to the jurisdiction of equity to decree specific performance in proper cases, is universally recognized and acted upon."

This is in accord with the earlier North Carolina decision of Heiser v. Mears, in which it was held that, where a buyer countermands his order for goods to be manufactured for him under an executory contract, before the work is completed, it is notice to the seller that he elects to rescind his contract and submit to the legal measure of damages, and that in such case the seller cannot complete the goods and recover the contract price.

. . . . It follows that there was error in directing a verdict for plaintiff for the full amount of its claim. The measure of plaintiff's damage, upon its appearing that notice was duly given not to build the bridge, is an amount sufficient to compensate plaintiff for labor and materials expended and expense incurred in the part performance of the contract, prior to its repudiation, plus the profit which would have been realized if it had been carried out in accordance with its terms.

Our conclusion, on the whole case, is that there was error . . . in excluding the testimony offered by the county to which we have referred, and in directing a verdict for plaintiff. The judgment below will accordingly be reversed, and the case remanded for a new trial.

Reversed.

DISCUSSION

What story do we understand from a first reading of this case? The board of commissioners for Rockingham County were sued for breach of contract, and they admitted to the breach. The Luten Bridge Company completed its end of the bargain by building the bridge and sued for payment under the contract. The trial court directed a verdict for the plaintiff for the full amount of its claim. [When you see a term you do not understand, look it up in your dictionary. In BLACK'S LAW DICTIONARY at 1592 (8th ed. 2004), a "directed verdict" is "[a] ruling by a trial judge taking a case from the jury because the evidence will permit only one reasonable verdict."]

It would seem that nothing could be simpler. But wait! This court's opinion, rendered by the Fourth Circuit Court of Appeals, reverses the lower court's decision and remands for a new trial. There is something wrong and the fault seems to lie with the Luten Bridge Company with the result that they are not going to get their contract price. This is strange! Does the Luten Bridge Company not have the right to all the money agreed to under its contract with the board of commissioners? What right does the appellate court have to deny this contract right? Go back now and read the case more carefully for what Luten did wrong. You will now be examining the problem (or what is called the issue) in the case. Ask yourself specifically what amount of the contract price the Luten Bridge Company may claim and why it is not the whole price.

This second, more careful reading of the case reveals that Luten is entitled to its expenses up to the time of the board's breach plus the profits it expected from performing the contract. Near the end of the case, the court specifically says the measure of damages "is an amount sufficient to compensate plaintiff for labor and materials expended and expenses incurred in the part performance of the contract, prior to its repudiation, plus the profit which would have been realized if it had been carried out in accordance with its terms." Profits are all monies in the contract beyond expenses; they are what the Luten Bridge Company makes on the deal. The case mentions that the expenses spent up to the time of breach were about $1,900 and the total contract price appears to have been about $18,300. It is not clear what monies were expended by the Luten Bridge Company between the time of breach and the conclusion of work (this is something that probably will be determined when the case is remanded for a new trial), but let us assume they were about $10,000. In such a case, total expenses would have been $11,900 and the expected profit would have been $6,400. Under the *Rockingham* decision, the Luten Bridge Company would be entitled to the $1900 expenses plus the $6,400 profit for a total of $8,300.

If the $10,000 figure is correct, the Company spent $11,900 but takes $8,300 from the deal. There is no profit. In fact there is a loss of $3,600. Why should the Company suffer this loss when the board of Rockingham County is the breaching party? This is the crux of the case: Regardless of the fact that the board was a breaching party, the Luten Bridge Company had a chance to mitigate the board's losses on the contract at no cost to itself if it had stopped work immediately upon notice of the board's breach. It would not have expended the additional $10,000 and it would have made its profit of $6,400. In the interest of preventing waste, the court called forth a rule for mitigation of damages that required the performing party to desist from expenditures that would produce no useful product and, if it did not, the performing party would be required to bear their cost. In other words, since the building of the bridge was useless after the board of Rockingham County rejected it, the court maintained that the Luten Bridge Company should have stopped its work in order to prevent waste, and since it did not mitigate the damages by stopping, the Company would be responsible for all the expenses incurred after notice of breach.

Now after reading this case closely enough to understand its story, its problem(s), the solution and the reason for the solution, we are ready to "brief the case":

Rockingham County v. Luten Bridge Co.
(4th Cir. 1929)

FACTS: P (Luten Bridge Co.) contracts to build a bridge for D (board of commissioners for Rockingham county). D breaches contract and notifies P to stop work before most of the work has been completed, but P completes the work and sues for the contract price. Lower court directs a verdict for P. This court reverses and remands.

ISSUE: To what damages is P entitled when a contract is breached by D with notice to P before work is completed?

HOLDING: P is entitled to its expenses up to the time of notice of breach plus the profits expected on the contract. P is not entitled to any expenses incurred after notice of the breach.

RATIONALE: Expenses by P after breach of the contract by D are wasted resources. This consequence should be avoided as a matter of good policy. Therefore, the mitigation of damages rule on which the court bases its decision above is enforced in contract law to discourage waste by putting the cost of the waste on the non-breaching party. There is no cost to the non-breaching party who ceases performance upon notice of breach and thus prevents waste.

We have digested our first case and now turn to the second. While *Rockingham* is a case in contract, *Roy* is a case in tort. Read through the case first for its story.

ROY v. ROBIN
173 So. 2d 222 (La. Ct. App. 1965)

TATE, Judge.

The defendant Robin struck the plaintiff Roy in the face in a dance hall fight. The plaintiff sues for personal injuries resulting from the fight. The trial court awarded the plaintiff $250 for minor cuts on the eyebrow. The plaintiff appeals this award as inadequate, contending that he is additionally entitled to recover for the subsequent loss of his left eye.

The evidence shows that the fight occurred near midnight on November 13th. The plaintiff and his wife testified that the chief initial injuries were three little cuts on the eyebrow, and that after the injury the plaintiff did not even sustain a black eye. About two days after the accident, however, the plaintiff's eye commenced to swell; and on November 21st about seven days after the accident, the plaintiff reported to a local physician because of the gradual development of extreme swelling of his eye.

The local physician testified that an infection in the eye had progressed so far, in the five or six days since it had commenced, that the physician immediately sent Roy on to Charity Hospital for hospitalization for treatment of the grave condition. The Charity Hospital records are in evidence and show the severity of an infection of unstated cause in the eyeball and surrounding tissues. Finally, after extensive treatment over some fifty days, the plaintiff's left eye was removed on January 12, 1960, that is, about two months after the fight in which the plaintiff's face was punched.

The trial court allowed recovery only for the initial slight facial injuries. It disallowed recovery for the severe infection in the eye area and the subsequent loss of the eye, reasoning that this aggravation of the initial very minor injury resulted solely from the plaintiff's failure to seek medical assistance sooner.

Able counsel for the plaintiff-appellant correctly points out, in our opinion, that the damages for the aggravation of the initial injury should not be minimized for this reason.

The general principle sought to be applied is that a person injured by a tortfeasor cannot recover damages for such subsequent results of initial injury as he could reasonably have avoided by the exercise of due care on his part. In the application of this principle, Louisiana decisions have held that an injured person who unreasonably refuses recommended medical treatment is not entitled to recovery for any aggravation of the initial condition resulting from the unreasonable failure to undergo medical treatment recommended by competent physicians. The tortfeasor has the burden of proving that damages should be minimized because of the injured person's unreasonable failure to seek medical attention earlier.

In the present instance, the injured plaintiff did not refuse medical treatment; he merely delayed securing same for some seven days after the injury. The infection did not set in until approximately two days after the fight, and the plaintiff and his wife at first attempted to treat it by home remedies for some five days before they reported to a physician for further treatment, after the infection had progressed gradually to a severe condition despite their efforts.

Considering the tortfeasor's burden of proof, we cannot say that the evidence sufficiently proves that the injured plaintiff unreasonably neglected to seek medical attention earlier: We cannot say that the aggravation of the injury was proved to be due to his failure to exercise ordinary, reasonable, or due care under all of the circumstances, including the relatively swift progression of the infection following its delayed inception, and including the absence of a showing that the plaintiff should reasonably have realized sooner that his initially minor injuries might become serious if he failed to secure expert medical attention rather than using home-care remedies.

The Louisiana cases allowing minimization generally involve some willful or deliberate failure of the injured person to avail himself of medical attention reasonably indicated. Here the plaintiff did not neglect care of his injury; rather the homecare remedy used by him of attempting to reduce the infection by epsom salts bathing was inadequate in the light of hindsight. There is no showing that reasonable care at the time demanded earlier consultation of a physician.

The defendant-appellee further contends, however, that no causal relationship has been proved between the blow to the eye area (which did not even produce a black eye), and the subsequent development of an infection behind the eyeball.

The commencement of this infection two days after the accident certainly might give rise to a serious suspicion in the lay mind that there was a causal relationship. Nevertheless, in the evidence before us, neither the initial attending physician's testimony or the Charity Hospital records — the only medical evidence in the record —, show any causal relationship between the blow to the face and the development of an infection within the eye some two to eight days later.

It is true that "A medical condition producing disability or death is presumed to have resulted from an accident, if before the accident the injured person was in good health or affected only with latent symptoms, but shortly after the accident the disabling or death-causing condition manifested itself; provided that the medical evidence shows that there is a reasonable possibility of a causal connection between the accident and the disability or death. * * *" In the evidence in the present case, however, there is not the slightest medical testimony to show how a blow to the eye area, which produced only cuts on the eyebrow and no black eye, could have produced interior tissue damage or otherwise produced or permitted the development of a massive eye infection such as was involved herein.

We think, therefore, that the defendant correctly contends that the plaintiff has not borne his burden of proving any causal relationship between the blow to the eye area and the subsequent development of a severe infection within the left eye, which, some two months later, resulted in the loss of this eye. Consequently, we find no error in the trial court's having awarded the plaintiff $250 damages for the only proven injuries, three small cuts above the eyebrow, resulting from the blow to his face sustained by him.

For the foregoing reasons, the judgment of the trial court is affirmed, at the cost of the plaintiff-appellant.

Affirmed.

DISCUSSION

Roy is analogous to *Rockingham* insofar as it raises the issue of mitigation of damages. The plaintiff (P) was the victim of a punch by the defendant (D). The lower court awarded P only $250 damages for three small cuts above the eyebrow but refused to award damages for loss of the eye. P had not sought medical attention for his eye and the lower court "reason[ed] that this aggravation of the initial very minor injury resulted solely from the plaintiff's failure to seek medical assistance sooner." The appellate court, which wrote the decision we read above, affirmed the lower court's decision. It seems to be a clear-cut case of waste by P for having failed to mitigate the damages of loss of his eye when he failed to seek medical assistance, even though D caused the loss of his eye through a punch.

But hold on! If you have concluded that P failed to mitigate damages, you have misread the case. Although the mitigation rule does exist in tort as confirmed by this court, the rule has a key element that is missing in this case. The court states that "an injured person who *unreasonably* refuses recommended medical treatment is not entitled to recovery for any aggravation of the initial condition resulting from the *unreasonable* failure to undergo medical treatment recommended by competent physicians." [Emphasis added] For the mitigation of damages rule to apply, the injured person must have refused to mitigate damages unreasonably, and the burden of proof of unreasonableness is on the tortfeasor. The court found that the defendant did not carry his burden of proof; the evidence was not sufficient to prove unreasonable neglect to seek medical attention earlier.

Then why did the court not reverse the lower court and remand the opinion to determine the full damages for loss of the eye? The case is affirmed on a totally different ground. The burden of proof to show a causal relationship between the punch and the loss of the eye was on the plaintiff victim. The plaintiff failed to provide sufficient evidence of this causal relationship, and, therefore, the damages for loss of the eye were denied. With this finding, the court relegates its discussion of the mitigation issue to dictum, but the dictum is still important to understand the rules concerning mitigation and how they are applied.

We now know the story of the case, the legal issues raised, and their solutions. The next step is to brief it.

Roy v. Robin
(La. Ct. App. 1965)

FACTS:	D punches P in the face and causes cuts to the eyebrow. Eye swells up after 2 days. P tries homecare remedies that don't work. After 7 days he sees a physician who sends him to hospital where his eye is removed 2 months after the fight. Lower court awards damages only for eyebrow cuts and not loss of eye. This court affirms.
ISSUE:	(1) Under mitigation of damages rule, is D responsible for loss of eye if P did not seek medical attention immediately? (2) What element of proof is missing in this case to allow damages for loss of the eye?
DICTUM:	Failure to mitigate damages must be an unreasonable act in order to prevent recovery for a tort, and the delay in seeking medical attention here was not unreasonable.
HOLDING:	P failed to prove that the loss of the eye was caused by the punch, and, therefore, damages are not allowed.

After writing the brief, the next step is to think about what questions the professor may ask in class concerning this case. The questions most likely will extend beyond identification of the facts, the issues, the dictum and the holding. For example, this case may provide an opportunity to discuss the practicalities of satisfying a party's burden of proof. Each of the parties carried a burden to prove certain facts in this case. The professor may discuss what that burden was and how each party could have presented evidence to establish the necessary proof. After discussing what could have been done to present a better case on each side, the professor may ask a more open-ended question about your opinion of the lawyering in this case. Did the attorneys who represented these parties handle the case properly? If it was improper, was it merely bad lawyering or did their actions border on malpractice? The court states that "there is not the slightest medical testimony to show how a blow to the eye area, which produced only cuts on the eyebrow and no black eye, could have produced interior tissue damage or otherwise produced or permitted the development of a massive eye infection such as was involved herein." The failure to present such medical testimony may have been the result of its failure to exist (in which circumstance this case should probably never have come to trial) or the result of the failure of the plaintiff's attorney to call the proper medical personnel to the stand. The decision in this case does not make it clear, but this ambiguity will not prevent a professor from exploring these issues through a series of hypotheticals designed to trigger your thinking.

Another example of an area for class discussion by the professor may be the elements of negligence. For negligence, one must prove duty, breach of duty, causation and damages. Causation is the crucial link between breach of duty and damages. This case may be the stepping stone to a discussion introducing these elements, giving a general background on the law of negligence, and exploring some of the issues that might arise later in specific cases in the course. The student usually is not expected to know more than the materials assigned in class, but she or he is expected to use common sense, logic, opinion, and other reasoning processes for discussing matters raised by the professor outside the specific bounds of the assigned materials. One quickly learns that in such discussions there usually are no "right" answers — just answers that make common sense, reasoned opinion, logical conclusions, etc. It is in these discussions that the student's creative spark is nurtured and the ability to "think like a lawyer" is developed.

The next case again raises the issue of mitigation of damages, only this time in property. In *Wright*, it is soon apparent that the mitigation principle in 1965 does not apply in a majority of jurisdictions when a lessee abandons a business leasehold. In other words, the lessor does not seek out a second tenant to take the lease for the remainder of the first tenant's lease in order to cut the cost of the lease to the first tenant. As you read the opinion, ask yourself WHY?

<h3 style="text-align:center">WRIGHT v. BAUMANN</h3>
398 P.2d 119 (Or. 1965)

O'CONNELL, Justice.

Plaintiffs seek to recover for a breach of agreement under which plaintiffs agreed to erect an office building and defendant, a dentist, agreed to enter into a lease of one of the offices after the building was constructed. Both parties waived a jury trial. Defendant appeals from a judgment for plaintiffs.

Defendant's principal assignments of error are directed at the trial court's rejection of evidence tending to show that plaintiffs had the opportunity to mitigate damages but refused to do so. Plaintiffs' objections to defendant's questions relating to mitigation were sustained by the trial court, apparently on the ground that the instrument signed by the parties was a lease rather than a contract and that, being a lease, the lessor had no obligation to mitigate damages. Defendant contends that the rule relied upon by plaintiffs is inapplicable because the "Agreement" in question is not a lease but is a contract to make a lease, and that therefore plaintiffs are required to mitigate as in any other contract case. Finally, plaintiffs counter with the contention that the case was tried by defendant upon the theory that the "Agreement" was a lease and that he is now estopped to assert that it is a contract to enter into a lease.

Defendant's offer of proof clearly indicates that he made a reasonable effort to mitigate the damages resulting from his refusal to take possession of the part of the premises intended for his occupancy. The offer of proof showed that plaintiffs notified defendant on August 27, 1956, that the building would be ready for occupancy on September 24, 1956. On September 6, 1956, defendant notified plaintiffs that he did not desire to enter into a lease of any part of the building. It was further shown that defendant informed two doctors that the space allotted to him was available and that during September, 1956, the two doctors had offered to lease the space allotted to defendant on the terms and conditions specified in the "Agreement" in question but that plaintiffs refused to lease the office space to them, giving no reasons for the refusal to do so.

1. A majority of the courts, including Oregon, hold that a lessor is not required to mitigate damages when the lessee abandons the leasehold. In a few states it is incumbent upon the lessor to use reasonable means to mitigate damages. If the transaction is a contract to make a lease rather than an executed lease, it is universally recognized that the landowner has an obligation to mitigate damages upon a breach of the contract by the promisor.

2. The majority view, absolving the lessor from any obligation to mitigate is based upon the theory that the lessee becomes the owner of the premises for a term and therefore the lessor need not concern himself with lessee's abandonment of his own property. That view might have some validity in those cases where there is simply a lease of the land alone with no covenants except the covenant to pay rent. But a modern business lease is predominantly an exchange of promises and only incidentally a sale of a part of the lessor's interest in the land. As 2 Powell on Real Property observes, the "growth in the number and detail of specific lease covenants has reintroduced into the law of estates for years a predominantly contractual ingredient" and that as a consequence "[i]n practice, the law today concerning estates for years consists chiefly of rules determining the construction and effect of lease covenants." These covenants in a modern business lease, particularly where only a part of the space in a building is leased, relate for the most part to the use of the space. The lessor's duties do not end with the execution of the lease. The case of *Whitaker v. Hawley* expresses this view as follows: "* * * a lease is in one sense a running rather than a completed contract. It is an agreement for a continuous interchange of values between landlord and tenant, rather than a purchase single and completed of a term or estate in lands."

3. The covenants in the instrument in the present case relate to the continuing obligations of the respective parties. The transaction is essentially a contract. There is no reason why the principle of mitigation of damages should not be applied to it. "* * * [I]t is important that the rules for awarding damages should be such as to discourage even persons against whom wrongs have been committed from passively suffering economic loss which could be averted by reasonable efforts * * *."

4. Lessors as well as contract promisors should be made to serve this salutary policy. To borrow again from McCormick, "the realities of feudal tenure have vanished and a new system based upon a theory of contractual obligations has in general taken its place." He reminds us that in disregarding the contractual nature of modern leases we have "neglected the caution of Mr. Justice Holmes, 'that continuity with the past is only a necessity and not a duty.'" Writing in 1925, McCormick predicted that eventually "the logic, inescapable according to the standards of a 'jurisprudence of conceptions' which permits the landlord to stand idly by the vacant, abandoned premises and treat them as the property of the tenant and recover full rent, will yield to the more realistic notions of social advantage which in other fields of the law have forbidden a recovery for damages which the plaintiff by reasonable efforts could have avoided." We believe that it is time for McCormick's prediction to become a reality.

5. It does not seem that the burden imposed upon a lessor in mitigating damages would ordinarily be any greater than that imposed upon promisees of contracts not relating to the occupancy of land. However, if it could be said that it is unreasonable to require the lessor to seek out other tenants, plaintiffs in the present case would not be

benefited by that argument because defendant presented a willing and, we may assume, suitable substitute tenant. If defendant had entered into possession and thereafter had offered the landlord a person willing to sublet the premises, plaintiffs under the terms of the "Agreement" could not have refused to accept the new tenant without reasonable grounds for doing so. The situation is essentially the same when the proposed new tenant is offered for the purpose of reducing the tenant's damages.

6, 7. Even if we were to perpetuate the distinction between a lease and a contract in the application of the principle of mitigation of damages, we would reach the same result. The agreement in question is a contract to make a lease rather than a lease. At the time the agreement was entered into the office building had not been constructed, and the office which was to constitute defendant's leasehold could not then be identified. Consequently, there was nothing that could constitute the subject matter of a conveyance at that time. Conceding that one may make a present demise of a term to begin in the future, it is difficult to conceive of the present transfer of the title (or a part of it in the case of a lease) when that which is to be transferred has no existence. The analogy to mortgages on after acquired property immediately suggests itself. Such mortgages do not transfer a legal estate or interest; they create only an equitable mortgage. And whether they are regarded as arising out of contract or conveyance, a court of equity should require the plaintiff seeking equity to do equity by making a reasonable effort to avoid damages.

8. Plaintiffs contend that defendant should not now be permitted to argue that the transaction was a contract to make a lease because the case was tried on the theory that the transaction was a lease. We have found nothing in the transcript indicating that defendant treated the instrument in question as creating a lease rather than a contract to make a lease. Neither defendant's pleadings nor his conduct in the course of trial clearly points one way or the other with respect to the character of the transaction. In his motion for a new trial defendant admitted that the question of the character of the instrument was not "squarely" presented to the court. But there was nothing to suggest that defendant was not relying upon the theory that the transaction was a contract to make a lease. On the contrary, it might be said that since all but three states have refused to require a lessor to mitigate damages defendant's offer of proof on the point of mitigation indicated that he was proceeding on the assumption that the transaction was a contract only.

The judgment is reversed and the cause is remanded for a new trial.

DISCUSSION

The first question that comes to mind when this case is contrasted with *Rockingham* and *Roy* is why the court should apply a different rule regarding mitigation of damages than is applied in contract and tort. What is it about property law that permits rejection of the mitigation of damages rule? Is it because the act of finding a new tenant is a burden on the lessor? In *Rockingham*, it is true, mitigation only required the stoppage of work, but in *Roy*, on the other hand, mitigation required the affirmative act of seeing a doctor when it became evident that professional medical attention was needed. How is finding a new tenant any more burdensome than seeing a doctor?

As we read into the opinion we find that the court speaks explicitly to the burden placed on the lessor: "It does not seem that the burden imposed upon a lessor in mitigating damages would ordinarily be any greater than that imposed upon promisees of contracts not relating to the occupancy of land." Furthermore, the court points out that in this case even the burden of finding a new tenant was absent because the lessee presented an appropriate substitute tenant.

The whole tenor of the court's discussion is to reject the existing exception to the mitigation of damages rule in property. A lessor may not have to mitigate damages for breach of a lease in a majority of jurisdictions, but it is a bad rule. This court finds no reason to differentiate between a contract and a lease in the application of the mitigation rule. Nevertheless, *stare decisis* is an important principle for deciding cases in our legal system. *Stare decisis* is defined as "[t]he doctrine of precedent, under which it is necessary for a court to follow earlier judicial decisions when the same points arise again in litigation." Implicit in this definition is that the prior decisions are only binding on the same court, or an inferior one.[3] In the presence of weighty reasons, however, a court might overrule a previous holding. Therefore, the Supreme Court of Oregon is reluctant to overrule the property exception to the mitigation of damages rule in this case. With a majority of jurisdictions still adhering to the exception, it is prepared only to speak against the rule, but not to overrule it as a basis for its holding in the case. Instead, the court finds an alternative path to the same result. It finds that in this case the agreement in question was a contract to make a lease and not a lease; therefore, the mitigation of damages rule can be applied without violating the exception.

How should a student read this case? How do we want to write the brief? What is the issue? If we concentrate on the holding we note that the mitigation of damages rule applies to a contract to make a lease, but this information does not tell us much more than we have already learned in *Rockingham*. Why would this case be placed in materials to prepare for class if it is merely repetitive of a previous case? Sometimes repetition helps drive a point home for students, but in this case we have additional information in the *dicta* of the court's opinion that gives us a better understanding of the mitigation of damages rule: this rule has an exception in property law for leases, and the exception appears to lack a rational foundation. The argument of the court against application of the exception in this case suggests that the court may overrule this rule in a future case. In fact, attorneys who read this opinion are put on notice of this possibility. Our brief of the case should focus on the court's *dicta* rather than on its holding.

We are now prepared to write the brief of this case. It should be possible to write the brief from memory. Then read over the full case one more time to ensure that everything you wanted is in the brief.

Wright v. Baumann
389 P.2d 119 (Or. 1965)

FACTS:	D (prospective lessee) negotiates a business lease with P (prospective lessor) and then breaches before the building contemplated in the lease is built and before he enters upon the lease. D offers P an appropriate tenant (two doctors to lease on same terms) but P refuses, charging D the full rent for the lease. Lower court finds for P on the ground that the agreement was a lease and therefore there was no duty on P's part to mitigate damages by accepting the new tenant. This court reverses and remands.
ISSUE:	Does lessor have a duty to mitigate damages by accepting an appropriate tenant for the remainder of an agreement for a business lease that is breached?
DICTUM & RATIONALE:	The majority of jurisdictions disallow the mitigation rule and for breach of a lease, based on the idea that the lessee becomes an owner rather than a contracting party. This rule is not overruled in this case, but it is a BAD RULE since there is no rational basis for a distinction. The character of a business lease is more an exchange of promises than the conveyance of property it was several years ago.
HOLDING & RATIONALE:	The issue whether the mitigation rule applies to leases is not and reached in this case because, before the building contemplated in the lease is built, the agreement is not a lease. The subject matter (building) of the lease must be in existence for there to be a lease. The agreement in this case is a contract to make a lease to which the mitigation rule applies.

Note that the brief does not follow the usual format of Facts, Issue, Holding and Rationale. There is no reason to do so if a different format helps you to recall the essence of a case more quickly and thoroughly. Use your own format and develop your own style

---

[3] BLACK'S LAW DICTIONARY 1443 (8th ed. 2004).

so that your brief becomes a powerful memory aid, not a perfunctory obligation. The briefs supplied in these pages are my own creation in my own style. You may have a different style that helps you more. Use it.

The court in *Wright* opposed the trend in property law to reject the mitigation rule in leases, but it found another ground on which to base its holding. In *Lefrak* the court faces the issue directly, and a summary reading of the case quickly shows that the court has decided to change the law. Read the case through and brief it on your own.

LEFRAK v. LAMBERT
89 Misc. 2d 197, 390 N.Y.S.2d 959 (1976)

HERBERT A. POSNER, J.

In the Book of Leviticus (ch. 19:15) it is written, "Ye shall do no unrighteousness in judgment: Thou shalt not respect the person of the poor, nor favour the person of the mighty: but in righteousness shalt thou judge thy neighbour."

If ever there was a classic case to test the mettle of a Judge's ability to live up to this time-honored precept, this is the case. We were faced with the vexing problem of balancing the common law with common justice.

This is an action for money damages in the sum of $5,462, allegedly resulting from the breach of a lease for an apartment in a multifamily dwelling. The plaintiff is well known and respected in this city as one of the largest (if not *the* largest) individual owner of residential apartment houses. The apartment in question is one of five thousand in the privately owned development known as "Lefrak City." The defendants are a young couple who were represented by the husband (Kenneth), appearing *pro se*; and responding to the complaint with an ingenuous answer. The answer, handwritten by Kenneth Lambert, stated: "My wife and I, left the apartment due to the new birth of my son and the loss of my wife's income. At the time we were two months behind in rent and had received a 30 day eviction notice. I wrote a letter to the mandalay leasing company explaining our problem. Our two month security covered the two months we lived there without paying. I will pay any *fair amount decided upon*" (emphasis supplied). Besides not being represented by counsel, the defendant sat mute during the entire trial and offered no evidence whatsoever in his own behalf. Since the trial, the court has received a memorandum of law from the plaintiff. The memo bears out the fact that the common law for centuries is that a landlord is under no obligation to mitigate damages stemming from the tenant's breach of the lease agreement. The defendant has not submitted any memorandum of law.

Since the defendant offered no defense to the issue of liability, the sole issue at the trial was the question of "damages." While the plaintiff's attorney claimed before the trial began that his client had no obligation to mitigate damages, he nevertheless presented one witness and several documents in an attempt to prove that an effort was made to rerent the apartment. The witness was an assistant manager in Lefrak City, who, while not directly involved in the rental office, exercised certain administrative duties in connection with the rental of apartments. He introduced into evidence the lease (a printed standard form) which showed a rental term of three years from September 15, 1973 to September 30, 1976 with rent payable in "equal monthly installments" of $258 per month. The witness testified that defendants moved out of the apartment on November 20, 1974 owing rent for October and November. The landlord had at that time a security deposit of $502. The apartment was vacant for 17 months and not rerented until May 1, 1976. During this period the defendants paid $45 in September, 1975. The plaintiff claimed (in his complaint) unpaid rent of $4,552 and $910 for legal fees, pursuant to a clause in the lease providing for 20% liquidated damages — resulting in a total claim of $5,462. However, the court's computation of 19 months rent at $258 per month less the security deposit of $502 and the $45 payment made in September, 1975 came to $4,355. There was no testimony of what the difference of $197 consisted of and the attorney's testimony of the value of his services (in justification of the 20% damage clause) only persuaded the court to the amount of $300 — resulting in a total of $4,655.

As to the efforts made by the landlord to rerent the apartment, the witness testified that the apartment went on an "availability" list November 25, 1974 and remained on that list until rented. He testified that the rental office consisted of five full-time employees who interview prospective tenants and show them apartments. In addition, advertisements are run daily in the major newspapers to attract tenants. Invoices totaling more than $124,000 were introduced into evidence. However, he could produce no witness nor records to show that an effort was made to rent the defendants' apartment, except for two documents (introduced into evidence) indicating that an application was received for this apartment on August 19, 1975 but rejected as a poor credit risk. The witness, himself, indicated no personal knowledge of the procedure and practices of the rental office, other than the fact that he approved credit for rental applications.

Based upon all the evidence presented by the plaintiff, the court came to the conclusion that he had failed to establish that he acted in good faith to rerent the defendants' apartment. This presupposes that by operation of law, he had a duty to mitigate his damages. The landlord had no duty to rent this apartment before he rented similar apartments that had become vacant prior to this one. However, he introduced not one shred of evidence as to what his rental policies were at the time. For all the court knows, he may have had a policy to first rent out apartments that became vacant upon expiration of lease, and to leave breach of lease apartments vacant. It is not for the court to speculate, but the burden of the plaintiff to prove he has a prima facie case. This is especially so when the facts are known only to him or employees under his control. The plaintiff's only witness testified that there were five employees working in the rental office. Not one of these employees was produced as a witness, though they obviously must know what the rental procedures were during the period in question. The law of evidence is well settled that failure to produce a witness under your control leads to an inference that the testimony of the uncalled person(s) would not support the plaintiff's version of the facts.

The plaintiff's evidence that he spent over $124,000 in advertising, during this period, and that he had five people working full time in the rental office, only proves that he generated a lot of prospective tenants *for* Lefrak City, *not* for this specific apartment. This court is in no position to speculate why it took the plaintiff 17 months to rerent this apartment with all that advertising and all those employees working in the rental office. This court finds, that as a matter of law, 17 months is an unreasonable period of time for a middle-class apartment in a middle-class neighborhood to remain vacant, absent proof by the landlord that a good faith effort was made to rerent.

Disposing of the factual determination was simple compared to the disposition of the legal question. As stated, heretofore, plaintiff's attorney claimed, before the trial even began, that a landlord is under no obligation to mitigate damages stemming from the tenants' breach of the lease agreement. As his authority, he cites Rasch as follows:

> "Therefore, it is well established that the usual obligation in the law of contracts to reduce damages has no application to a contract of leasing, and a landlord is under no obligation or duty to his tenant to relet, or attempt to relet, abandoned premises in order to minimize his damages.

> "A lease grants in praesenti a term which the tenant thereof agrees to pay for. It is like the sale of specific personal property. Title has passed, and all that is left is liability for the purchase money.

> "The tenant's absolute liability, therefore, is unaffected by a landlord's refusal to relet the premises."

To support this ancient rule of law (dating back to feudal England), he cites a 1964 lower court case (*Fermaglich v Warshawiak*), a 1927 Appellate Division First Department case

(*Sancourt Realty Corp. v Dowling*), and a 1876 Court of Appeals case (*Becar v Flues*). However, let it not be said that a valid rule of law does not survive time and changing circumstances. The paramount question is whether this rule of law deserves to be validated or summarily abandoned. Law is justice and justice must be the foundation of the law. The Hon. Judge IRWIN SHAPIRO in a recent article entitled, "The Law: Yesterday, Today, Tomorrow" wrote:

> "The law not only helps formulate and strengthen the beneficial institutions of our way of life but also, like those institutions, grows and alters to meet the needs of our society for a system of justice that accords with the changing patterns of morality and custom which our improved technology continually brings about in our life."

There is no longer good reason — if there ever was — why leases should be governed by rules different from those applying to contracts in general. The greatest strength of the common law is its ability to adapt to changing conditions. It is a living, growing, changing thing and nowhere is that growth and that change more evident than in the law of landlord and tenant. Courts across the Nation are rejecting the conveyance theory of landlord-tenant law in favor of simple contract law. That trend was recently recognized by this court in *Cohen v Werner*. My colleague Judge CHARLES H. COHEN approached the problem head on saying: "In recent years, however, traditional rules of law involved in the landlord-tenant relationship have been changing. In general, this has involved the recognition of a lease not as a conveyance of land but as a contract involving mutual obligations in which the principle of interdependency of covenants should be applied * * * 'The assault upon the citadel' surrounding the traditional concepts of the law of landlord and tenant 'is proceeding these days apace' * * * in accordance with 'the adaptability of our judicial system and its resilient capacity to respond to new developments.'" If ever there was good reason to treat leases as a conveyance, that reason no longer exists. With the possible exception of cooperative and condominium apartments where our income tax laws require some vestige of ownership, residential landlords and tenants do not consider the renting of an apartment as a conveyance. It is the owner who keeps title, takes depreciation, deducts real estate taxes and interest and maintains all of the indicia of ownership. A tenant does no more than contract for a package of goods and services to be supplied. (*Javins v. First Nat. Realty Corp.*)

The modern concept of a lease, as viewed both by the courts of this State and the Legislature, is that a lease is a contract and that the contract principle of interdependency of covenants should be applied. Further, recognition has been given, that the landlord and tenant are not in equal bargaining positions. Both the courts and the Legislature have applied these principles in matters dealing with (1) the right to sublet; (2) the warranty of habitability and (3) in striking out unconscionable clauses. The only major area not yet dealt with by the appellate courts and Legislature of this State is this question of "Mitigation of Damages." A number of other States have responded judicially. American Jurisprudence states: "On the other hand, there is direct authority, as well as dicta, which takes the view, respecting the duty of the landlord in this regard, that it is the duty of a landlord on wrongful abandonment of the premises by his tenant, to make reasonable efforts to reduce the damages from the breach by reletting the premises to a new tenant." "According to considerable authority, also, if the landlord reenters in pursuance of a forfeiture or under a provision of the lease permitting him to do so after his tenant has abandoned the premises, he must then use diligence in seeking a new tenant in order to lessen the damages."

If the lease is now viewed as a contract, then all the rules of law regarding contracts should apply, including the requirement that the injured party make a reasonable effort to mitigate damages. It is interesting to note, that, even though the plaintiff's attorney did not point out the clause in the lease, there is a clause, entitled, "Remedies of

Landlord," which give contractually to the landlord the same rights he is claiming under the common law. The clause is so unconscionable on its face that even without the recently enacted statute (and applicable to all leases, regardless of when executed), this court would have ruled it unenforceable. Governor Carey in his memorandum of approval, acknowledged that, "The concept of unconscionability is not new to the law of this state. The Uniform Commercial Code, at the time of its enactment in 1962, codified the doctrine as it related to the law of sales. It has, however, had limited applicability in landlord and tenant disputes until recently. The doctrine is only now beginning to be judicially applied in such cases. This bill would codify the doctrine and establish a defense of unconscionability in landlord and tenant proceedings."

A colleague of mine, in this court, in a decision dated April 27, 1976 disagreed with the opinion expressed in *Parkwood Realty Co. v Marcano* that a change in the law is warranted. He stated that, "Such a change, if a change is warranted, should be made either by our appellate courts or the Legislature." But how will the appellate courts have an opportunity to change an unjust law if a court of the first instance does not present them with a case that sharpens the issues and provides a clear opportunity for the appellate courts to deal with the merits of the rule of law. Rarely, if ever, will the tenant appeal. He who must breach a lease for lack of funds and defends himself, will hardly be able to take an appeal. As for waiting for the Legislature "to make the change," are we an independent branch of government or not? Do we have to wait for another branch of government to tell us when we are wrong? Judge-made law should be changed by Judges, not legislators. Though admittedly, they came very close this year when the Assembly (by a vote of 113 to 25) passed a bill that would have made the landlord's duty to mitigate damages a statutory one. Alas, it did not get out of committee in the Senate, perhaps to give the courts an opportunity to right their own wrong. Judge FULD writing for the majority in *Bing v Thunig* in striking down a rule of law that had been in existence for over a hundred years, stated, "The rule of nonliability is out of tune with the life about us, at variance with modern-day needs and with concepts of justice and fair dealing. It should be discarded. To the suggestion that *stare decisis* compels us to perpetuate it until the legislature acts, a ready answer is at hand. It was intended not to effect a 'petrifying rigidity,' but to assure the justice that flows from certainty and stability. If, instead, adherence to precedent offers not justice but unfairness, not certainty but doubt and confusion, it loses its right to survive, and no principle constrains us to follow it. On the contrary, as this court, speaking through Judge DESMOND in *Woods v. Lancet*, declared, we would be abdicating 'our own function, in a field peculiarly nonstatutory,' were we to insist on legislation and 'refuse to reconsider an old and unsatisfactory court-made rule.' "

There is something basically unjust, basically unreasonable and, therefore, basically not legal about a landlord in an urban society with a housing shortage having no obligation to try to rerent an apartment and mitigate damages. There is something unfair about permitting tenants to be in a different category than other persons entering into a contract. To be sure, a tenant should be required to pay every penny of damage actually sustained by a reasonable landlord acting to mitigate damages but to allow what is really a draconian remedy is foreign to our modern concept of justice.

Since the plaintiff has failed to establish that he acted in good faith to mitigate damages, the court finds that he was entitled only to a reasonable period of time in which to rerent. In this case that was three months. Therefore, adding the three months to the two months unpaid at the time tenants vacated and subtracting the $502 security plus $45 payment made in September, 1975, plaintiff is entitled to a judgment in the sum of $743 for unpaid rent and $148 for legal expenses (20% of $743) for a total of $891 with statutory costs.

DISCUSSION

It is interesting to note that two years later on appeal the judgment in this case was "modified by increasing the amount of plaintiff's recovery." Without deciding whether the lower court was right to have changed the law on the applicability of the mitigation rule to leases, it held that the plaintiff had satisfied any duty to mitigate that might exist by making responsible and diligent efforts to rerent the apartment. See Lefrak v. Lambert, 93 Misc. 2d 632, 403 N.Y.S.2d 397 (N.Y. App. Term 1978).

As you prepare to brief the court's opinion above, you might want to guess what types of questions the professor would be likely to ask in class on this case. For example, why did the plaintiff lessor, who was not the wrongdoer, have the burden of proving a prima facie case that he satisfied a duty to mitigate? What was the duty to mitigate? Is the court right to imply in one of its statements that the duty to mitigate does not allow the lessor to rent out all other vacant apartments before renting out the vacant breach-of-lease apartments? Why should a lessor not be allowed to rent out his other units before a breach-of-lease apartment? How much effort must the landlord expend to rerent a breach-of-lease apartment and what costs for this effort can he charge to the lessee? How does the application of the mitigation of damages rule in this property case differ from its application in a contract or torts case? On a more general level, what do you think about a court changing law in the face of a refusal to act on the part of the legislature?

These are all questions that are fair game in the classroom. They cannot be answered by relying solely on your brief of the case. Remember that the brief is there only to help you recall the case as you seek to analyze it in line with questions such as those just presented. You need to be familiar with your case beyond just the summary lines in your brief, and you need to be prepared to use your mind to explore issues in class that you may not have anticipated on your own. Therefore, get involved, make the case your own, and find a study group or partner with whom you can argue the issues and questions raised by the assigned materials.

Topic III
ATTEMPT
(1 Assignment)

ASSIGNMENT 1
Briefing and Statutory Interpretation:
Examples in Criminal Law

One feature about the U.S. judicial system that must be remembered is that it includes 51 sovereigns (the federal sovereign and one from each state) and therefore 51 different systems. While the Federal system may have final say over certain decisions, such as those based on federal law or those based on the federal constitution, states retain much authority to interpret their own laws and may do so in different ways. While you might be convicted of a crime in one state in the absence of certain kinds of evidence, you might be found not guilty in a different state under the same circumstances. This topic will explore and compare various authorities for the crime of attempted robbery and will highlight different approaches to determining whether a defendant actually committed an attempted robbery. Furthermore, this topic will look at the important role that courts play in the interpretation of congressional law.

Before we get into the discussion, it might be helpful to understand the basics of an attempted crime. An attempted crime is called an inchoate crime because it punishes a party before the actual crime is committed. A person cannot be charged, let alone convicted, for attempt unless there also exists an underlying crime on which the attempt is based. "Everyone seems to agree that it would be a perversion of the institution of punishment to convict for thoughts alone,"[1] therefore, as Oliver Wendell Holmes stated, "The law only deals with conduct."[2] Consequently, the two basic elements required to convict for attempt are: (1) intent and (2) conduct. It is the second element, conduct, that will be the primary focus of this topic.

More specifically, this topic will focus on the overt acts required to prove that the conduct has gone far enough for a court justifiably to convict a person for attempting a crime that they were unable to complete. These overt act requirements differ from state to state and may arise from different statutory definitions or interpretations of those definitions by courts.

The first case from Kentucky contains a statutorily created definition for "overt act." It provides one form of what is called the "substantial step" test to determine whether sufficient conduct has occurred to warrant a conviction for "attempt." First read the case to get an understanding of the story. Then read it again for details you may have missed and brief the case.

COMMONWEALTH v. PRATHER
690 S.W.2d 396 (Ky. 1985)

Gant, Justice.

On January 11, 1983, in Louisville, Kentucky, a paid police informant contacted a member of the Louisville Police Department and advised an officer that he had been approached by Robert Andrew Prather and solicited to assist Prather in an armed robbery at the Executive Inn in Owensboro, Kentucky. Respondent Prather had obtained information concerning the hotel and certain plans thereof from his uncle, a former security guard at the facility. In essence, the plan called for the informant to drive, for Prather to enter the van on its way to the bank with a deposit, to force the occupants to drive out of town where the robbery would be completed, and to "dispose"

---

[1] George P. Fletcher, *On the Moral Irrelevance of Bodily Movements*, 142 U. Pa. L Rev. 1443, 1452 (1994).

[2] Oliver Wendell Holmes, The Common Law 65 (1881).

of the occupants. This plan was known to the police from the informant and from clandestine tape recordings of the conversations between the informant and Prather.

On January 14, the informant advised the Louisville police that they were leaving for Owensboro in order to "case" the job and the Kentucky State Police in the Owensboro area were immediately notified. The latter replaced the regular couriers of the Executive Inn with two officers in plain clothes, and at 2:00 p.m. that date Prather and the informant were observed at the Executive Inn. Carrying out their assumed roles, the two officers took the deposit and drove in the company van to the depository bank. The car containing Prather and the informant followed the van to the bank and the two men were observed in that vehicle.

Upon his return to Louisville, the informant apprised the police that the robbery was scheduled for the following Monday, January 17. Prather had obtained a sawed-off shotgun for use in the crime, which the informant brought to the police in order that they could file down the firing pin, rendering it incapable of discharge. The gun was then returned to Prather, and on Monday the two men returned to Owensboro.

They continued to discuss the robbery on arrival and waited in the parking lot at the Executive Inn for the "couriers" to depart for the bank. Again, the plain clothes officers had been substituted. Prather was given the unloaded weapon and had gone to the company van and tested the door handles to ascertain that they would open. The officers entered the van, with the deposit bags, and drove several hundred feet from the front door of the Executive Inn to the street on which the property abuts. Prather and the informant followed closely and when the van was forced to stop at a stop light, they pulled in behind it. It was at this point that the arrest was made.

Prather was indicted, tried and convicted of criminal attempt to commit first degree robbery, and sentenced to 15 years imprisonment as a first degree persistent felony offender. The Court of Appeals, in a 2-1 decision, reversed the Daviess Circuit Court and we granted discretionary review.

The statute involved herein is KRS 506.010, which reads:

(1) A person is guilty of criminal attempt to commit a crime when, acting with the kind of culpability otherwise required for commission of the crime, he:

*   *   *

  (b) Intentionally does or omits to do anything which, under the circumstances as he believes them to be, is a substantial step in a course of conduct planned to culminate in his commission of the crime.

(2) Conduct shall not be held to constitute a substantial step under subsection (1)(b) unless it is an act or omission which leaves no reasonable doubt as to the defendant's intention to commit the crime which he is charged with attempting.

*   *   *

At the conclusion of the evidence of the Commonwealth, Prather moved for a directed verdict on the ground that there was no proof of a substantial step which left no reasonable doubt of intent, as required by KRS 506.010(2), which motion was denied. The Court of Appeals found this to be error, but we disagree and reverse.

Numerous jurisdictions have examined the standard delineated by similar statutes on the crime of criminal attempt. The commands of the statute are well defined in *State v. Woods*, 48 Ohio St. 2d 127 (1976), which states that the substantial steps directed by the statute are overt acts " . . . which convincingly demonstrate a firm purpose to commit a crime, while allowing police intervention, based upon observation of such incriminating conduct, in order to prevent the crime when criminal intent becomes apparent." We adopt this standard. *State v. Workman* requires that the steps be "strongly corroborative." *State v. Pearson* declares that the emphasis should be on what acts have been carried out and not on what additional acts would have been even more convincing.

There is no absolute applicable to this statute except to say that the overt acts, the substantial step, must be considered under all of the circumstances of the case to discover whether they manifest a clear intent to commit the crime. Under that precept, let us examine the current case. The evidence of the plan was overwhelming and undisputed. We must then categorize the substantial step mandated by the statute. The plan was to conduct a reconnaissance operation in order to carry out the robbery. The overt acts, fully observed by the police, were: (1) drove from Louisville to Owensboro, going directly to the Executive Inn; (2) conducted a surveillance of the surroundings; (3) noted the modus operandi involved in making the deposit by use of the van; and, (4) determined the route between the Executive Inn and the bank by following the van. The plan was to carry out the robbery on Monday, January 17. The overt acts, again fully observed by the police, were (1) again drove from Louisville directly to the Executive Inn in Owensboro; (2) parked and waited for the couriers to appear; (3) tested the doors on the van; and, (4) followed the van several hundred feet and pulled behind it at the traffic light.

It is our opinion that these overt acts, considered under the circumstances of this case and not as isolated occurrences, convincingly demonstrated a firm purpose to commit a crime, and we further find that the police, upon observing such incriminating conduct, properly intervened to prevent the crime.

It is our opinion that the "no reasonable doubt" requirement imposed by KRS 506.010(2) is a matter for jury determination and that it was properly submitted to them upon denial of the motion for a directed verdict of acquittal.

As an additional argument attempting to uphold the opinion by the Court of Appeals, Prather contends that double jeopardy attached when the Court of Appeals reversed the conviction because of their opinion that there was insufficient evidence to withstand a motion for directed verdict. As authority for this position, respondent cites *Commonwealth v. Burris*. That case related to an appeal by the Commonwealth from a judgment n.o.v., and in no way relates to the discretionary review by this court from an opinion of the Court of Appeals.

The Court of Appeals is reversed and the judgment of the Daviess Circuit Court is affirmed.

DISCUSSION

So what is the story? Prather conspired with a paid police informant to carry out an armed robbery of the Executive Inn in Owensboro, Kentucky. The informant would drive and Prather would enter and rob the courier van while on route to the bank. Because the informant kept the police up to date on the activities of the conspiracy, the police were able to track and observe many acts in which Prather and the informant took part in preparation for the robbery. These acts included driving to Owensboro, Kentucky in order to scope the job and track the van, and then returning to Owensboro three days later to carry out the plan. On the second trip to Owensboro, the police were aware that Prather possessed a sawed-off shotgun, and observed that he checked the handles of the courier van, then followed the van and stopped behind it at a stoplight while the van was on route to the bank.

At the end of the trial, Prather moved for a directed verdict. The trial court denied Prather's motion, thereby determining that a jury could find that the facts were sufficient to convict Prather. Prather appealed, and the appellate court decided that the facts were insufficient to find that Prather was guilty. The decision that you read came from the supreme court of Kentucky, who agreed with the trial judge that the facts were sufficient on which a jury could find Prather guilty of attempted armed robbery.

In determining whether the particular facts in this case were sufficient, the court needed to interpret the state statute on attempt and specify the standard on which to interpret what is meant by a "substantial step" that left "no reasonable doubt of the defendant's intention." It adopted Ohio's standard and found that a substantial step occurs if the facts "considered under the circumstances of this case and not as isolated occurrences, convincingly demonstrated a firm purpose to commit a crime." It then determined that the particular facts in this case were sufficient for a jury to find that a substantial step had occurred.

Be sure to recognize the difference between a finding that a substantial step has occurred and a finding that the facts are sufficient to determine that a substantial step has occurred. The court did not find that a substantial step had occurred. Instead, the court said "that the 'no reasonable doubt' requirement . . . is a matter for jury determination and that it was properly submitted to them." What difference does this make? The difference is that even though the supreme court determined that a jury could find that the facts were sufficient to find that a substantial step had occurred, it was the jury, as fact finder, that made the decision. If the fact finder had acquitted Prather, this decision would not be in conflict with the supreme court's decision. The supreme court merely found that the facts were sufficient to satisfy the statutory definition and therefore gave the finder of fact the freedom to determine the factual question.

Would the result have changed if the informant had not told the police about the conspiracy until after the first scouting mission to Owensboro? In this case, the police were lucky because they had the luxury of being informed of a possible crime before any acts had taken place and therefore were able to observe most of the preparation. What if the police had been unaware that Prather possessed a gun? What if the only thing that the police had observed was that Prather had pulled up behind the van on route to the bank? Would the supreme court have decided that pulling up behind the van alone was a sufficient overt act which left "no reasonable doubt" as to Prather's intent to commit armed robbery? Probably not; pulling up behind a courier van at a stoplight could have been done by an innocent person without the slightest thought of robbery.

What if the police had observed Prather only from the time he got out of his car to test the handles of the courier van? Would that have sufficed as a sufficient overt act? Possibly, but remember how the court decided. Even if the court determined that this was sufficient, this does not mean that Prather would have been found guilty. The jury may have determined that simply trying the handles of the van was not sufficiently convincing of his guilt and did leave reasonable doubt as to Prather's intent. Perhaps Prather had another intent when he checked the handles of the car. Without the other overt acts, the jury decision might have been different.

Now that we have sufficiently digested the case, brief it on your own, if you have not already done so, before looking at the sample brief below. After you have created your own, compare it with the following sample.

Commonwealth v. Prather
690 S.W.2d 396 (Ky. 1985)

FACTS:	Prather (Defendant) conspired with a paid police informant to conduct an armed robbery of the Executive Inn's courier van while on route to its bank. They drove to the Executive Inn on Jan. 14, surveyed the surroundings, determined the courier van's route, planned to carry out the robbery, drove a second time to the Inn on Jan. 17, tested the doors on the courier van, waited for the couriers, and, armed with a sawed-off shotgun, followed the courier van on route to the bank and pulled in behind the van at a stop-light. When they pulled in behind the van, Prather was arrested. He was convicted and appealed to this court. This court affirmed.
ISSUE:	What overt acts are sufficient to satisfy the "substantial step" language under Kentucky's definition of attempt under KRS 506.010?
HOLDING:	Overt acts, such as those listed above, which convincingly demonstrate a firm purpose to commit a crime, satisfy the "substantial step" requirement under KRS 506.010.

RATIONALE: The statute limited a "substantial step" to conduct (overt acts) that leaves "no reasonable doubt as to the defendant's intention to commit the crime which he is charged with attempting." To interpret this statute, the court adopted Ohio's standard, which required that the overt acts "convincingly demonstrate a firm purpose to commit a crime." The court determined that the jury was permitted to find guilt, based on the adopted standard, because the combination of listed facts under the circumstances was sufficient to make such a finding.

What if Prather had committed this crime in a different state such as New York? Unlike Kentucky, New York's definition of attempt does not include the words "substantial step." Would the outcome change? Read the Kentucky statute below and compare the wording of New York's definition from McKinney's Penal Law.

Kentucky: KRS § 506.010

(1) A person is guilty of criminal attempt to commit a crime when, acting with the kind of culpability otherwise required for commission of the crime, he:

(a) Intentionally engages in conduct which would constitute the crime if the attendant circumstances were as he believes them to be; or

(b) Intentionally does or omits to do anything which, under the circumstances as he believes them to be, is a substantial step in a course of conduct planned to culminate in his commission of the crime.

(2) Conduct shall not be held to constitute a substantial step under subsection (1)(b) unless it is an act or omission which leaves no reasonable doubt as to the defendant's intention to commit the crime which he is charged with attempting.

McKinney's Penal Law § 110.00 (attempt to commit a crime)

A person is guilty of an attempt to commit a crime when, with intent to commit a crime, he engages in conduct which tends to effect the commission of such crime.

Instead of requiring a substantial step towards the commission of a crime, New York merely requires that the conduct "tend[] to effect the commission of such a crime." What does this mean? Does New York's statute make it easier to convict?

In the next case, *People v. Hirniak*, a man is arrested with a knife in his hand while he is taking money from the office of a gas station. As you read *Hirniak*, think about the similarities and differences between the facts of this case and the facts in *Prather*. Consider whether the defendant in *Hirniak* would be convicted under Kentucky law, but also whether Prather would be convicted under New York law. Once you have read the case for the story, re-read the case to pick up any details you may have missed and create your brief.

PEOPLE v. HIRNIAK
467 N.Y.S.2d 345 (N.Y. Supp. 1983)

DANIEL F. McMAHON, Acting Justice.

The defendant is charged in a three-count indictment with the crimes of attempted robbery first degree, burglary second degree and criminal possession of a weapon third degree, all alleged to have been committed on the 21st day of July 1982 at a Mobil Gas Station, located on the Saw Mill River Parkway near Tompkins Avenue in the City of Yonkers.

More particularly, the evidence showed that at about 4:40 P.M., the only attendant on duty at the station was a 16-year-old, John McDonald. He was seated on a wall near a gas pump on the southwest corner of the property. He observed the defendant jogging from the northwest corner of the property into the station office. The defendant had a cloth mask covering his face and his right hand clenched on a kitchen knife. He did not see the attendant. The complaining witness, John McDonald, then approached the entrance of the office and observed the defendant therein. He had switched the knife to his left hand and was riffling through desk drawers which contained money belonging to McDonald. The defendant was observed to have had money in his right hand. McDonald then rushed over to a police officer who was coincidentally parked in a patrol car on the south side of the station building observing traffic. The police officer immediately went to the office; drew his gun and arrested the defendant.

The defendant sought a trial order of dismissal on each of the three counts. The Court denied the motions with respect to counts 2 and 3, but has carefully considered the motion with respect to the first count charging attempted robbery first degree and finds a significant issue presented. The defense argues that the crime of robbery first degree requires either violence or the threat to use violence or physical force against a victim. He further argues that the complaining witness was not in the office nor was any other individual. Since the crime of robbery could not be committed, the attempt could not be committed.

The Assistant District Attorney countered by relying on Penal Law, Section 110.10, which reads as follows:

> "If the conduct in which a person engages otherwise constitutes an attempt to commit a crime . . . . it is no defense to a prosecution for such attempt that the crime charged to have been attempted was under the attendant circumstance, factually or legally impossible of commission, if such crime could have been committed had the attendant circumstances been as such person believed them to be."

The law relating to the crime of attempt has gone through considerable evolution. Under common law, impossibility of the completed crime was for most purposes a defense to the charge of attempt to commit a crime.

Thereafter, a distinction was made between factual impossibility (an attempt to pick a pocket which was in fact empty), and legal impossibility (receiving stolen property which in fact was not stolen). The provisions of Section 110.10 changed the distinction and rejects both types of impossibility of performance as a defense upon the theory that neither detracts from the culpability of the defendant. Former Penal Law, Section 2, which was in effect until September 1, 1967, defined an attempt to commit a crime as: "an act, done with intent to commit a crime, intending but failing to effect its commission, is an attempt to commit that crime". Our present Penal Law, (P.L. Section 110.00) defines an attempt as follows:

> "A person is guilty of an attempt to commit a crime when, with intent to commit a crime, he engages in conduct which tends to effect the commission of such crime."

Under the old law, it was necessary in order to be found guilty of an attempt to commit a crime to "carry the project forward within dangerous proximity to the criminal end to be attained." Thus, the distinction between the two definitions (the old and the new) are the words tending "but failing," which words have been omitted in the new definition.

The evolution of the law of attempt based on impossibility to complete the substantive crime has continuously narrowed the defense available to the defendant. However, this Court finds the mere showing of an intent to commit a crime coupled with some act, or acts, in furtherance of the intent, does not necessarily trigger the operability of this statute.

The Assistant District Attorney relies on *People v. Dlugash.* In that case, the defendant was convicted of attempted murder. The evidence clearly showed his intent to murder and his firing of several shots into the head of the victim. However, unknown to the defendant, another individual previously fired shots into the chest of the victim and there was no proof that the victim was alive before the defendant fired. This case is distinguishable from the case at bar in that a victim was present, the defendant shot the victim and there was a closer proximity to the defendant's acts accomplishing the intended crime.

In *People v. Cullen*, the Court held that the defendant's *plea* (emphasis added) of guilty to attempted robbery in the first degree should not have been accepted, where defendant's statement to Court did not indicate that there had been any forcible taking of property from the victim or that the defendant had used or threatened immediate use of a dangerous instrument.

As can be seen from the above, the gravamen of a robbery charge under our Penal Law (Section 160.15), is the *forcible taking* (emphasis added) of property, by the use of or by threatening the immediate use of a dangerous instrument.

Taking the evidence in the most favorable light to the People, as we must for this motion, the Court would find the defendant clearly had the intent to rob "someone" in the office of the gas station. The Court would further find the acts and conduct of the defendant were in furtherance of that intent. However, to prove his case, the Assistant District Attorney must further show that the defendant used force or threatened to use immediate force against the individual named in the indictment or some other individual. This element (force) constitutes the gravamen of the crime of robbery first degree. This the Assistant District Attorney has been unable to do.

Accordingly, the motion for a trial order of dismissal as to count one, attempted robbery first degree, is granted.

DISCUSSION

You may have noticed that the court spent a considerable amount of time talking about the history of attempt, the defense to attempt, and a comparison with certain cases. Many cases you read will contain information that is not essential to either the main story of the case or the direct rationale that leads to the binding decision. Were you able to stay focused, find the story, and locate the essential elements that you need for your brief? Even if you were able to locate the essential elements of the case, you should still not ignore the rest of the discussion. Not only is the entire case fair game for questions in class, but the dicta, or non-essential elements of the case, could be just as important (and sometimes more important) as the holding itself.

With that in mind, what is the story in this case? A defendant, who by the looks of it, intended to rob someone, found no one to rob and therefore proceeded to look for money to steal in the gas station's office without the use of force. Without the crucial element of force, or threat of force, taking money does not amount to robbery, but rather to mere larceny, or theft. Here, the defendant never threatened or used force against anyone; rather, the police arrested him while he was committing larceny. Therefore, the appellate court above decided that the motion to dismiss the charge of attempted robbery should be granted.

While this seems simple enough, compare it to the facts in *Prather*. In *Prather*, Prather never used force against the people in the courier van; Prather was arrested before he attacked, just after he pulled up behind the van at the stoplight. Under these facts, would Prather have been acquitted in New York? The defendants in neither case used force. Therefore, it would seem that a New York court might have acquitted Prather since he, like Hirniak, did not manifest the essential force element of the crime of robbery.

What if Hirniack was tried under Kentucky's law? In *Prather*, even though the police had an opportunity to observe Prather's preparation, they arrested him before he had the chance to take any property or use/threaten to use force. In contrast, Hirniack already had his weapon out and had already taken money. The court in *Hirniack* even stated that "the defendant clearly had the intent to rob 'someone' . . . [and] the acts and conduct of the defendant were in furtherance of that intent." Were these acts, however, which were "in furtherance of that intent," enough to satisfy Kentucky's standard, which required a convincing demonstration of a firm purpose to commit the crime? Does it matter that the police in *Prather* observed all the other preparatory overt acts and had the police informant's testimony that the plan was to rob and not merely to steal, while the police in *Hirniack* merely witnessed the defendant riffling through the office with a knife and money in hand? It seems at least possible, if not likely, that a Kentucky court would have determined that Hirniack's conduct was sufficient to demonstrate convincingly a firm intent to rob.

If you have not already done so, create your own brief of *Hirniack*. A sample brief is included below for comparison after you have attempted making one by yourself. Remember that the briefing process becomes easier with every brief you create; it will only become easier, however, if you attempt to make these briefs on your own, before you examine the sample. The brief below will provide you with a way to check your work, but should not be used as a substitute for your own brief, or as a substitute for reading the case. In school, you may think that buying commercial outlines and/or briefs will save you time, but commercial products will not refresh your memory as effectively as a brief you create for yourself. In addition, your job as a lawyer will require that you read cases, not briefs; therefore, learning to read cases and create your own briefs will make you a better lawyer.

People v. Hirniak
467 N.Y.S.2d 345 (N.Y. Supp. 1983)

FACTS:	Hirniak (defendant), jogged into a Mobil Gas Station's office in Yonkers while holding a knife and wearing a mask. The gas station attendant, unnoticed by the defendant, observed the defendant going through the desk looking for money and also holding money that he found. The attendant notified a nearby police officer who proceeded to arrest the defendant. This court granted the defendant's motion to dismiss the charge of attempted robbery.
ISSUE:	What overt acts are necessary to prove attempt under N.Y.'s statute which states that the conduct must "tend[] to effect the commission of such a crime?"
HOLDING:	To convict for attempted robbery in N.Y., the overt acts by the defendant must include force or the threat of force against an individual.
RATIONALE:	The court based its reasoning on the decision from *Cullen*, which rejected a guilty plea for attempted robbery based on a lack of evidence showing force or the threat of force. The *Hirniak* court clarified the meaning of this precedent by requiring that the force or threat of force be directed against an individual.

The next case involves Arizona law. Note how the court uses cases from other jurisdictions to support its own rationale. First read the Arizona statute that defines "attempt" and look for differences between it and the Kentucky statute.

Arizona: A.R.S. § 13-1001

A. A person commits attempt if, acting with the kind of culpability otherwise required for commission of an offense, such person:

   1. Intentionally engages in conduct which would constitute an offense if the attendant circumstances were as such person believes them to be; or

   2. Intentionally does or omits to do anything which, under the circumstances as such person believes them to be, is *any step* in a course of conduct planned to culminate in commission of an offence; . . .

(emphasis added)

Arizona's statute may look identical to the first part of Kentucky's statute, but a closer reading reveals what might be a major difference in wording: Kentucky uses "substantial step" while Arizona uses "any step." Additionally, Arizona is not restricted by the phrase "leaves no reasonable doubt" with regard to the step required, as in Kentucky. What are the implications of these differences? Will the Arizona courts have an easier time convicting? Do the words "any act" create an easier burden of proof than "substantial step," especially in light of the "leaves no reasonable doubt" language in section (2) of Kentucky's statute?

Read the following case, *State v. Clark*, for the story first. Keep in mind the facts and outcomes of the previous cases we read, especially *Prather*. What effect, if any, does the "any step" language have on the ultimate outcome of the case? After you have a grasp of the situation, re-read the case to pick up details you may have missed and then create your own brief.

STATE v. CLARK
693 P.2d 987 (Az. App. 1984)

KLEINSCHMIDT, Judge.

Appellant Kenneth Allen Clark, was charged with two counts of aggravated assault, first-degree burglary, attempted armed robbery and misconduct involving a weapon. The burglary charge was dismissed. After trial to a jury, appellant was found guilty of the four remaining counts. The aggravated assaults and attempted armed robbery were found to be dangerous offenses by the jury. Appellant moved for new trial, on the basis that the state failed to properly serve subpoenas for witnesses requested by the defense. His motion was denied after an evidentiary hearing. Appellant was sentenced to 7.5 years, the presumptive term on the aggravated assault and attempted armed robbery convictions, and to 1.5 years for the misconduct involving a weapon conviction.

The basic facts of the case are as follows. At about 4:00 a.m. on January 22, 1983, Donald Frank, a nightwatchman at a Texaco Station near Ehrenberg, Arizona, noticed a person who appeared and disappeared several times around the station. Frank went to the station owner, Paul Flannagan who was in the office of the station, and told him what he had seen. Frank obtained a pistol and the two proceeded to search the premises. Flannagan entered the men's restroom and encountered the appellant, masked, gloved, and pointing a sawed-off shotgun at him. Flannagan ran out, calling to Frank that appellant had a gun. Appellant emerged from the restroom, pointing the shotgun at Frank. Frank shot first, wounding appellant who collapsed in the doorway of the men's restroom. A deputy sheriff was called and arrived to find the appellant still lying by the restroom doorway. Appellant told the deputy he had been rabbit hunting prior to entering the restroom.

Appellant's first argument is that the trial court erred in denying his motion for judgment of acquittal on the charge of attempted armed robbery. Appellant's argument is that the evidence will not support the conclusion that he undertook any overt act toward the commission of the crime of attempted armed robbery beyond the point of mere preparation.

In determining whether or not there was sufficient evidence of an "overt act," we view the evidence and inferences therefrom in the light most favorable to sustaining the verdict. A.R.S. § 13-1001(A), defines attempt, in relevant part, as:

> A person commits attempt if, acting with the kind of culpability otherwise required for commission of an offense, such person . . .

> 2. Intentionally does . . . anything which, under the circumstances as such person believes them to be, is any step in a course of conduct planned to culminate in commission of an offense.

The trial court instructed the jury in accordance with the above statute. The essential elements of an attempted robbery are (1) intent to commit robbery and (2) an overt act towards that commission. In determining whether a defendant is guilty of attempted robbery, the court must examine the particular facts in each case to determine whether the defendant's acts have advanced beyond the stage of mere preparation. The fundamental reason behind the requirement of an overt act in an attempt case is that until such acts occur, there is too much uncertainty as to whether the design is actually to be carried out.

The evidence of the necessary overt act is as follows. Donald Frank had observed the appellant appear and disappear around the corner of the restroom building several times. This activity persisted for 30–40 minutes. No customers were at the station. The time was 3:30 a.m. Surprised by Flannagan in the restroom, the appellant pointed the gun at him. The appellant was wearing a stocking cap with eye holes cut in it pulled down over his face and he wore gloves on his hands. As he left the restroom, he encountered Frank, who testified that appellant pointed the shotgun at him. Appellant's gun was an illegal sawed-off shotgun. The weapon was fully operable and a shell was in the chamber ready to fire. An expert witness, Richard Beaudry, from the State of Arizona Game and Fish Department, testified that it is not typical to hunt rabbits with a sawed-off shotgun and that one so hunting is not likely to kill a rabbit.

While it is true that the Arizona cases cited by appellant all involve some statement by the defendant to the victim indicating an intent to rob the victim, no such statement is necessary for the commission of the crime of attempted robbery. All that is required is an overt act. The above actions were sufficient steps in a course of conduct planned to culminate in a robbery. We conclude that the actions were sufficient to prove the "overt act" requirement of the crime of attempted armed robbery.

Although we have found no cases with similar facts in Arizona, our reasoning is supported by several opinions from other jurisdictions. In *People v. Burleson*, 50 Ill.App.3d 629, 8 Ill.Dec. 776, 365 N.E.2d 1162 (App.1977), the defendant and his accomplice did not enter the bank building, which was their alleged target, but they were in possession of a shotgun, a suitcase and were wearing disguises consisting of nylon stockings and stocking caps. The duo was scared away and shortly thereafter arrested. The court found that the defendants' acts constituted a "substantial step" toward the commission of an armed robbery of the bank. 50 Ill.App.3d at 633, 8 Ill.Dec. at 780, 365 N.E.2d at 1166.

In *People v. Vizcarra*, 110 Cal.App.3d 858, 168 Cal.Rptr. 257 (App.1980), the defendant approached a liquor store with a rifle and attempted to hide on a pathway immediately adjacent to the store when observed by a customer. The court found this to be a "sufficient direct act toward the accomplishment of the robbery." 110 Cal.App.3d at 862, 168 Cal.Rptr. at 259. The court stated:

> It is sufficient that the overt acts reach far enough for the accomplishment of the offense to amount to the '*commencement* of its consummation.' [Emphasis in original.]

110 Cal.App.3d at 862, 168 Cal.Rptr. at 259.

In *State v. Ward*, 601 S.W.2d 629 (Mo.App.1980), the defendant's acts consisted of going up to the door of the motel office, while masked, with shotgun in hand and with a getaway car waiting. The court stated:

> An overt criminal act is one going beyond mere preparation and done after and in furtherance of a prior plan to commit a crime. . . . We agree with the trial court's conclusion that overt acts were shown.

601 S.W.2d at 630.

We find no basis to distinguish the above cases. We conclude that the trial court did not err in denying appellant's motion for judgment of acquittal.

. . .

For the foregoing reasons, the judgment and sentence are affirmed.

DISCUSSION

First, as always, lets get the story straight. In this case, Clark (the defendant) roused the suspicion of the night watchman and station owner of a Texaco gas station in Missouri when he kept appearing and disappearing from around the premises of the station in the middle of the night. The owner and watchman looked for Clark, and eventually the owner encountered Clark in the bathroom. Clark wore a stocking cap with eye-holes cut out and had a sawed-off shotgun pointed at the owner. Upon the owner's cry for help, the watchman was able to shoot Clark down. Soon after the shooting, the police arrived and arrested Clark. Clark argued that he had not committed any overt act beyond mere preparation that was sufficient to satisfy the "any step" requirement under section A(2) of the Arizona statute defining attempt.

Whether an act goes beyond mere preparation is a factual inquiry. Similar to the analysis in the Kentucky case above, this court focused its discussion on whether the conduct had gone far enough, past mere preparation, to corroborate the intent of the defendant. Unlike New York this court did not focus on whether the overt acts included an actual use or immediate threat of force. Furthermore, the Arizona court considered all the facts under the circumstances, just as Kentucky had done. Arizona did not identify any single overt act that satisfied the statute, but rather it listed a full paragraph of facts that in total satisfied the overt act requirement.

Recall that, as the court stated, "The fundamental reason behind the requirement of an overt act in an attempt case is that until such acts occur, there is too much uncertainty as to whether the design is actually to be carried out." On the other hand, it is important not to set the bar of the overt act requirment too high that it makes it difficult to stop crimes before they happen. In this case, the court determined that a fact that had existed in all the Arizona cases cited in the arguments (a statement of intent by the defendant to the victim indicating an attempt to rob the victim) was not necessary to satisfy the overt act requirement.

Do not make the mistake of thinking that Arizona overturned precedent to make this determination. Simply because previous Arizona cases involved a statement of intent does not mean that the statement was the determining factor in those cases. Furthermore, do not make the mistake that Arizona merely adopted the law of other states. Here, Arizona came to its own conclusion and cited cases from Illinois, California, and Missouri only to strengthen its position.

If you have not done so already, brief *State v. Clark* now and then compare your brief with the sample brief below.

State v. Clark
693 P.2d 987 (Az. App. 1984)

FACTS:	Clark (defendant), was spotted several times over the course of 30–40 minutes appearing and disappearing around 3–4 a.m. near a Texaco Station by the night watchman. The watchman and station owner searched the premises, and when the owner encountered Clark in the bathroom, Clark wore a stocking on his head with eye holes cut out, and had a loaded sawed-off shotgun pointed at the owner. After the owner called for help, the watchman shot and wounded Clark, who was later arrested for attempted robbery. Clark appealed his conviction, and this court affirmed.
ISSUE:	What act, or acts, by the defendant satisfies the "overt act" requirement contained in the statutory language "any step?"
HOLDING:	"Any step," under A.R.S. § 13-1001, is any overt act that goes beyond mere preparation, and does not require a statement that indicates an intent to deprive the victim of property.

RATIONALE: Similar to Kentucky, this court did not specifically define what is meant by "overt
                      act beyond mere preparation," but simply noted that the facts in this case were
                      enough to satisfy this standard. Key in its determination was the decision about
                      what is not required. There is no requirement that the defendant make a verbal
                      statement that indicates intent to deprive the victim of property. Additionally,
                      unlike N.Y., the overt act did not need to include an actual showing of force or
                      immediate threat of force.

Does the Arizona statute, which contains the word "any," make it easier to convict for attempt than the Kentucky statute, which contains the word "substantial?" Despite the reasoning in the cases above, the question is still not an easy one to answer. If Clark had been tried under Kentucky's "substantial step" statute, it is arguable that the evidence could have been found to "convincingly demonstrate [] a firm purpose to commit a crime." Clark came even closer to committing the robbery than Prather because Clark had his gun pointed at the station owner while Prather was arrested before pulling out his gun. What if Prather was tried under Arizona law? Neither Prather nor Clark made any verbal statement to the victim indicating his intent to take property, but did Prather's actions manifest an "overt act beyond mere preparation?" Prather was arrested before making any attack on the van, and had the informant not warned the police, pulling up behind the van at a stoplight would not necessarily appear to be a step beyond mere preparation.

Even though the statutory words are "substantial" and "any," in order to evaluate the facts, a lawyer must look to the cases defining these standards. A court's interpretation of the words may differ from a layman's definition. In these cases, a layman might consider "substantial" more difficult to satisfy than "any," but what about "convincingly demonstrates a firm purpose to commit a crime" and "overt act beyond mere preparation?" Statutory provisions, even when they appear clear on their face, are subject to continued interpretation on the basis of new arguments and changing perspectives on the law.

The final case we will consider in this topic comes from Wisconsin. The statute that defines attempt in Wisconsin has some similarities with the other statutes we have considered so far but also some significant differences. When reading this case, notice how the court's rationale is dependent on the specific wording in the binding statute. At the same time, notice how the rationale is strikingly similar to the rationales in the other cases we have read despite the differences in statutory language.

No sample brief is provided for this case. Brief the case on your own and be prepared to discuss it in class.

STATE v. STEWART
420 N.W.2d 44 (Wis. 1988)

SHIRLEY S. ABRAHAMSON, Justice.

This is an appeal from an unpublished decision of the court of appeals filed on March 18, 1987, reversing a judgment entered by the circuit court for Milwaukee county, John F. Foley, circuit judge. The court of appeals reversed the conviction of defendant Walter Lee Stewart for attempted robbery, party to a crime, in violation of secs. 943.32(1)(b) (robbery), 939.32(3) (attempt), and 939.05 (party to a crime), Stats. 1985–86. The court of appeals concluded that the trier of fact could not be convinced beyond a reasonable doubt that the defendant would have committed robbery except for the intervention of another person or extraneous factor pursuant to sec. 939.32(3).

Sec. 939.32(3), Stats. 1985–86, the attempt statute, provides as follows:

An attempt to commit a crime requires that the actor have an intent to perform acts and attain a result which, if accomplished, would constitute such crime and that he does acts toward the commission of the crime which demonstrate unequivocally, under all the circumstances, that he formed that intent *and would commit the crime except for the intervention of another person or some other extraneous factor."* (Emphasis added.)

We interpret sec. 939.32(3) as follows: to prove attempt, the state must prove an intent to commit a specific crime accompanied by sufficient acts to demonstrate unequivocally that it was improbable the accused would desist of his or her own free will. The intervention of another person or some other extraneous factor that prevents the accused from completing the crime is not an element of the crime of attempt. If the individual, acting with the requisite intent, commits sufficient acts to constitute an attempt, voluntary abandonment of the crime after that point is not a defense.

Viewing the evidence in the light most favorable to the prosecution, we conclude that a rational trier of fact could find in this case that the state proved the essential elements of the crime beyond a reasonable doubt. Accordingly we reverse the decision of the court of appeals and affirm the conviction.

I.

The only evidence at trial was the testimony of the complainant, Scott Kodanko. The complainant testified that he was waiting for a bus at about 4:30 P.M. on a Saturday, after leaving work. He was alone in a three-sided plexiglass bus shelter open to the street in downtown Milwaukee. Two men, Mr. Moore and the defendant, entered the bus shelter while a third man, Mr. Levy, remained outside.

Moore and the defendant stood one to two feet from the complainant. The complainant was in a corner of the shelter, his exit to the street blocked by the two men. Moore asked the complainant if he wanted to buy some cigarettes. The complainant responded that he did not. Moore then said, "Give us some change." When the complainant refused, the defendant said "Give us some change, man." The defendant repeated this demand in an increasingly loud voice three to four times. The complainant still refused to give the two men change. The defendant then reached into his coat with his right hand at about the waist level, whereupon Moore stated something to the effect of "put that gun away." At that point Levy, who had been waiting outside the bus shelter, entered and said to the defendant and Moore "Come on, let's go." Levy showed the complainant some money, stating, "I don't want your money, I got lots of money."

The three men left the bus shelter together and entered a restaurant across the street. A few minutes later Moore returned and made "small talk" with the complainant. The three men were arrested a short while later. It appears from the record that the complainant did not report the incident to the police. The record does not reveal who called the police.

The complainant testified that he felt threatened throughout the encounter, which lasted less than three minutes. None of the men ever touched him or raised a hand to him, and at no time did he attempt to leave the shelter.

In a bench trial, the circuit judge found the defendant guilty of attempted robbery. The circuit judge at first expressed doubt that the state had proved the elements of the charge because he believed the defendant's abandonment of the criminal enterprise negated the intent necessary for attempted robbery. After the parties submitted briefs on this issue, the circuit judge found the defendant guilty.

The court of appeals reversed the conviction, reasoning that "the evidence clearly demonstrates that even if Stewart had the requisite intent to commit attempted robbery, he voluntarily terminated his participation in such a crime."

The defendant makes three arguments urging the court to affirm the court of appeals' reversal of his conviction. First, he argues that the evidence at trial was not sufficient to prove he acted with the requisite intent. Second, he argues that the evidence at trial was not sufficient to prove that he had taken sufficient steps in furtherance of the crime of robbery for his conduct to constitute an attempt because the state failed to prove beyond a reasonable doubt that the intervention of another person or an extraneous factor aborted the commission of the crime. Third, the defendant argues that the state failed to prove beyond a reasonable doubt that he did not voluntarily abandon the commission of the crime. We shall discuss each of the defendant's arguments in turn.

II.

The defendant claims that the state failed to prove beyond a reasonable doubt that he intended to commit the crime of robbery as defined in sec. 943.32(1)(b), Stats. 1985–86.

[This section, which discussed the defendant's first argument regarding intent, has been omitted. The court concluded that the evidence was sufficient to find intent.]

III.

The defendant next argues that the evidence at trial was not sufficient to prove that he had committed sufficient acts in furtherance of the crime of robbery for his conduct to constitute an attempt because the state failed to prove beyond a reasonable doubt that the intervention of another person or an extraneous factor aborted the commission of the crime.

. . . .

We disagree with the court of appeals interpretation of sec. 939.32(3). This court has concluded that sec. 939.32(3) does not require the state to prove the existence of an extraneous factor as a third element of the crime of attempt.

In *Hamiel*, the court said, "[W]hether another person or some other intervening extrinsic force are present and actually frustrate the accused person's attempt is not material to the inquiry of the defendant's guilt." Similarly in *State v. Berry*, the court stated that the requirement of sec. 939.32(3) that an actor would commit the crime except for the intervention of another person or some other extraneous factor "does not add an additional, separate requirement that the attempt be thwarted by an outside force."

The court has stated that the statutory language "necessitates a determination whether under all the circumstances it was too late for the person to have repented and withdrawn." The import of sec. 939.32(3) is, according to this court, that "the defendant's conduct must pass that point where most men, holding such an intention as the defendant holds, would think better of their conduct and desist."

The court's interpretation of sec. 939.32(3) as not requiring the state to prove that the accused was actually interrupted by the intervention of another person or an extraneous factor comports with legislative intent. The legislature intended to punish individuals who have exhibited a dangerous propensity toward committing a crime because these individuals are as dangerous as a person who completes the crime contemplated.

Because the legislature intended sec. 939.32(3) to address the accused's manifest dangerousness, we conclude that the legislature did not intend to require an actual interruption of the accused's conduct by intervention of another person or an extraneous factor in order for there to be an attempt under the statute. When the accused's acts demonstrate unequivocally that the accused will continue unless interrupted, that is, when the acts demonstrate that the accused will probably not desist from the criminal course, then the accused's dangerousness is manifest. Accordingly we reject defendant's assertion that sec. 939.32(3) requires the state to prove the intervention of another person or an extraneous factor.

The purpose of the language in sec. 939.32(3) relating to intervention of another person and extraneous factor is to denote that the actor must have gone far enough toward completion of the crime to make it improbable that he would change his mind and desist. The conduct element of sec. 939.32(3) is satisfied when the accused engages in conduct which demonstrates that only a circumstance beyond the accused's control would prevent the crime, whether or not such a circumstance actually occurs. An attempt occurs when the accused's acts move beyond the incubation period for the crime, that is, the time during which the accused has formed an intent to commit the crime but has not committed enough acts and may still change his mind and desist. In other words the statute requires a judgment in each case that the accused has committed sufficient acts that it is unlikely that he would have voluntarily desisted from commission of the crime.

The *Hamiel* court suggested that the accused's acts be viewed as a film in which the action is suddenly stopped, so that the audience may be asked to what end the acts are directed. "If there is only one reasonable answer to this question then the accused has done what amounts to an 'attempt' to attain that end. If there is more than one reasonably possible answer, then the accused has not yet done enough." The aim of this "stop the film" test is to determine whether the accused's acts unequivocally demonstrate an intent to commit the crime rendering voluntary desistance from the crime improbable.

If the defendant had been filmed in this case and the film stopped just before Levy entered the bus stop and the three men departed, we conclude that a trier of fact could find beyond a reasonable doubt that the defendant's acts were directed toward robbery. The film would show the defendant demanding money and appearing to reach for a gun. This evidence is sufficient to prove that the defendant had taken sufficient steps for his conduct to constitute an attempted robbery.

In *Jacobs v. State*, a case involving attempted robbery, the court applied a similar analysis of the accused's acts:

> "The attempt was complete when the defendant, with intent to commit a robbery, took action, to wit, pointing the gun and demanding the money, in furtherance of such intent. Pointing the gun and telling the store proprietor to 'give me that sack' were unequivocal acts, accompanied by intent, sufficient to complete the crime of attempted robbery. The unanticipated set of circumstances, including the store owner stating he had no money and to go ahead and shoot, . . . the accomplices suggestion that they leave and his leaving, combined to influence the defendant to abandon the robbery, but *only after attempted armed robbery had been unequivocally completed.* (Emphasis supplied.)

We conclude that the evidence was sufficient for the trier of fact to find beyond a reasonable doubt that the defendant's conduct in furtherance of the defendant's intent to commit robbery had proceeded far enough toward completion of the crime to make it improbable that the defendant would desist. The state proved the second element of the crime of attempt.

IV.

[This section, which discussed the defendants third argument involving voluntary abandonment has been omitted.]

For the reasons set forth we conclude that the decision of the court of appeals should be reversed and the judgment of conviction of the circuit court affirmed.

The decision of the court of appeals is reversed.

Topic IV
UNCERTAINTY
(1 Assignment)

ASSIGNMENT 1
Briefing: Examples in Tort and Contract Law

Damages may not be awarded in a case where the source of the harm for which damages are sought is too uncertain. In most cases it must be proved by a preponderance of the evidence that the defendant caused the harm. This standard of proof has been explained as a greater than 50% chance that the defendant caused the harm. If the standard is met (and the other elements of proof in the case have been satisfied), the plaintiff is awarded the full measure of damages. If the standard is not met, the plaintiff receives nothing. The first case in this assignment discusses the implications of this standard of proof. Harm did occur, and breach of the standard of due care would most likely have been proved in *Cooper* if the case had gone to the jury, but causation could not be proved by a preponderance of the evidence. Therefore, the case did not go to the jury and no damages were awarded.

On the other hand, damages have been awarded in cases where the extent of the harm for which damages were sought was uncertain. It was not necessary to prove by a preponderance of the evidence that a specific amount of damages had occurred. *Mange* involved the loss of a chance of benefit; *Locke* involved the loss of profits; and *Rideaux* involved the loss of earnings. What is interesting in these cases was the willingness of the courts to consider awarding damages in proportion to the probability that a certain situation would have occurred if the harm from breach of contract had not occurred. A question to keep in mind during your reading and briefing of the cases in this assignment is why the courts have not used the same approach for determining the existence of causation in a case like *Cooper* as they have in determining the existence of damages in cases like *Mange, Locke* and *Rideaux*. In other words, why did the court take the case from the jury in *Cooper* despite the fact that defendants' negligence, if proved, could have had some chance of causing the harm?

Before reaching these major questions raised by the cases, however, it is necessary to understand what the cases tell us about the law. Each case must be analyzed for its relevant facts, the issue it presents, how it is resolved in the holding of the court, and what rationale is given by the court for its resolution of the issue. Read the *Cooper* case first for its story and then reread it to determine in brief form its facts, issue, holding, and rationale.

COOPER v. SISTERS OF CHARITY OF CINCINNATI, INC.
27 Ohio St. 2d 242, 272 N.E.2d 97 (Ohio 1971)

This case originated in the Court of Common Pleas as a wrongful death action brought by Margaret Cooper, administratrix of the estate of her son, Theodore Grant Cooper.

Sometime in the early afternoon on July 22, 1965, Theodore Grant Cooper, age 16, was struck by a truck while riding a bicycle. Later that afternoon at about 2:00 p.m., his mother saw him at the home of a relative. Theodore stated that he had hit his head, hurt his back, and complained of a slight headache. He had vomited prior to his mother's arrival and again after her arrival. Mrs. Cooper observed a red mark on the back of his head.

In the early evening of July 22, 1965, Mrs. Cooper accompanied her son to the emergency room of Good Samaritan Hospital. He was able to enter the hospital unaided. While waiting to be attended, the decedent vomited again.

A lady came from an office in the emergency room, asked for, and was given certain information by Mrs. Cooper. Mrs. Cooper informed her of her son's name, address, and how he was hurt.

The boy and his mother then entered an examining room where appellee, Dr. Hansen, began his examination.

The doctor was given the history of decedent's accident, vomiting, and complaint of headache. Dr. Hansen examined the decedent about the stomach and the top of his head; tested his reflexes and grip, examined his eyes with a light; looked into his ears; and ordered X-rays, the results of which did not reveal a skull fracture.

At all times during the examination Mrs. Cooper was present, except when decedent was taken to the X-ray room. She testified that her son was lying down on a movable cart throughout the examination, and that she called the physician's attention to the fact that it was the back of the boy's head that was hurt, but he did not examine the back of the boy's head.

Dr. Hansen did not utilize an opthalmoscope, did not test decedent's gait, did not perform a Romberg test, nor did he conduct any other diagnostic procedures.

Concluding his attendance, Dr. Hansen advised that the patient be taken home, put to bed, and awakened every hour during the early part of the evening to make sure that he could be awakened. Thereafter he was to be awakened every two hours throughout the remainder of the night. Mrs. Cooper was told that if she were unable to awaken him or if he vomited more than twice, or if she recognized any other change in his condition, she was to return him to the hospital. Upon leaving the hospital the decedent had to be assisted in walking.

When appellant and her son returned to her apartment, the boy went to bed. He remained awake with no apparent change in his condition until he became restless just before his death, which occurred early the next morning.

Appellant's witness, Dr. Frank Cleveland, Hamilton County Coroner, performed an autopsy and stated at trial that, in his opinion, the cause of death was a basal skull fracture and a swelling of the tissues in the back of the decedent's head, causing intracranial pressure and hemorrhage as the result of an injury to his head.

Dr. Hansen did not determine decedent's vital signs; i.e., temperature, respiration, pulse, and blood pressure. Mrs. Cooper testified that none of these tests were conducted while she was with her son at the hospital. Dr. Hansen testified that although he had no personal knowledge of his own as to whether the vital signs of the decedent were taken at the hospital, taking such signs were mandatory routine procedures in the emergency room. He testified further that at present he did not know what decedent's vital signs were that night, but that he was sure that he had known them at that time.

The appellant filed this action in the Court of Common Pleas against the Sisters of Charity of Cincinnati, Inc., doing business as Good Samaritan Hospital; the Emergency Professional Service Group of Good Samaritan Hospital, an unincorporated association; Richard Weber, that group's codirector; and Dr. Robert Hansen. The petition alleges that the Sisters of Charity had represented to appellant, and to the public, that the persons rendering medical care in the emergency room were doing so on behalf of the hospital, and that the appellant's decedent's death was "directly and proximately caused by the negligence and carelessness of the defendants" in their diagnosis and treatment of decedent's injuries.

. . . .

Dr. Cleveland testified that, in his opinion, the swollen tissue and external discoloration from decedent's injury would have appeared within a brief period after such injury, and should have been found upon examination. Although there is a near certainty of death when an injury, such as suffered by decedent, goes untreated, Dr. Cleveland stated that "there is no possible way for a physician or anyone else to ascertain with any degree of certainty whether with medical intervention, the individual would have survived or died." Such a finding would require, he concluded, pure conjecture or speculation.

Dr. DeJong, chairman of the Department of Neurology at the University of Michigan medical school, testified for appellant by deposition. He related that contemporary medical standards, both in Ann Arbor, Michigan, and Cincinnati, require that the "vital signs" should have been checked in this kind of case, and that the decedent's vomiting should have given rise to a more complete examination than was performed including in-hospital observation for a period of time. Injuries to the brain may be evidenced by changes in those vital signs. He testified further that while there is practically a 100% mortality rate without surgery for patients with similar injuries as decedent's, *"there certainly is a chance and I can't say exactly what — maybe some place around 50% — that he would survive with surgery."* With regard to appellee Hansen's failure to examine the knot on decedent's head, or to test his ability to sit up, stand, or walk around, Dr. DeJong opined that "the evaluation concerning these two factors was not complete."

. . . .

At the close of appellant's case, the court granted appellees' motion for a directed verdict. The trial court entered separate findings of fact and conclusions of law. Among others, the following findings of fact were made:

"8. The normal hospital procedure was that the nurse would take the vital signs before the patient was taken to the doctor. Dr. Hansen did not take the vital signs and they were not taken in his presence. He had no knowledge of what they were, if taken. When the admission sheet reached the doctor, only the typewritten portions appeared on it."

"15. At the time of the examination of plaintiff's decedent by Dr. Hansen, in the opinion of Dr. Cleveland within reasonable medical certainty, a swollen and discolored area would have existed and would have been apparent and sensitive to palpatation [sic] on the back of decedent's head and should have been found on examination at the emergency room."

"21. Dr. Cleveland described the vital signs to be blood pressure, pulse, temperature and respiration, and as a matter of course must be checked where there is injury to the head."

"24. Dr. DeJong said that in the condition of the decedent death was inevitable without surgical intervention. Even with the best surgical intervention no one could say with any certainty that there would be recovery; that there is no possible way for a physician to ascertain with any degree of certainty whether with further medical attention the decedent would have lived or would have died and that it is a matter of pure speculation and guess to render any opinion concerning the chances of recovery."

The trial judge's conclusions of law are as follows:

"From the facts adduced it is the conclusion of the court that the evidence of proximate cause was insufficient to make a prima facie case for submission to the jury as against defendant, Dr. Hansen, his employer, the Emergency Service Group of the Good Samaritan Hospital, or Sisters of Charity of Cincinnati, Inc.

. . . .

"Based upon the foregoing, it is the conclusion of the court that the defendants were entitled to judgment in their favor as a matter of law."

The trial court's judgment was affirmed by the Court of Appeals. This court is reviewing the case pursuant to the allowance of a motion to certify the record.

DUNCAN, J. Reasonable minds could arrive at differing conclusions as to whether Dr. Hansen was negligent in rendering professional medical services to plaintiff's decedent, and there is sufficient evidence for the submission of that issue to the jury. There is ample evidence in the record supportive of the trial judge's findings of fact that Dr. Hansen did not take the vital signs that they were not taken in his presence, and that he had no knowledge of what they were, if taken. Those findings, considered together with other expert testimony, provide a basis from which a jury could properly determine that Dr. Hansen's conduct regarding Theodore Cooper did not satisfy the standard that a physician in the community should observe under like circumstances.

The more problematic issue of proximate cause looms from these facts as a reminder of past difficulties this court has experienced with this issue in malpractice cases.

It has been established, and we now reaffirm the principle that: "Even though there is evidence of malpractice sufficient for submission to the jury on that issue, a verdict must be directed in favor of the defendant where there is no evidence adduced which would give rise to a reasonable inference that the defendant's acts of malpractice was the direct and proximate cause of the injury to the plaintiff." Paragraph two of the syllabus in *Kuhn v. Banker.*

In his opinion in *Kuhn*, Judge Williams stated that "the patient cannot recover damages unless the act of malpractice is the direct and proximate cause of injury. Loss of chance of recovery, standing alone, is not an injury from which damages will flow." In so stating, Judge Williams disagreed with, and relegates to *obiter dictum*, the conflicting view expressed in *Craig v. Chambers* that "any want of the proper degree of skill or care which diminishes the chances of a patient's recovery * * * would, in a legal sense, constitute injury."

In *Hicks v. United States*, construing Virginia law, it is expressed:

"When a defendant's negligent action or inaction has effectively terminated a person's chance of survival, it does not lie in the defendant's mouth to raise conjectures as to the measure of the chances that he has put beyond the possibility of realization. If there was any substantial possibility of survival and the defendant has destroyed it, he is answerable. Rarely is it possible to demonstrate to an absolute certainty what would have happened in circumstances that the wrongdoer did not allow to come to pass. The law does not in the existing circumstances require the plaintiff to show to a *certainty* that the patient would have lived had she been hospitalized and operated on promptly."

Although the words "substantial possibility" are employed as articulating a standard of proof, the facts in *Hicks* reveal that plaintiffs' evidence satisfied a much higher standard of proof. The court also stated:

"The government further contends that even if negligence is established, there was no proof that the erroneous diagnosis and treatment was the proximate cause of the death, asserting that even if surgery had been performed immediately, it is mere speculation to say that it would have been successful. The government's contention, however, is unsupported by the record. Both of plaintiff's experts testified categorically that *if operated on promptly, Mrs. Greitens would have survived,* and this is nowhere contradicted by the government expert." (Emphasis added.)

A rule, which would permit a plaintiff to establish a jury question on the issue of proximate cause upon a showing of a "substantial possibility" of survival, in our judgment, suffers the same infirmity as a rule which would permit proof of a "chance of recovery" to be sufficient. While the substantial possibility concept appears to connote a weightier burden than the chance of recovery idea, both derogate well-established and valuable proximate cause considerations. Traditional proximate cause standards require that the trier of the facts, at a minimum, must be provided with evidence that a result was more likely than not to have been caused by an act, in the absence of any intervening cause.

Lesser standards of proof are understandably attractive in malpractice cases where physical well being, and life itself, are the subject of litigation. The strong intuitive sense of humanity tends to emotionally direct us toward a conclusion that in an action for wrongful death an injured person should be compensated for the loss of any chance for survival, regardless of its remoteness. However, we have trepidations that such a rule would be so loose that it would produce more injustice than justice. Even though there exists authority for a rule allowing recovery based upon proof of causation by evidence not meeting the standard of probability, we are not persuaded by their logic. The following authorities appear to require the establishment of proximate cause by evidence of probability: . . . .

We consider the better rule to be that in order to comport with the standard of proof of proximate cause, plaintiff in a malpractice case must prove that defendant's negligence, *in probability*, proximately caused the death.

In this case, we are convinced that in order for the jury question to be presented, giving plaintiff's evidence, and inferences reasonably deductible therefrom its most favorable consideration and indulgence, there must be sufficient evidence that Dr. Hansen's negligence denied plaintiff's decedent the *probability* of survival. Appellant has not produced such evidence.

Dr. Cleveland, plaintiff's witness stated that "there is no possible way for a physician or anyone else to ascertain with any degree of certainty whether with medical intervention, the individual would have survived or died." Dr. DeJong stated that, if untreated, the condition from which Theodore Cooper died had practically a 100% mortality rate without surgery for patients with similar injuries as decedents. He then stated that "there certainly is a chance and I can't say exactly what — *maybe* some place *around 50%* — that he would survive with surgery." (Emphasis added.)

Dr. Cleveland's opinion furnishes no suggestion of a probability of survival. Dr. DeJong's opinion bears closer examination. Probability is most often defined as that which is more likely than not. Dr. DeJong's opinion that, with surgical intervention, decedent's expectation of survival was "Maybe * * * around 50%," in our judgment does not provide a basis from which probability can reasonably be inferred. The use of the words, "maybe" and "around," does not connote that there is probability; those words, in the context used, could mean either more than 50%, or less than 50%. Probable is more than 50% of actual. In view of the requirement that proximate cause, in this type of case, is a matter demanding medical expert testimony, there are no facts available in this case from which a juror could infer that survival would have been more likely, than not, if surgery had been performed. A juror could as reasonably infer from Dr. DeJong's testimony that survival would, under the circumstances, have been somewhat less than probable.

As stated in *Davis v. Guarnieri*, "It is legally and logically impossible for it to be probable that a fact exists, and at the same time probable that it does not exist."

Plaintiff's cause of action was brought under R.C. 2125.01, under which compensation may be awarded "when death is *caused* by a wrongful act, neglect or default * * *." (Emphasis added.)

In an action for wrongful death, where medical malpractice is alleged as the proximate cause of death, and plaintiff's evidence indicates that a failure to diagnose the injury prevented the patient from an opportunity to be operated on, which failure eliminated any chance of the patient's survival, the issue of proximate cause can be submitted to a jury only if there is sufficient evidence showing that with proper diagnosis, treatment and surgery the patient probably would have survived.

. . . .

For the foregoing reasons, the judgment of the Court of Appeals is affirmed.

Judgment affirmed.

O'NEILL, C. J., SCHNEIDER, CORRIGAN, STERN and LEACH, JJ., concur.

HERBERT, J., dissents.

DISCUSSION

Theodore Cooper was hit by a truck while riding his bicycle. According to Cooper's mother, the doctor in the emergency room did not perform a number of procedures that might have led to lifesaving surgery. The patient was sent home and died the following morning. The mother sued the hospital, the doctor, and others. The court stated at the beginning of its opinion that there was ample evidence for submission of the issue of negligence to the jury. But a verdict was directed [look up "directed verdict" if you do not know the term] in favor of the defendants. In other words, the judge took the case away from the jury and decided it in favor of the defendants. Why? Towards the end of its opinion, the court stated that there was insufficient evidence that the doctor's negligence "denied plaintiff's decedent the *probability* of survival."

The issue in this case is not negligence; it is causation. Did the negligence of the doctor cause the death of Theodore? More specifically, what is the standard of proof for establishing whether the negligence of the doctor caused the death of Theodore, and did the plaintiff carry its burden to prove causation under this standard? The standard is not proof beyond a reasonable doubt. That standard is the one used in criminal cases. The standard used here is the traditional standard of proof in civil cases "that a result was more likely than not to have been caused by an act, in the absence of any intervening cause." Stated again by the court, "the standard of proof of proximate cause" requires that "plaintiff in a malpractice case must prove that defendant's negligence, in *probability*, proximately caused the death." The court directed a verdict for defendants because it found that there were "no facts available in this case from which a juror could infer that survival would have been more likely, than not, if surgery had been performed."

If the standard of proof in this case was the traditional one, why did this case come up on appeal to the Ohio Supreme Court? There was a dispute in this case over whether the traditional standard should be applied. The court spent part of its discussion on a case called *Hicks v. United States*. Dictum (a term to look up in the dictionary if you do not know its meaning) existed in that case to the effect that if a defendant destroyed a person's substantial possibility of survival, the defendant would be liable. This dictum suggested that liability could be found even if a person's substantial possibility of survival was less than 50% in the absence of negligence, as long as it was found that the defendant's negligence destroyed that possibility of survival. Such a standard would be contrary to the traditional standard that causation must be proved by a preponderance of the evidence, meaning that there must be a greater than 50% chance that defendant's negligence caused the harm. But the court in *Cooper* rejected this dictum from *Hicks* on the ground that it was not the holding, that is, the rule that governed the decision in that case. The *Hicks* court found the uncontradicted evidence to be that in the absence of the negligence, the victim of the negligence would have survived. Therefore, the facts, which governed the holding of the *Hicks* case, were sufficient to establish that there was a greater than 50% chance that the negligence caused the harm. The dictum could be ignored because the precedential value of a case is tied to its facts, and the facts in *Hicks* supported the traditional standard of proof, that is, proof by a preponderance of the evidence.

Now that we have the story of this case and have explored the questions it has raised and answered, we can take a stab at writing a brief. Remember that a brief should be just that — brief. It is designed to refresh your memory concerning the case on later occasions when you review your notes. Write your own brief and then compare it with the one below. The brief below is not the only way to write a brief but it should give you some basis on which to evaluate your own style and content.

Cooper v. Sisters of Charity of Cincinnati, Inc.
272 N.E. 2d 97 (Ohio 1971)

FACTS: Cooper boy hit by a truck, treated in an emergency room, sent home, and died the next morning. Mom sued for damages from doctor's negligence. There was ample evidence for submission of negligence issue to jury. Lower court directed verdict for defendants, the Court of Appeals affirmed, and this court affirmed.

ISSUE: Was there sufficient evidence for submission of causation issue to jury?

HOLDING: No. There was insufficient evidence that the doctor's negligence "denied plaintiff's decedent the *probability* of survival."

RATIONALE: The standard of proof for causation is whether the "defendant's negligence, in *probability*, proximately caused the death." If the victim of the negligence had a substantial possibility of survival without the negligence occurring, but the possibility was less than 50%, death by the negligence cannot be proved by a preponderance of the evidence because there is a greater than 50% chance that the death occurred from other causes. In this case there were no facts from which a juror could infer that survival would have been more likely than not if the negligence had not occurred.

The next case turns attention from the element of causation to the element of damages. Although *Cooper* denied the plaintiff a right to recover based on the uncertainty of causation between the defendant's wrong and the harm, *Mange* allows the plaintiff a right to recover despite the uncertainty of the extent of the harm that occurred when the defendant's wrong caused the harm. Read *Mange* with the following question in mind: How are damages determined when it is uncertain how much harm is caused by a breach of contract?

MANGE v. UNICORN PRESS, INC.
129 F. Supp. 727 (S.D.N.Y. 1955)

Irving R. Kaufman, District Judge.

Defendant seeks summary judgment in an action for breach of contract. To stimulate sales of its New Funk & Wagnalls Encyclopedia (hereafter the Encyclopedia), the defendant initiated a Puzzle-Quiz contest in 1950. With each volume of the Encyclopedia, one Puzzle-quiz consisting of several rebus type puzzles and several quizzes pertinent to the contents of that volume were sent to contestants. All parties agreed to be bound by the Official Rules of the contest. Rule 3 stated that each question or puzzle would have only one correct answer or solution, each earning contestant a designated number of points. Those tied with the greatest number of points would be entitled to compete in tie-breaking puzzles. Rule 5 established the Encyclopedia as "the final and deciding authority on all quizzes contained in the puzzle quizzes" and stated that "Facts not found in the Encyclopedia will not be recognized as the correct answers to the quiz questions." Rule 9 stated that "the contestant * * * agrees * * * that the decision of the Publishers shall be final and conclusive in all matters concerning the conduct of the contest, the judging of answers and solutions to Puzzle Quizzes * * *, the making of awards, * * * and the measures invoked to insure individual effort and equal opportunity in fairness to all contestants." However, in an issue of the Contest News sent to all contestants, the judges' job was described as "merely a matter of tallying."

Plaintiff's complaint deals with Puzzle-Quiz No. 16B in which the contestants were required to check "correct statements" about the giraffe. One sentence in the puzzle sheet sent to plaintiff read: "It is timid and, having no vocal chords, is mute." This form was sent to 75,000 contestants, but in a later printing, sent to 200,000 others, the word "chords" was spelled "cords." In the "controlling" Encyclopedia the identical sentence appears but the word is spelled "cords." Plaintiff contends that because of this spelling variance he did not check the statement as correct. He affirms that he found this spelling variance to be a critical problem; *i.e.* he was unsure of whether it was a typographical error or a deliberate substitution of an incorrect phrase and, unable to find the spelling "chords" used in an anatomical sense any place else in the Encyclopedia, he chose the latter interpretation. He contends that he was guided in this choice by Rule 3 which states that there is only one correct answer to each quiz and by a statement in defendant's "Guide for Answering Quizzes and Solving Puzzles" which warned: "always read and reread the quiz-questions very carefully. If you grow careless in reading them and overlook the exact meaning, you may make a foolish mistake." He also claims that he thought there was a difference between being asked if the statement was "correct" or "true."

Plaintiff urges that in marking his answer wrong, defendant violated Contest Rule 5 making the Encyclopedia the controlling authority and hence breached its contract; and further, that in sending him a puzzle with a variant spelling of a key word, defendant gave him a more difficult question than that posed to other contestants in violation of its agreement to give equal treatment to all. Had plaintiff not been marked wrong with respect to Puzzle 16B he would have been eligible to enter the tie-breaking stages of the contest as all his other answers to the 36 Puzzle-Quizzes were correct.

Defendant bases its request for summary judgment on the theory that, absent an allegation of fraud or gross mistake, the decision of the Publishers against plaintiff was made final and conclusive by Rule 9.

. . . .

At this stage of the litigation, the Court cannot peremptorily hold that a decision of the Publishers under Rule 9 was clearly intended to be conclusive on the issue here presented, particularly in view of: (1) the language of Rule 5, rendering the Encyclopedia "the final and deciding authority on all quizzes," which appears *prima facie* to be inconsistent with plenary power in the Publishers; (2) other language in the contest rules and in a publication distributed in connection with the contest which seem to imply that the Publisher's powers in this regard were intended to be merely of a ministerial nature; and (3) the policy expressed in Minton v. F. G. Smith Piano Co. of resolving ambiguities against the publisher-offeror.

> "It is enough to notice that there is a substantial doubt about that and such an involved question is so bound up with the particular facts and circumstances that it is better first to let them be fully developed at a trial and findings made after that has been done."

Defendant's final contention is that any award of damages would be merely speculative. It points out that 23,548 contestants entered the tie-breaking stages and that only 210 prizes were awarded, first prize being $307,500. Of course, the number of tiebreaking contestants might be different if plaintiff's contentions as to the proper solution to Puzzle 16B are fully accepted, but the number of contestants would still undoubtedly be in the thousands. Defendant relies on a series of New York cases not involving contests, and a series of out-state cases involving contests to support its contention that such speculative damages cannot be the basis for an award. It is unnecessary to reach the merits of the question whether plaintiff can establish actual damages in order to reject the contention that a denial of actual damages entitles defendant to judgment. Awarding judgment to the defendant would foreclose the plaintiff from possibility of recovering at least nominal damages. Furthermore, with respect to whether actual damages can be awarded to plaintiff, although there is substantial authority denying recovery, there appears to be a liberal trend towards allowing the jury to determine the value of the chance of which plaintiff was deprived. This is the English rule and has been followed a few times in America. The rationale behind these cases is that plaintiff's chances of success would have had some market value especially since there was no risk of out-of-pocket loss offsetting the possibility of gain. The question of speculative damages in contest cases does not seem to have been definitely decided in New York.

Motion denied. So ordered.

DISCUSSION

What happened in this case? The plaintiff was precluded from winning a cash prize because he was marked wrong in a puzzle-quiz. He complained that it was not wrong, notwithstanding the decision of the Publishers. The defendant sought summary judgment on the ground that the Publishers had the final decision on this matter and that "any award of damages would be merely speculative." The court denied the motion for summary judgment on which this case was brought, because it found that there was sufficient evidence to go to trial on the issue of the finality of the Publishers' decision, and that the issue of speculative damages was yet to be decided because "there appears to be a liberal trend towards allowing the jury to determine the value of the chance of which plaintiff was deprived."

This summary of the case does not jump out at the reader. It requires more than one reading. You might try a summary reading and then search for the component parts of your brief. The first sentence of the case reveals that it was one for summary judgment. (You need to find the term "summary judgment" in the law dictionary if you do not know what it is.) Then, skipping to the end of the opinion, the reader finds that the motion was denied. Therefore, the plaintiff won the right to go to trial on the issues. The first part of the opinion reveals one reason why the defendant claimed that there was no issue for trial. The defendant claimed that the breach of contract asserted by the plaintiff was ruled on by the Publishers in a final and conclusive decision, leaving no room for appeal to this court. This court disagreed. In any case, you may decide to give this issue less attention since it does not pertain to the issues addressed in this assignment. The second issue, which is the issue relevant to this assignment, was whether the damages would have been speculative. The discussion on this issue occupies the last full paragraph of the opinion. (You can gather from the opinion that speculative damages are not allowed, but you can also confirm this rule by checking out a hornbook on Contract.) It may take some time to skip around the case to find these component parts and to put them in understandable form. Once you have understood the case, you are ready to brief it.

Mange v. Unicorn Press, Inc.
129 F. Supp. 272 (S.D.N.Y. 1955)

FACTS:	Plaintiff precluded from becoming one of 23,548 contestants who had a chance to win one of 210 cash prizes (first prize being $307,500) because he was marked wrong in a puzzle-quiz. Defendant sought summary judgment on the ground that the Publishers had the final decision on this matter and that "any award of damages would be merely speculative." Court denied motion for summary judgment.
ISSUE:	Are damages for loss of a possibility of a prize speculative?
HOLDING:	They are not necessarily speculative.
RATIONALE:	"[T]here appears to be a liberal trend towards allowing the jury to determine the value of the chance of which plaintiff was deprived. . . . The rationale behind these cases is that plaintiff's chances of success would have had some market value especially since there was no risk of out-of-pocket loss offsetting the possibility of gain."

The next case raises a similar issue to the one in *Mange*. It discusses whether the value of a chance for profits is measurable such that a court may be allowed to value the lost opportunity.

LOCKE v. UNITED STATES
283 F.2d 521 (Ct. Cl. 1960)

JONES, Chief Judge.

This is a suit . . . for lost profits resulting from an alleged breach of a requirements contract held by plaintiff with the General Services Administration. The contract covered the repair of typewriters in the San Diego, California, area. . . . The case comes before the court on the parties' cross-motions for summary judgment under Rule 51, 28 U.S.C.A.

I

. . . The plaintiff, Harvey Ward Locke, was the owner of a typewriter-repair company doing business variously under the names "Ward's Typewriter Repair" and "Allied Typewriter Company." As Ward's Typewriter Repair, of San Diego, California, plaintiff was awarded GSA Federal Supply Schedule Contract GS-09S-1329. The contract covered the repair, maintenance and reconditioning of manual typewriters in the San Diego area for the period July 1, 1955, through June 30, 1956. Similar typewriter-repair contracts were awarded to three other local companies covering the same period of time. These contracts provided that upon an acceptable bid and a showing of responsibility the contractor's name, address, and telephone number would be placed in a Federal Supply Schedule which was widely distributed to Government installations in the area. Apart from certain exceptional conditions not pertinent here, it was mandatory upon the various departments of the Executive Branch of the Federal Government in the area to use contractors whose names appeared in this schedule when typewriter-repair services were desired. (The Department of Defense was specifically excluded.) However, these agencies were at liberty to choose *any* name from the schedule and were not bound to proceed in the schedule in a given order. In addition to "mandatory use" all agencies of the Federal Government, particularly the Department of Defense, optionally might order repair services from contractors appearing in the schedule. Each bidder whose bid was accepted and whose name was listed in the schedule was obligated to perform all the services for which he contracted that resulted from the "mandatory" provisions of the contract. However, contractors were at liberty to decline those progressive awards which arose from the "optional" provisions of the contract.

Plaintiff operated under his contract for several months and received some business from the Government. But on February 2, 1956, the Government's contracting officer terminated the contract for default and plaintiff's name was stricken from the schedule. Other contractors in the schedule continued to receive Government business until the expiration of their contracts. Plaintiff filed an appeal with the Board of Review, General Services Administration, and following a full hearing, the board rendered the following decision:

"1. Contract No. GS-09S-1329 was terminated for default on February 2, 1956, without proper cause.

"2. The Appellant's claim for the payment of $30,000 as compensation for lost profits is denied.

"3. The Appellant's claim for the payment of $60,000 as compensation for alleged defamation of character and loss of other business is denied."

Following this denial of relief the plaintiff filed his appeal to this court.

The question brought to this court for determination is what if any compensable damage did plaintiff suffer as a direct result of the Government's improper termination of plaintiff's contract. The Government says no damage has occurred and has moved to dismiss the complaint for failure to state a cause of action upon which relief can be granted. The plaintiff, appearing *pro se*, has alleged in his jumble of testimony, less explicitly but no less expressively, that various forms of damages have occurred. He has asked "this Court to assist him to see that justice does not suffer miscarriage under American Jurisprudence."

Simply phrased, the defendant takes the position that while the contract may have been improperly terminated no loss of profits is recoverable because the contract was a "requirements contract" and did not guarantee that *any* minimum requirement would exist. Furthermore, where a requirement did in fact occur, the contract by its terms did not guarantee that the Government would give all or any part of this requirement to the plaintiff. The contract merely provided that plaintiff's name would appear in a Federal Supply Schedule along with other typewriter-repair contractors. Certain Federal agencies could select typewriter-repair companies from the schedule to fulfill their requirements, if any. Furthermore, since plaintiff could not have demanded business while he remained in the schedule, he cannot now be heard to complain that he received no business, albeit he may have been improperly removed from the schedule. With this we cannot agree.

It is now beyond question that contracts for requirements do not lack mutuality and are enforceable. In every case it is the reasonable expectation by both parties that there will be requirements on which the bargain is grounded. The facts, as alleged, show that plaintiff in the past had received substantially all of his business from Government agencies under similar contracts. We cannot believe that in this instance plaintiff bargained merely to have his name printed in the supply schedule. It appears more important that being in the schedule created a reasonable probability that business would be obtained. Particularly is this so when it is noted that among the four San Diego repair companies originally put in the schedule plaintiff was the low bidder.

We agree that nothing in the contract would have prevented the Government from enlarging its own repair facilities to fill completely its needs. This would have left nothing to be awarded under the Federal Supply Schedule contracts. But the facts as alleged show that the Government did have some service requirements beyond its own capacity. Presumably, these requirements were awarded to contractors in the schedule. Plaintiff's chance of obtaining some of these awards, by being in the schedule and competing with the other contractors, had *value* in a business sense. The Government by its breach deprived plaintiff of this value.

The defendant further takes the position that the fact of damage as well as the amount that resulted from the removal of plaintiff's name from the schedule is too speculative to permit of proof. But the constant tendency of the courts is to find some way in which damages can be awarded where a wrong has been done. Difficulty of ascertainment is not to be confused with right of recovery. Nor does it exonerate the defendant that his misconduct, which has made necessary the inquiry into the question of harm, renders that inquiry difficult. The defendant who has wrongfully broken a contract should not be permitted to reap advantage from his own wrong by insisting on proof which by reason of his breach is unobtainable. It remains true, however, that the plaintiff must meet a higher standard of proof to establish that he has sustained *some* injury than to fix the amount.

If a reasonable probability of damage can be clearly established, uncertainty as to the amount will not preclude recovery. The amount may be approximated if a reasonable basis of computation is afforded. "All that the law requires is that such damage be allowed as, in the judgment of fair men, directly and naturally resulted from the breach of the contract for which the suit is brought." Certainty is sufficient if the evidence adduced enables the court to make a fair and reasonable approximation of the damages. In circumstances such as these we may act upon probable and inferential as well as direct and positive proof.

> "Any other rule would enable the wrongdoer to profit by his wrongdoing at the expense of his victim. It would be an inducement to make wrongdoing so effective and complete in every case as to preclude any recovery by rendering the measure of damages uncertain. Failure to apply [this rule] would mean that the more grievous the wrong done, the less likelihood there would be of a recovery.

> "The most elementary conceptions of justice and public policy require that the wrongdoer shall bear the risk of the uncertainty which his own wrong has created."

We are here concerned with the value of a chance for obtaining business and profits. The last time this question of recovery for a lost chance at business was put to this court, recovery was denied. However, that case is not governing for there the court expressly found that the plaintiff never had *any* chance to obtain business. Here it appears that the plaintiff did have a chance of obtaining at least one-fourth of the total typewriter-repair business let by the Government. It is true that plaintiff's reasonable expectations might have been disappointed by the happening of diverse contingencies. We should not, however, overlook the fact that the plaintiff gave valuable consideration for the promise of a performance which would have given him a chance at business and profit. We believe that where the value of a chance for profit is not outweighed by a countervailing risk of loss, and where it is fairly measurable by calculable odds and by evidence bearing specifically on the probabilities that the court should be allowed to value that lost opportunity.

Therefore, we direct the trial commissioner to determine the following facts:

1. The total amount of typewriter-repair business let by the Government for which plaintiff would have been eligible under his contract but for the Government's breach. (This should be easily obtained from the Government's records.)

2. Whether there were any material facts that would have tended to prevent plaintiff from receiving his proportionate share of such business.

3. The average per unit cost normally incurred in performing repair work of the type here involved.

4. Expenses plaintiff necessarily incurred in preparing to fulfill his obligations under the contract. The expense of preparing the bid should not be included.

In view of the small amounts involved it is suggested that most of the above facts may be stipulated by the parties.

. . . .

. . . As to the California contract, both motions are denied and this case is remanded to the trial commissioner for further proceedings consistent with this opinion.

It is so ordered.

DURFEE, LARAMORE and MADDEN, Judges, concur.

WHITAKER, Judge, took no part in the consideration and decision of this case.

DISCUSSION

The first paragraph reveals that plaintiff is suing for lost profits due to the Government's breach of the California contract. The last paragraph of the opinion before the order reveals that plaintiff won the right to proceed. With this basic knowledge about where the case is going, we can turn to a more careful analysis of what happened.

It appears that plaintiff had a contract along with three other companies to repair typewriters for Government agencies who could choose among the four companies for their repair work. Before the contract was over, the Government terminated it for default. On appeal with the Board of Review, it was found that the default was "without proper cause," but no damages were awarded. The plaintiff appealed to this court for damages, and the Government claimed that there were no damages because the plaintiff was not guaranteed any work under this contract. This court disagrees with the Government's position and finds that there was "a reasonable probability that business would be obtained" and that this chance "had *value* in a business sense." The Government claimed that this value was too speculative, but this court finds that "[i]f a reasonable probability of damage can be clearly established, uncertainty as to the amount will not preclude recovery." The "value of a chance for profit" should be determined "where it is fairly measurable by calculable odds and by evidence bearing specifically on the probabilities."

Try your hand at a brief and then compare with the brief below.

Locke v. United States
283 F.2d 521 (Ct. Cl. 1960)

FACTS:	Plaintiff sues for lost profits due to an improper termination of his requirements contract with the Government. The requirements contract gave P a chance along with three other companies to repair typewriters for government agencies. No work was guaranteed but it was reasonably probable. This court denies D's motion for summary judgment and remands.
ISSUE:	Are damages for loss of the possibility of work under this contract too speculative?
HOLDING:	They are not too speculative "[i]f a reasonable probability of damage can be clearly established," and the court suggested that such proof could be established easily in this case.
RATIONALE:	"[T]he constant tendency of the courts is to find some way in which damages can be awarded where a wrong has been done. Difficulty of ascertainment is not to be confused with right of recovery."

As you learn to produce briefs for the cases you prepare in each of your classes, you will find that different professors have different approaches to their subject matter. Accordingly, you will need to alter your style of briefwriting to accommodate the information needs demanded by your professors. Some professors pay a great deal of attention to the facts and the procedure in a case; others are particular about the manner in which the issue is stated; yet others focus on an extended discussion of the rationale behind the cases and how the cases fit together in the assignment. Remember that there is no one correct method for writing a brief. Any method is correct that produces a brief that will help you recall the essential information you are required to learn from each of your cases. Pay attention to the professor's focus on her cases; train yourself under her guidance to find what information is essential; and develop a style of briefwriting that will give you instant recall of this essential information days after you have completed its study. Remember also that the brief is not the whole of your knowledge. It recites in shorthand form the essential information of a case, but you must have read the case often enough to recall this information beyond the brief. Take enough time with your cases to get to know them thoroughly. Avoid the mistake of rushing through your assignments with only a cursory reading that produces a brief that recalls nothing.

The next case follows the same direction as the previous two but with regard to loss of earnings.

RIDEAUX v. LYKES BROS. STEAMSHIP CO., INC.
285 F. Supp. 153 (S.D. Tex. 1968)

Hannay, District Judge.

On October 24, 1963, the Libelant, Mrs. Louise Rideaux, a widow, an American Citizen, residing in Houston, Harris County, Texas, filed suit against the Respondent Lykes Bros. Steamship Company, Inc., a foreign corporation, doing business in the State of Texas and engaged in interstate commerce and the owner of the S.S. Thompson Lykes. The Respondents will hereinafter be referred to as Lykes. Libelant's action is to recover compensatory damages by reason of the death of her husband, Howard Rideaux, on or about July 15, 1963, while working as a longshoreman in Hatch Number Three of the S.S. Thompson Lykes and discharging forty-foot long steel "I" beams. She was the sole beneficiary of Howard Rideaux. The slings holding a load of beams, parted, or broke, permitting the beams to fall and crush the Libelant's decedent. Libelant alleges that the death of her husband was caused by the negligence of Lykes and the unseaworthiness of the slings ("snodders") used in the discharge operation. This action is brought under the Texas Wrongful Death Statute, Article 4671 et seq., Vernon's Annotated Texas Civil Statutes, and the Texas Survival Statute, Article 5525, Vernon's Annotated Texas Civil Statutes.

[The case came to trial before the court without a jury. Lykes in its brief admitted liability for the death of Howard Rideaux. The issue of indemnity from Paulsen-Webber is omitted.]

Considering first the question of damages. Libelant alleges that Howard Rideaux was fifty years of age and that he had a life expectancy of many years according to the United States Life Tables and that he was a kind, considerate and dutiful husband and provided well for his wife and that he would have, in all reasonable probability, continued during his natural life to have so provided for Libelant. It is also alleged that he was hard working and industrious and earned approximately $7,200.00 per year and that in all reasonable probability his income would have increased. This was later changed by Libelant to $6,300.26. Libelant alleged that he contributed greatly to her, that she was wholly dependent upon him for support and that she had sustained damages by the reason of the death of her husband including $15,000.00 for his conscious pain and suffering, the total amount of Libelant's claim being in the sum of $200,000.00.

Considering first Libelant's claim for conscious pain and suffering. Inasmuch as Howard Rideaux was struck a terrific blow from the rear crushing his skull, breaking his neck and injuring his chest, causing his death instantly, no allowance for conscious pain and suffering should be or is allowed.

The correct measure of recovery of damages herein should be equivalent to actual compensation for the deprivation of the reasonable expectation of pecuniary benefits that would have inured to Libelant for continued life as under the evidence could be expected of her husband Howard Rideaux. "Pecuniary benefits" as applied to Libelant meant not only money, but anything that could be valued in money including reasonable pecuniary value of counsel, protection, advice, services, care and attention that she would have in reasonable probability have [sic] received from her husband. Testimony regarding prospective wage scale raises and cost of living increases is speculative and of little help.

In Har-Pen Truck Lines, Inc. v. Mills, in a personal injury and death case decided by the Fifth Circuit in 1967, the Court, speaking through Judge Goldberg, said:

> "* * * Past earnings are indicative but not conclusive, and defendants would have us stare fixedly at the past with no thought of change in the future. * * * If the jury were restricted to the past for its answers, its computation of loss might have to be purely arithmetic; but the jury may look forward as well as backward, as long as it relies on such relevant and appropriate evidence as is available."

Claim was made by Libelant in its last brief for interest at the legal rate from the date this cause of action arose.

She also desires the question of vacation pay and average yearly wage increases to be taken into account.

This is an admiralty case and the question of pre-judgment interest is discretionary with the court.

Lumping and considering all of the factors to be decided in arriving at damages, including the decedent's age, health, condition in life, habits of industry and sobriety, mental and physical capacity, disposition to frugality, customary and probable earnings in the future then as well as the past and the use made of them (discounted for present payment) decedent's life expectancy and his work expectancy, and without any allowance for Libelant's loss of decedent's companionship, or as solace for grief, I find and decide that Libelant is entitled to receive from Lykes as reasonable, fair and just damages the total sum of $54,350.00 with interest at the rate of 6% per annum from date of judgment until paid. . . .

. . . .

The above and foregoing shall constitute the findings of fact and conclusions of law herein.

The Clerk will notify counsel.

DISCUSSION

This case is rather simple to brief. Respondent admits liability for the death of plaintiff's husband and the only question in the case appears to be the correct measure of recovery of damages. The court defines these damages as "equivalent to actual compensation for the deprivation of the reasonable expectation of pecuniary benefits that would have inured to Libelant [look up this term if you do not know it] for continued life as under the evidence could be expected of her husband."

How is the court to determine these damages? The husband was fifty years old at the time of his death. He earned approximately $6,300 a year with the likelihood of an increase in his income over time. The court did not allow damages for his pain and suffering, but pecuniary benefits that would have inured to the wife were stated to include the "reasonable pecuniary value of counsel, protection, advice, services, care and attention that she would have in reasonable probability have received from her husband" in addition to the benefit of his income. The court considered "the decedent's age, health, condition in life, habits of industry and sobriety, mental and physical capacity, disposition to frugality, customary and probable earnings in the future then as well as the past and the use made of them (discounted for present payment) decedent's life expectancy and his work expectancy." It did not state how it valued these factors but concluded rather summarily that damages were $54,350. The uncertain nature of these damages is evident, but the court does not find them speculative.

Rideaux v. Lykes Bros. Steamship Co., Inc.
285 F. Supp. 153 (S.D. Tex. 1968)

FACTS:	Libelant's husband, a longshoreman, was killed while working for the Respondent Steamship Co. The husband was fifty years old and making $6,300 a year at the time of his death. Respondent admits liability when action is brought in admiralty. Court finds liability for damages of $54,350.
ISSUE:	How are damages measured when they are uncertain?
HOLDING:	Damages are "equivalent to actual compensation for the deprivation of the reasonable expectation of pecuniary benefits that would have inured to Libelant for continued life as under the evidence could be expected of her husband." These damages include the "reasonable precuniary value of counsel, protection, advice, services, care and attention that she would have in reasonable probability have received from her husband" in addition to the benefit of his income. These damages are determined by taking into account "the decedent's age, health, condition in life, habits of industry and sobriety, mental and physical capacity, disposition to frugality, customary and probable earnings in the future then as well as the past and the use made of them (discounted for present payment) decedent's life expectancy and his work expectancy."

As you finish this fourth and last case of the assignment, give some thought to what the cases tell you about the law of evidence dealing with causation and the law of evidence dealing with damages. This is a higher level of discussion than the analysis of individual cases and is likely to be the focus of discussion in the classroom. At this level of discussion, you should not hesitate to make comparisons between the cases that might suggest a different outcome in a case based on an analogy with other cases in the section. Think critically and question rationales. For example, would you have decided the *Cooper* case any differently based on the other three cases, or is there a sufficient reason to differentiate it from the rest?

Appendix A

HOW TO READ A CASE CITATION

Reading your first case citation may feel like reading an encrypted code. Once you learn the basics, however, it becomes very clear. This appendix will give you the basics on how to read a case citation, but is by no means an exhaustive explanation. You will learn more about citations during your first year of law school, especially during your legal writing class.

Proper legal citation can be found in THE BLUEBOOK: A UNIFORM SYSTEM OF CITATION (18th ed. 2005). This book is what many, if not most, law school journals rely upon when editing, and it is a worthwhile investment for every law student.

Here is an example of a typical case citation:

United States v. Johnson,   425 F.2d 630   (9th Cir. 1970).
       A   B   C   D

A: The Case Name/Name of Parties

B: Official Citation

C: Court that decided the case

D: Year in which the case was decided

A: The case name usually takes the form as the one above. Depending on where you see the citation, the case names may also be underlined or in plain text. Most of the cases you read will be appellate cases, and therefore the name of the party listed first (e.g., United States) is the appellant and represents the party who appealed the lower court's decision.

Be sure to distinguish the appellant and appellee from the plaintiff and defendant. An appellant is simply the party who makes the appeal, and may have been either the plaintiff or the defendant. Consequently, from the order of the case names you should be able to determine who prevailed in the case below. In this case, the trial court must have decided favorably for Johnson with respect to the issue on appeal because the United States appealed.

B: The official citation includes three parts:

the volume (e.g., 425)

the reporter that published the case (e.g., F.2d)

the page on which the case starts (e.g., 630)

The citation is simply a shorthand way to locate the case. Think of it as an informative file number. Sometimes you will see multiple citations from multiple reporters. The case remains the same, but the citation is simply telling you that the case can be found in multiple places.

Although the page number seems straightforward enough, suppose you encounter the above citation with the following change: " . . . 425 F.2d 630, 637 (9th Cir. 1970)." Notice that "637" is added. This means that the citation is directing you to an exact page within the case; this is called a "pinpoint" cite.

The reporter that publishes the case indicates the geographical region in which the case was decided and whether it was tried in federal or state court. For example, if the reporter is F.2d, you know that the case is a federal case. The system of reporters includes the following examples:

A. and A.2d: The Atlantic Reporter
N.E. and N.E.2d: North Eastern Reporter
So. and So. 2d: Southern Reporter

The three reporters listed above are regional reporters, which publish state cases from that region.

U.S.:   United States Reports (only publishes
                                cases from the U.S. Supreme Court)
F. and F.2d: Federal Reporter (only publishes federal
                                cases)
Fla.:   Florida Reports (only publishes Florida
                                cases, although Florida cases are also re-
                                ported in the Southern Reporter)

Compare the first citation above to the following example:

Karafiat v. State, 6589 S.E.2d 801 (Ga. Ct. App. 2008).

Unlike the first example, this case comes from a state court. You can tell because the reporter (S.E.2d) is a regional reporter that reports state cases. We also know it is from a Georgia appellate court (not the supreme court) from the parenthetical information.

The examples in the "Test Your Knowledge" section below will continue to explain the case citations even further.

Test Your Knowledge:

Review the following hypothetical examples, and try to figure out which party prevailed on the appealed issue in the court below the one cited, in which precise court the case was tried, and to which page the citation refers.

State v. Johnson, 157 P.3d 198 (Or. 2007).

In this case, the lower court held for Johnson because the first party listed (State) appealed the case to this court. When you see a party named "State," you know that the party is the government, in this case Oregon. We also can tell from the parenthetical that the decision comes from the supreme court of Oregon because the only abbreviation in the parentheses is of the state itself. Finally, the citation refers us to the entire case, starting on page 198. When a pinpoint reference is not listed, the citation refers to the entire case in general. The briefs you create will not have pinpoint references because your briefs will cover the entire case.

Rousey v. Jacoway, 544 U.S. 320, 321 (2005).

In this case, Jacoway prevailed in the lower court on the issue being appealed in this court because Rousey is the first name listed and is therefore the appellant. From the reporter "U.S." we can tell that this case was decided in the U.S. Supreme Court. When a U.S. Supreme Court decision is cited, the parenthetical information will contain the year alone. Finally, the citation refers us to page 321, even though the case started on page 320.

Carter v. Adams, 877 N.E.2d 1015, 1015–17, 1020 (Ohio Ct. App. 2007).

In this case, Adams prevailed in the court below because Carter, being the first name listed in the case, is the appellant, the party who appealed. This case was tried in an Ohio state appellate court. Although the case starts on page 1015 of volume 877, the citation pinpoints a reference to pages 1015–17 and to page 1020 of the opinion.

Appendix B

Additional Reading[*]

A. The Study of Law

Arnett, J. Robert, Coon, Arthur & DiGeronimo, Michael, *From Here to Attorney: The Ultimate Guide to Excelling in Law School and Launching Your Legal Career* (Belmont: Professional Publications, 1993).

Bonsignore, John J., *Before the Law: An Introduction to the Legal Process* (8th ed. Boston: Houghton Mifflin Co., 2006).

Bradley, Gerard V. & Andrews, Cory L., *A Student's Guide to the Study of Law* (Wilmington: ISI Books, 2006).

Burton, Steven J., *An Introduction to Law and Legal Reasoning* (3d ed. Austin: Wolters Kluwer Law & Business; New York: Aspen Publishers, 2007).

Carey, Christen Civiletto & Adams, Kristen David, *The Practice of Law School: Getting In and Making the Most of Your Legal Education* (New York: ALM Pub., 2003).

Cooper, Charles, *Later-in-Life Lawyers: Tips for the Non-Traditional Law Student* (Honolulu: Fine Print Press, 2006).

Coughlin, George Gordon, *Your Introduction to Law* (4th ed. New York: Barnes & Noble Books, 1983).

Covington, J. S., *The Structure of Legal Argument and Proof: Cases, Materials, and Analyses* (2d ed. Buffalo: William S. Hein, 2006).

Currier, Katherine A. & Eimermann, Thomas E., *The Study of Law: A Critical Thinking Approach* (New York: Aspen Publishers, 2005).

Deaver, Jeffery, *The Complete Law School Companion: How to Excel at America's Most Demanding Post-Graduate Curriculum* (Rev. and updated ed. New York: Wiley, 1992).

Frank, J. Steven, *Learning the Law: Success in Law School and Beyond* (1st Replica Books ed. Bridgewater: Replica Books, 1999).

Grossman, George S., *The Spirit of American Law* (Boulder: Westview Press, 2000).

Gillers, Stephen & Society of American Law Teachers, *Looking at Law School: A Student Guide from the Society of American Law Teachers* (4th ed. New York: Meridian, 1997).

Griffin, Lissa, Gershman, Bennett L. & Pace University, School of Law, *The Law School Experience: Law, Legal Reasoning, and Lawyering* (White Plains: Pace University, School of Law, 2000).

Hricik, David, *Law School Basics: A Preview of Law School and Legal Reasoning* (Los Angeles: Nova Press, 2000).

Kennedy, David & Fisher, William W., *The Canon of American Legal Thought* (Princeton: Princeton University Press, 2006).

Kissam, Philip C., *The Discipline of Law Schools: The Making of Modern Lawyers* (Durham: Carolina Academic Press, 2003).

Krieger, Lawrence S., *The Hidden Sources of Law School Stress: Avoiding the Mistakes That Create Unhappy and Unprofessional Lawyers* (Tallahassee: Krieger, 2005).

Llewellyn, Karl N., *The Bramble Bush: On Our Law and Its Study* (New York:

---

[*] Prepared by Katie Brown, Faculty and Student Services Librarian, St. Thomas University Law Library.

Oceana Publications, 1996 reprint of 1960 ed.).

McAlinn, Gerald Paul, Rosen, Daniel Allan & Stern, John Peter, *An Introduction to American Law* (Durham: Carolina Academic Press, 2005).

McFadden, Patrick M., *A Student's Guide to Legal Analysis: Thinking Like a Lawyer* (Gaithersburg: Aspen Law & Business, 2001).

McKinney, Ruth Ann, *Reading Like a Lawyer: Time-Saving Strategies for Reading Law Like an Expert* (Durham: Carolina Academic Press, 2005).

Mertz, Elizabeth, *The Language of Law School: Learning to "Think Like a Lawyer"* (Oxford England; New York: Oxford University Press, 2007).

Miller, Robert H., *Law School Confidential: A Complete Guide to the Law School Experience: By Students, for Students* (Rev. ed. New York: St. Martin's Griffin/Thomas Dunne Books, 2004).

Moliterno, James E. & Lederer, Fredric I., *An Introduction to Law, Law Study, and the Lawyer's Role* (2d ed. Durham: Carolina Academic Press, 2004).

Munneke, Gary A., *The Legal Career Guide: From Law Student to Lawyer* (4th ed. Chicago: ABA Law Practice Management Section, 2002).

Nygren, Carolyn, *Starting Off Right in Law School* (Durham: Carolina Academic Press, 1997).

Schwartz, Michael Hunter, *Expert Learning for Law Students* (Durham: Carolina Academic Press, 2005).

Spizman, Justin, *The Insider's Guide to Your First Year of Law School* (Avon: Adams Media, 2007).

Stuckey, Roy T., *Best Practices for Legal Education: A Vision and a Road Map* (New York: Clinical Legal Education Association, 2007).

Sullivan, William M. & Carnegie Foundation for the Advancement of Teaching, *Educating Lawyers: Preparation for the Profession of Law* (San Francisco: Jossey-Bass/Wiley, 2007).

Turow, Scott, *One L: The Turbulent True Story of a First Year at Harvard Law School* (Warner Books ed. New York: Warner Books, 1997).

Zitrin, Richard A. & Langford, Carol M., *The Moral Compass of the American Lawyer: Truth, Justice, Power, and Greed* (1st trade paperback ed. New York: Ballantine Books, 2000).

B. Surviving Law School

Darrow-Kleinhaus, Suzanne, *Mastering the Law School Exam: A Practical Blueprint for Preparing and Taking Law School Exams* (St. Paul: Thomson/West, 2007).

Dernbach, John C., *Writing Essay Exams to Succeed (Not Just to Survive)* (2d ed. New York: Aspen Publishers, 2007).

Fischl, Richard Michael & Paul, Jeremy R., *Getting to Maybe: How to Excel on Law School Exams* (Durham: Carolina Academic Press, 1999).

Good, R. Stephanie, *Law School 101: Survival Techniques from Pre-Law to Being an Attorney* (Naperville: Sphinx Pub., 2004).

Hirshman, Linda R., *A Woman's Guide to Law School* (New York: Penguin Books, 1999).

Horwitz, Jeremy B., *Law School Insider: The Comprehensive 21st Century Guide to Success in Admissions, Classes, Law Review, Bar Exams, and Job Searches, for Prospective Students and Their Loved Ones* (Amherst: Lion Group Publication, 2002).

Iijima, Ann L., *The Law Student's Pocket Mentor: From Surviving to Thriving* (Austin: Wolters Kluwer Law & Business/Aspen Publishers, 2007).

Mitchell, Evangeline M. & Bell, Derrick A., *The African American Law School Survival Guide: Information, Advice, and Strategies to Prepare You for the Challenges of the Law School Experience* (Houston: Hope's Promise Pub., 2006).

Noyes, Shana Connell & Noyes, Henry S., *Acing Your First Year of Law School: The Ten Steps to Success You Won't Learn in Class* (Littleton: Fred B. Rothman, 1999).

Ramy, Herbert N., *Succeeding in Law School* (Durham: Carolina Academic Press, 2006).

Reinhart, Susan M., *Strategies for Legal Case Reading and Vocabulary Development* (Ann Arbor: University of Michigan Press, 2007).

Shapo, Helene S. & Shapo, Marshall S., *Law School Without Fear: Strategies for Success* (New York: Foundation Press, 2002).

Stropus, Ruta K. & Taylor, Charlotte D., *Bridging the Gap Between College and Law School: Strategies for Success* (Durham: Carolina Academic Press, 2001).

Tonsing, Dennis J., *1000 Days to the Bar, But the Practice of Law Begins Now* (Buffalo: W.S. Hein & Co., 2003).

Whitebread, Charles H., *The Eight Secrets of Top Exam Performance in Law School: An Easy-to-Use, Step-by-Step Program for Achieving Great Grades!* (Chicago: BAR/BRI Group, 2003).

Yianilos, Christopher J., *The Law School Breakthrough: Graduate in the Top 10% of Your Class, Even if You're Not a First-Rate Student* (Franklin Lakes: Career Press, 2005).

C. Legal Research

Armstrong, J. D. S. & Knott, Christopher A., *Where the Law Is: An Introduction to Advanced Legal Research* (2d ed. St. Paul: Thomson/West, 2006).

Atkinson, Valerie J., *Legal Research Via the Internet* (Albany: West/Thomson Learning, 2001).

Bae, Frank, *Searching the Law* (3d ed. Ardsley: Transnational Publishers, 2005).

Berring, Robert C. & Edinger, Elizabeth A., *Finding the Law* (12th ed. St. Paul: Thomson/West, 2005).

Brostoff, Teresa & Sinsheimer, Ann, *Legal English: An Introduction to the Legal Language and Culture of the United States* (2d ed. Dobbs Ferry: Oceana Publications, 2003).

Glaser, Cathy, *The Lawyer's Craft: An Introduction to Legal Analysis, Writing, Research, and Advocacy* (Cincinnati: Anderson Pub. Co., 2002).

Johnson, Nancy P., Berring, Robert C. & Woxland, Thomas A., *Winning Research Skills* (2007–2008 [ed.] Eagan: West, 2007).

Kunz, Christina L., *The Process of Legal Research* (6th ed. New York: Aspen Publishers, 2004).

Mersky, Roy M., Dunn, Donald J. & Jacobstein, J. Myron, *Fundamentals of Legal Research* (8th ed. New York: Foundation Press, 2002).

Murray, Michael D. & DeSanctis, Christy Hallam, *Legal Research Methods* (New York: Foundation Press, 2006).

Neacsu, Dana, *Introduction to U.S. Law and Legal Research* (Ardsley: Transnational Publishers, 2005).

Oates, Laurel Currie & Enquist, Anne, *Just Research* (New York: Aspen Publishers, 2005).

Putman, William H., *Legal Research* (Clifton Park: Thomson Delmar Learning, 2006).

Roberts Bonita K. & Schlueter, Linda L., *Legal Research Guide: Patterns and Practice* (5th ed. Newark: LexisNexis Matthew Bender, 2006).

Simonsen, Craig B. & Andersen, Christian R., *Computer-Aided Legal Research (CALR) on the Internet* (Upper Saddle River: Pearson/Prentice Hall, 2006).

Sloan, Amy E., *Basic Legal Research: Tools and Strategies* (3d ed. New York: Aspen Publishers, 2006).

Stevens, Anne M., *Finding, Reading, and Using the Law* (Albany: West/Thomson Learning, 2002).

D. Legal Writing

Armstrong, Stephen V. & Terrell, Timothy P., *Thinking Like a Writer: A Lawyer's Guide to Writing and Editing* (2d ed. New York: Practising Law Institute, 2003).

Bronsteen, John, *Writing a Legal Memo* (New York: Foundation Press; St. Paul: Thomson/West, 2006).

Charrow, Veda, Erhardt, Myra K. & Charrow, Robert, *Clear and Effective Legal Writing* (4th ed. Austin: Wolters Kluwer Law & Business, Aspen Publishers, 2007).

Clary, Bradley G. & Lysaght, Pamela, *Successful Legal Analysis and Writing: The Fundamentals* (2d ed. St. Paul: Thomson/West, 2006).

Drennan, William, *Advocacy Words: A Thesaurus* (Chicago: American Bar Association, 2005).

Garner, Bryan A. & Black, Campbell Henry, *Black's Law Dictionary* (8th ed. St. Paul: Thomson/West, 2004).

Garner, Bryan A., *A Dictionary of Modern Legal Usage* (2d ed. Oxford; New York: Oxford University Press, 2001).

Garner, Bryan A., *The Elements of Legal Style* (2d ed. Oxford; New York: Oxford University Press, 2002).

Garner, Bryan A., Newman, Jeff & Jackson, Tiger, *The Redbook: A Manual on Legal Style* (2d ed. St. Paul: Thomson/West, 2006).

Goldstein, Tom & Lieberman, Jethro Koller, *The Lawyer's Guide to Writing Well* (2d ed. Berkeley: University of California Press, 2002).

Kimble, Joseph, *Lifting the Fog of Legalese: Essays on Plain Language* (Durham: Carolina Academic Press, 2006).

Neumann, Richard K., *Legal Reasoning and Legal Writing: Structure, Strategy, and Style* (5th ed. New York: Aspen Publishers, 2005).

Oates, Laurel Currie & Enquist, Anne, *The Legal Writing Handbook: Analysis, Research, and Writing* (4th ed. New York: Aspen Publishers, 2006).

Oettle, Kenneth F., *Making Your Point: A Practical Guide to Persuasive Legal Writing* (New York: ALM Media, Inc., 2007).

Rambo, Teresa J. Reid & Pflaum, Leanne J., *Legal Writing By Design: A Guide to Great Briefs and Memos* (Durham: Carolina Academic Press, 2001).

Ray, Mary Barnard, *The Basics of Legal Writing* (St. Paul: Thomson/West, 2006).

Ray, Mary Barnard & Ramsfield, Jill J., *Legal Writing — Getting it Right and Getting it Written* (4th ed.St. Paul: Thomson/West, 2005).

Volokh, Eugene, *Academic Legal Writing: Law Review Articles, Student Notes, Seminar Papers, and Getting on Law Review* (3d ed. New York: Foundation Press, 2007).

Wydick, Richard C., *Plain English for Lawyers* (5th ed. Durham: Carolina Academic Press, 2005).

E. Legal Citation

Barris, Linda J., *Understanding and Mastering The Bluebook: A Guide for Students and Practitioners* (Durham: Carolina Academic Press, 2007).

Dickerson, Darby & Association of Legal Writing Directors, *ALWD Citation Manual: A Professional System of Citation* (3d ed. New York: Aspen Publishers, 2006).

Dworsky, Alan L., *User's Guide to the Bluebook* (Rev. for the 18th ed. Buffalo: William S. Hein, 2006).

Harvard Law Review Association, *The Bluebook: A Uniform System of Citation* (18th ed. Cambridge: Harvard Law Review Association, 2005).

Prince, Mary Miles & Bieber, Doris M., *Bieber's Dictionary of Legal Abbreviations: Reference Guide for Attorneys, Legal Secretaries, Paralegals, and Law Students* (5th ed. Buffalo: W.S. Hein, 2001).

Prince, Mary Miles, *Prince's Dictionary of Legal Citations: A Reference Guide for Attorneys, Legal Secretaries, Paralegals, and Law Students* (7th ed. Buffalo: William S. Hein, 2006).

Appendix C

On the Lighter Side

The following cases are actual decisions written in a variety of unique styles.

FISHER v. LOWE
122 Mich. App. 418, 333 N.W.2d 67 (1983)

J.H. GILLIS, J.

We thought that we would never see
A suit to compensate a tree.

A suit whose claim in tort is prest
Upon a mangled tree's behest;

A tree whose battered trunk was prest
Against a Chevy's crumpled crest;

A tree that faces each new day
With bark and limb in disarray;

A tree that may forever bear
A lasting need for tender care.

Flora lovers though we three,
We must uphold the court's decree.

Affirmed.*

UNITED STATES v. SATAN AND HIS STAFF
54 F.R.D. 282 (W.D. Pa. 1971)

MEMORANDUM ORDER

WEBER, District Judge.

Plaintiff, alleging jurisdiction under 18 U.S.C. § 241, 28 U.S.C. § 1343, and 42 U.S.C. § 1983 prays for leave to file a complaint for violation of his civil rights in forma pauperis. He alleges that Satan has on numerous occasions caused plaintiff misery and unwarranted threats, against the will of plaintiff, that Satan has placed deliberate obstacles in his path and has caused plaintiff's downfall.

Plaintiff alleges that by reason of these acts Satan has deprived him of his constitutional rights.

---

* Plaintiff commenced this action in tort against defendants Lowe and Moffet for damage to his "beautiful oak tree" caused when defendant Lowe struck it while operating defendant Moffet's automobile. The trial court granted summary judgment in favor of defendants pursuant to GCR 1963, 117.2(1). In addition, the trial court denied plaintiff's request to enter a default judgment against the insurer of the automobile, defendant State Farm Mutual Automobile Insurance Company. Plaintiff appeals as of right.

The trial court did not err in granting summary judgment in favor of defendants Lowe and Moffet. Defendants were immune from tort liability for damage to the tree pursuant to § 3135 of the no-fault insurance act. MCL 500.3135; MSA 24.13135.

The trial court did not err in refusing to enter a default judgment against State Farm. Since it is undisputed that plaintiff did not serve process upon State Farm in accordance with the court rules, the court did not obtain personal jurisdiction over the insurer. GCR 1963, 105.4. [Footnote from opinion].

We feel that the application to file and proceed in forma pauperis must be denied. Even if plaintiff's complaint reveals a prima facie recital of the infringement of the civil rights of a citizen of the United States, the Court has serious doubts that the complaint reveals a cause of action upon which relief can be granted by the court. We question whether plaintiff may obtain personal jurisdiction over the defendant in this judicial district. The complaint contains no allegation of residence in this district. While the official reports disclose no case where this defendant has appeared as defendant there is an unofficial account of a trial in New Hampshire where this defendant filed an action of mortgage foreclosure as plaintiff. The defendant in that action was represented by the preeminent advocate of that day, and raised the defense that the plaintiff was a foreign prince with no standing to sue in an American Court. This defense was overcome by overwhelming evidence to the contrary. Whether or not this would raise an estoppel in the present case we are unable to determine at this time.

If such action were to be allowed we would also face the question of whether it may be maintained as a class action. It appears to meet the requirements of Fed. R. of Civ. P. 23 that the class is so numerous that joinder of all members is impracticable, there are questions of law and fact common to the class, and the claims of the representative party is typical of the claims of the class. We cannot now determine if the representative party will fairly protect the interests of the class.

We note that the plaintiff has failed to include with his complaint the required form of instructions for the United States Marshal for directions as to service of process.

For the foregoing reasons we must exercise our discretion to refuse the prayer of plaintiff to proceed in forma pauperis.

It is ordered that the complaint be given a miscellaneous docket number and leave to proceed in forma pauperis be denied.